SAILORS'
SECRETS

SAILORS' SECRETS

Advice from the Masters

Michael Badham and Robby Robinson

INTERNATIONAL MARINE
CAMDEN, MAINE

International Marine

A Division of The **McGraw·Hill** Companies

8 9 10 11 12 13 14 15 DOC/DOC 0 9 8

Copyright © 1997, 1999 International Marine

The Library of Congress has cataloged the hardcover edition as follows:

Library of Congress Cataloging-in-Publication Data
Robinson, Robby.
    Sailors' secrets / Robby Robinson and Mike Badham.
      p.   cm.
    Includes bibliographical references (p.   ) and index.
    ISBN 0-07-039088-6
    1. Boats and boating—Maintenance and repair.   I. Badham, Mike.
II. Title.
VM322.R63 1996
623.88'23–dc21
                             96-47681
                             CIP

The ISBN for the paperback edition is 0-07-134869-7

Publishers' permissions appear on page 309.

Questions regarding the content of this book should be addressed to
    International Marine
    P.O. Box 220
    Camden, ME 04843
    http//www.internationalmarine.com

Questions regarding the ordering of this book should be addressed to
    The McGraw-Hill Companies
    Customer Service Department
    P.O. Box 547
    Blacklick, OH 43004
    Retail customers: 1-800-262-4729
    Bookstores: 1-800-722-4726

Unless otherwise specified, illustrations by Rob Groves
Design and Production by Dan Kirchoff
Edited by Jonathan Eaton, Don Casey, Tom McCarthy, Scott Kirkman
Printed by R.R. Donnelley, Crawfordsville, IN

To Doug Terman, who first came up with the idea for this book.
      —Michael Badham

For Marty Luray, editor, mentor, and true friend. I've tried to answer your call.
      —Robby Robinson

CONTENTS

PREFACE

This book began as *101 Ways to Get Your Boat Really Ready to Go to Sea*. We set out to gather nuggets of preventive maintenance, outfitting, and forehanded seamanship. We chose charter-boat skippers as our experts because they tend to maintain their own boats, spend only what's necessary, keep "down time" to a minimum, and operate far from home. We picked their brains.

After sifting through the first three or four hundred suggestions, we decided to widen our scope. There is more to sailing than getting ready for sea, and sailors outside the charter fleet also know a thing or two. You'll find well over 1,000 tips, suggestions, evaluations, and pieces of advice in *Sailors' Secrets*. We started with a short list of "gems" that we each, out of our combined century and more than 60,000 miles on the water, wanted

to share. To those we added things that surprised, delighted, and instructed us. Not everything in this book will be new to you, but if you don't find at least a fistful of useful things you didn't know, you should be writing books.

With no particular debt to Moses or Letterman, we organized the book around 10 principles . . . things to do to get more from your boat. From "Keep It Simple, Sweetheart" to "Be Safe," we listed "commandments" for sailing better, cheaper, safer, and happier. This book is our selection of the best of what more than 300 sailors say about how they turn those principles into reality.

Michael Badham
Bath, ME

Robby Robinson
Marshfield, MA

ACKNOWLEDGMENTS

Family and friends have helped, prodded, even snickered along the way. May what enjoyment and enlightenment they might find here prove some small recompense. The unstinting and willing help of the many contributors is thankfully and gratefully acknowledged.

We hasten to add that in the interests of brevity, continuity, and sometimes entertainment, we have taken liberties in relaying their comments and ideas. We tried mightily in the course of our editing not to alter original intent, and if we have failed anywhere in that effort, we apologize. In any case, all of the information in this book has passed through our filter, so even if an idea is credited to someone else, the full responsibility for any inaccuracies rests squarely on our shoulders.

KEEP IT SIMPLE, SWEETHEART

If there is a first principle for sailors, shouldn't it be the KISS principle? It is a golden guide through much of life; it shines with special brilliance in the world of boats.

Olin Stephens was hardly a simple man. Few designers enjoyed success (six America's Cup–winning designs, etc.) to rival his. Perhaps one of the secrets of that success was that he kept it in perspective. He was a pioneer in tank testing, a leader with computers, an innovator of superlatively efficient structures, a wizard to whom rating rules were self-evident equations, yet he wrote, "for fun it is likely to be best to think small and simple so that you get the pure fun of sailing without the hassle."

Susan Hiscock and husband Eric never carried a two-way radio on their cruises and circumnavigations. Shortly before her death in 1995, she wrote "electrics don't tolerate salt water. Most people own boats because boats provide *independence*; don't fill up your boat with gadgets that make *you* dependent upon *them*."

Simple solutions offer elegant results. With all due respect for tradition, technology, and the realities of modern boating, we've gathered here solutions whose simplicity makes them elegant—and then some. "Keep it simple, sweetheart." KISS.

I could not simplify myself.

—*suicide note left by Neshdanov in Ivan Turgenev's* Virgin Soil

*If you can't repair it,
maybe it shouldn't
be on board.*

—*Lin and Larry Pardey*

THE FIRST THING   *(Jimmy O'Cain)* I never
leave the dock without at least one 5-gallon bucket. My all-purpose
buckets have handles with ropes attached to scoop water on deck.
They're big enough to serve as emergency heads (few moving parts),
and there's no bailing system quite as efficient as a scared sailor with
one of these in his hands.

BLOWN DRY   Humphrey Barton, a lifelong voyager,
crossed the Atlantic alone aboard *Vertue XXV* and is perhaps best
known as the founder of the Ocean Cruising Club. Mary, his widow
and mate through thousands of ocean miles, says "maintenance was not
my part of our partnership. One birthday I was delighted to receive an
electric hair dryer . . . delighted, that is, until I discovered that it was to
be used primarily to blow dry the varnish work so that Humphrey
could apply the following coat as soon as possible."

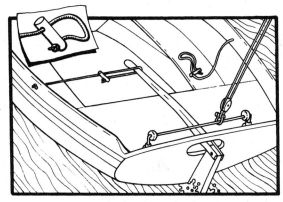

*Self-steering made easy!
Captain Carlton Poulnot's
Tiller Master.*

TILLER MASTER   Over 50
years at the helm have made Captain Carlton Poulnot of Charleston, SC, quite aware of the "tyranny
of the tiller." He finds, though, that "an inexpensive
ax handle from the hardware store can make a superb emergency tiller." He has equally straightforward ideas about self-steering: "I simply made two
homemade 'tent-peg tensioners' by drilling blocks of
wood with holes sized to my small line. I rig the line
(with tensioner) between the gunwale and the
tiller—port and starboard. It can then be adjusted
positively and smoothly and fast."

OUT OF TEAK OIL?   *(Jo Anna Brown)*
For preserving interior teak trim, clear lemon oil works fine, doesn't
darken appreciably, and smells nice.

SIMPLIFY   *(Robert W. Merriam)* "If I had more time,"
Cicero, the Roman orator, once wrote, "I'd have sent you a shorter letter." The great practical engineers of our time, too, recognized simplicity's virtue. James Watt's mine-pumping engines were so brilliantly conceived and executed that many of them ran continuously for more
than a century. In one sweep of genius in 1878, Thomas Edison picked
the line voltage we still use today, designed the fuse system, and created
the screw-in lamp base to launch modern electric power. These men
had simple ideas that worked—and have kept on working for most of
this century.

　　You don't have to give up sophisticated solutions to problems, just
reduce those sophisticated solutions to simple terms. Modern loran and
radar are two good examples. Choose gear that performs its prime func-

tion reliably and well. As it said on the sign hung above Edison's workbench: "Simplify, Simplify, Simplify!" [Could it be that Edison was a disciple of Thoreau, who is most often credited with this admonition?—eds.]

KEEP THEM BURNING
If you use oil lamps on a boat, especially if you use them as an anchor light hung in the rigging, the danger is that they may go out. Most often that occurs due to the oil in the base sloshing around and disrupting the wicking action that feeds the flame. A simple solution is to fill the fuel reservoir with caulking cotton, thereby making the whole into a "wick."

ECONO-LITE
(Art Loya)
For $5.00 I purchased a small white "back-up light" from Western Auto intended for a trailer, and from Radio Shack I bought a toggle switch for $1.00. If your boat doesn't have an engine room light, it can . . . very cheaply, very easily.

GIVE IT THE BOOT
(Doug Terman)
To replace or renew a leaking mast boot:

1. Obtain an Ace bandage from a pharmacy.
2. Purchase a can of Dip Whip at a ships' store.
3. Wrap the mast with the elastic bandage.
4. Paint the bandage with three coats of Dip Whip.

Flexible, attractive, and waterproof, the new boot is good for seasons of use.

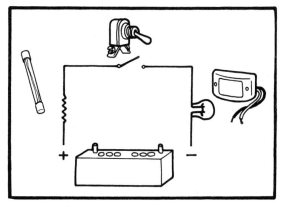

Econo-Lite

DUDS AND SPUDS
To collect the essentials of good seamanship, John Rousmaniere (*The Annapolis Book of Seamanship*) needed more than 300 pages. The essentials of what to wear aboard a boat, however, take just three phrases: tough fabrics; double-seamed; and loose fit. Rousmaniere does add that high collars are good for fighting off wind, sun, and spray. "And you should remember potatoes. What could be better than a baked potato hot from the oven to take on watch with you? It warms your hands and your pockets and, when it cools, you eat it."

TOPSIDE APRONS
Fenders pick up grime and can grind it into your hullsides. We like the solution put forward by English designer Ian Nicolson: simply hang a canvas apron between hull and fenders. You'll require stout grommets in the corners into which you may tie lines and stretch the apron smoothly over the boat's side.

To make his aprons even easier on the hull, Floridian Don Casey

Modern conveniences become inconveniences at sea. Simplify the inventory. Everything (except flares and safety gear) that hasn't been used for 6 months, goes ashore.

—Dick Newick

sews terry cloth—a bath towel—to the inner surface, leaving the bottom edge unsewn.

TURN, TURN

(Dynamite Payson) Given a 50-50 chance of doing things either the easy way or the hard, my experience tells me that I'll find a way to find the hard way. I'm a little on the short side. That's good for rowing standing up in my peapod, but when it comes to stepping the mast in *Bobcat,* my 12-foot catboat, as my lanky friend Peter Spectre says, I'm a step too short for stepping. At any rate I don't manage much leverage. After dropping the spar twice, though, it finally dawned on me. I tipped the boat on its side and slid the damn thing in on the level.

BOX YOUR BOAT

At lay-up time place a few boxes of cat litter below. Not only does the litter absorb moisture and reduce the chances of mildew, it sops up odors, too.

BOX YOUR BERTH

(Arne Brun Lie) Boats sweat, especially when you're trying to live aboard in relatively cold weather. It can be awful! Moisture on the overhead, behind the cushions, even in your bunk. I've discovered corrugated cardboard, the kind they give you in boxes at the supermarket. I line the hull sides around my bunk. It gives insulation, absorbs moisture, and, when it gets soggy, I just get more, for free.

WHEN THE LIGHTS GO OUT

Once you've tried all of the breakers, it's time to remember that more than one component can be on the same circuit. To find the culprit that is shorting out and tripping your breaker, turn off all of the components on each circuit. Turn them on again one at a time until your breaker trips. You have found the culprit.

DISPATCHING FISH

An article in the Ocean Cruising Club journal *Flying Fish* tells how to dispose of your catch without the messy business of bashing it on the head

with a winch handle. Just give it a drink. Booze down the piscatorial throat (by way of about a capful of anything stronger than wine poured in the gills) quickly puts an end to all that tiresome thrashing and beating about.

LET THERE BE LIGHT

The main companionway sliding hatch in a yacht is almost always made of solid timber or fiberglass. To add cheer to the cabin interior, especially when everything's shut up tight during protracted periods of rain or heavy weather, a large oval decklight of Plexiglas let into the hatch can work wonders. Simpler still is Bob Anderson's idea: fit a new top board for your companionway, then hang a flap of clear dodger material below it to cover the rest of the opening. You might go farther and substitute Plexiglas for the teak or mahogany washboards in the companionway. A solid piece of thin Plexiglas (not individual boards) works great and is easily stored under a bunk.

Ocean voyager and championship sailing coach Toby Baker suggests, "when you're tied up in a marina or riding in a crowded anchorage, drape mosquito netting over the companionway and position a light to shine on it. This creates an opaque curtain that maintains privacy while letting the breeze in."

SMALL STUFF

(Richard Dey) Always have on hand, somewhere near the binocular case, half a dozen pieces of ⅛-inch or ³⁄₁₆-inch light line, up to 6 feet in length, for lashing things down in a hurry.

HOSE GUARDS

If a piece of hose or tubing is positioned where it might be vulnerable to chafe or crushing, tie-wrap a backup piece of suitably sized hose around it for protection.

THE "WATCHLIN"

(Susan Hiscock) An old sea captain named Watchlin presented us with a rectangular 3 ft. x 6 ft. piece of waterproofed canvas with grommets at the corners and along the edges. It became an

invaluable part of our deck equipment. It could be used as a shelter, an awning, a dodger, a rain catchment, even a knee-cover when on watch. In truth we found the proverbial 101 uses for it.

EVER-READY PAINTBRUSHES

(Doug Terman) Dave Stickley, an old Caribbean hand, taught me this one. When he finishes painting or varnishing, he works all the excess paint or varnish out on a newspaper, then places the brush in a wide-mouthed PVC jar with a screw lid. The jar is three-quarters filled with a 50-50 mixture of diesel fuel and Penetrol. When he wants to use the brush again (obviously each brush is dedicated to a specific color and type of paint or varnish), he merely brushes out the excess liquid and starts painting or varnishing directly. The bristles are lubricated and thus preserved by the liquid, and there is no dried paint or varnish on the brush. Dave has some 20-year-old badger-hair brushes that look and perform like new.

WINCH HER OFF

(Will Robinson) I usually can push my 15-footer into the water from her trailer, but on some of the flatter ramps I've had to use, I've found a way to winch her off the trailer. I just take a snatchblock (stolen from Dad's boat) and clip it to the trailer frame somewhere back by the wheel. I slack off the trailer-winch cable and lead a bight through the block. Then I button up the block, winch on the cable, and enjoy a powerful mechanical advantage cranking the boat off the trailer into the water.

THE "NO HANDS" FLASHLIGHT

(Lin and Larry Pardey) We've finally come up with the perfect gift for friends setting off on a cruise. It's small, it costs less than $3, takes less than 20 minutes to build, and it's indispensable. Start with a soft-bodied, water-resistant flashlight. Cut a strip of strong, stiff plastic (about 4 in. by 1½ in. by ⅛-in. thick), and use thread-reinforced packing tape to attach it to the barrel of the flashlight. Customize (with regular plastic tape or a tooth-grip of choice)

the end of the plastic strip and you have . . . a flashlight you can hold in your mouth. Don't laugh; it'll fall out.

EASY-DRIVE FASTENINGS

For easier driving and—if need be—unscrewing, lubricate screw threads with waterproof marine grease before you install them. Avoid using soap; it's corrosive.

SADDLE THE RODE

(Dr. Claud Worth) The yacht was dragging her anchor with the warp coming taut from time to time with a twang like a bowstring. So we got up a 70-pound pig of lead, tied a rope round it, and made a becket round the warp. We let the pig slide down the warp, paying out about 15 fathoms of small line secured to it. The weight of the lead acted to deepen the catenary, and the yacht ceased to drag and snub.

Riding to a chain instead of a rope, we would not have been able to make a rope becket slide down—or up—the chain. So, for future use, I had an iron traveler fabricated, somewhat in the form of a large shackle, with curvature being carried right out to the sides so the lips don't bind on the chain. From such a cable saddle, hang a weight, even as light as a quarter of [the weight of] the anchor you have down, and lower it to maximize your holding power and greatly dampen surge.

—*adapted from* Yacht Cruising

THE SEAGOING COAT HANGER

Why take a metal coat hanger to sea? Because it can:

- hook something out of an inaccessible area of the bilge
- poke blockages out of hoses
- replace a cotter pin in a pinch
- be twisted into a temporary tie-down
- keep your jacket hanging smoothly
- help you get into the family car locked shoreside with the keys inside when you return

New Eyes

Reading the small print on the chart is never as easy as it used to be. Steve Colgate advises in *Steve Colgate on Cruising*, "turn a pair of binoculars upside down. Put the eyepiece on one side very close to the print. Look through that lens, wrong way through, and the print will be magnified many times."

Burn-Proofing the Cook

High-waisted oilskin trousers are good protection against burns and scaldings that can come from tending the stove in heavy weather. A well-secured galley belt is another lifesaver. It frees both hands to manage the meal and protects against lurches that might spill the chef.

Free Boards

Floorboards love to swell together. According to British naval architect and surveyor Ian Nicholson, the best solution is to simply bevel the boards slightly, about 10 degrees or so. They still swell together, but a slight tug will bring them up.

—*adapted from* Customize Your Boat

Guarding the Gunwale

Fitting a skiff or dinghy with gunwale guards can be satisfying. Mike and Anne Adair have cruised the Caribbean for years and know what works. "You can buy ready-made fendering material (at up to $5/foot) or improvise. One good solution is a length of line. Use the largest diameter you can afford. Manila looks good but we prefer the durability, softness, and look of braided nylon. You can bolt line on (tightening the bolts to compress the line and form protective 'dimples'), but we prefer lashing the line in place. We drill holes 6 inches apart all round the gunwale and lace the new rubrail in place."

Crew Alarm

(Charlie Pickering) We were delivering a schooner across the Pacific and we were shorthanded. That's why the guy at the wheel had a line running below. It was tied (supposedly) around his watchmate's foot. All he had to do was yank when he

needed help. Meantime everyone else got some sleep. My watchmate was a bit irritated when I tied the line around the table leg instead of my own. Nowadays you can install a waterproof button by the wheel that sounds an alarm below that even I would be hard-pressed to ignore.

One, Two, Three

(Clifford Chew, Jr.) More years than I can remember were spent both in the wheelhouse and engine room of North Atlantic draggers. (I am now age 72.) Three things stand out real big in trouble-free maintenance:

- Keep a clean engine room.
- Keep a well-lighted, well-painted engine room.
- Keep a dry engine room.

Often having "green" men aboard, I used color coded pipes and valves for fuel, fresh water, salt water, hydraulic, lube oil, bilge, etc. All of these ideas are within reach of all vessels and save money and time.

Hot and Spicy Barnacles

When Ken Fischer bit into a deviled egg liberally laced with Tabasco, a new antifouling preparation was born. Fischer's teary-eyed brainstorm was to blend the oils of cayenne peppers—environmentally kind yet death to crustaceans—with an epoxy paint. Fischer has applied for a patent, and a spokesman for the navy, which is testing the product in a South Carolina shipyard, says he thinks it has potential. [Pepper paint is in production but combined with copper, so the actual effect of the pepper is unclear.—eds.]

Caulking Bind

(Dan Spurr) It's a dilemma. Caulk liberally enough to prevent all leaks and you're left with a mess. Bed sparingly enough to have no clean-up and you risk having to do the job again when the leaks persist. I figure it's simpler to clean up than re-do and re-bed. Whether it's a portlight, hatch, or whatever, I have on hand a number of cloths that are of contrasting color with the sealant. That

way it's easy to see where I've got sealant on my rag and avoid wiping it back onto the fitting or lens. Tape around the perimeter to capture the excess (fun disposing of, especially in a wind). Use 3M General Purpose Adhesive Cleaner. It's the best.

—adapted from Spurr's Boat Book

GHOSTING

(Gary Jobson) In light air, especially if there is a swell or chop, all boats tend to hobbyhorse, losing energy and having difficulty moving through the water. In these conditions I find it very helpful to place the weight of my crew and gear as low as possible. I make sure all unused sails are packed tightly and stowed amidships, over the keel. Then I invite all the crew I can spare to move below onto the pile. It makes a big difference.

FINGER-TIP CONTROL

(MB) I always keep an empty fingernail polish bottle (complete with brush) full of my favorite varnish. It's very handy to cover scratches, dents, and the like before the wood discolors.

PERFECTLY POURED

Many container cans have their screw-on caps to one side of the top. The temptation is to pour the contents with the spout at the lower side, but this usually means wastage. Pour with the can reversed, so that the spout is on the upper side. This allows air to get in above the liquid level, and you can empty the can completely without splashing.

Perfectly Poured

NO-TEARS CRATE

(Bob Noyes) Once when I went off cruising, some groceries came aboard in an onion crate. Instead of throwing the crate overboard, I kept it on deck, and it proved so useful that I've never been without one since. In fact, my new yawl has a permanent onion crate bolted to her cabin house. It is a lovely thing, built of beautifully varnished teak, but it is essentially an onion crate. Sail stops, spare lines, and all the loose gear that customarily clutters up the deck are thrown unceremoniously into the onion crate. They cannot blow out or fall overboard, yet there is free circulation of air through the slats, and any water drains overboard instantly.

—adapted from Yachtsman's Omnibus, *H. A. Calahan*

STAINLESS TEST

When purchasing stainless steel fittings, test them with a magnet. Do the same with bronze and brass; if there's any attraction, the fitting is probably plated steel.

PINHEAD

When a wrench can't get a grip on a burred or rounded bolt head, drill a hole through the head and insert a stainless steel pin. That gives the wrench something to grab.

ANCHOR CHAIN SNUBBER

In gusty and choppy conditions anchor chain can jerk up taut, making noise and putting undue strain on both boat and ground tackle. One solution is to rig a snubber to provide the elasticity the chain lacks. With a chain hook or a rolling hitch, attach a 20-foot length of nylon rope to the cable. Ease the chain a few feet and take the strain on the snubber. The shock-absorbing effect of the nylon renders the slacks and strains of the chain shock-free and silent.

GET A GRIP

Available at RV supply stores, illuminated grab handles are excellent for use on a boat. The 12-volt fixtures can be fitted with red bulbs and installed near companionways, over the chart table, or wherever else a handy night light/grab handle combination would prove convenient.

THE LITTLE THINGS

(RR) More than 25 years ago Carol and I bought our first cruising boat. The choice of a 25-foot Westerly Tiger came down, I must admit, to my preference for a single design feature: clear plastic sliders that enclosed and "organized" the cabin stowage areas above her settee/berths. We have that same boat today. We might have chosen one of her rivals but never mind. We've enjoyed years and miles galore on both sides of the Atlantic. Little things may not mean a lot, but at least they help you make up your mind.

ANCHOR TRICKS

(David Bill) Stowing an anchor rode so that it's ready to run free when you need it is important. I make the rode up in a coil, then lash it at its "four corners" with stops made of light line. That keeps it organized and prevents it from getting fouled in its bin or locker.

Used tennis balls don't look that salty, but I use them as protective "mothballs" over the stocks and/or flukes of deck-stowed anchors. The balls save scratches, snagged lines, and stubbed toes, and they're easy to replace.

KEEP YOUR HEAD

(RR) Vietnam vet, novelist, and charter skipper Mike Lewis is a friend of mine with a full bag of tricks—and then some. His approach to going overboard to unfoul a prop has always stood me in excellent stead: "What you need is common sense, good communication, a tether, and the right tools (the best underwater cutting device I've found is a hacksaw blade). I tape a towel to my head, like a helmet. Strapped on much like an ice bag, it offers some aid and comfort for those inevitable times, even in remarkably little seaway, when the boat comes down hard on your head."

PLASTIC PAILS

The wonders of Tupperware containers have been celebrated far and wide. For excellent stowage in larger-size containers, though, try plastic pails (like those in which you might buy detergent, fertilizer, lime, etc.) that come with snap-on lids.

WELL-SEATED SOLUTION

Galway Blazer II was holed by a great white shark south of Australia during Bill King's circumnavigation. He tacked to raise the hole above the waterline but, as he writes in *Adventure in Depth*, "though I tried everything I could think of, I couldn't mend the hole. Fremantle lay only three days away, but I was lengthening, not decreasing, the distance by this enforced tack towards the South Pole. Darting between the pump and trying to position the storm jib over the damaged area, I slipped below to inspect the result. It wasn't working. The edges of the canvas were acting not as a collision mat but as a water scoop. After a day or two, though, a fever of improvisation beset me, and this is when I came up with a pair of waterproof trousers—yellow, shiny, strong. I ran ropes through the legs, nailed them along the bottom edge of the damage, and hauled them taut. They were just the right consistency to stop the leak. My lovely boat in oilskin trousers! It was ludicrous, but it worked."

PUNCTURE-PROOF

(William Hodsdon) Carry an automobile tire inner tube. For emergency patching of a "not-too-big" hole in the hull, cut the tube to overlap the hole, insert control lines (bulked up by figure-eight knots or suitable washers) in the four corners of the patch, and stretch it over the hole. Both water pressure and tension on the lines will minimize leakage and allow you to limp home.

FREE-SHAKING SALT

(Jo Anna Brown) We tried to get the salt to come out of the shaker—rice in with it, switch to iodized salt, snap-topped shakers, heated salt to drive the moisture out. . . . Finally we remembered the Mexican roast-corn vendor. He had a bottle of salt brine handy for sprinkling on the corn. Now we do the same thing. We put a saturated salt solution into an empty soy-sauce bottle, and out it comes, in drips.

STUFFING BOX RX

(Jarvis W. Newman) To remedy the nuisance of a leaking stuffing box, whether the boat is power or sail and whether the gland is on a propeller shaft or a rudder post, use a wrench that fits and tighten the nut until the drip from the box is down to one or two per minute. If you haven't the proper tools, you can try tightening the adjustment nut by holding a screwdriver to the proper corner and tapping it *carefully* with a hammer. [If *we* were building boats, we'd have two open-end wrenches the appropriate size mounted right by the stuffing box, and we'd feature them in our ads.—eds.]

RENEWING CHAIN

Re-galvanizing is expensive. To restore a chain whose galvanizing has been worn away, end-for-end the cable, wire brush it thoroughly, and soak it in boiled linseed oil for as long as possible.

HAMMOCKS

One way to add stowage painlessly is to use nets suspended from cup hooks and shock cord. They can be custom designed to utilize many unoccupied spaces, you can see what's in them, you can use them to localize each crewmember's gear, they offer superb ventilation, and they're amazingly stuffable. Hammocks!

WATER WICK

(Chris Way-Nee) The water that sits on the rim of a portlight can insinuate itself below. To minimize the problem I jam a piece of wool yarn in the portlight so that one end sits in the water and the other hangs down the cabin side. The wool will wick away standing water.

TARP TOGGLES

(Ron Richard) If you've tried to cover anything with those ubiquitous blue plastic tarps, you have probably discovered that while such covers are durable and a good value, their grommets typically are poorly reinforced and inconveniently far apart. An answer I have found is to cut ¾-inch hose into inch-long toggles. Where you'd like to tie on to the tarp, gather it into a loose bunch around a toggle. Tie your line (a clove hitch is best) around the "neck" of the bulge the toggle forms in the tarp: secure, custom-tailored tie-downs.

STICKWARE

(June Vigor) I've admired (and even owned) those purpose-designed mugs, dishes, and plates that come with skidproof rubber rings on the bottom and cling to tables and counters at impressive angles of heel. I made my own by simply painting the bottoms of ordinary boatware with thick layers of rubber cement. It dried to a good, firm, nonskid finish.

COTTER PINS

(Roderick Stephens, Jr.) A cotter pin can provide a very safe way to secure many connections in the rig, but because of failure to live up to several simple expedients, the cotter pin is universally disliked. For good results the pin should be cut so that, seen from below, its length will be about one

Another use for parbuckling. In addition to working docklines or hoisting cargo, parbuckling could help you retrieve an overboard crewmember in the bunt of a headsail, as shown on page 264.

and a half times the diameter of the clevis pin. The ends must then be rounded with a smooth flat file so that there are no sharp corners. When cotter pins have been put in place, they should be opened slightly (each side bent back only about 10 degrees). Never bend the ends sharply back because it makes them difficult to remove and/or reuse. To protect lines, sails, and people, tape the pins. For extra protection, mask the end with a gob of silicone sealer before taping.

PARBUCKLED?

With a heavy boat secured but being blown off the dock, you can get her close enough alongside to board or load using the parbuckle system. Make one end of a stout rope fast to the dock somewhere about amidships and pass it around the bow line. Bring the working part back to near where the bitter end is secured and haul away with increased mechanical advantage. Once the bow is properly secured alongside, repeat the operation on the stern line.

BLOWN AWAY

(Richard Van Voorhis) When teak cleaner or any other powder is being blown away by the wind as you apply it, make it into a light syrup in a bowl and then wipe it on.

SIMPLE STEERING

(Herb McCormick) In sailing, as in life, the most truthful truths are the simple ones. And it follows that often the best advice, especially for newcomers to the sport (or those trying to explain the sport to newcomers), is of the simple, straightforward variety.

I well remember one of the first times I took the tiller of a fast sloop sailing to weather. My friend passed me the magic stick and said, "She's in the groove. Just keep her there." Simple enough, but the *karma* must have been off. The boat wandered like a tipsy jaywalker, our wake spritzed and splashed in tortured meander; what little I had understood of the groove I lost instantly.

There began a crash course in reading jib tell-tales. How to read those signs: which airflow? what slot effects? where the tiller? how the flutter? It was a classic (and ugly) information overload. Then my friend's girlfriend, who'd been watching with quiet amusement, suggested, "Just steer away from the one that's fluttering."

Oh, the sweet wisdom of simplicity.

ACE IN THE HOLE

(Bob Johnson) Few people know it, but we make every Island Packet with a hole in its rudder. It's a well-chamfered hole at the top of the trailing edge of the blade. It's there so that, should the regular and emergency steering systems fail, you could fish a lashing through the hole and control your rudder via a bridle of lines to the cockpit winches. No one has, to my knowledge, ever needed to use it, but the hole's there, just in case.

SIMPLE SELF-STEERING

(John S. Letcher, Jr.) To get a sailboat to steer herself with fore-and-aft sails is not hard. I have tried any number of configurations and enjoyed varying degrees of success. Looking back over that process, the following common features stand out:

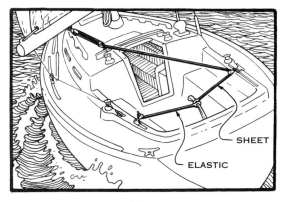

Self-steering

- Some part of the running rigging, most always a sheet, though a downhaul or vang might serve, is led to exert a pull—with or without mechanical advantage—to windward on the tiller. That line should pull harder as the boat luffs, slack off as she falls to leeward.
- The windward pull is more than enough to counteract weather helm, so the *excess pull* should be balanced by elastic of some sort run to the leeward side. This arrangement guarantees that added weather helm will be provided as the wind freshens.
- The elastic should always be positioned so it becomes slack when the tiller is centered (or just to the lee side). You can then adjust sensitivity to wind strength out of the system by experimenting with elastics of various thickness. (Surgical tubing of various weights provides an ideal range for boats under 40 feet.)

These rigs take experimentation, but the price is right for hours of relief from "the tyranny of the tiller." If a set-up doesn't work, figure out why. Keep at it, keep refining!

—*adapted from* Self-Steering for Sailing Craft

HANDY BILLY

A handy billy is a pre-rove tackle, and it has a number of uses on a boat. Sir Francis Chichester rigged handy billies to his sheets to let him make small adjustments in trim precisely and easily. Typically this sort of tackle should have a snap-shackle attached to the block at one end and a lanyard at the other—which gives you lots of ways to make it fast. You can tie it into a clew grommet, use a rolling hitch to attach it to a sheet or halyard, shackle it to the dinghy, or even use it to hoist a man overboard back aboard.

CONSTANT STAR

For a relatively quick read in a crossing situation at night, note the position of the vessel you are observing in relation to a star. If she and the star remain in the same relative position for long, that signals a constant bearing and gives warning to start taking evasive action.

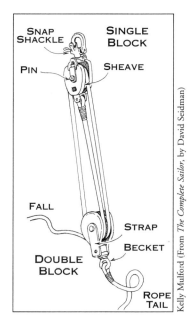

Handy Billy

Kelly Mulford (From *The Complete Sailor*, by David Seidman)

OUT, OUT

To protect that skin, thoroughly wash your hands with soap before painting. Forsaking rinse water, rub the soap into the skin until it dries, then go ahead and paint. When it comes time to clean your hands, the paint will slide right off.

INSTANT WOOD RESTORATION

(Suzanne McHutchison) To repair a shallow dent in wood, place a wet towel over it and apply a hot iron. The moist heat will swell the wood back to its pre-dented shape.

SMILING SHINE *(Bernard Gladstone)* Rather than attacking cosmetic blemishes with abrasives or harsh chemicals, try rubbing scuffs and marks in your gelcoat with a rag dipped in toothpaste.

SMOOTH HEADINGS

After much thought concerning the bubble of air in his compass, creative cruiser Glen MacLeod poured out the old mixture, let the compass dry out for a few days, and refilled it with good old Johnson & Johnson Baby Oil. "It has worked flawlessly for eight seasons—no clouding, freezing, layering, or leaking," he says.

CONTACT! *(Steve Callahan)* I'm sure I'm not the first person to think of it, but I use contact cement relatively often for emergency sail repairs. When you need to stick a rag back together without a machine, just coat the area to be repaired and the back of the patch, and voilà! Just make sure you have the cloth stretched flat and located where you want it before you press the pieces together.

Russ Brown had a jib that was patched so often with the stuff that people used to ask him if it was Kevlar. I don't know how the fancy, new water-soluble stuff works on sails (you can guess). At any rate, I always carry a can of the old smelly stuff in my kit.

SMALL CHANGE

(Jim Archer) After more than 30 years of twirling wrenches and dealing with manufacturers, I guess the most useful thing I might say is to cut down the recommended intervals and change your filters more often. I'd reduce the time between fuel filter changes by something like 30 percent. Where it says a full season for oil filters, I'd use 100 hours of running as my rule of thumb.

NO USE IS ABUSE

(Jan and Bill Moeller) One of the main reasons sailors have so many problems with their engines is that they do not run them enough. Engines are designed to be run, not to sit idle and rust. The weekender who uses an engine only to get in and out of the slip is asking for trouble. The engine needs to be run. [But no-load running can be even harder on your engine than not running it. If you run it at the dock, put it in gear, and run it long enough to reach operating temperature.—eds.]

—*adapted from* Living Aboard: The Cruising Sailboat as a Home

SOAK YOUR HEAD

(Peter Edles) Marine heads are essentially rugged, uncomplicated, and trouble free. Unless you're more fortunate than the sailors who have gone before, though, sooner or later there will be a problem and it will be *your* head poking into a disassembled Marine Sanitation Device.

To forestall that confrontation I suggest a routine of lubrication for the perishable moving parts inside your toilet. Keep rubber valves, seals, piston O-rings, and leathers flexible by periodically (twice a season) pouring into the head a half ounce of mineral or baby oil dissolved in a half bowl of warm water. Close the manual lever to flush, and pump just until the mixture disappears. Let stand for half an hour or more, and the internal workings will get the full benefit.

PRESSURE-COOKER BREAD

(Carol Robinson) I don't know why more people don't use pressure cookers on their boats. Granted, they aren't easy to stow, but they cook fast, save fuel, and are very convenient. They're also the safest thing going to cook underway because they lock up so tight. Some people, too, don't know how versatile they are. Here (right) is a recipe for bread:

THE SHORT LIST

(Jerome K. Jerome) They were only about to set off for a week in a rowing skiff down the River Thames, but they knew that they needed a list. So they wrote down everything that they'd like to take. When they saw the list it became clear that they couldn't go at all. They had left no room in the boat for themselves. "You know," said George, "we are on the wrong track, altogether. We must not think of the things we could do with, but only of the things can't do without." They gathered the items on that short list and rowed happily off together.

—*adapted from* Three Men in a Boat

4 CUPS FLOUR
2 TBSP. SUGAR
1 1/2 CUPS SEAWATER (OR WATER WITH 1 TSP. SALT)
1 TBSP. MARGARINE
1 OR 2 PACKETS YEAST

Heat the water to 125°F and add all the ingredients, mixing thoroughly before adding flour. Knead slightly, then put in a greased and floured pressure cooker, allowing at least 2 hours to rise.

Bake for ½ hour over low flame with the cooker top on but the jigger valve off. Open to turn bread over, then bake for another ½ hour. Let stand to cool before serving.

FIGURE EIGHT

(RR)

When Morris Sherwood taught the *figure eight* to me donkey's years ago, he emphasized that you could always break the knot open by sliding the back loop up the standing part—no matter what the strain. It's a stopper knot, so tie it near the end of a line.

Kelly Mulford (from *The Complete Sailor*, by David Seidman)

② KNOW YOUR STUFF

There are Jonahs, there are good men and women to have aboard, and there are those with "the right stuff." Fate, personality, and genetics all play some part in who is "chosen," but ask a true sailor, it's simpler than that.

"Like the New York cabby said when I asked him how to get to Symphony Hall, 'practice.' It's an old joke, but if you're talking about knowing your stuff, you're talking about practice." Buddy Melges knows his stuff. Just ask generations of snaffled opponents, loyal crewmen, and a grateful America (for which, wrestling with Bill Koch for the helm of America[3], he retained the Cup in 1992). Just ask the crowd who have bought enough Melges 24s to make Buddy's creation the hottest one-design of the '90s.

"You can give me Arnold Palmer's clubs; I won't play Arnold Palmer's game. You've got to know how to use what you've got. In sailboat racing you've got to know where the bow plate is. That lets you maneuver with confidence. But, to get out front of the bow plate . . . that's something else. Get ahead of your boat and you meet Mother Nature on her own terms. There's no instrument I know of that can do it. Only you and the time and effort that you put into your boat can get you there—out ahead of your boat."

It's not so much God or Nature, then. It's a process: Get things right inside the boat and you'll be able to get ahead of your boat (and of the others). Know what to do and where to look; know your stuff.

Says Buddy, "Planning and locating sail controls so they work conveniently and well is all very nice, but that's not all there is to the story. You should have a picture of what's going to happen when you pull a particular string." That picture doesn't come to some because they are blessed and not to others. You *put* the right image into your mind by knowing what to look for.

"It's natural to look at the sail when you're making a sail adjustment," says Melges, "but when you do, all you see is blue sky. Look at the horizon! If you're looking for power, you can tell that the adjustment works if the boat heels more. If she heels less, you're on the wrong track."

Know your stuff.

They were suffered to have rope enough till they had haltered themselves.

—*Thomas Fuller,*
1639

KNOW THE ROPES

GO FIGURE
Working *strains* are the greatest loads that may be put on a line continually without shortening its life. They are computed as a percentage of the breaking strain and vary from 11 percent with nylon and Dacron stranded lines to 20 percent with Dacron double braid.

Working *loads* on docklines and anchor lines are a product of windage, tidal current, and wave surge as they affect a boat. A rough measure of maximum loads generated by small boats is:

LOA	15	20	25	30	40	60
BEAM	5	7	9	11	13	15
LOAD (IN LB.)	250	360	700	1,200	1,600	2,000

(NOTE: SELECT THE DIMENSION OF YOUR BOAT THAT PRODUCES THE GREATER LOAD.)

Once you figure the loads which your boat exerts on her docklines (or ground tackle) you can more intelligently size your lines to do the job:

WORKING STRAINS FOR DOCKLINES (IN LBS.)

LINE SIZE	NYLON (3-STRAND)	DACRON (3-STRAND)	NYLON (BRAIDED)	DACRON (BRAIDED)
¼"	182	182	420	350
⁵⁄₁₆"	281	281	680	560
⅜"	407	407	960	750
½"	704	704	1,630	1,400
⅝"	1,144	1,100	2,800	2,400
¾"	1,562	1,375	3,600	3,000
⅞"	2,200	1,980	5,300	4,800
1"	2,750	2,420	6,260	5,600

FIGURES TAKEN FROM THE *AMERICAN BOAT & YACHT COUNCIL'S SAFETY STANDARDS.*

THE BAGS

(Brian McSweeney) To organize our cockpit we carry a number (three to each side, to be exact) of canvas bags. They are "balloon seat" cut—much fuller in the body than at the mouth. I have shock cord (hopefully suitable to the strain in each case) sewn in the mouth of each. We stuff the tails of sheets, halyards, guys, preventers, you name it, in the bags. If you stuff in big flakes the line doesn't seem to snarl much. We've been "bagging it" for years.

REMEMBER YOUR FENDERS

(Marty Luray) There are lots of things to know about fenders: allow an inch of diameter for every 5 feet of boat length, for instance. If you're into spherical fenders, make that rule of thumb 1 inch per every 3 feet of boat. Buy fenders not only for coverage, but for stowage—they've got to reside somewhere. Keep in mind to protect the wide part of the boat first and to hang the fenders to water level. You can always raise them. Finally, when you cast off, remember to bring your fenders aboard.

STRONGER STRONG POINTS

(Larry Pardey) In 1982 a fierce storm struck the anchorage at Cabo San Lucas in Mexico. Bernard Moitessier and a number of other well-prepared cruisers were driven ashore. One of the common problems highlighted by the disaster was the tendency of windlasses to pull away from their fastenings. One of the lessons of Cabo San Lucas is "fit your windlass with an oversize backing plate."

SPLICED TOGETHER

(MB) I noticed my daughter making a birthday present for her boyfriend. It was to be a seaman's knife on a lanyard, and she had spliced the lanyard directly onto the knife's becket. I suggested she put eyesplices at both ends of the lanyard instead, then loop the splice through the becket and take the standing part through the eye rather than making the union "permanent." She saw that the knife could be taken off the lanyard (and the wearer) that way. In many places a shackle or looped lanyard makes more sense than an elegant—but all too permanent—eyesplice.

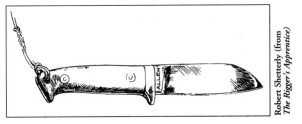

Loop the lanyard on itself.

GETTING IT BACK

(Jimmy O'Cain) Always tie a retrieving line to the head of your anchor and buoy it. That makes it a simple matter to pull the flukes out backwards rather than prying and trying to lift your anchor free from an obstruction. Less elegant but sometimes necessary (in the absence of the retrieval line that you should have bent on) is the tactic of drawing the anchor rode up taut to the bow, taking it around a cleat, and using the wave action to let you gain more and more line. Use the buoyancy of the boat to do your lifting. In an emergency come ahead over the taut rode, but make the strain even and the added power gradual.

HURRICANE HOLDING GEAR

(MB) Being anchored in 12 feet of water to a 75-pound Danforth on 30 fathoms of ⅜-inch chain and in good holding ground might seem enough for a 43-foot vessel, but a hurricane watch was in effect. To deal with Hurricane Esther's reported 150-mph winds, I'd assembled a motley but rugged assortment of gear, though to deploy it all by myself (never mind getting it back out of the mud) gave me pause.

Finally I shackled a 65-pound fisherman anchor to the inboard end of that first chain. To that anchor I shackled a second bow chain, ranged it on deck so it could run free, then took its bitter end several times around the mast and shackled it on itself. Now, when it started to blow, *Westering* would be tied to a 75-pound anchor with a 65-pound fisherman suspended halfway along its chain to deepen the catenary.

My next move was to prepare a third anchor to drop underfoot. I dug out a 30-fathom length of ⁷⁄₁₆-inch wire rope and shackled it to a second 65-pound fisherman. I rigged a plastic anchor float and secured the wire to the Samson post.

Readying the boat on deck, I struck all the sails below, tied off all running rigging to strong points, and clamped wooden shutters in place over the wheelhouse windows. I put the canvas hatch covers in place and laid out tools, seizing wire, spun yarn, and sharpened knives.

Common sense dictated sleeping now in the calm before the storm. Seven hours later I wrote in the log, "No bloody wind whatever." But advisories were heating up. The first rain began to fall at dusk. The rain thrummed down, the breeze built, and before long *Westering* was snatching furiously at her lines. I started both main engines, running them slow ahead to ease the strain on the holding gear, and stood by to see what the next hours would bring. By 0815 the dinghy was completely swamped. Force 11 winds, I would guess, were having their way—the tops whipped off waves, horizontal rain, the harbor churned to a froth.

By mid-morning wind and rain had yet to taper off. We had passed our baptism under fire and now I was eager to get the whole thing over. I cut the engines. Not till midnight did the glass improve and the wind subside a bit. It put me in mind of all that holding gear. I started picking it up around 0900. By 1330 I had it hosed off (somewhat) and was riding to that same Danforth on just 10 fathoms of cable.

FLAKING

(Eric Mino) To make sure the anchor hits bottom when and where the skipper wants, the anchor should be slung outside the stem to drop free and the anchor rode should be flaked (not coiled) on deck. One loop of a coiled line will often pick up another as it pays out and cause a jam. Flaking is a series of figure eights and allows the line to run out freely.

HOLDING TOGETHER

(RR) The best we could do for a refuge when we heard that Hurricane Bob was on the way was the rustic Annisquam Marina in the Annisquam River (at the base of Cape Ann near Gloucester, MA). Hard by a railroad bridge, its floats looked spindly but welcome. Protection was pretty good for the opening winds from the northeast, but as I was

adding a twelfth spring line to *Shere Khan*, I heard some ominous creaks. Then planks began to wrack, timbers split, and brackets pull loose. The storm was twisting the "T" dock; the long finger pier that formed the "stem" of the T (and was the anchor for most of the marina slips) was coming apart.

A handful of large powerboats were cinched up against the outside of the T. I cursed their weight; I could see that as they were swept by the 80-knot gusts, the strain was bowing the finger pier and pulling the marina apart. But as I was cursing them, one after the other they fired up and slid into gear. Their churning props, choreographed by the harried marina owner, turned together to take the strain off the dock. Slowly they straightened out the stem of the T. Idling there, they kept it straight until the breeze died down.

When the storm passed, the wind veered into the southwest and came in strong again. The dock started to bend the other way, but the boats shifted into reverse and revved together to balance things out again. Except for a few splintered planks and pulled-out cleats, the marina (along with us aboard *Shere Khan*) made it.

LIVE END

(Dr. David Lewis) Rather than fixing the bitter end of an anchor chain by shackling it to a strong point below, tie the chain to a length of stout rope long enough to let the whole chain be hauled up through the hawse. This way twists and kinks in the chain can be worked out and, should you need to slip your anchor in an emergency, you'll be able to do it quickly with a sharp knife rather than laboriously with a hacksaw.

—*adapted from* The Voyaging Stars

OUT OUT

(Tim and Pauline Carr) The humble candle has more than a brief moment of usefulness doing ropework. It heat-seals the ends of line without wasting matches or butane. It can be substituted for beeswax in treating sail thread. It even gets pressed into service to ease the opening and closing of drawers, the push and pull of handsaws, and the glide and cut of planes.

WIRE STOPPERS

Mechanical wire stoppers are effective, but you must size them to your wire and be careful not to crimp or kink the wire you attach them to. To take up strain on virtually any wire in an emergency, like when a halyard winch has overriding turns, have a braided stopper line handy. Tied in a rolling hitch, the stop grabs remarkably well. Once properly set, it will hold tenaciously under load, comes off easily, and leaves your wire meathook free.

QUICK AND DIRTY BRAIDED EYE-SPLICE   *(David Seidman)* I hate making eyesplices in braided line. Here's an alternative. It may not be as strong as the conventional splice, but it's not much weaker:

1. From a splicing kit used for braided line select a hollow fid that will accept the full width of the line you are using.
2. Push the fid and line through the standing part to make an eye of the desired size, with an extra 9 inches left over towards the end. Make sure you pass through the line leaving equal portions of braid on either side of the hole.
3. Count three pairs of strands up the standing part and tuck the fid in again.
4. Pull the tucks tight and serve the free end to the standing part.

TIGHTENING THE EYE

The knot we have here is nearly as strong as a splice, having very fair leads and being of symmetrical shape when properly hove up. Heave it taut around the thimble; then spring open the crotch of the thimble (by levering it with a fid or other tool), to seat the thimble as firmly as you can.

To get the knot tight enough, pull it as tight as possible by hand, then put it on deck with an iron bar through the eye. Stand on the bar with the knot between your feet and, with knees and body bent at about 45 degrees, bring the rope over the left hip (if right-handed), round the lower part of the back, and down onto itself. Frap a few turns, hold tightly together, and straighten the knees. Three or four heaves like this and you cannot pick the knot out with a spike.

The Gordian Knot he will unloose, familiar as his garter.

—*Shakespeare,* King Henry V

Tightening the Eye

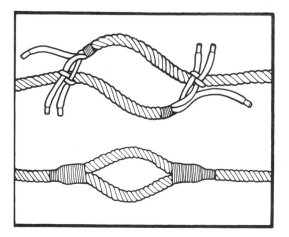

Cut Splice

CUT SPLICE

For suspending, bridling, lifting, and any number of other uses, a line with an eye in its center is handy. A bowline in a bight serves the purpose, but here is a neater and more permanent solution. Make the cut splice by overlapping two lines (equal size is best), then splice the end of each into the body of the other. Whip the splices, and you end up with a "single" line with a very useful eye in the middle.

COW HITCH

A *cow hitch* is a knot that slips as a result of not being tied properly or of not being a recognized maritime knot.

FLAMING SWORD

(Richard Van Voorhis) Now there is a knife that heats rapidly to 420°C for sealing the ends of line. It is portable and needs no batteries—just butane—giving an hour's continuous heat from a cigarette lighter refill. A soldering iron tip that screws in to replace the knife blade is available. (Sutronics, 62 Park Rd., Swanage, Dorset, BH19 2AE, England.)

WHIPPING

Whether you are whipping synthetic or natural-fiber line, rub the whipping twine with beeswax. It will be a lot less likely to come adrift.

QUICK AND DIRTY WIRE-TO-ROPE SPLICE

(David Seidman)

Ever splice wire to braided line? It's something you won't try twice. If you really have to get it done, try my way:

1. Swage a stop sleeve to the end of the wire.
2. Remove 8 to 10 inches of the core from the braided line.

Quick and Dirty Wire-to-Rope Splice

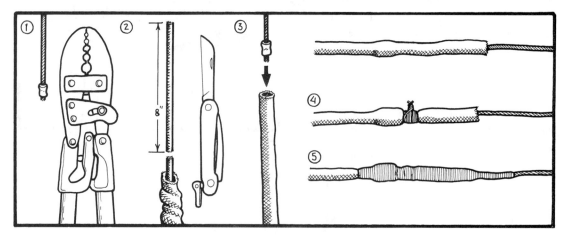

3. Insert the end of the wire down the hollowed rope.
4. Make a very tight service behind the swaged stop with Monel or stainless steel wire.
5. Starting just ahead of the stop sleeve, tightly serve the full length of the splice with strong nylon whipping thread.

[Since the wire just butts against the core, this "splice" is only as strong as the outer cover.—eds.]

ROPE-TO-CHAIN SPLICE

A shackle at the end of an anchor rode ofttimes forms a weak link. If it is small enough to pass inside the chain links, it is measurably weaker. A spliced eye in the rope creates a bulge that may be difficult to pass through the hawse. With a three-strand rode, however, you can:

1. Pass two of the strands from opposite directions through the second link.
2. Pass the third strand through the end link.
3. Splice the strands back up the rope in the normal fashion.
4. Serve over the "loose" area between rope and chain.

Rope-to-Chain Splice

BUNGEE MOORING

The idea of substituting a new-fangled bungee pennant for a tried-and-true nylon pennant made Steve Bunnell, the General Manager of McDougal's Boatyard in Falmouth, Massachusetts, a little uncomfortable. But after tripping over the thing in his office for several months, Bunnell said he decided, reluctantly, to put it on one of the boats in the harbor to see how it would fare against the rapidly approaching Hurricane Bertha. The boat he "volunteered" for his experiment, a 45-foot LeCompte sailboat, happened to belong to his service manager.

Bunnell had heard that a Hazelett bungee pennant stretched more than its traditional nylon counterparts, much more, which tended to restrain a boat's inclination to "sail" back and forth on its pennant in heavy weather. Instead of sailing, a boat on a Hazelett pennant was supposed to ease back whenever the wind strengthened and then glide slowly forward as the wind abated. Bunnell had also heard that a boat on the stretchy new pennant wouldn't yank at its mooring like it would with a nylon pennant. Bunnell remained skeptical right up until the remnants of Hurricane Bertha came sweeping up the coast and he watched from his office window as the Hazelett pennant behaved exactly as advertised. While other boats in the harbor tacked back and forth in the 65-mph gusts, dragged their mooring balls underwater and yanked violently at their pennants, the LeCompte eased backward and then forward, backward and forward, with the mooring ball always clearly visible in front of the boat. It seemed to be riding out an altogether different storm than the other boats in the crowded harbor.

Bunnell says he's a believer now, and that he plans to try Hazelett pennants on some of the smaller fin keel boats with spade rudders, the same boats that had the most difficulty ("those babies were flying everywhere") during Bertha. (For more information about Hazelett rodes and pennants, contact Seacure Solutions, PO Box 119, Milford, NH 03055; telephone (603) 672-7260; fax (603) 672-1855.)

—*adapted from "Seaworthy," BOAT/U.S.*

A PROPER PENDANT   *(Howard Barnes)*

The mooring pendant [sometimes spelled and always pronounced *pennant*—eds.] is a vital mooring component. The part to let go in a storm is not likely to be the shackle, the mushroom, the swivel, or the chain. It's the pendant. Four of my son's fellow club members lost boats in the same blow to chafed-through nylon mooring pendants. [The only time that my boat went wandering was for the same reason.—MB]

Nylon resists chafe poorly, but its stretchiness still makes it the ideal mooring line. Your pendant should be about a third of your boat's overall length. It should be the thickest line that will pass through your bow chock after it has been served and given a leather sleeve. For the mooring-chain end of the pendant make an eyesplice around a thimble, using five tucks. At the other end make a soft eyesplice long enough to fit through your bow cleat and drop over the horns.

To protect the pendant, serve it. One large ball of marlin will serve 8 to 10 feet of ¾-inch line. Stretch the line between strong points at about elbow height. Wrap the marlin using a serving mallet or marlinspike. To finish off the serving, lay a pencil along the nylon. Wind ten or so loops around the pencil. Cut off the ball, pull the pencil, and fish the end inside the pencil loops. Now cinch it tight with pliers.

Next cut leather to form a sleeve long enough to protect the pendant where it passes through the chock. Punch matching holes along the opposing long edges. With a length of waxed nylon whipping twine, thread two sail needles and, working out from the middle, stitch (using baseball stitching) the leather around the nylon.

A Proper Pendant

—*adapted from* The Backyard Boatyard

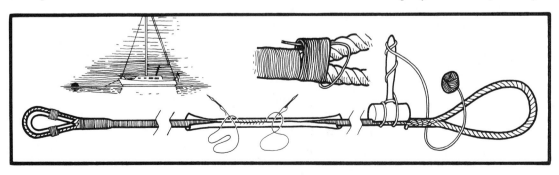

SET THE HOOK

Conditions are not always ideal, but an anchor sets best if you *lower* it from the stemhead rather than throwing or dropping it. Positioned in the water by a boat making just the slightest sternway, an anchor will lie on the bottom with its rode downwind of it. Take a strain to the point of moving the anchor, then ease off. By applying increasing strain as you drift backwards (always easing at the point when you feel the anchor beginning to give), you can "set" your hook to best advantage. Let out more scope than you plan to ride to, then take a strain and back down easily, burying the anchor. The extra scope provides a more horizontal pull. With the anchor firmly set, shorten up again to an appropriate scope for your anchorage. About five times water depth is usually adequate, but more may be required to deal with rough weather, strong tide, or poor holding ground.

GANTLINE HITCH

The *gantline hitch* is used to allow a man aloft in a bosun's chair (see "One Hand for the Margarine Can," page 40) to lower himself under control. He unjams the knot by lifting the hanging halyard tail, which allows the rope hitch to surge smoothly.

DOUBLE UP *(George Trautman)*

Set a second anchor and you can shrink your swinging circle by more than half, increase your holding power, and make sure you'll swing clear of the beach, dangers, or other boats. First, set your main anchor using plenty of scope. Next, come ahead on a course about 60 degrees to leeward of the true wind. Bring the spot where you dropped your first anchor abeam and drop your second. Set it, then tend the rodes to put the boat halfway between. Pick them up in reverse order.

Gantline Hitch

SCREWED TO THE BOTTOM

Comparison tests off Martha's Vineyard between concrete mooring blocks and the corkscrew "helix" mooring (from David Merrill of Helix Mooring Systems, Inc., Stonington, CT) involved 8- and 10-inch diameter helices fitted with mooring heads and shackles. While it took just 2,100 pounds of pull from a tug to move a 3,000-pound block, and even a 6,000-pounder was dislodged, the helices repeatedly withstood full towing force. MIT, the Vineyard harbormasters, and Boat/U.S. conducted the tests. Helix moorings are being installed commercially throughout New England. (1-800-866-4775)

ROCK RESISTANT

(*Chris White*) Multihulls generally are good boats at anchor; they have no lead hanging from them, so they don't develop the pendulum motion from a small beam swell that troubles monohulls. When monohulls start to roll, it's often not that the swell is so big but that its period is so close to the boat's own roll period. Aboard *Juniper* (my trimaran) I've often had idyllic anchorages to myself because they were too rolly for everyone else.

Multihulls do tend to "sail" around their anchors, though. They provide the cure in their beam. Just bridle the anchor rode and you'll limit sashaying to 10 degrees either side of head to wind.

—*adapted from* The Cruising Multihull

SURGE ABSORBER

We were intrigued by the idea John Whiting (*On Deck*) espouses of buoying your anchor rode to increase holding power. This seemed at first to decrease scope. However, a significant float in the anchoring system serves as a shock absorber and lessens the likelihood that the jolt of wave action will break the anchor loose. It will also help to keep the strain on the rode from burying the boat's bow and "pinning her into" the waves.

HANDLE YOUR BOAT

In the old days navigators used magic to make themselves strong. But I make myself strong by thinking, *just thinking.*

—*Mau Piailug,*
The Last Navigator,
by Stephen Thomas

BY THE NUMBERS

(*Bob Anderson*) The wind can gradually pipe up without your noticing until it is past time to reef. Rather than depending upon the time-honored seat of your pants, simply sail with a clinometer. Once you've determined the heel angle that's best for speed and handling, the clear reading will unfailingly tell you you've reached the point to shorten sail—without question, prevarication, or procrastination.

GIVE THE PICTURE

If you're voyaging, you might do well to take snapshots of your boat's underwater profile along with you. While most yard operators can do pretty well with lines drawings, it's helpful to give whoever hauls your boat as clear an idea as possible of her hull shape. A further help might come from making chalk lines on the hull exterior to indicate where strength bulkheads are and so assist in the placement of blocks and supports.

THRUST ISN'T A MUST

(*Bob Payne*) As most helmsmen know, a single-screw boat with a right-handed prop can be more than a little uncooperative about backing to starboard (or backing straight, for that matter). The reverse thrust is, of course, pushing the stern to port. The conventional solution is to get up enough sternway so that the boat will steer with her rudder. Unfortunately it is not unknown for this tactic to head me into the opposite bank or to closer association than I had wished with a neighbor. Another solution, particularly effective on sailboats or powerboats with good-sized rudders, is to gather a bit of sternway and then put the prop in neutral. When the prop stops turning, it stops pulling the stern sideways. Given enough momentum, you can then point your stern and have it go where you want it to.

GETTING THE FEEL

(Gary Jobson) Boats differ, but a good helmsman can get the best from almost any of them. It starts with being observant and open to what you're feeling through the helm, what results you're getting, and what surprises you're finding. As you get to know a boat, you'll get a feel for how she accelerates, how her helm changes as she heels, and how much rudder takes how much speed off. Remember, the best steering is often no steering at all. My favorite references to use, in order of priority, are listed at right:

1. ANGLE OF HEEL
2. THE SAILS
3. THE NEXT PUFF AS IT APPROACHES THE BOAT
4. THE MASTHEAD FLY
5. OTHER BOATS
6. MY COMPASS

SAVING FUEL

(George Lundgren) In terms of miles per gallon, the basics still apply. Slow down. Sometimes you can double your miles per gallon by easing off as little as 15 percent on the throttle. Keep your engine cool. Clean air filters, clear intakes, and general good airflow are important, and they pay off in good performance. Slow-turning, large-diameter props can add as much as 30 percent to your efficiency.

Propeller "thumps" and noises signal inefficiency. Make sure you keep your propeller clean and that you file nicks and cuts smooth. Cutting weight and cleaning the bottom are further things that will cut fuel consumption. Weight distribution is also important; a properly trimmed boat will run better than one that's down by an end.

HEED YOUR WAKE

It follows you wherever you go. Sail or power, calm or storm, you pull a wake. Good seamanship, common courtesy, and the law of the land all demand that you pay attention to the waves you make. Slow down so that they don't wreak havoc. Slow down soon enough so that all that others feel is your good intentions.

STAMP OUT WORK

(Peter Isler) Whether it's saving strength in your crew, saving time when you're shorthanded, or just "doing it right," the helmsman can do a lot to make work easy for the crew.

- Dropping a genoa or large headsail, bring the boat dead downwind if you have sea room. With the wind sucked out of it by your boat speed, the headsail should float docilely onto the foredeck.
- Hoisting a genoa benefits equally from running off.
- If you have the choice when hoisting the main, it all works better if you steer so that the hoister is on the windward side.

- Set and douse the spinnaker on a *deep* downwind course where you'll benefit from the lee of the main.

WITH THE FLOW

Maneuvering with the current behind you is difficult because steering power is proportional to water flow over a rudder. It is deceiving. If you're making 5 knots over the ground in a 2-knot following current, the rudder is only "feeling" a flow of 3 knots and will steer with only 60 percent of the power you'd expect. You must be going faster than the current speed or the rudder feels "dead water" and stops working.

BREAKING FREE

(H. A. Calahan) Getting free when you are aground in deep mud is a problem. Poling, pushing, kedging—none of the standard remedies work well with ooze. In soft mud, however, a boat can be made to wallow. Jump from one side to the other. Try to rock the boat. The keel should excavate a hole for itself, and you may well be able to back free.

—*adapted from the* Yachtsman's Omnibus

RIDING GUIDE

If a vessel is to go aground while secured alongside a dock or pier, take precautions to insure that she lists inwards (where the quay will give her support). If you will be aboard, lead a spinnaker halyard (main and jib halyards will saw across their sheaves) to a strong point on the dock and apply strain enough to create a slight inboard list. The halyard must, of course, be tended with the changing tide. If you must leave the boat unattended, fix a block to a strong point on the dock. Run a masthead halyard through the block and then take it tight to the deck. The block will exert an inboard pull yet allow the boat to rise and fall to the tide.

TAKING STRAIN

To move a substantial, displacement vessel off a shoal or take her under tow for an open-water passage, take a well-padded hawser or heavy rope right around the vessel's hull. Secure it in various places with fairleads, but the idea is to put the load into the stern quarters. Secure this bridle at the stemhead or bow roller as evenly as possible. Normal strong points such as Samson posts, the mast base, or a series of deck winches may not be able to stand the strain. A "full-body" towing hawser distributes the load best.

MAIN LINE

(Harold Cudmore) While this situation isn't likely to occur every day, having thought about it some might pay off when it comes: You've lost your rudder. You still have full sail and power capabilities, but you're drifting onto a lee shore. Why not drop the jib, sheet the mainsail in hard, and engage the engine. The boat will make her own way forward and to weather in a series of scallops, tacks, or oscillations that should carry you clear of the danger.

APPROACH ANGLE

Docking, picking up a mooring, or even anchoring under sail, your approach angle is critical. Tempting as it is to "shove the boat into the eye of the wind" and let her drift to a stop precisely where you'd planned, not many of us are that good or lucky that often. It makes most sense to approach, if possible, on something like a 60 degree angle to the true wind. That way you can ease sails to slow down *or* trim sails to speed up. In boats up to maxi-boat size, backing the main boom is an effective, if inelegant, means of applying the brakes. If you are already pointed into the wind, though, there are no gimmicks (short of the engine) that will let you accelerate.

TURNING TECHNIQUE

A boat turns around her axis. A boat (under power or sail) will rotate on a point roughly one-third of the way aft from the bow. The bow and stern therefore follow different arcs, the stern scribing a path that is wider than the bow's. Beware stern swing!

TOWING ALONGSIDE

To control a towed vessel in harbor or other tight quarters, take her alongside. This is problematic in a seaway, so wait for calm water if you can. "Corners" on either boat can do damage to the opposite number before you know it. The towboat should be made fast with its stern—steering and power unit—aft of the stern of the towed boat. This gives you steering and maneuvering leverage. Fender the two boats well.

A towing spring (from forward on the towboat aft) is your primary controlling line. Next get a backing spring (from aft on the towboat forward) in place. Bow and stern lines should be cinched taut to prevent wracking. If you encounter a wake, don't slow suddenly; that will cause your lines to slack and the boats to twist together. Use the towed boat's steering system in conjunction with the towboat's to make maneuvering easier.

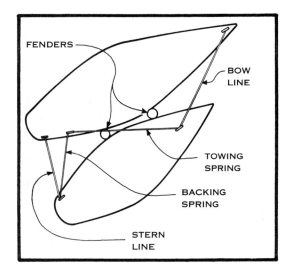

Towing Alongside

ONE SPOKE AT A TIME

(Herb McCormick) The adjustment from tiller to wheel steering wasn't so hard, I thought. We were delivering a boat down Long Island Sound. We were in convoy with a "mother ship" that had everything—the food, the girls, the charts. It was blowing healthily from the East, and we labored mightily to keep up as the night got darker and their lights got smaller. But as it got late and cold, and as I tried to concentrate on their stern light in the waves, I found myself wandering. I found myself slinging the wheel one way and then the other to compensate for the following sea. Pretty soon my gyrations—now to anticipate, now to compensate—were maddening, and they were getting worse.

Dan, the best sailor of our ragged bunch, came topside. "Damn, man, you're oversteering like crazy. Settle down. You don't need much helm action. If you get off course, bring it back slow. Just steer one spoke at a time."

Last summer I was helping some friends bring a sweet 41-foot semi-custom racing boat back from Bermuda. As we closed the coast the wind died and blank fog set in. We were powering through the murk. I was below pushing buttons at the nav station when I realized the repeater compass was spinning like a top. I went on deck to gray nothingness. At the helm, my buddy, no stranger to all of this, was staring at the compass card as if it held the secret to life itself. The wheel was hard over. "I think I'm a bit disoriented," he said. "Mind taking it for a few."

I asked the course, took the wheel, and got us headed right again.

He was right: driving through the deep soup was a bitch. I handed him back the wheel. "It ain't so bad. Don't overcorrect though. Just steer her one spoke at a time."

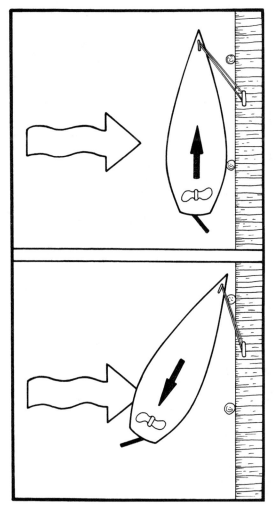

Springing Off

AROUND THE DOCK

A controlled and elegant way to leave a dock when wind and/or current are pressing you onto it is to take a back spring from the bow to the dock. Snub it tight, then come gently ahead against it with the helm toward the dock. Your stern will swing out from the dock. Now reverse, recover the spring, and back clear. You can do the opposite by taking a stern spring forward and coming aft against it until your bow swings away from the dock (but watch the prop). Well-positioned fenders complete the maneuver.

A boat's only "brakes" are her reverse gear. Current and wind and rudder action all can be used to slow her down, though. Given the choice, land upstream and upwind. When wind and current are in opposition, point into the stronger of the two. The paddle effect (right-handed engines pull the stern to port in reverse) is a consideration. It means you won't stop in a straight line, but it also gives you sideways control in tight situations—the ability to "walk" your stern to port when you're portside-to.

TIPS ON TOWING

(John Mellor)

• Even inshore, no tow should be shorter than four boat-lengths (of the towed boat).
• Secure the towline on the towboat as close to amidships as possible for maximum maneuverability.
• Towing a boat off the ground, anchor upwind, then ease back to hook up. Use a combination of anchor windlass and engine power to pull the boat off.
• Adjust boats so that they both crest and fall on waves at the same time.
• Minimize jerks in the tow rope with suitable catenary.
• Establish and maintain communication (VHF, flags, hand signals, etc.).
• Use horn signals (one long, two short) to alert traffic in fog. At night display two white lights (visible forward to 22.5° abaft the beam), one above the other.

RUNAWAY ROMANCE

(Bill Biwenga) Friends of mine were married on a large sailboat and were returning to the dock in a celebratory mood. The skipper made his approach sure in the knowledge that a quick thrust of reverse would stop the boat where he wanted her. His eyes and those of the onlookers from the dockside restaurants widened, though, when the control cable jumped off its bracket and the boat continued briskly toward the dock. Crewmembers heroically snagged cleats on the dock as the boat slid by, only to have them ripped out of the wood by her progress. Only when a line was dropped to a passing Zodiac did quick action put on the brakes.

CHOREOGRAPHY

(David Bill) Orchestration of a landing, with crew or singlehanded, involves preparation, judgment, and timing. Your goal is to stop the boat precisely *in* the spot where you want to tie her. Get a feel for your boat's "carry" and "drift" at slow speeds. Come in with steerageway only, using reverse against the boat's momentum to stop her. Pick a spot, play wind and current and propeller effects, and arrive.

Most landings deteriorate from here. Have your fenders out before you approach. Tie them fore and aft from the boat's widest point on your dockside side. Come in parallel to the dock. Having someone with a loose fender to "troubleshoot" is a good idea.

Smoothness, speed, and precision in tying up are the real measures of a good landing. Bow line, aft spring (running aft from the bow), forward spring (running forward), and stern line are not all always necessary, but they might be. The order for sending them ashore will vary, but the plan should be discussed and modified calmly and well in advance. Send the bitter end of the line ashore. Make adjustments from the boat. Unless you're tying to a float, allow for tidal rise and fall. The longer a dockline, the greater the range of up and down movement it will allow.

PROPERTIES

The single propeller normally will run "right-handed" (in a clockwise direction when viewed from aft), but left-handed props are not uncommon. Check your direction. There are five main propeller effects:

- Forward thrust.
- Sternward thrust.
- Sideways thrust. This is also called the paddle effect or propeller effect. The lower blades move denser water, so a right-handed propeller in forward gear will tend to "paddle" the stern to starboard. The opposite occurs in reverse.
- Slipstream effect. When the slipstream from the propeller strikes one side of the rudder, it enhances steering effect. The greater the force of the stream, the greater the turning power. Thus, to tighten your turning circle, gun the engine momentarily. You increase the slipstream force on the rudder without necessarily moving much ahead.
- Propeller race effect. With a right-handed prop at high revs, the port-hand blades pick up dense water and deliver it to the starboard side, so that the stream hitting the starboard side of the rudder is denser than that on the port side. This causes a slight swing of the stern to port.

TOWING A DINGHY

It's usually wise to stow the dinghy onboard, but that doesn't mean never trail one astern. Bridling the towline is a good idea. Running the painter to a block traveling a line between stern bitts is particularly neat. Tying a line to the painter with a rolling hitch also can create a bridle.

Try to get dinghy and towboat "in sync." Adjust the painter so that the dinghy parks atop the second wave aft. Whatever's in the dinghy might go in the water. Lash oars and bailers. Oarlocks? Take cushions out, etc. An outboard mounted on the transom of a trailing dinghy is risking immersion.

You will shift into reverse before you remember to shorten your dinghy painter, but not twice. Some people secure two lines (led from separate strong points on the dinghy to separate quarter cleats on the towboat) together with plastic cable ties, the idea being that if one painter snaps, the other will be a back-up.

LINES ON A DINGHY

"For every force there is an equal and opposing force" —Isaac Newton, Second Law

Any time you step in or out of one,
    thinking you're sure-footed,
it will, having a mind of its own,
    step away from you, uprooted.

A dinghy trails behind, a quiet dog,
    to be at hand when you claim it.
And when, in calm or gale or thick fog,
    it knocks the hull, who can blame it?

When you go ashore it stays behind,
    like a horse outside a frontier saloon;
and when you return, late and in a bind,
    it drifts away, waving "See ya soon!"

In it, with any luck, you're in-between
    the drain and charge of amps,
at ease; but this of course is precisely when,
    in a passing wake, it swamps.

And this says nothing of how to tow
    a dinghy, or where, on the boat, to stow
what, once out of the water, transforms
    from Siamese cat to water buffalo.

Though dangled, dragged, cast adrift, bailed,
    capsized, or just sitting pretty;
though rowed, motored, paddled, sculled, or sailed,
    it never loses *its* dignity.

And a dinghy, no matter what you do,
    gets the final word—you know:
"Like, without me, where would you
    have gone, be now, or hope to go?"

—*Richard Dey*

SAILING THROUGH CHOP

(Duncan Brantley) When it seems like waves are originating from an infinite number of sources, when words like "slop" and "trash" are on your tongue, when you're pounding, getting wet, and going nowhere— that's chop. In a powerboat you can try to pick up speed and plane over it. Sometimes the waves are small enough and close enough together so that you can skip relatively neatly from one to the next. Chances are, though, that you'll need to give your back teeth a break and slow down.

With waves there's a percentage in playing the throttle. With chop there rarely is. As long as wind and chop are lined up truly, the driest course is dead into the breeze so that spray blows clear to either side. In a sailboat you need power to deal with chop. Steep-sided waves will stop you if you let them. Start sheets and drive off to keep momentum and steering control. In light air and chop, heel the boat, hold the boom, and put a paddle where you want the pocket in your sail. Docking or picking up a mooring in slop, the waves shorten your boat's carry by about half.

Know What to Cut

(C. S. Forester) Pretty Jane shuddered and lurched drunkenly as a mass of water came in over her bow. The wind shrieked at them, and the combination of wind and wave laid the little ship over until the deck was almost vertical. There were four men at the mainmast already, but after clawing across the heaving deck, he was able to make Barbara fast there.

Pretty Jane was lying in the trough of the sea, not lying with her bows to the waves. She was rolling wildly and ever-more-deeply: she could not be expected to survive this for long. Something was needed to keep her bow into the sea. In the normal way, just a small area of canvas exposed aft would bring this about, but no canvas would stand against this wind. The foremast should be cut away. Then pressure on the mainmast back aft would bring her into the waves. The loss of the mast would probably ease her rolling, too.

It was awkward to consume precious time fastening the lanyard of his sheath knife to his wrist, but otherwise he risked wasting his effort in ridiculous failure. At last he was sawing desperately at the shroud. It parted and he moved to the next. Four minor shocks followed by a major one came next as the four remaining shrouds parted under the strain and the mast snapped off 8 feet above the deck. Almost instantly a change in *Pretty Jane*'s motion became apparent. The seas seemed to quiet, the roll smoothed almost away. Hornblower noticed then that the broken spar was trailing in front of *Pretty Jane* as she made sternway—a sort of sea anchor.

—*adapted from* Admiral Hornblower in the West Indies

Grounded!

(RR) It's never elegant, but running aground needn't be the end of your world either. If you poke into out-of-the-way spots, if you enjoy "gunkholing," sooner or later the gunk is going to get you. Maintaining your calm is key, but swift action is also a good passport to regaining your freedom. So before you bump to a stop, think about what you'll do when it does happen.

Know the state of the tide. If it's rising, relax. If it's falling, act fast. How long until low water? It helps to have these answers written out—day by day, hour by hour—either in your logbook, tide book, or on your chart.

The way you got in is often the best way out. Making sure not to back over your trailing dinghy, use a good burst of reverse as soon as practicable. You know that the water you just traversed is deep enough to float you, so try backing into your track.

The more you heel, the less you draw, so your next step is to reduce your draft by heeling the boat (with sails, with crew weight, or with a halyard taken to an anchor, a steaming dinghy, a tree, etc.). Remember, though, that seacocks for sinks and toilets will backfill on the down-heeled side, so close them. Ports, too.

If you're still stuck, take the time to sound the surrounding water to find where it's deep, then sit back and make a plan about how to get there. If you have my luck, chances are you'll have about 11½ hours of tide cycle to wait.

Climb the Wind

(Richard Bode) "In this light breeze you want to sit down here on the lu'ard side," the captain said. He settled in the lee corner of the cockpit. He sat on the floorboards with the tiller held lightly between thumb and forefinger, as if he were listening to the sound of the water rising through the rudder post and into his fingers. "You've got to climb the wind. When you sail a boat, you've got to climb the wind all of the time. Sail with the jib. Let the boat climb the wind until the jib luffs, way up high. Then ease off a hair until the flutter goes away."

Through the years I've encountered innumerable sailors who understood the theory of sailing and had no compunctions about explaining it to me. The only trouble was that either they couldn't sail or the sheer poetry of a boat in motion passed beyond their ken. But it was from the captain— "climb the wind"—that I first perceived the balance between myself, my boat, and the sea.

—*adapted from* First You Have to Row a Little Boat

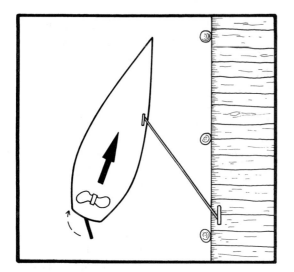

The midship spring is the most important mooring line.

THE SPRING   *(Don Street)*

When handling under power, a good seaman does not need a large crew to throw lines, fend off, or heave the bow in by force. He remembers that a spring line rigged amidships is the most effective line in the boat. If a spring line is correctly rigged and the engine is set to slow ahead, most boats can be brought to lie alongside the dock with no other line over.

—*adapted from* The Ocean Sailing Yacht

POINTING SHIP

(John Mellor) Not long ago I sailed a pretty 70-foot schooner into a winding creek near my home. We picked up a visitor's mooring, had a good supper, and enjoyed a fine sleep. In the morning, however, with wind and tide both coming downstream, we were pointed the wrong way to exit. With boats moored close on either side and not much clearance anywhere, I was loath to try to turn around under power. So I employed a little trick I learned years ago in the Navy.

What we did, quite simply, was to run a long warp from the schooner's stern, outside everything, to the mooring buoy. We then slipped a line from our bow through the mooring buoy ring and back aboard. At this point we set loose the mooring pendant. By hauling on the stern line and veering the doubled bow line, we controlled our swing as wind and tide turned the schooner end for end.

"Pointing ship" works to turn a boat on her own anchor, too. Attach a stern line (passed outside everything, as before) to the anchor rode with a rolling hitch; slack the rode and haul on the stern line and, with wind and tide doing the work, you can turn your boat the opposite way.

TIDEWATER EMERGENCIES

After going aground in confined water, shut the engine down immediately and check the inlet strainer and water circulation. Don't let mud or weed clog the cooling system. If the engine runs "lumpily" at normal revs, check for weed around the prop. A few bursts in reverse may spin it clear, or you might prune it with a boathook.

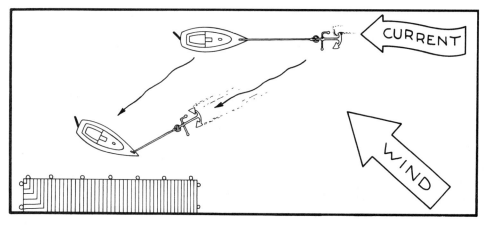

TIGHT SPACES

(Patrick Ellam) Beating up a river or narrow channel presents difficulties. I have found a bit of an advantage by headreaching along the bank or channel edge. Come nearly head-to-wind before making your tack across channel. The "bulge" of current between you and the bank will keep you from making leeway, and you can run out your momentum to the limit before you have to make your tack.

It sometimes seems that there's no way of getting there. Your berth is downwind and the current is running strong downstream. It takes some time, but "dredging in" can be used to get you safely alongside. Drop your anchor upstream of your berth. Veer cable until the boat is just upstream of your spot and then begin to steer toward the dock. To accomplish this most elegantly, shorten the anchor rode as you approach the dock. Done with perfection, you can shorten scope and let the anchor walk across the bottom so you arrive in your berth under control, then haul the anchor back aboard.

DRUM ROLL

(Norrie Hoyt) Retired on the St. John's River in Florida, my friend bought and launched his 36-foot sloop. She was, alas, too deep for the river in front of his home and too tall for the bridges betwixt him and deep water. When we fitted her with several 55-gallon oil drums (filled with water and hung from the end of her swung-out main boom), however, the boat heeled enough to get through the shallows and under the bridges and find freedom of the seas.

ON THE BOW—NOW!

(Will Robinson) We were stuck in fairly soft sand. We had strayed from a deep-water channel astern and were on a broad reach when we hit the bank. To jibe and put the wind on the beam to head back toward deeper water, we needed to pivot the boat about 120 degrees to starboard. Engine power, crew running up and down, even my father neck-deep in the water pushing produced no results.

Then it occurred to me to give us a finer pivot point. We put the whole family up forward. The keel dug its forward end in—and lifted its after half out. With maybe a third of the keel to turn through the mud, we swung right around. That made it a simple affair to heel the boat and slide back to deep water.

HEAVING DOWN

(James E. Minnoch) You reduce a boat's draft by heeling. By heeling a lot, you can get a grounded sailboat to float free. One of the best ways to do this is to set an anchor out abeam with maximum scope. Attach a snatch block to the end of a spinnaker halyard (main and jib halyards will pull across the sheave), then feed the anchor line through it. Hoist the block to the top of the mast, then crank in on the anchor line to simultaneously heel the boat and haul it free.

—adapted from Aground

BACK-UPS

(Tom Dove)

- My 11,000-pound boat won't handle at all in reverse with a 200-pound crewman on the bow. The slight bow-down trim keeps the prop from biting properly.
- Always approach a dock port-side-to if you can. The paddle-wheel effect from your (right-handed) prop working in reverse will help "walk" your stern to port.
- As you back, the force of the water will try to slam the rudder to one side. Notice, too, that your boat accelerates much more reluctantly in reverse; it's designed to go forward. This is doubly true with folding props.
- Because your prop is pulling you rather than pushing you, it is more precise to back into a slip. You can stop with a small, efficient burst of forward; you can kick your stern either way; and you can judge when you're "in" from close range. Try backing in.

GET BEHIND YOUR BOAT

(Buddy Melges) When I was preparing for the Olympics (in Solings), I spent a lot of time chasing my boat in a runabout. I'd have the crew on board make an adjustment and I'd watch the flow of water off the stern. If the flow moved aft, that meant the waterline lengthened and we were going faster. I call that plowshare engineering.

KNOW THE RULES

Experience will guide us to the rules.

—Antoine de St.-Exupery, Night Flight

FAST FISH—LOOSE FISH

(Herman Melville) Perhaps the only formal whaling code authorized by legislative enactment was that of Holland. It was decreed by the States-General in 1695. Though no other nation has ever had any written whaling law, yet the American fishermen have been their own legislators and lawyers in this matter. They have provided a system which for terse comprehensiveness surpasses Justinian's Pandects and the By-laws of the Chinese Society for the Suppression of Meddling with Other People's Business. Yet these laws might be engraven on a farthing or the barb of a harpoon and worn round the neck. They are:

I. A fast fish belongs to the party fast to it.
II. A loose fish is fair game for anybody who soonest catch it.

—adapted from Moby Dick

POINT OF VIEW

The *Rules of the Road* are an ancient and honorable tissue of legalities, but they are rendered just the slightest bit moot when one of the parties is invisible. To the big ship plodding the trade routes of the world or staking out a maritime battleground, the yacht is not just "no more than a speck," it's often not there at all.

Take a US Navy destroyer with a bridge 40 feet above sea level. Amid 4-foot cresting whitecaps our white hull and sail hardly jump out at the observer, even on the best of days. At dusk or pre-dawn we disappear against a dark sea, with running lights too dim to be seen at all unless it's totally dark and perfectly clear. On even the most sophisticated radar, targets as small as our boats are exceedingly difficult to track inside the 1-mile circle. Our speeds are so slight that big ships perceive us as dead in the water. As radar targets we come up so weak and intermittent that we get lumped with flotsam. Still, the religiosity with which we hoist and orient our radar reflectors has its reward. On 5-mile radar, the contact point we make without a reflector is about the size of the period ending this sentence. With a reflector it jumps to twice that size.

All small boats are undetectable, by *either* human eye or radar, in heavy rain. Big ships, on the other hand, make big targets—visually, on radar, even by ear. Whatever the burdened/stand-on relationship, it makes excellent sense for people in little boats to institute evasive maneuvers when dealing with big ships.

REDRESS

(H. A. Calahan) There is a fairness at the center of the *Rules of the Road*. They endeavor to give the right to the vessel that needs it most. In the case of two sailboats on the same tack, the close-hauled vessel has the right of way over the vessel sailing free. The *Rules* were formed at a time when most vessels were square-riggers. It is relatively easy to handle a square-rigger when she is running free. It is harder to sail her close to the wind. Thus the *Rules* give the priority to the vessel LEAST able to maneuver with ease.

—adapted from The Yachtsman's Omnibus

MNEMONIC MADNESS

It is helpful to turn navigational, weather, and *Rules of the Road* wisdom into easily recalled sayings, complete with rhyme and deep maritime significance. "Red right returning" is a good one—unless you're talking about international buoyage, and then it's a death trap. How about the passing protocol:

GREEN TO GREEN		GREEN TO RED
RED TO RED	OR IS IT:	RED TO GREEN
PERFECT SAFETY		WHAT THE HELL
GO AHEAD.		GO BETWEEN?

Here lies the sailor Michael O'Day

Who died maintaining his right of way;

His course was clear, his will was strong,

But he's just as dead as if he'd been wrong.

—anonymous

QUICK READING

The couple were cruising off the Swedish coast where ferry traffic was brisk. She had the wheel. He was taking bearings. They had been commenting to one another, "she'll pass astern" or "that red one will cross us," until a monster hove into view. The man was lining up a bearing on the super-ferry when his wife said, "Never mind, she's going to cross us."

"How can you tell so quickly?" he asked.

"Because I'm going to let her," she replied, turning the wheel hard-over.

RULE NUMBER ONE

The primary authority for the *Rules of the Road* in the United States is the *US Coast Guard Navigation Rules (COLREGS) 1990*. Rule 1 authorizes separate regulations for inland waters. International Rule 2 therefore is the first rule to speak to mariners' responsibilities: "Nothing in these *Rules* shall exonerate any vessel, or the owner or master or crew thereof, from the consequences of any neglect to comply with these *Rules* or the neglect of any precaution which may be required by the ordinary practice of seamen."

—*adapted from* American Merchant Seaman's Manual

POWERBOATS CROSSING

(John Rousmaniere) Boats that approach each other without meeting or overtaking are crossing. Both *COLREGS* and *Inland Rules* say that when two boats cross, "the vessel which has the other on her starboard shall keep out of the way." Therefore the vessel to the left is the *give-way* vessel while the vessel to the right is the *stand-on* vessel.

—*adapted from* Annapolis Book of Seamanship

EXCEPTIONS

(Peter Kemp) Any ship overtaking another must keep clear (including a sailboat overtaking a powerboat). Otherwise all power-driven vessels must keep clear of boats under sail—except when

a sailing vessel is approaching a ship in narrow waters, in which case the sailboat should give way.

—*adapted from* The Oxford Companion to Ships and the Sea

SALVAGE

(George H. Reid) The law in Admiralty Court differs markedly from the common law ashore. There are several criteria that apply which determine whether an act can be legitimately classified as *salvage*. If these criteria are met, any legal action that follows is considered *maritime* in nature and falls within the jurisdiction of the federal court.

1. It must take place on navigable water.
2. It must be volunteer action.
3. It must be successful.

Once the parties agree to a salvage effort, they may not also agree upon the compensation. Normally, unless otherwise stipulated, a standard agreement calls for "no cure, no pay." In other words, payment is made only upon a successful outcome.

A salvor may work under what is known as "pure salvage." Under this arrangement the salvor rescues the vessel without a previous agreement made as to compensation. In this case, a successful salvage gives the rescuer a maritime lien on the salvaged object. The salvor must make his claim to the courts if the involved parties are unable to arrive at a mutually satisfactory agreement.

If the parties enter into a salvage contract, they may agree to the amount of compensation. Failing that, they may enter into a Lloyd's Standard Form contract. Such an arrangement usually calls for arbitration in London or some other agreed upon place. However, a recent US court ruling affirms that in the case of small-craft salvage, arbitration overseas *may not be an enforceable requirement*.

The salvor may lien the salvaged object to guarantee payment for his efforts. In maritime law, attaching or arresting a vessel (commonly known as "plastering the ship") does not give ownership rights to the salvor. In effect, the court takes custody of the vessel to protect her and insure orderly payments of any judgments. Attaching a ship is a complicated and sometimes costly effort requiring the services of a maritime lawyer.

—*adapted from* Marine Salvage:
A Guide for Boaters and Divers

What's Up?

(Barry Peale) Every time I see someone towing a trailer boat down the highway with her ensign taped in a ball to her backstay, I try to tell myself that flag etiquette isn't worth bothering about. I'm still not convinced. Part of the enjoyment of being on the water is having a sense of what's traditionally and aesthetically right. Proper flag-flying provides pleasure for the spectator (me). Flying my own flags in tune with what's expected and what went before gives me a kick. Try it, you'll like it.

- Make your ensigns big enough—an inch of fly (horizontal dimension) for every foot of boat is the rule—but err on the generous side.
- In the old days ensigns were flown from stern staffs while sailing as well as in port. That tradition is coming back. Powerboats fly them from staffs or from the peak of the signal-mast gaff.
- Burgees fly from the mainmast. Use a staff that lets the pennant rotate and fly free.
- Dropping flags at sunset is the tradition. Burgees are sometimes exempted but ensigns should always come down.
- Arriving from overseas, hoist the yellow "Q" flag (meaning "my vessel is healthy; I request free practice") to the starboard spreader and leave it aloft until you clear customs.
- Sailing in foreign waters, after clearing customs hoist the courtesy ensign of your host country to the starboard spreader.

Sailboat Racing 1-2-3!

(Abbot Fletcher) First, it's a management, planning, preparation process. Everything—sails, navigation equipment, documentation, handicap certificate, accessible through-hull valves, secure stowage, weather reports, knowledge of the course, foul-weather gear, crew assignments, a watch system, food, meal plans—must be there at the starting line. There's no going back to get them.

Second, sailboat racing is a scientific technical process. A sailboat is a fluid-flow machine. You need a good hull, and you need to keep provisions, people, and whatever weight you can in the middle of the boat to reduce pitching. The boat needs to be weight and wind balanced.

Third, the crew needs to sail the boat to its highest speed under any and all conditions, *and* it needs to avoid giving away distance by poor tactical choices or delayed sail changes. Seek out big-gainer courses and digressions when they present themselves.

Admiral's Orders

(Phinneas Sprague) Admiral Chester A. Nimitz offered the following words to the Pacific fleet: "The time for taking all measures for a ship's safety is while still being able to do so. Nothing is more dangerous than for a seaman to be grudging in taking precautions lest they turn out to have been unnecessary. Safety at sea for a thousand years has depended on exactly the opposite."

Ulysses Quotient

His Roman name is Ulysses, but in the original Greek he was Odysseus. Literally translated, the Greek word *odysseus* means *trouble*. It's a poetic connection. As Odysseus wandered the seas, he was faced with troubles the winds, the gods, and the odd monster stirred up. If you are wondering whether or not to cast off and become a full-time voyager, much of your doubt will center, no doubt, on the "troubles" that await you.

In *Sell Up and Sail*, Bill and Laurel Cooper write about having done what their title urges. They analyze their own experiences and set up guidelines that should help you decide whether moving aboard is the move you should make. After all, says Bill, it takes "a certain sort to wander off in a small boat for years without actually getting anywhere much." And it takes a certain amount of cash, no matter how adaptable and resourceful you might be.

The Coopers devised a tongue-in-cheek-but-pertinent self-assessment system. See how you stack up. Your Ulysses Quotient encompasses attitude, experience, finances, and a good deal more. Free and candid with the realities of their experience, the Coopers make good guides to deciding whether to undertake full-time cruising.

KNOW WHAT TO SAY; KNOW WHAT TO DO

He always thought of the sea as la mar . . . *Some of the younger fishermen speak of her as* el mar. *They speak of her as a contestant or a place or even an enemy. But the old man always thought of her as feminine, and as something that gave and withheld great favors.*

Ernest Hemingway,
The Old Man
and the Sea

THE FRIENDLY KNIFE   *(MB)* I was at a meeting not so long ago in the office of a magazine for which I occasionally write. The editor produced a bundle of copies of the current issue fresh from the printer, securely tied with string. "You carry a knife, don't you Mike?" my friend inquired.

I cut the bonds and we handed out the issues. Later I took it upon myself to berate the boss, seaman to seaman, for appearing in what seemed to me a naked state. "Have you considered how many times, even driving this desk, you'll need a sharp cutting edge? And not just for slitting open letters. How about for fixing your typewriter carriage, for slashing through interminable packing, for defending yourself perchance against a rabid rat?"

"Uhm?"

"I'm serious. I just can't believe there are people, especially sailors, who go around without a knife in their pockets. Have I told you about David Gregory?" Of course I hadn't, so I gave him the essentials.

"I was scheduled in the submarine *Untiring* to rendezvous with *Sidon* off the Dorsetshire coast one morning. She didn't show up, so I signaled back to base asking what the delay was. I was told to return to harbor and anchor off. The relevant happening was that the squadron Captain, David Gregory, seated in his depot-ship cabin doing paperwork, was suddenly assailed by a deafeningly loud explosion. He leapt to his feet and out to the side deck, to see *Sidon* still alongside but heavily down by the bow. He raced across the gangway to the boat's after hatch, donned a breathing mask and bent on a safety line, then made his way forward to the scene of the disaster. The Court found later that a loaded torpedo had exploded and blown out the front door of the tube. One of the survivors reported that David said, 'Hurry lads. Everyone to the back of the bus. All change!'

"Last to leave the compartment, he started to follow his men aft when his safety line and breathing tube snagged on an invisible obstruction. He found himself securely anchored in the bow of a fast-sinking submarine."

I paused.

"Well?" offered my editor friend at last. "What happened?"

"David," I intoned, unbearably patronizing, "like any sensible seaman, had a knife in his pocket—even when doing paperwork. He cut free his bonds and made it to safety just before *Sidon* went under."

RETRIEVING LOST HALYARDS

(Victor Koechl) You may be able to retrieve a lost halyard by using another, higher halyard. If you can lead a higher halyard to pass in the proper direction close by the loose halyard:

1. Secure the two ends of the higher halyard to form a loop.
2. Form a noose of soft wire that is securely fastened to your halyard loop and protrudes 6 to 8 inches sideways.
3. Lead the other end of the noose through a part of the higher halyard.
4. Attach twine to this movable end of the wire noose. The twine should be long enough to let you close the noose from the deck.
5. Haul the noose assemblage into contact with the lost halyard shackle.
6. Tighten the noose. Snare the lost halyard. Bring it safely to deck.

FREEING A PROP   Fouling a prop is most likely when you're entering a harbor whose entrance is carpeted with lobster pots or fish traps, or when you're docking and a rope gets dropped into the water. In the first case there's not much to do but go over the side with the carving knife. One thing first: disarm the battery or take the key so that no one, however well-meaning, can start her up while you're in the water.

When docking, you might insure that the springs are short enough so they can't reach the prop. You should have a "cut" signal to tell the helmsman to put the engine in neutral as soon as rope hits water. If you were in reverse when you fouled the line, put the engine in neutral and haul back as much as you can. Then, with the line taut and as close to the prop as possible, haul it in while gingerly engaging the prop in forward. It might work.

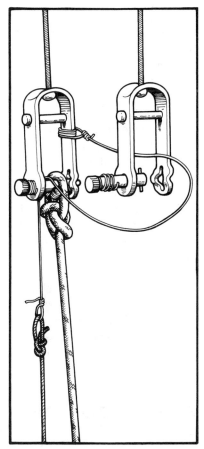

Retrieving Lost Halyards

ONE HAND FOR THE MARGARINE CAN

(Eric Newby) The ship was running 9 or 10 knots steadily. The sky was grey, the sea cold. Through it *Moshulu* drove like a thread of a screw. The bosun's chair was suspended from the stretcher of the crosstrees, and a bight of its hoist passed through the eye of the thimble, over the chair itself, and was drawn taut, held in a half-hitch quite safely (so long as the weight of the occupant was sufficient to jam it). To lower oneself it was only necessary to take some weight off the chair, ease the half-hitch, and descend cautiously. Tossed by the wind, buffeted by a 14-pound margarine can full of oil and tallow swinging beside me, I greased the cables. In rigging the chair I foolishly allowed the ends of the fall to drop on the lee side of the topgallant staysail. Without considering what I was doing, I began to overhaul it, but I neglected to jam the half-hitch.

There was a shrill whistle and a blurred vision as rigging rushed past and I began hurtling, hugging my margarine can, bomb-like toward the deck. I opened my mouth to cry out but only succeeded in biting my tongue as, at that moment, the chair fetched with a terrific jerk as the bight of line I'd overhauled jammed in the thimble. Shaking with terror, partly because of my narrow escape and partly because I was expecting to find that I'd fouled the captain's private piece of deck by the charthouse, I made my way, with burnt arm and bitten tongue, to the deck.

—adapted from The Last Grain Race

WORKING ALOFT

(Dodge Morgan) I didn't relish going aloft, but the gear I had helped. For one thing, my bosun's chair was attached to a three-part tackle which made it easy enough to haul myself up. Phil Weld had a fright when he dropped the fall from his tackle and it snagged so that he couldn't let himself down. I kept the tail of my tackle in a canvas bag. A third thing that was very successful was a piece of luff tape with a grommet in it that rode the

mast groove. I cinched the chair to it and that minimized swinging.

HAND SIGNALS

(Don Street) My wife Trich and I developed hand signals more than 30 years ago that let us communicate from bow to stern when we're anchoring, docking, or picking up a mooring. When *Iolaire* had no on-deck controls, I used to have to signal to an "engineer" below. One finger forward, two fingers neutral, three reverse. I still use the system.

It doesn't matter what the signals are, though, just work them out—for pilotage from the pulpit or the spreaders, for maneuvering in tight quarters, for heavy weather, (with a flashlight) for nighttime sail trimming. Shouting is not only inelegant, it's inefficient. Clear signals universally understood are the best way.

—adapted from The Ocean Sailing Yacht

SWEEP ANTENNAE

(Phinneas Sprague) Depending on your own evaluation of your preparation, there is no moment more terrifying—or more reassuring—than when the last remnant of land disappears beneath the horizon. At sea there is no bluff, no good line of bull. Either the situation is under control or it isn't.

A wonderful lady named Frances Wright taught many grateful students celestial navigation and "lifeboat navigation" over the years at Harvard and through the Museum of Science in Boston. Her motto was *Constant Vigilance*. As her student I might be excused for adding "foresight"—*Constant Foresight and Vigilance*.

Vigilance means maintaining the highest level of alertness. Foresight means never having to experience that which hasn't been contemplated in advance. If foresight has never imagined what vigilance detects, the line between luck and competence blurs, and you touch base with your own personal deity. On the other hand, if you have foreseen your problem and recognized it soon enough to implement a plan, you're in a good spot to make a "straight A" response to the test.

COLONIALLY COLLOQUIAL

(RR) With the spare tire in the boot, the engine beneath the bonnet, and the steering wheel in the shotgun seat, the car must be English. Ask him to open the trunk or pop the hood; if he's confused, he must be English. We all speak English, but there are two sides to the Atlantic and at least two brands of the "Mother Tongue." With ecumenical good cheer Mike and I have cut through most of our differences and hope we've found language that rings true on either side of the ocean. Still, in pursuit of clarity, we offer these transatlantic translations:

UNITED STATES	GREAT BRITAIN	UNITED STATES	GREAT BRITAIN
AIRFOIL	AEROFOIL	HOSE CLIP	JUBILEE CLIP
ALUMINUM	ALUMINIUM	WIRE CLAMP	BULLDOG GRIP
MARCONI RIG	BERMUDAN (BERMUDIAN) RIG	LAPSTRAKE	CLINKER
FLOTATION	BUOYANCY	RANGE	LEADING MARK
JIBE	GYBE	CHOCK	FAIRLEAD
TRUNK	COACH-ROOF	SPREADER	CROSSTREE
COTTER PIN	SPLIT PIN	STERN PULPIT	PUSHPIT
DAY BEACON	DAYMARK	BOOM VANG	KICKING STRAP
GUNKHOLING	DITCHCRAWLING	HEAD	HEADS
FRP (FIBERGLASS REINFORCED PLASTIC)	GRP (GLASS REINFORCED PLASTIC)	KEROSENE	PARAFFIN
		MURPHY'S LAW	SOD'S LAW
FIGURE EIGHT KNOT	FIGURE-OF-EIGHT	WRENCH	SPANNER
FLAMMABLE	INFLAMMABLE	TURNBUCKLE	RIGGING SCREW
FLOOD (CURRENT)	FLOOD STREAM	START (SHEETS)	CHECK OR EASE
BURDENED	GIVE-WAY	WILDCAT	GYPSY
HARD-ALEE	LEE-O	GYPSY	WARPING HEAD
HAZARD	DANGER	HARDEN	AFT

STOWING THE MAIN

(RR) How do you furl your main? Do you get it all the way down, take it out of the mast, and roll it into a neat and shapely tube? Do the stops you use to tie it up with have little bowlines on the end so you can cinch them up tight and use quick-pull bow-knots? Do you perhaps flake your mainsail in plaits of no wider than 30 inches and layer them precisely one upon the

other atop the boom as the sail descends? Do you position flat, strapping-like stops in evenly tensioned clove hitches to hold the sail on its perch without putting puckers in the Kevlar?

Perhaps you pull the lower part of the leech forward to form a sort of bag into which the loose folds of the rest can be bundled. You then, don't you, pull out the bottom fold, push down the remaining loose sail, and tie it up with sail ties.

Aha! You simply make a lengthwise ball of the sail and slap it into place with bungee cord zigzagged over and back between a tasteful number of hooks and eyes.

I can see the virtues (and the occasional vice) of each of these methods. On my boat, though, you get the sail down, pull everything aft, point the battens aft, and roll the whole up around the battens into an ever-tightening window shade. You cinch it firmly with clove hitches locked off with half-bows. And that's the way you do it!

FURLING WEB

(Joe Maggio) Finding the sail ties may not be the biggest problem that you encounter at sea, but it is one of the most persistent. Aboard our schooners we've developed something that solves all of that scurrying about and aggravation. Clumped all together in a predictable place, we have *Furl-o-way*, our champion sail-tier. It is simply a boom-length piece of stranded line with snap shackles at either end and sail ties rove through it at decent intervals along its length. When it's time for furling, we just grab the "thang," snap it in place at either end of the boom, then cinch up the sail with its prepositioned ties.

FREEING FASTENERS

Screws. Don't use excessive force on any fastener you're not sure about. Corrosion is usually to blame for a seized-up screw, but corrosion causes metal to become brittle. Brass screws loose their zinc (signaled by a telltale reddish hue) in a salt environment, which leaves them brittle. Take it easy!

Apply penetrating oil to soften the corrosion. Allow a couple of days for it to work—if you have the patience. Choose the biggest screwdriver that fits the slot, filing it square and flat if necessary. Apply a firm mallet blow to its handle to jar and loosen the threads. The trick now is to induce just the minimum of twist to the screw. If the blade slips out of the slot, the screw head will probably be irreparably damaged. Put your full weight on the driver and lean down on it while at the same time imparting a minute twist. [This is how an impact driver functions, and it is the most likely to succeed.—eds.] If unsuccessful at first, give another mallet blow. Repeat the efforts and be satisfied to proceed slowly in small increments. If need be, get another person involved. One person pushes hard on the driver while the other turns it slightly with Vise-Grip pliers. Wait for that first slight movement, then follow it up carefully.

Nuts, Bolts, and Studs. Penetrating oil must be given time to work—about two days in the ideal world. A rag soaked with diesel is effective, but that requires waiting a week. Your wrench or socket must be an *exact* fit. If not you will almost assuredly ruin the flats of the fastening. Be cautious about applying force on a frosty day; cold makes threads even more brittle. Use a single hammer blow to jar the threads, but you risk real damage if you overdo it.

Apply steadily increasing force, perhaps sleeving a pipe to the wrench handle for better power. If this doesn't work, sheering the fastening will probably follow, so resort to heat. A small pointed flame is best. Surround the work with moist rags and have a fire extinguisher at hand. Apply the flame evenly all around the nut. You are trying to expand it. Fumes from penetrating oil are toxic.

When a nut and bolt turn together and you cannot access the other end of the bolt, hacksaw a suitable groove in the bolt end and use a screwdriver to turn it while you hold the nut with a wrench. In a broken-off stud, drill two holes close together in a line, then take an old screwdriver as a chisel and rupture the bridge between the holes. Now back the stud out as if it were a screw.

If you can't reach a nut with a wrench, use a

sharp cold chisel to cut a deep nick in the middle of one of the flat sides. Fit a square-ended punch to the nick and smack it *hard* with a heavy hammer to get the nut turning.

Stainless steel threads generate a "welding" effect when they are forced. They must be "babied" with easing to and fro, lubrication, heat, and time to cool.

THE BIG PICTURE

(Tink Martin) My stomach was churning as I heard the wind whip the palm trees outside my window. It was a norther, and even sailing inside the Gulf Stream promised to be rough. I settled into my pillow, relaxed completely, and let my whole being soak up the rhythm of wind and waves. I began mentally trimming sail, quartering up the waves, finding the fitting S-pattern with a light touch of the helm. As the relaxation became deeper, I felt myself at one with this boat I'd never sailed.

For more than 10 years I've churned out a monthly column for *Offshore* magazine called "Boating Mishaps." The incidents are hypothetical, framed from cases, reports, and experiences. This extreme focus on the "bad side" of boating has helped me realize that the people involved in these mishaps are overwhelmingly *not* doing the daredevil, drink-too-much, playing chicken sorts of things we might expect. They are somewhat knowledgeable, somewhat experienced, and mostly responsible. But a good number have trouble with the big picture.

Good seamanship is more than just experience; it's seeing the connections. Lightening water color; breaking wake—*shallow water*. Trouble comes when we pick things up in isolation (like a bluebird weather forecast) and ignore the full picture (like purple-gray streaks of cloud, a drop in temperature, and a shift in the wind).

Imaging can improve your seamanship. Golfers picture the perfect shot, skiers master championship courses in their minds, cancer patients draw health from imaging healthy bodies. It's not crazy and it's not magic. Imaging allows and encourages the full interrelation of thought, skills,

senses, and feelings. Relax. Open all of your resources. Just *be*.

Forehandedness is a pillar of seamanship, and imaging is thinking ahead. But it's more than that. It takes our experience and knowledge, integrates it, and projects it forward. Imaging is a way to keep from doing the same dumb things over and over.

BREAKING THE LAW

(Gary Jobson) Sailing has more than its share of rules. Over the years I've found the willingness to break them from time to time has paid off.

- It's O.K. to have wrinkles in a sail if the shape is what you want.
- I find it acceptable to luff your sails a bit if you're being overpowered.
- Sailing downwind it often pays to sail by the lee for a short while rather than doing extra jibes.
- Overshoot the weather mark occasionally to arrive at the rounding with extra speed.

No matter how right you are, I've found you only win 50 percent of your protests. Avoid the protest room at all costs.

ALPINE LINE

(Bill Biwenga) There are many ways to rig a main-boom preventer for sailing offshore. One of the slickest is to attach a length of climbing rope, of suitable diameter and about two-thirds of the boom's length, between the end of a normally rigged (through a block forward and aft to a winch) preventer and the end of the boom. Climbing rope stretches up to 60 percent of its length, so it provides a safety margin should you bury the boom in a wave. The combination controls the boom well under normal conditions. Fix the climbing rope in place and you have a convenient attachment for the preventer even when the boom is let all the way out.

CHAFE CONTROL

(Bill Biwenga) Slick, durable Delrin pads and strips are a good answer for fighting many kinds of chafe. A Delrin pad cut larger than the radius of a block keeps it from scraping the deck and deadens the sound of its banging. Delrin strips on the bottom of the boom will eliminate wear from light-sail sheets sawing against the underside. Drill and tap narrow strips to spreader surfaces. Countersink the fastenings and you have a light, streamlined answer to spreader chafe. Install a wide Delrin strip from the hawse hole to the bow anchor in the way of the anchor chain to keep it from chewing up the deck. Deck-mounted Delrin can often be held in place by marine sealant. In heavy-traffic areas use a few fasteners.

There are other tricks, too. Try making a chafe guard to protect a line from a turning block, cringle, or fairlead by taking a piece of braided cover from a larger diameter line and sewing it in place. Braided cover can also be installed over lifelines where they rub the foot of the jib. I put "boots" over stanchion tops just like I do over spreader tips. I also wrap stanchions, something like an Ace bandage, with sticky-back Dacron sail tape.

A final thought: chafe guard often hides chafe beneath it. Check beneath your protectors.

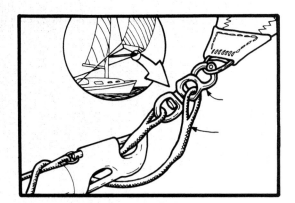

Spinnaker Trip-line

> *Designing cruising boats primarily, I still pay close attention to the deck layouts of racing boats, where convenience and efficiency are truly important.*
>
> *—Bob Perry*

SPINNAKER TRIP-LINE

If you're tired of taking fid (and life) in hand and teetering on the pulpit to get your spinnaker guy released from the sail so you can douse the sail, use a "trigger-loaded" Sparcraft snapshackle—or equivalent—(standard in most spinnaker set-ups) to gain remote control over the process. Whitbread-Round-the-World-Race boats, says Bill Biwenga, use variations of this technique to free the chute from the guy for dousing or changing. It should work just as well on a gusty afternoon on the bay. Tie a trip line into the Sparcraft (through the hole against the trigger). Snap the Sparcraft to the chute, with the afterguy made to the Sparcraft. Once the sail is set, lead the trip line over the pole, down to a block on the rail, and to a convenient winch. The trip line ought to be about the size of a light spinnaker sheet. Maintain slack in it until you want to douse the spinnaker, then tension the line until it releases the trigger and sets the sail free.

MAKE IT EASY

(Peter Isler) In most sailhandling instances, the easy way is the right way.

- Take a full turn around the base of a horn cleat. That takes the strain and prevents the figure eight or locking turn from jamming.
- When working a winch, you are stronger pulling rather than push-

ing. Set up for the grinding/ratchet process accordingly.

- For quick, temporary control of a loose headsail on a wet, breezy foredeck, simply twist the middle of the sail in one direction on itself—like a piece of taffy.
- Don't try to move a lead block or rail car under load. Take the strain onto a short sheet (using the weather sheet is fine) before you make the adjustment.

CATCH THE WAVE

(Gary Jobson) To surf on a wave, you want to steer as perpendicular as possible to its course. Set up to be upright and moving fast when you get on course with the wave. You want as little pressure as possible on the rudder as the wave passes beneath your hull. Point the bow into the deepest trough and steer just enough to keep the boat headed straight down the wave. Let your trimmers know whether you're heading up or bearing off to catch the wave so they can keep full power in your sails. Keep the boat flat and go!

REEF EARLY

(RR) I always wonder how to take the stories of solo sailors. I mean no one else was there. Well, in this case there were a few other sailors there, but they spoke only Arabic.

I'm talking about the famous incident in which Joshua Slocum (*Sailing Alone Around the World*), having decided not to try the Suez, has turned back from the Straits of Gibraltar and is coasting Saharan Africa on his way south toward Cape Town. A felucca filled with swarthy, cutlass-rattling individuals spies *Spray* and gives chase. Beneath its monster sail, the pirate boat gains hand-over-fist on Captain Slocum, but not so fast that he ignores a line of cloud appearing dirtily on the horizon. Despite the momentum of the onrushing felucca, Slocum drops his main and tucks in two deep reefs.

You can almost see the villains closing the gap and getting ready to board, but then the squall strikes. Double-reefed, *Spray* revels in it like a barnyard goose, snapping off the end of her boom but barreling on. Overcanvased, the felucca loses her mast (and the pirates their chance at *Spray*). Meanwhile the solitary skipper sails off toward the South Atlantic under canvas well-suited to the weather.

GIVE IT THE SLIP

Don't look down on slipknots. Writing in *Sail* magazine, Bill Beavis tells us that the *slipped clove hitch,* for instance, is an elegant solution for combining security and flexibility along the rail where you want to place and replace your fenders. A slipped loop not only allows quick release, it is an antidote to jamming. Witness the *slipped reef knot*—elegant for furling. The *slipped bowline* has all the virtues of the regular bowline but in quick-release form. Put a toggle in the loop and you've got the best of everything—a non-jamming, quick-tying, easy-releasing, forever-holding knot.

Hervey Garrett Smith (from *The Arts of the Sailor*)

3 TREAT YOUR BOAT RIGHT

The word came down to Noah: "Build an ark! And thou shalt pitch it within and without with pitch." Care and maintenance of our boats has been with sailors ever since. We've come well beyond oakum and tar, and it's been a while since most of us holystoned a deck, but boats still demand a goodly amount of care.

It seems ironic. Today's paints, finishes, coatings, and cleaners are so good that minimal investments of time and skill can yield pleasingly professional results. On the other hand, these same maintenance aids present a bewildering smorgasbord of choices that sets loose dark concerns about our skin, lungs, and eyes, not to mention the boat and the environment.

In the simpler times of the 1940s, H. A. Calahan set forward (in *The Ship's Husband*) a timeless ideal—to make and keep the ship ready for sea. It's traditional, it's romantic, and it's helpful. Every boat needs someone to make and keep her ready to sail. It's a noble principle.

The reality of husbandry today means doing the right

thing—in terms of economy, in terms of elegance, in terms of safety, in terms of *results*. We offer the following reports and recommendations to help you toward better results.

Treat your boat right.

BOTTOM PAINTS AND VARNISH-WORK

A Coating by Any Other Name

(Hank Hinckley) The level of sophistication of today's bottom coatings is such that some are recommended for professional application only. This may be as much a reflection of the dangers of handling the materials and residues (which are genuine) as it is of the difficulty of application. At any rate, the technology available now includes *permanent* bottom-coating systems of 100 percent copper either sprayed or applied in sheets. This has come about because tin and TBT (tributyl tin) products have been legislated out of use on pleasure boats. Special tin-based products are still available for use on aluminum boats and outdrives, but for all other applications copper seems to be the answer today—the more the better. Foil applications aside, the copper is usually painted on, combined with a relatively new vehicle like polypeptide polymer, controlled solubility copolymer, or epoxy polymide, or with more familiar alkyd enamel or modified epoxy paint.

Bottom coatings divide into two general groups. One works through the leaching of the toxicant as the material ages. The other exposes new toxicant as the coating *ablates*, or wears off.

The leaching group is made up of coatings with increasing degrees of surface hardness. Softer paints are for slower-moving boats in less severe fouling conditions. Harder paints cost more and are targeted for faster or racing boats.

Ablative paints are less subject to the vagaries of temperature and salinity, they are better at fighting slime, and they require little surface sanding for recoating. They also are not affected by exposure to air, so you can put them on well before launching. They are at the high end of the price range.

Using an epoxy-based primer/barrier coat under the bottom paint will improve the bond and increase the longevity of the coating that you choose (as well as provide a measure of protection for the laminate against

> *The boatkeeper's most grievous problem is his/her/our tendency to re-invent the wheel.*
>
> —*Richard Van Voorhis, Tabor Academy*

water penetration). The choice in bottom paint today goes well beyond the old "red, blue, or green."

PAINT THE PROP

(Chris White) Walk through any boatyard and you'll see more fouled props than clean ones. It's tough to make antifouling stick to props, but there's a right way to do it. Etch the metal with rough sanding first, then paint the prop, shaft, and strut with a zinc-chromate primer. Regular antifouling will have no trouble adhering to the primer. I usually apply two different colors so I can tell when the first coat is wearing off. Even a little slime can mean as much as ½-knot loss under power, so put potent paint on your prop.

PROTECT YOURSELF

Bottom coatings contain toxins. Use these guidelines when you're working with *any* paint or coating that might be toxic:

- Don't spray it. If it must be sprayed on, let the pros do it.
- Wear tight-fitting industrial-quality goggles.
- Wear a quality respirator, and change the filter elements often.
- Apply paint outdoors or in a shop where there is free airflow.
- Get away from the paint at the first sign of an adverse reaction. Headache, nausea, breathing difficulties, and chest constriction are all signs that you should stop painting immediately.
- Wet-sand whenever possible to minimize dust.
- Keep the substance off your skin as much as possible. Wear gloves, protective clothes, a hat, etc.
- Shower after applying or removing bottom paint.
- Read and heed the cautions that come on the can.

DIVE IN

(Dave Gerr) Take a quick dive into antifouling terminology and see what you come up with:

- *Ablative, self-polishing, copolymer,* and *sloughing* paints (or coatings) are all *soluble,* i.e., they work by allowing their surface layer to dissolve or "slough" away into the water. Soluble paints

are the old reliables of the bottom paint business. Their big drawback, though, is abrasion. Even simple scrubbing wears them away.

- *Non-soluble* antifouling paints like the one-coat *epoxies, modified epoxies, epoxy esters,* and *vinyl-based paints* all contain a biocide that dissolves into the water through the pores of the coating while leaving the paint film relatively unaffected.

Hard-surface non-solubles are usually the best choice if you're going to scrub your bottom regularly or if you have a high-speed powerboat or racing sailboat. Vinyl paints aren't compatible with other coatings. Soft, soluble paints are generally best for displacement-speed craft that aren't scrubbed often.

Ever see a dolphin with barnacles? Interlux has released an antifouling system designed to emulate the dolphin. Called Veridian 2000, it's based on silicone-elastomer technology, is applied by professionals in five coats, and results in a slightly rubbery, softish surface that's extremely smooth and slippery. Current cost for an average 45-footer is about $12,000, and the coating is meant to last at least three seasons. Dive right in?

PAINT COVERAGE

One gallon of most paints and varnishes will cover about 500 square feet. Antifouling covers less, about 300 square feet per gallon. Estimate a boat's bottom area by multiplying length times beam times 0.90.

GO WITH THE FLOW

(Brodie MacGregor) Around the yard (Concordia in South Dartmouth, Massachusetts) people are always asking me about antifouling. A surprising number leave the choice up to us.

- One thing that's true of all antifoulants is that a stationary boat keeps them from working properly. When the paint is undisturbed, an oxide film forms on the surface that inhibits—actually it just about neutralizes—the action of the antifouling agent.
- This season, more out of desperation than anything, I've applied regular epoxy (with no an-

tifouling) to my Etchells; it's smooth and hard enough to withstand all the scrubbings I give her.

- Some people around here are pretty excited that there's finally a copper-based white paint for racers.
- I see vinyl paints less and less, though they are still used on Beetle Cats because wood boats flex and swell a lot.
- All around I'd have to say we put on more Awlstar (from U.S. Paint) than any other brand.

PAINTING TIPS
(Ferenc Maté)

- Spread the toxin (copper) evenly through the coating by stirring constantly as you paint.
- Long-haired rollers get too heavy when soaked with bottom paint. Short-haired rollers work best.
- Spraying bottom paint isn't a great idea. Remember, you're spraying liquid poison.
- Put the sacrificial zinc on the shaft or whatever other underwater metal you are protecting before you apply paint. That allows for good electrical contact between the zinc (don't paint it) and the underwater metal (which you should paint—except, of course, beneath the zinc).
- Store paint cans upside down. That prevents air from seeping in and hardening the mix.

—adapted from Shipshape

PICK YOUR PAINT

Ask around to find out what works well in specific areas. Water temperature, salinity, movement, and pollution are all factors, so do some research to find what works best where you are. Know the type of antifouling already on your boat because some paints, particularly vinyl-based coatings and some epoxies, are not compatible with other paints.

DOWN UNDER

(RR) In my experience, there is no way of painting a boat's bottom without besmirching most of yourself with antifouling. The closest thing to a secret for keeping self-coating to a minimum is "less time, less mess." The longer you're beneath the boat, the more time the drips have to get you. Preparation is the key—not only to achieving smooth and durable results, but to limiting the accumulation of mess on your person. Fairness thus takes on at least two meanings when you're painting a bottom.

Getting old bottom paint off is tough. Heat guns, orbital sanders, and strippers are all messy and spread more toxins about than you'd like, but hand sanding and scraping aren't much safer, and they're a whole lot slower. From this unattractive assemblage I tend to choose a "safe stripper," one that contains no methylene chloride. They're just as effective as other strippers, they just take longer to do the job. Peel-Away takes up to 48 hours, but it's my stripper of choice.

If you have doubts about a stripper and how it will affect your hull and/or your environs, use something else. Otherwise, mask carefully, apply with cheap bristle brushes (foam disintegrates), and avoid scouring with steel wool (which, among other sins, leaves bits and grits behind that will rust). Wear gloves (rubber rather than latex), good goggles, and protective clothing. Plastic sheets or drop cloths taped over areas covered with stripper concentrate the vapors on the surface and accelerate the action. Most people waste up to half the potency of their chosen stripper by scraping it off before it has a chance to complete its reaction with the paint. If the paint peels to the hull surface, it's ready. If not, WAIT! After the paint is off, wash the hull, either with a solvent wipe or with water.

The best way to prepare a hull for bottom coating is a thorough machine sanding and then one or two coats of epoxy primer. The primer is much more effective than gelcoat as a water barrier, and it's hard enough to allow for wet-sanding the bottom to achieve genuine smoothness.

Before priming, fair gouges with an epoxy-based fairing putty. Use a portable hair dryer to make sure the dings and gouges are clean and dry before you put on the fairing mix. If the fairing compound is harder than the surrounding surface, it will create hollows; an epoxy/microballoon mixture just dense enough to hang on a vertical surface without sagging is ideal.

You can apply epoxy primer by brush, roller, or spraying. One of the best ways is to put it on with a smooth roller while someone follows behind with a wide foam brush smoothing out the roller nap marks. However you apply it, make the coat as smooth as you can; sanding out surface irregularities in epoxy paint isn't easy.

Try 220-grit paper, used wet, to sand the primer. To fair the surface, use a rubber sanding block, like those sold for auto-body repairs. For a surface with lots of irregularities, try a fairing board—a 2-foot by 3-inch strip of ¼-inch Masonite or plywood to which you staple sandpaper. Like battens, these "long boards" conform to the curves of the hull to help you achieve a fair surface.

WHAT'S UP FRONT COUNTS

Skin friction is the major form of hydrodynamic resistance sailboats encounter at low and medium speeds. Laminar flow reduces skin friction. Laminar flow occurs only over the forward third of the hull. Given these tenets of rudimentary hydrodynamics, does it not then make sense that the forward third of the shape (hull, rudder, keel, etc.) should be faired to the highest perfection possible to promote increased slipperiness through the water—with attendant speed and efficiency rewards?

POP OFF YOUR BOTTOM PAINT

Some time back we heard about a boatowner who removed a nine-year accumulation of bottom paint from his 33-footer in just three hours. Here's how. He connected a sandblasting rig to a commercial compressor, then filled the hopper with ground-up corncobs instead of sand. Reportedly corncob is coarse enough to wear off bottom paint, but soft enough not to damage gelcoat. It sounds awfully good, but we are sure this will work on soft paints only, not on epoxy-based coatings.

VARNISHING WITH AN AIRBRUSH

(Doug Terman) This is a way of laying on five coats of varnish in one day without sanding between coats. Prepare the area to be varnished in the normal manner: sanding, wiping down, tack ragging, and masking. Then take a high-quality varnish such as Epifanes, cut it with 30 percent Japan drier, then airbrush it on. After finishing the first coat, go back to where you started. If the varnish is dry enough to touch but leaves the imprint of a fingertip, start to spray on the second coat. On a sunny summer day in New England with temperatures in the mid 70s, five full coats can be laid on, and the effect is mirror-like.

SIX!

(H. A. Calahan) I recommend strongly that all new varnish work should be built up with at least six coats. By six I do not mean five. Five coats of varnish are not sufficiently waterproof to prevent the moisture from attacking the surface of the wood underneath and discoloring it. If you build up six good coats, you will have enough varnish to protect the wood and, by occasional light sanding and adding a fresh coat, you can keep your varnish in perfect condition for several seasons.

—*adapted from* The Ship's Husband

VARNISHING TIPS

(Ferenc Maté)

- Varnishing calls for a good, dry day. On the East Coast an offshore breeze, light enough not to raise dust, is ideal.
- Sand old varnish thoroughly. Use 100-grit paper and always sand with the grain.
- Don't sand in the afternoon if evening dew might raise the grain of the wood before you varnish.
- Thin your first coat by at least 10 percent so it will penetrate the wood.
- Short-bristled brushes let you spread the varnish quickly and allow more time to *tip off* before the varnish sets up.
- Sand lightly between coats with 220-grit paper.

Work for an even surface pattern.

- Don't varnish out of the can the varnish comes in; pour what you need into a small clean container.
- Strain varnish through a nylon stocking to remove grit and dust.
- Don't stir or shake.
- Don't varnish in direct sunlight.
- Don't move varnished work from shade into the sun.

—adapted from Shipshape

TURN OFF THE BUBBLE MACHINE

(Bob Payne) Bubbles are one of the banes of the varnisher's existence. If they break while the varnish is still wet enough, they cause no problems, but if they don't break until after the varnish has begun to set up, they create depressions that look something like the craters on the moon. Avoid bubbles by remembering you are working with a paint brush, not a scrub brush. Wipe your excess varnish at the start of each stroke gently on the *inside* of the can. When you wipe your brush on the rim it aerates the bristles; thus you not only foment drips down the outside of the can, you foster bubbles.

THREE WAYS SLICK

(RR) My personal runny, blotchy, drippy track record is grim enough that it makes me quake to offer advice in the arena of awe-inspiring varnish-work. However, *by observation* I know that consistently sparkling brightwork is a matter of attention to detail and a determination not to take shortcuts. For more specific advice I identified a yachtsman, Jonathan Lewis, and a professional, Roger Crawford, whose results spoke for themselves, and I asked them to fill in some of the steps they took on their respective ways to excellence.

- A store-bought tack rag to pick up dust from the surface that you're working on is inexpensive and handy. If you want, you can make your own by dampening a piece of old undershirt or other soft cotton cloth with whatever solvent (thinner) your varnish calls for. Then trickle on a little

varnish and wring it so that the thinner and varnish get mixed. Fold the rag into small squares. Use one square at a time to assure that you are always wiping the surface with a dust-free rag. When the rag is full of dust, throw it away and break out a new one. (JL)

- If the wood is weathered and blackened to the point where normal sanding won't remove the blotches, bleaching is the answer. The traditional bleach is a solution of oxalic acid crystals dissolved in ½ cup of warm water. Wipe this solution on the bare or blackened spots. Go lighter with the solution toward the outer edge of the discoloration to help blend spots into the rest of the surface. Make a solution of 1 cup of borax dissolved in a quart of warm water. When the discoloration has disappeared, wipe on the borax solution to neutralize the bleach. Allow to dry 10 to 12 hours before sanding. (RC)
- With your wood bleached and sanded, you may need to fill and/or stain the surface before you varnish. Stains have a watery consistency, but fillers usually come as thick paste, which needs to be thinned according to product directions. Rub or paint the filler or stain (or filler/stain mix) on and let it stand for 10 to 15 minutes. Then rub hard across the grain with an old towel or piece of burlap to remove everything that has not penetrated into the grain. Don't apply filler to too large an area or you won't be able to rub it all off before the paste dries completely. (RC)
- Brushes must be either the cheapest type of disposable polyfoam brushes or the most expensive ($15 top-of-the line) badger bristle. There is, I have found, no middle ground. The most important advice is to use a brush that is perfectly clean and pliable. (JL)

WHICH WAY STEINWAY?

(Ralph Naranjo) When I am asked what sort of finish to use on exterior teak, I recommend a good-quality spar varnish. It is true that there are complicated two-part solutions which, when sprayed on the wood, give it the gloss of a freshly

rubbed Steinway, but unfortunately that gloss is short-lived. Teak might just have been invented by Murphy (he of Murphy's Law) to lift the shipkeeper's best finishes. Seeing eleven precisely applied coats of urethane or varnish separate from the wood at the very bottom layer can ruin anyone's day. Ergo spar varnish. It's not as hard as the synthetics, so you won't need a jackhammer to get it off when the time comes.

Another possibility is to seal the teak. The promise here is also greater than the performance, however. While the wood looks good after you have done it, some sealers with overmuch linseed oil darken quickly, others wash away and bleach out discouragingly fast. Cetol and Epifanes are, I have found, the best of the lot at delivering attractive results that last. Use masking tape and a throwaway brush, remember that two thin coats are better than one thick one, and avoid drips onto the gelcoat.

BASIC BRUSHING
(Don Casey)

- Dip the tip of the brush into the paint—never deeper than ⅓ the bristle length.
- Unload one side by dragging the brush over an edge. For small jobs it's okay to use the edge of the paint bucket. For larger painting projects, install a piece of stiff (coat-hanger) wire through punched holes in the can. It should prevent most paint from finding its way outside the bucket. A straight wire also introduces fewer bubbles into varnish.
- Apply the paint—loaded side first—just beyond the wet edge. Use several straight back-and-forth strokes to join the paint to the previously painted area and to spread it evenly. You can brush enamel as much as you like, but when applying varnish, limit your strokes to the absolute minimum.
- Finish by blending the new paint into the previous brush load. The usual method is to brush into the previously painted area, lifting the brush while the stroke is still in motion, but the best finish is achieved if the final stroke is out-

ward. Start this stroke 6 inches behind the old, wet edge, but don't let the bristles actually touch the paint until a couple of inches inside the wet edge. Think of landing an airplane—very softly. Continue this light stroke to establish a new wet edge. The advantage of this outward stroke is that it pushes excess paint forward rather than back into the previous application.

—*adapted from* Sailboat Refinishing

A FINISH TO DIE FOR

(Ron Gray) I was never happy with the look of my interior teak until I sanded the wood (smoothly and evenly). People with bare wood should cut the first coat of varnish by 10 to 15 percent with thinner. I was working over old varnish so I applied the first coat of satin-finish urethane full strength. Next I brushed on 6 or 7 coats of the same stuff. I let each coat dry (usually overnight) but I didn't bother to sand between coats. Finally I began to sand using 600-grit paper wet, attacking stubborn spots with bronze wool. I rubbed parallel to the grain, working with paper and the bronze wool, until I had a perfectly smooth surface, satiny to the touch. Even though I had sanded the gloss and weather-resistance from the varnish, I was still left with a smooth, velvety, lustrous surface that will last for years, especially if I grace it with a light coat of wax from time to time. [Wax may prove a problem later.—eds.]

SOLE SURVIVAL

(Hank Hinckley) Teak and holly soles are deservedly popular, but they present a maintenance dilemma. The teak veneers are rarely thick enough to stay put without some protection for the glue that holds them in place. They look like hell, too, if you let them gray out. On the other hand there is virtually no coating to put on the sole that will yield a secure footing when the sole is wet. Therefore the best you can do is use a satin-finish polyurethane floor varnish and dust it with the barest amount of fine non-skid grit near the foot of the companionway, in the galley, and outside the head.

A MEANS FOR THE ENDS

Even varnished masts should be painted at their very top and butt to protect the end grain in those areas.

COATING AND CLEANING

ORDERLY PAINTING

In painting, use only a little paint on the brush and never paint cross-wise; that is, never make the strokes cross; they should always be parallel to one another. Put paint on in thin coats. It will dry quickly and form a hard surface.

When painting topsides, always start from the windward side. This assures that no paint or dirty water will be blown onto the finished work. When painting the mast or tarring down rigging, a simple way to control the paint or tar is to fit the paint can inside a bucket and pack it around with rags.

—American Merchant Seaman's Manual

WHITE WHITE WHITE   To give a long-lasting snowy brightness to interior enamel, add half a teaspoon of royal blue to every new quart of white and mix in thoroughly.

EUREKA   *(Dynamite Payson)* Having built my share of plywood boats over the years, sealed with the best of sealers and painted with Woolsey's best yacht paint laid on with the best badger-hair brushes, I've come to the conclusion it was all a waste of time. No matter how good the preparations, base coats, and all, boats left outdoors were a mess in no time, with paint cracking and peeling off the plywood. Ah, but on fiberglass the paint was perfect and stayed that way regardless of the weather. Now I glass the whole outside (not the interior) and use latex-based paint inside and out. Why didn't someone tell me about that 30 years ago?

PLASTIC OVER WOOD?   *(Doug Templin)*

"Wood's got to breathe" my boatbuilder friend exclaims, explaining why he'd *never* put a linear polyurethane coating on the hull of his wooden boat. I've had this sort of discussion hundreds of times in my years of coating sales. Intelligent, skilled, knowledgeable people like my friend simply cannot imagine covering wood with "plastic." I've painted my 36-foot wooden ketch with two-part polyurethane (just three times

If it moves, salute it.
If it doesn't, paint it!

—*sailors' wisdom circa WWII*

in the past 10 years). She continues to turn heads, and I'm way ahead on seasonal yard bills. It's the way to go.

The common denominator in objections to these coatings seems to be that they impede the wood's need to take in and release moisture. What about spar varnish? Doesn't it, in fact, isolate the wood from its environment? Urethanes, owing to their dense, chemically cross-linked structures and substantial adhesive properties, do the same job. They just do it much better. With fewer, smaller spaces between pigment particles and resin molecules, they offer greater obstruction to water molecules, vastly superior gloss, color, and shine retention, and much greater coating durability. But over wood?

Urethane coatings are, in fact, only appropriate for wood that is uniformly dry and has reached equilibrium with the environment. There should be no manifestation of excess moisture, like blistering paint. Healthy, properly dried, dimensionally stable wood is what you need. Hardwoods produce the most predictable success. Problems can develop with "pissin' pine" that continually bleeds sap from its many knots.

If you have an area where there is a good deal of shear movement between planks (like a deckhouse), don't urethane there. Any hull whose seams have worked in the past is likely to do so again, shortening the life of the finish, even urethane. Be sure all butt joints, scarfs, and cracks are sealed tightly. A polymer coating is no more resistant than any other to moisture migrating behind it and attacking the bond. Unless your existing finish is in exceptional condition, you will get much more of the gloss and durability that the urethanes offer by "wooding" your hull.

Surface preparation is always critical. With these coatings it is doubly important because they are so thin that even the barest flaw beneath them mars the finish coat. Whether you use unfilled epoxy resin (two or three coats applied with a roller and rough-sanded and cleansed) or a high-build epoxy primer (mixed 1:1 with catalyst and brushed, rolled, or sprayed until the coats are thick enough

to bring low spots up to the highs) as your base coat, you will find them very hard to sand. Don't be duped into a softer finish, though, because ease of sanding means ease of denting. A firm foundation makes for a long-lasting finish.

Fairing comes next. Mix microballoons and epoxy, or use a store-bought epoxy fairing compound. (Don't use polyester putties on wood.) Apply with a squeegee and sand. Finally apply a finish-sanding surfacer and finish-sand to the 220-grit stage.

Spray application shouldn't be attempted unless you've already developed familiarity and some spraying skill. [More than that, you need a full pressure suit to spray safely.—eds.] Brush-on results can be surprisingly good, though. Mix the color base with the catalyst according to the instructions from the manufacturer. Then add the recommended amount of brushing thinner to make the paint flow. Use good bristle brushes—lots of them; foam brushes just don't work with urethane. Clean with MEK solvent.

Keep epoxies off your skin and employ good air flow and respiratory protection to keep fumes out of your lungs. Fresh, activated charcoal filters on a tight-fitting respirator mask offer a good bit of protection; a positive-pressure fresh-air supply respirator offers more.

BRINGING IT BACK

When your polyurethane finish begins to show the effects of exposure and/or ham-fisted helmsmanship, you might be able to resuscitate it. With light hand pressure, wet-sand the scuffed or lackluster areas with 3M 1500-grit color paper. Machine-buff the sanded areas with Finesse-It *liquid* buffing compound (from 3M). Don't expect to restore the shine more than once or twice in the life of the paint, so protect that shine when you get it back. If you had put fenders out to start with. . . .

BRUSH BIN

(*James R. Neal*) To make an overnight brush-storage container, drill holes just large enough for a wire to pass through in either side of a coffee can.

(Make sure you've got the plastic snap-on lid.) You can drill holes at different heights to hang different-size brushes and keep them immersed. Hang brushes on the appropriate wire, pour in turpentine or thinner, and snap the lid on. Your brush will keep well until you return, but clean it more completely for permanent put-away.

SPAR WARS

(Joe Maggio) To maintain the hundred-foot sticks in *Heritage of Miami* and *William H. Albury*, we tried a number of things. Over the years we settled on a concoction of Deks Olje, linseed oil, Japan dryers, and a bunch of other stuff. When I was docked at Mystic in 1986, I asked one of the shipwrights what they used on the spars of the *Dutton*—what research showed about tending wood in her era. He laughed and handed me a bottle of petroleum jelly. Vaseline! I thought he was putting me on, but he said that they simply sluice their masts with Vaseline. It protects, keeps water out of the wood, and can be removed very easily. We do that now, and it works beautifully, though we've modified the routine a bit to include using a little Deks Olje first, purely for cosmetic purposes.

DRIPS AWAY

To clean drips and runs of varnish, teak oil or sealer, or paint from your topsides, start with a mild solvent like mineral spirits. Nastier blemishes will require an escalation of your attack. Acetone is the next weapon, then toluene. Use these only with good ventilation, and wear protective gloves. Rubber kitchen gloves provide good feel and fine protection; latex gloves can succumb to some solvents.

Once you've removed all the stain you can with solvent, there is always abrasion. Rubbing compound isn't great for the finish, but applied judiciously it can return your hull to presentable status.

This whole exercise is a superb reminder of the invaluable adage: "An ounce of prevention sure beats all that pounding around trying to cure the mess you made in the first place!"

SQUEAKLESSLY CLEAN

(Hank Hinckley) You can use a moisture-barrier lubricant like WD-40 or CRC to clean tar and grit from fenders, decks, shoes, or topsides. Spray on liberally, let sit for a couple of minutes, and then wipe off. Repeat as necessary.

ON & OFF

(Alice Robinson) For a general hull cleaner that won't harm fiberglass yet is tough enough to remove rust stains, yellowing, and barnacle rings, On & Off is my choice. It's made by MaryKate Boat Care Products (Bohemia, New York), and it's worked well in Caribbean and New England climes over the years. It contains hydrochloric, phosphoric, and oxalic acids. For general cleaning, pour it into a plastic container, apply it full strength with a natural-bristle brush, then hose off or rinse with water. For rust stains, apply directly to the stain, let stand for 60 seconds, then rinse. Reapply if necessary. For barnacle "footprints," apply, wait a few minutes, scrape, and they're off!

IT CAME FROM AEROSPACE

Boeing Aviation developed a metal protectant that works well on boats. Its developers say, "Experience told our aerospace engineers that Teflon, silicone, and other synthetic products evaporated too quickly to work well against rust, while thicker coatings were too messy for aircraft application." So they formulated Boeshield T-9 from a combination of solvents and oils (to assure penetration) and a wax (that remains as a dry barrier film after the other ingredients have evaporated). Because of its initially thin viscosity it has the ability to penetrate metal pores and assembled components and displace moisture while dissolving minor corrosion. It then leaves a resilient (but removable) coating that lasts for months. Use it to protect engines, deck hardware, and steering linkages. It is non-conductive so it can also be used on electronics, fuse panels, electrical circuits, batteries, and wiring connections. Boeshield T-9 is also an excellent lubricant.

A Yankee ship came down the river;

Blow boys, blow.

Her hull and spars they shone like silver.

Blow my bully-boys, blow.

—*sea chantey*

RUST BUSTER

Wearing rubber gloves, apply muriatic acid with a rag to gelcoat rust stains. Let it work for a minute or so, then rub the stains away. When the gelcoat is clean, rinse the area with plenty of water. Muriatic acid works well on stains on wooden-boat enamel using the same technique.

CLEANING VINYL

(Warren C. Graumann)

To clean a vinyl interior, wipe it down with a mixture of ammonia and water. Follow with a warm-water rinse. Soap and liquid cleaners seem to allow mildew to get a foothold in vinyl fabrics.

AS SMOOTH AS . . .

Few materials are as absorbent when used for cleaning spills, soaking up oil, or polishing and buffing as babies' cloth diapers.

AN OLDIE THAT'S A GOODY

(Warren Graumann) There's a simple, economical, and pleasing way to treat your gelcoat: apply one or two coats of a good auto polish (Nu Finish). My boat is 19 years old and her topsides still look great.

HOME TEAKBREW

(Don Casey) Before teak can be oiled (or given any other coating, for that matter), it must be completely clean. Use the mildest cleaner that does the job. Start with a 75/25 mixture of Wisk laundry detergent and chlorine bleach (no water), boosted with TSP. Apply with a stiff brush, scrubbing lightly with the grain. Leave the mixture on the wood for several minutes to give the detergent time to suspend the dirt, and the bleach time to lighten the wood, then rinse thoroughly by flooding and brushing.

—*adapted from* Sailboat Refinishing

NO ENEMIES

Bar Keepers Friend does a fine job of scrubbing the counters down at Duffy's Tavern. It may also be the best teak cleaner you'll ever use. Bar Keepers Friend is cleansing powder containing oxalic acid, so it bleaches the teak as well as cleaning it. You can find it in many supermarkets—or maybe Duffy will give you a can in recognition of your dedicated patronage.

THE FOAMING CLEANSER

If you can't find Bar Keepers Friend (what kind of sailor are you?), try plain old Ajax powder, which also contains oxalic acid. It not only "washes the dirt right down the drain," it brightens teak. You may wonder why you've been paying six times the price all these years for some fancy-smancy cleaner with a boat on the label.

XYLOL

(MB) Tarting up my little boat preparatory to putting her on the market, her white fenders, it struck me, had turned an unacceptable shade of gray. A note in a boating journal suggested using solvent formulated for vinyl paints to clean vinyl fenders and rubrails. I went in search of the solvent, but one hardware store after another failed to come up with the right stuff. Finally one enterprising salesman suggested Xylol. He warned me that it was "fierce" and, indeed, there are no directions for use on the can, only a series of dire warnings and a last note: *"for professional/commercial use only. Keep out of reach of children."* Armed with latex gloves, and with a minimum of bare skin showing, I got to work. Xylol proved quite effective for removing stubborn stains from vinyl boat accessories.

I CAN SEE CLEARLY NOW

(Bernard Gladstone) The care of plastic bridge curtains and dodger windows is a delicate thing. I've had good luck with this maintenance procedure:

1. Wash in fresh water and a mild detergent, using a sponge.
2. Dry with paper towels.
3. Apply a light coat of clear wax. [Pledge does a good job.—eds.]
4. Buff vigorously with a soft, clean cloth.

WAX WISDOM

Waxes are not a big expense, but if one can last twice as long or cut waxing time in half, that makes a difference. Surprisingly there is no clear understanding of what "wax" really is. Still, most "waxes" include some wax, some silicones, some solvents, and some abrasives. Most professionals say carnauba wax (made from the leaves of the carnauba palm tree) is the best because of its hardness. It is so hard, however, that it needs to be "softened," so the margin of difference over other waxes isn't that great.

Solvents are used to soften solids, but they act as cleansers, too. The primary cleaner in most waxes, however, is an abrasive. The major difference between boat (fiberglass) and car (paint) wax is that boat waxes contain more and coarser abrasives. Despite all of the additives, preparations, and even pre-preparations, boat wax is really quite simple: on an older, rougher boat, use a mix that contains more cleaner than wax; on a newer, smoother boat, use more wax than cleaner.

NATURAL ELEMENTS

THE BREATH OF LIFE

(Richard Morris Dey) If there is any one thing that is the key to keeping the lady on top of her form, it's *ventilation*. I never go aboard without dropping below and opening up first the forepeak and lazarette hatches, then some of the sole hatches, and finally lockers wherever they are—in the galley, the cockpit, the head, and so forth.

It also helps to keep the temperature cool below if you slosh a bucket or two of seawater on deck.

I would fain die a dry death.

—Shakespeare, The Tempest

RESUSCITATORS

(Jim McHutchison) When C. Raymond Hunt began work on the 40-foot sloop for himself and his family that eventually led to his famous Concordia yawl, he envisaged an "ideal" bunking arrangement: four adult-size berths in the body of the boat and two "coffin" berths aft beneath the cockpit seats for his two boys. That part of the design became one of the most complex, though, because he had to design a ventilation system to make sure that the coffin berths did not literally function as such for his heirs.

THE BLUES

(Dave Gerr) One of the saddest things I see as winter rolls around is the unventilated boat covers so many people drop over their prides and joys. The most common and simplest cover, of course, is the blue poly tarp. They're everywhere! You see them haphazardly lashed, installed without frames, and very often fitted with no ventilation whatsoever. Ventilation, even for fiberglass boats, is vital.

Without fresh air in abundance you'll get mildew, increase corrosion, and cook up temperatures beneath the tarp that can reach better than 140°F. Frames are so simple that you really have no excuse not to build one. Also install a pair of Nicro boat-cover vents high up at the peak. They fit any cover, plastic or canvas, they don't cost much, and they can be reused over and over for years of good airflow.

OPENING PORTS

The simplest form of ventilation, opening ports are also insidious. Forget to close them and you're breathing in water. Experience at sea in small boats has taught us a lot about the proper configuration of ports. Few have more offshore time than Bermuda Race-winner (in the Concordia yawl *Malay*) Dan Strohmeier. He says that a port set into an inward-sloping house, for instance, must have a down-sloping lower rim so that water doesn't collect on its lower lip to join you below when you open it. Most modern designs feature eyebrows or deep Lucite watersheds above ports to shield them from heavy water. Don't locate ports above elec-

tronics (or electronics below ports). An architect, Strohmeier points out that while ports play a big part in the "look" of a boat, it is wisest to give functional considerations such as light and air first priority when deciding where to put them.

MILDICIDE DISCS

(Bruce Bingham) Use wax mildicide discs to fight mildew spores during the sailing season. Put one in every drawer and locker. To be doubly tough on mildew, wash down those interior surfaces first with a mildicide solution. Well-stocked in hardware stores 15 years ago, these discs are hard to find now. If you see them, grab some.

RAIN SHIELD

(Tina Sherman Harnden) Beckson, well-known for its plastic ports, has had success selling a rain shield. It's louvered plastic and fits inside the opening of an opening port. The shield reduces airflow somewhat but won't admit any but the hardest-driven rain. You can dog the normal window tight with the shield in place.

VENTILATE!

(Meade Gougeon) The single worst problem with the overwhelming majority of today's boats is excess moisture trapped below decks. When a boat sits on the mooring, there is usually a big differential between the temperatures inside and outside. This is because boat decks can reach 120°F or more (darker colors can reach 170°) on sunny days, even if air temperature is only 75°. The hot deck heats the interior air, which, without ventilation, can reach high temperatures.

This in itself would not be a problem without a ready source of moisture, the worst being a wet bilge that can quickly create 100-percent humidity inside the boat. Air 100° or hotter at 100-percent humidity can support 18 grains of moisture per cubic foot of air. In comparison, the 75° air outside a boat at a normal 60-percent humidity would hold less than 6 grains of moisture.

Unless this large disparity is corrected with appropriate ventilation, dire consequences will result. Moisture vapor in combination with air is a potent gas that can permeate most materials, such as fiberglass and wood, with surprising rapidity. The carnage resulting from this subtle and little-understood enemy is huge. In fact, it may be the major contributor to the aging process of today's fleet.

Even without a wet bilge, the large difference in temperatures inside and outside of the boat can act as a "moisture pump." Warming air inside the boat will suck in moisture from the outside, which it then drops as condensation when the air cools. Repeated cycles of this process can quickly turn a dry interior into a very wet one.

I use solar-powered ventilators on my boat, enough of them to change interior air every few hours. Nicro makes a good one, and they are not expensive. Other makes are on the market, but I have not tried them. They are the best solution modern technology has yet developed to combat the ventilation problem. They are cheap insurance against one of the more difficult problems modern boats face.

HATCHES AND DORADES

(Rod Stephens) Any hatch should be absolutely watertight when it's shut. It should also provide some waterproof ventilation when it's open. The best way to accomplish both of these requirements, apart from having strong hold-downs on a good gasket and having the hatch at least moderately raised from the surrounding deck, is to fit a tent-type cover over the hatch. This should be absolutely tight on both sides and across the forward edge, secured by a bolt tape in a groove running around these sides. On the after edge it is loose enough to hang well over the open hatch. This permits the hatch to be opened up to 30 degrees or thereabouts and makes it an effective exhaust ventilator that will shed water from any direction except aft.

Getting air below in adverse weather is a difficult proposition. *Dorade* ventilators are still one of the best answers to the problem. Unfortunately the *Dorade* vent is only effective when it is well-designed. To make them appear streamlined and appeal to the boatshow public, the vent boxes are too often built too low. The cowls also are too low, and the scuppers are often too small. Both box and cowl must be high to function properly. That means you should select their location carefully in order not to interfere with visibility, handling sails, or flaking lines.

Ideally vents should be on the centerline, where they interfere least

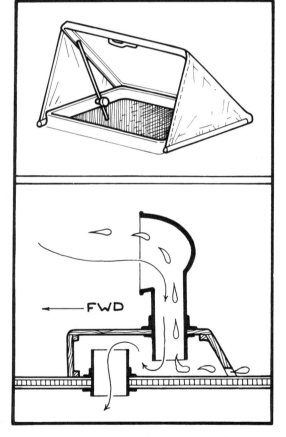

Hatches and Dorade

with visibility and where solid water is not a regular expectation, though this isn't always possible. Large-cowl vents with good-sized boxes and large, well-sited scuppers will provide all-weather ventilation very satisfactorily.

STORM BOARDS

(Dan Spurr) Any port larger than 6 inches across should have a storm shutter made of ⅜ to ½-inch plywood, ⅛-inch aluminum, or 5⁄16 to ⅜-inch Lexan to protect it in heavy weather. Adlard Coles points out in *Heavy Weather Sailing* that it is more common for lee-side ports to break from the cabin slamming against the water than for those on the weather side to succumb to waves breaking full-force against them. [The need for storm shutters depends on the material and mount of portlights. For example, ½-inch Lexan portlights bolted to the cabinside won't need them.—eds.]

—adapted from Upgrading the Cruising Sailboat

NATURAL ENEMIES

The sea never changes, and its works, for all the talk of men, are wrapped in mystery.

—*Joseph Conrad,* Typhoon

YOU SEE, MILORD . . .   *(Nigel Warren)*

In the year of the realm 1763, a group of gentlemen reported to their Lordships of the Admiralty on the success and failure of an experiment whereby HMS *Alarm* had been copper sheathed underwater and sent to tropical waters. Success because the copper had indeed prevented fouling and attack by teredo and gribble worms. Failure because of the effect the copper had upon *Alarm*'s iron fastenings, rudder pintles, and other underwater items which were "as corroded and eaten that they could not have continued of sufficient strength and that, with respect to the false keel, it was entirely off." Since that time many others have been "greatly surprised" by the rapidity and destructiveness of galvanic corrosion.

—adapted from Metal Corrosion in Boats

IF YOU HAD A HAMMER

(A. B. Fraser-Harris) I would like to offer a tip to boatowners anxious about blistering. There is nothing to allay your fears about the onset of the osmotic pox so completely as a thorough examination. In many cases it is wise to call a professional surveyor, but there's also no reason not to examine your boat yourself. The tip I wish to convey, learned from my experience as a surveyor of both fiberglass and wooden hulls, is the use and value of *sounding hammers*.

I use two, both with transparent yellow solid-resin heads. The first is light, about 4 ounces, with an 8-inch hardwood handle. The second weighs 9 ounces and has a steel handle 9½ inches long with a hard rubber grip. The lighter hammer is my standard tool for use on average fiberglass laminate or lighter wooden construction; the heavier is used, for example, on solid wooden beams or heavy glass members. I prefer the plastic head to steel, and it is much kinder to the surface being tested. I use these tools to establish the hardness or texture of the material being surveyed.

Apply a tap or a series of taps to solid laminate and you will get a sharp note, and the hammer head will bounce. Apply the same tap to an area where there is moisture and/or delamination in the fiberglass and the sound will be more of a dull thud, the rebound of the head less lively. Lay the hammer lightly between thumb and forefinger with the shaft lying in the palm of the hand. Allow it to bounce, pivoting about the thumb and finger grip. You will soon learn what a sensitive instrument it is. It is a wonderful exploratory tool, and the early detection of incipient defects can save major repair bills.

MULTIHEADED MENACE

(Meade Gougeon) I've given up trying to find a single cause for osmotic blistering. I can think of at least ten causes. That makes the monster that much tougher to slay. All of the experts aren't in agreement, and that's because they're all looking at a number of different things. The really sad thing is that a small percentage of boats that have been peeled and dried and ventilated and coated just perfectly *still* go back to blistering. No one knows why. I do know that hull blisters are connected to bad ventilation. Of the batch of Valiant 40s that were made with fire-retardant resin and blistered, one didn't. It was a liveaboard boat kept in cold water. Keeping a dry interior can really retard blistering.

Blisters are more than cosmetic. I can think of a used boat that had blisters. It was peeled, recoated, the whole 9 yards. Within 100 hours of hard sailing from being launched, the forward third of her hull delaminated to the point where the bulkheads threatened to come loose. When a laminate starts to disintegrate in shear, there's less and less of it to take more and more stress. The plies of glass begin to crack, and when those cracks reach a critical length, all strength is lost. Good ventilation is a great investment in your hull's future as a structure.

SURPRISING RESULTS

Rick Strand's Comtex Development Corporation has spent the last 15 years investigating blistering, its causes, and some cures. Many of their conclusions challenge accepted ideas about the pox. First, while gelcoat is oft-cited as the weak link in fiberglass construction, Comtex has determined that it isn't the quality of gelcoat but the bond between it and the laminate that has most to do with determining a hull's resistance to water permeation. In 22 percent of the samples tested, blistering was caused by the failure of this gelcoat/laminate bond. And 31 percent of the samples blistered due to a "dry bond" or silica trapped at the interface *between the first and second layers* of the laminate. Conclusion: state and quality of the glass laminate is more likely than that of the gelcoat to be the cause of blistering.

In the past, glass fiber, being somewhat inert, had been thought not to contribute much to blistering. Now, though, it is seen as being a big part of the process. Chemical treatments applied to the glass fibers can, Comtex discovered, be hydrolyzed by water to form chemical by-products that are not only harmful to the laminate but attract water into it via osmosis. And, when the sizing used to help the filaments cling together is broken down by invading water, that in turn creates an instant moisture path and promotes more infiltration. It has long been clear that dry cloth—not properly wet-out with resin—provides the same migration route without hydrolyzation.

Finally, hand-laid fiberglass has always been the premier method of production fiberglass building, while chopper guns were considered quick and ugly. Surprise, then, that laminates built up of sprayed material have proven better at resisting blisters. Sprayed hulls are better at avoiding shearing between the laminates than hulls built and wetted out by hand.

Says Strand, "To ultimately solve the blister problem, moisture must be kept from entering the laminate. We can now do this by employing a better fiber, more-moisture-resistant gelcoats and resins, and improved building methods. The laboratory can help to continue to determine the proper fix."

BLISTERCURE

(Jim Archibald) [Over the years people have attacked osmotic blistering in myriad ways. Jamestown Boatyard, Jamestown, Rhode Island, has long been a leader in dealing with pox and stands behind the treatment described here with a 10-year warranty. Other yards have developed different approaches, but Jamestown's "cure" is representative of the precision, technology, experience, and range of products available to today's boaters in dealing with blisters.—eds.]

We use both hand-held and robotic peelers for getting the infected material off and getting down to healthy laminate. We feel they give us a much fairer surface than sanding or grinding, and they also save time and labor. We peel beyond the depth of the deepest blister. This is essential to dry the boat properly.

We dry the hull until we bring its moisture level to where we want it. In some cases we tent boats and dehumidify them, but the fastest way to dry a boat is to use catalytic infrared heaters that heat portions of the hull to 130° or 135°F without affecting the interior or the wood. That takes between two and three weeks. We look for a reading of 5 percent on a Sovereign moisture meter, but that is more of a relative indicator than an absolute guide. Still, we're very reluctant to recoat a boat if we can't get the moisture content down to 5 percent because that increases the odds of further blistering.

When we recoat a boat, we go over her whole hull with 24-grit paper—just lightly to give the surface some tooth and make it easier to establish a secondary bond with the coating. We wipe the hull with acetone (to clean it), then styrene (to prepare it to bond and lower its hardness). Recoating begins with vinylester resin applied by spray (chopper) gun with a continuous strand of roving. Where the hull has been deeply peeled, we build it back to its original depth. Overall we apply at least 60 mils of the vinylester coating over the whole surface.

We follow by spraying from 50 to 60 mils of Duratek sealer coat mixed with microspheres and extender. We are able to vary the amount of balloons in the mix to create a skin that is tough where it goes on and easier to sand as it builds up. This is essentially our fairing compound. From there the boat goes into the post-cure tent—forced hot air for 48 hours. That removes the solvents from the vinylester and makes it compatible with epoxy primers. We use Interlux 2000/2001 (proper thickness per the directions is important) that goes on wet-on-wet and is followed by wet-on-wet vinylester antifouling.

GALVANIC CORROSION

(Dermot Wright) Seawater is an excellent electrolyte, and any metal immersed in such a saline solution has voltage potential. If this potential exceeds 0.25 volts between two immersed metals in contact, electrolytic action will take place. Current flows from the anode (the metal with the lesser potential) to the cathode, with a loss of ions from the anode into the solution.

Although the phenomenon is normally thought of as occurring with dissimilar metals, it can occur as well among identical metals because local conditions such as pressure, heat stress, mill scale, and differences in paint surface can create differing potentials. For example, in a steel-hulled ship the rivets, because of the heat and stresses endured during formation, have a lower potential than the hull. This causes them to act as anodes (to the cathode of the hull), and galvanic corrosion will take place.

A basic law of electricity is that for every anode there is a complimentary cathode, and that the path of least resistance between them is the one chosen. Corrosion is most severe when an anode is small and a cathode large. For example, pin pricks or imperfections in a painted surface will function as anodes if there is a difference in potential between the unpainted and the painted surface.

In order to prevent loss of metal from anodic areas, make them cathodic. There are two ways to do this:

- impressed (controlled external) current
- sacrificial anodes

—adapted from Marine Engines and Boating Mechanics

THE HOLE
IN THE BRASS RING

(H. A. Calahan) What happens to brass is this: It is an alloy of copper and zinc, with actual pieces of metallic zinc held in suspension by the surrounding copper. When brass is put into salt water, little electric currents are formed between the copper and the isolated particles of zinc with the result that the zinc is eaten away and the brass becomes so soft, porous, and at the same time brittle that you can cut it easily with a knife. Brass which thus loses its zinc becomes reddish in color. If you set out to buy a boat that is brass-fastened, examine the screws for color. If you see red, don't buy the boat!

—*adapted from* The Ship's Husband

ENEMY
NUMBER ONE

(John Marples) The most common fault in the boats I have surveyed in the past 10 years is lack of proper corrosion protection for metal fittings, both above and below the waterline. Since we sail in an electrolyte, lack of protection underwater can reduce stainless steel, for instance, to something resembling Swiss cheese. Above-water activity happens more slowly, but it is there: blistered paint, pitted winch pads, fasteners frozen with festering oxide. Fortunately, prevention is neither complicated nor expensive. It is, however, necessary.

First, use metals that are compatible with each other whenever possible (see attached list). For example, brass or bronze in contact with aluminum is a bad choice. That's a common problem and difficult to avoid. How do you mount a winch (with its bronze baseplate) on an aluminum mast without bringing incompatible metals together? You can do it if you insert a plastic isolation disc between the two active metals. It should extend at least ¼ inch beyond the edge of the base to prevent salt build-up from bridging the gap between the two metal surfaces. Use a disc of strong, non-conductive nylon or polypropylene (even Formica) to separate the two. It should be a minimum of ½₂ inch thick.

Stainless steel is shown in the table to be compatible with aluminum, but for real-life

Galvanic Compatibility

LEAST NOBLE / ANODIC (ACTIVE)

Magnesium and its alloys
Zinc
Galvanized steel
Galvanized wrought iron
Aluminum alloys
Cadmium
Mild Steel
Wrought Iron
Cast Iron
Ni-Resist
Stainless steel, 13% chromium, type 410 (active in still water)
Lead tin solder (50-50)
Stainless steel, 18-8, type 304
Stainless steel, type 316 (active)
Lead
Monel (70% Cu, 30% Ni)
Tin
Muntz metal (60% Cu, 40% Zn)
Manganese bronze (58.5% Cu, 39% Cn, 1%Sn, 1%Fe, 0.3% Mn)
Naval brass (60% Cu, 39% Zn)
Nickel (active)
Yellow brass (65% Cu, 35% Zn)
Aluminum bronze (92% Cu, 8% Al)
Red brass (85% Cu, 15% Zn)
Copper
Admiralty brass (71% Cu, 28% Zn, 1% Sn)
Aluminum brass (76% Cu, 22% Zn, 2%Al)
Silicon bronze (93% Cu, 0.8% Fe, 1.5% Zn, 2% Si, 0.75% Mn, 1.6% Sn)
Bronze, Composition G (88% Cu, 2% Zn, 10% Sn)
Bronze, Composition M (88% Cu, 3% Zn, 6.5% Sn, 1.5% Pb)
Nickel (passive)
Stainless steel, 13% chromium, type 410 (passive)
Stainless steel, 18-8, type 304 (passive)
Stainless steel, type 316 (passive)
Hastelloy C
Titanium
Platinum

MOST NOBLE / CATHODIC (PASSIVE)

protection, stainless steel fasteners should be coated with an antiseize compound. The oxide build-up would otherwise make them hard to remove. Above-water or below, simplify your corrosion protection by choosing metals with good galvanic compatibility.

—*courtesy of* WoodenBoat *magazine*

POINTS OF PREVENTION

Fighting galvanic corrosion is a time-honored and somewhat mysterious endeavor, but basic defensive maintenance against the scourge is relatively simple:

- Underwater hardware should be fastened with screws or bolts of the same metal. If there is no difference in electrolytic potential, there will be no electrolysis.
- When hardware is eaten away the metal loss is usually just a small fraction of its mass. When the same deterioration occurs in a fastener, however, it's gone!
- Paint underwater hardware with non-metallic paint (to shield the metal from galvanic activity). A metal-based anti-fouling will react with the metal in the hardware.
- Situate dissimilar metals so that current can pass between them *only through the water.*
- If you can't accomplish this, the opposite tack (bonding them all together with heavy (#8 or better) wire works *provided* that you protect them all by making them all cathodic.

Provide individual protection for underwater hardware in the form of sacrificial zincs. In *Your Boat's Electrical System*, Conrad Miller goes into further detail on keeping underwater activity under control.

BARE FACTS

(Robert W. Merriam) Should you paint:

- a zinc? Never. Also make sure the zinc and the hull or shaft or strut it's attached to are both polished clean so good contact is maintained between them.
- a ground plate? Yes. It makes no difference to radio reception, but it makes a big difference to the barnacles.
- a transducer? In theory, according to the cloistered engineers, no. In practice, give the face of the transducer one swipe with thin bottom paint. A depthsounder is useless if it has to struggle through a fistful of growth, but keep the face of the transducer free of grease; that prevents a close contact with the water and causes distorted depth readings.

ZINCS

Making sure that there is good contact between the sacrificial zinc and the hardware it's protecting is essential. Zincs should have cast-in plates and fasteners to ensure that the tie between them and the hardware remains firm even when the zinc begins to be eaten away. It is wise to use the biggest zinc that fits, because protection decreases underway. On wooden hulls, insulate the zinc and its fasteners from the hull to guard against alkali attack (which causes wood to deteriorate with alarming speed). Protection only extends as far as good conductivity; a greased joint is a very poor conductor. Use a connecting strap or wire by-pass to connect the zinc to material on the far side of the joint.

TIES THAT BOND

(Nigel Warren) You should have a ground plate on the underside of the hull and well away from propellers, etc. Heavy-gauge insulated wire or a non-insulated metal bonding tape should run fore and aft above the level of the bilge water. Run short branches from the main tape to all large metal items, connecting them together and tying them to the ground plate. The object is to avoid electrical disparity (and so the potential for galvanic corrosion) between the various metallic parts of your boat—engine, fuel tanks, radio cabinets, generator, etc.

To minimize resistance, connections should be

soldered or brazed. If they must be bolted, avoid bolting dissimilar metals together because galvanic corrosion will quickly lead to an impedance across the joint.

—*adapted from* Metal Corrosion in Boats

NO MORE BONDING

(Giffy Full) The basic idea is that bonding will prevent galvanic corrosion. However, something almost always goes wrong and eventually a very minor electrical leak penetrates the system and causes unnecessary deterioration in the parts the system was designed to protect. Over more than 30 years of surveying, all of the older boats I've examined or sailed in that never showed any electrolysis problems of consequence had one thing in common—no bonding. The boats where I've noted deteriorated structural members, bolting, etc. turned out to be bonded. I have extensive records of boats that were bonded where I recommended the removal of those systems. In the cases where the system was removed, the problem was in most instances alleviated.

It is my very firm belief that bonding is a generally poor practice that should be discontinued. If any sort of galvanic action appears in any boat—wood, aluminum, steel, or fiberglass—there is a specific cause. Bonding almost always masks the facts. Do a thorough analysis, find the problem, and correct it—period!

BONDING?

(Nigel Calder) [Experts of impressive experience and credentials differ about bonding. We've just heard ardent cases for and against. Here is Nigel Calder's even-handed overview of the practice.—eds.]

Bonding *completely and well* is an effective antidote to galvanic corrosion of underwater metals and can also suppress radio frequency interference, minimize the consequences of AC leaks onboard, and help with protection against lightning strikes. However, to be effective, a bonding circuit needs electrically perfect connections with conductors that ensure no voltage difference between bonded fittings. With bonded electrical equipment, if the DC negative cable fails, the bonding circuit may become the full current-carrying conductor, so the rule of thumb is to size the bonding cable the same as the DC negative or AC neutral (which means, in the case of any connections to or between engines, *the bonding cable must be rated to handle the full engine cranking load*).

Proper attachment of zincs is also crucial. A stainless steel bolt attaching a zinc will corrode where it contacts the zinc and loosen the connection. Zincs should have cast-in plates and fasteners if they are to maintain good electrical contact throughout their service life.

Grounding propeller shafts, especially those with flexible couplings, also needs special attention. A jumper wire should be connected across the coupling and a spring-loaded bronze brush set up against the shaft and tied into the bonding strap.

Further, when two dissimilar pieces of metal, such as a stainless steel propeller shaft and a copper radio ground plate, are immersed in seawater, *bonding the two will make precisely the circuit needed to promote galvanic corrosion!* However, if the bonding system is in turn connected to a piece of zinc immersed in seawater, the zinc will be the object to corrode, providing protection to all of the more noble metals on the galvanic scale.

Zinc surface area and weight have to be matched to the job. Depending on the amount of metal to be protected and its distribution, more than one zinc may well be necessary. The use of several anodes rather than one larger one will provide better current distribution.

The opposite approach to bonding and cathodic protection is to unbond all underwater fittings, isolate them electrically, and allow them to reach equilibrium at their own voltage. More prevalent in Europe than the US, this practice necessitates top-quality underwater fittings (e.g., bronze), and they must be insulated from all electrical circuits. In practice, most hose-connected through-hulls in fiberglass boats are insulated already. Through-hulls in metal boats should be mounted on insulated blocks to reduce galvanic action between hull and fittings.

An unbonded hull will still need zinc anodes in spots. Steel hulls and rudders will need their own zincs. Unbonded hulls will need electrical systems of the insulated-return type (which should be mandatory in boats in any case).

We had an unbonded boat in warm tropical and semi-tropical waters for 12 years with no signs of corrosion save minor pitting around the knot-meter impeller and a trace of corrosion between the bronze propeller and its stainless steel shaft. Part of our success was undoubtedly due to the fact that our internal circuits were wired to high standards with heavy wire, and we had no external radio grounds or other potential sources of stray current.

—*adapted from* Boatowner's Mechanical and Electrical Manual

NATURAL WONDERS

Let us a little permit Nature to take her own way; she better understands her own affairs than we.

—*Michel de Montaigne*

WOOD WISDOM
(H. A. Calahan) All wood is porous. It is the function in the life of the tree for the softer layers to act as does the wick in an oil lamp, drawing up moisture and circulating sap. Before wood is placed in a boat, it must be seasoned. Seasoning is the slow removal of moisture and sap from green wood by drying. Green wood is very easy to work. It would be very easy to fashion a boat from green wood, but it would have a lamentably short life.

In the early 1600s, before they understood the seasoning of wood, the British Navy almost ruined the country financially by building battleships that rarely lasted more than a year. Often dry rot set in before they were launched. This is why today some cheaply built boats have pathetically short lives. A single green timber may ruin the whole thing.

Dry rot is apt to start inside a boat when the outside air is dry but the inside air remains humid. Ventilation is thus a primary insurance of keeping your planks and timbers sound. When paint is applied to green timber or to an area of the boat where dry rot exists, the paint seals the moisture in the wood and accelerates the rot. There is really only one remedy—prompt surgery.

—*adapted from* The Ship's Husband

EXPOSE YOUR BOTTOM
Careening is the ancient and honorable art of bringing your boat's underwater surfaces to light. If you need to get at the underside of your boat, drying her out on the tide can be cheaper and more convenient than a conventional boatyard haulout. Pick a spot where the bottom is flat and level and where you will be protected from wakes and severe tidal current. Organize your materials beforehand so you can paint or clean or repair as fast as possible within the framework provided by the tides.

You can choose to tie off to a dock or other man-made structure, you can build a temporary frame, or you can let your boat lie on her side as she dries out. Use the tidal range to your advantage, be it a foot or over 30 feet (as it is in Brittany and the Bay of Fundy). Even if there is no rise and fall, you can still haul down on a halyard to heel the boat and get at her bottom.

EVER-READY GRIT

(Jack and Charlotte Clementson) When cleaning *Eleuthra*'s bottom, when roughing up the topsides, or when preparing to paint the dinghy—just about all of the time—we use real sand instead of sandpaper. What makes it work is using a sanding block of scrap Styrofoam. Whether in sheets or in the form of discarded floats and net buoys, Styrofoam comes ashore along just about every beach. We harvest it and shape it to fit the job. We take our work to the beach where there is a natural selection from coarse to fine grains of sand along the gradient. The sand can be wet or dry. Once we've chosen our "grit" we slap some on, wet the block, and go to work. The cutting power and return on elbow grease that we get this way continue to amaze us.

EIGHT WAYS CLEAN

Next time you rub yourself raw with mineral spirits or glop up to your elbow with hand cleaner, just remember—you could have had a vegetable wash. It's true. Vegetable oil removes paint and varnish from your hands and tenderer parts. It works quickly, safely, thoroughly, and smoothly.

LANOLIN

(RR) Time-tested as a waterproofing agent, this wondrous, anhydrous stuff is also a skin cream and healing balm that helps make life on the water easier and more elegant. In stitching, on clothes and shoes, on swagings, as a salve, and as an all-purpose lubricant, it seems a miracle product.

When I learned via explorer Tim Severin that Irish monk St. Brendan probably used this "wool grease" to keep the seawater from attacking the oak-tanned ox-hide hull of his *curragh* more than 1,000 years ago, it gave me new respect not only

for this over-the-counter wonder from the corner drugstore, but for seamen of old. If the sailors of medieval Ireland were clever enough to discover lanolin, then maybe the notion that they crossed the Atlantic to discover the New World circa 800 AD might hold some water, too.

THE WAYS OF THE WIZARD

(L. Francis Herreshoff) Said Goddard, "Where there is not a free circulation of air you will often find rot, and this is particularly so on yachts where the cabin floor or cabin sole runs way out to the planking."

"What do you think of painting all of the interior parts?" inquired Briggs.

"Well," Goddard mused," that is a great question. Old George Lawley [North Shore of Boston builder circa 1920—eds.] used to say, 'Wood has to breathe and should not be painted on both sides,' while N. G. Herreshoff was very particular to have bilges well painted-out and have butt-blocks set in white lead. In fact he tried to have all of the surfaces of every piece of wood either painted or varnished. The yachts built by these men have outlasted all others in America. Who's to say who's right?"

—*adapted from* The Compleat Cruiser

VINEGAR

(Chuck Phillips) Use vinegar to wash down the insides of lockers and bilges to get rid of mildew and musty odors. Wash down your sunburn with vinegar (to alleviate pain without drying your skin). White vinegar is an excellent cleaner of epoxy spills and surfaces. Make a hair rinse using 2 tbsp. in a pint of fresh water to cut through soap and salt water. Even though it tastes terrible, ½ tsp. of vinegar in a glass of warm water makes a good laxative.

SHINING WIPE

To clean interior varnish, add a tablespoon of malt vinegar to a small bowl of fresh water. Wipe this on the varnished surfaces and then pat dry with toilet paper.

GREASE CUTTER

(*Dave Gerr*) For cleaning really baked-on grease on the engine block or in the galley, sprinkle vinegar and then a layer of baking soda on the surface. Let it sit for several minutes, then rub the tough spots with bronze wool. This mix will also work on bilges, ovens, stove tops, and ceramic tiles. For heads, sprinkle the baking soda in first, drip in the vinegar, then scour.

SPRAY AWAY

Many of us worry about using chemical cleaners on our teak decks. A sailor we know reports that he tackled the task with a pressure water cleaner similar to that used to clean bottoms. Removing three years of dirt took about three hours, but the deck dried blotchy. He gave it a second pass, this time spraying one plank full-length at a time. The result was "a gleaming teak deck." [Caution: This can wear the soft wood from the grain prematurely if hull-cleaning pressure is used.—eds.]

FROM BEES AND TREES

(*Ken Textor*) Two items I make sure I take along on any cruise are beeswax and pine tar. They sound like anachronisms, but I make good use of both. They can add comfort to life aboard and longevity to a surprising number of things that you ordinarily depend on.

Beeswax is used primarily as a sealant, as it has been for centuries. For instance, I had an old cotton Bimini top that, toward the end of its years, began to suffered from leaks in places where it had been abraded. By melting some beeswax into these thin spots, I was able to stop the leaks and use the top for another five years. I've since used this technique for leaks in a canvas deck, a winter cover, some faded foul-weather gear, and even an old sou'wester. It seems to work just as well with new, synthetic fibers as with cotton cloth.

Beeswax also works beautifully as a non-toxic putty for pressure joints in the freshwater system. Warmed in your hands, it's pliable enough to fill just about any space. I have also used it as a coating on unrefrigerated eggs. The eggs stayed good for months! But it must be beeswax. Canning paraffin or other wax substitutes don't have the same versatility, and beeswax has a stickiness that's all its own. You should find it easily in your hardware store or any natural food store.

Pine tar is another old-time item. It is best used as a preservative for cordage, and it's particularly good for seizing ropework like macramé thump mats, hemp fenders, safety netting, marline seizing, and the like. If you use it in areas where it will be handled often, cut it 50-50 with turpentine. That helps the pine tar penetrate and does away with just about all of the sticky residue. When you use pine tar in the rigging, though, use it full strength. It will double the life of almost anything that you put it on. It's no longer available in chandleries, but tack and horse shops still carry it. [Caution: Pine tar will stain sails.—eds.]

A SAILOR'S SOLUTION

(*Bruce Bingham*) An "old salt's" formula for fine wood oil: ⅓ turps, ⅓ linseed oil, and ⅓ carnauba wax. Shake well, wipe on, let set for an hour, wipe off.

DEW IT RIGHT

(*L. Francis Herreshoff*) After they had moved out into the cockpit again, the sun was drying up the dew so that Weldon hurried as much as he could, wiping off the brightwork, while Jim, who was now fully awake, asked him why he liked to chamois the morning dew so much. He explained: "The dew has been settling on the brightwork all night and has softened up the films of dirt, salt, and gum that are on the surface of the varnish." Weldon then chamoised a place in the shade where the dew still remained and it came out as smooth as a piece of amber. Then he wiped a place where the sun had partly dried off the dew so that there were drops between dry places. Here the surface was mottled after wiping, for in the dry places the film of dirt and gum had dried on again.

When Weldon did this early morning chamoising he kept a hand basin of fresh water near him, and occasionally rinsed out the chamois. The water in the basin was black by that time, so Weldon commented: "You would not think all that dirt was on the brightwork, but it is just this sort of wiping off that makes a boat look yachty, while the one that is wiped off with salt water or even if done later in the day with soap and water, always looks grimy."

—The Compleat Cruiser

CLEANING BRASS
Rub the brass with a lemon dipped in salt. Wipe on, wipe off!

TIPS, TRICKS, AND TOOLS

PORTION CONTROL   *(Hank Hinckley)*
Sometimes when I would be mixing a small quantity of polyester resin I would get inconsistent results. It dawned on me then that the stirring stick is quite absorbent. When stirring the hardener into the resin, the stick would absorb some of the hardener and mess up the proportions. The answer is to wet the stick thoroughly in the resin before you put the hardener in the cup.

A man's boat ought to be as long (in feet) as he is (in years).

—*Uffa Fox*

MIRROR FINISH   Did you know that a two-part
teak cleaner (such as Tip Top Teak) will also brighten discolored stainless steel? Try the acid part on stainless hardware and railings; it works wonders.

RUST REMOVER   Liquid teak cleaners will re-
move rust stains from gelcoat or from laminated plastic countertops. These stains turn up if you leave cans on a galley counter or tools on a fiberglass deck. Teak cleaner is hard on plastics and should not be left on the surface you're cleaning for long. Apply the teak cleaner, let sit for 30 seconds, then wipe off. Repeat as necessary to remove the stain. Flush well with water when you are through.

SEALANTS   Modern marine sealants can be from three
different families: polysulfides, polyurethanes, and silicones.

- Polysulfides have high bonding strength, resist cleansers and oils with good success, take a relatively long time to cure (accelerated, though, in the presence of water), and can be sanded and painted after they cure.

- Polyurethanes are the strongest adhesive and produce strong, re-silient joints. Teak cleansers soften them, though, and their curing time is the longest of the three types of sealant. You can sand them and paint over them.
- Silicone sealant lacks the adhesive strength of polysulfide or polyurethane, but silicone's cohesive strength makes it a superior "gasket" for bedding deck fittings. Silicones are resilient and resist solvents admirably. They can't be sanded or painted, though, and they're not a good choice for filling large voids. They have also been known to discolor when exposed to the elements.

There is no "right" formula for a marine sealant, but the more you know about how each of these chemical confections performs, the like-lier you are to pick the right one for the job you have in mind.

NAME GAMES
Put the name on your boat yourself. It's relatively straightforward when you use self-adhesive vinyl. The ad-vantage of using this thin "sticky-back" plastic (made by 3M and others) is that the art work takes place in a studio instead of atop a ladder.

Clean the hull where the name will go (Windex works well on fiber-glass). Wet the area with a detergent/water solution, wet down the name and scrim, peel off the adhesive protector, and place the graphic on the hull. Once you have it positioned where you want it, squeegee the water out. When everything is dry, peel off the application scrim to leave just the name in bright, long-lasting vinyl.

SOFTPACK
(David Seidman) Hard toolboxes are handy, but not so much so on a boat. They chip, gouge, and hunker. They slide and clutter. I love my canvas tool carrier. It accommodates odd-shaped gadgets, it keeps tools manageable even underway, and it stows just about anyplace. For the past 12 years mine (homemade by yours truly) has served me well and drawn praise wherever we go. Make yours with width and depth to suit your needs. Even, if you're really or-ganized, devise a series of smaller rolls that incorporate into one big one.

Softpack

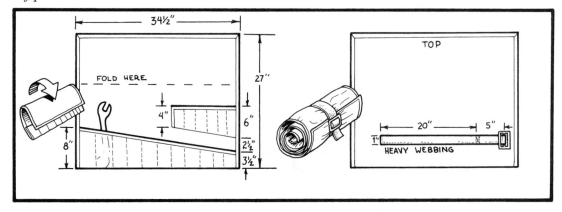

FIX-IT KIT

(Art Loya) Since I started using West System epoxy, I have found that a 2-ounce jar half full of resin with a bit of one of their fillers or very fine sawdust, and another 2-ounce jar with the appropriate amount of hardener, keep very well together in my spares locker—there at all times for those small jobs that come up when I'm out on the boat and need some handy epoxy for a quick, strong fix.

EVERBRITE TOOLS

Keeping tools corrosion-free in the damp environs of a boat is a formidable challenge. Keeping them in a gasketed toolbox is a start, but you can substantially improve your chances of long-term success if you line the box with chemically impregnated rust-inhibiting paper, such as Brookstone's Everbrite. If any of your tools are in pouches, also slip a half-sheet of this paper inside the pouch. Replace the paper once a year. You can order it from Brookstone's, Nashua, NH, 800-926-7000 (catalog # 1588.3).

ZAP

(Phillip Morawa) Zap has almost unlimited uses. It is actually cyanoacrylate adhesive (commonly called CA by model builders). It comes in various viscosities: Zap is water-thin; Zap-a-Gap is semi-gel; and Flexi-Zap is flexible when cured. I always use Kicker, their spray cure accelerator, which makes Zap-cure happen in seconds. It can take up to a minute if you don't use the spray—depending on the viscosity you're using.

Some Zap-uses I've found:

- Run it around the rim of a fixed port to stop leaks.
- Apply it to broom handle threads for an elegant, long-lasting connection to mop or broom.
- Repair a broken tape recorder drive belt or fashion a correct-size O-ring. The adhesive will glue skin in seconds, so be neat.

Once opened, the stuff has a shelf life of about four months.

SCULPTING A DING-FREE KEEL

(J. R. Watson)

1. Clean, and de-scale the wounded areas.
2. Tap out the bulges around the edges of keel depressions with a ball-peen hammer. (Many light, sharp blows are more effective than a few heavy whacks. Save as much lead as you can.)
3. Plane the bulge flush. (Coat the lead liberally with petroleum jelly to facilitate planing.) Make sure the plane blade is sharp. Adjust it for a medium-fine cut.
4. Acetone the planed area and scrub with a wire brush.
5. Mix epoxy enough to coat the exposed area, roll it on, then scuff up the mix with a wire brush. This promotes adhesion to the lead. (For keel sculpting use a low-viscosity epoxy, such as West System 105/206.)
6. After the wire-brush treatment, mix a 50-50 combination of colloidal silica and low density filler into blended epoxy to make a non-sagging putty. Trowel that mixture onto the surface and sculpt to fit. Voids bigger in volume than a golf ball may require several applications; epoxy in a thick mass can heat up and may form bubbles.
7. When the necessary build-up has cured (at least 12 hours at 70°), give it a final shape with 50-grit sandpaper.
8. Coat the filled area and perimeter with three coats of epoxy (no filler added).
9. You may apply bottom paint after about 24 hours.

LAYERING OVER VARNISH

(Doug Terman) For a long lay-up or a rough passage, you can help preserve your varnished exterior surfaces by painting over them with a thin coat of latex house paint. When the passage is over, sand the surfaces and revarnish. You would have had to sand them anyway. This way you'll find the existing varnish well worth working with.

INFLATABLE LEAKS

(MB) I got a tip once from a fellow charter skipper in the Caribbean on how to trace those frustratingly invisible holes in inflatable bottoms, the ones that are always weeping just a little bit. First, pick a warm, sunlit day and take the rascal to the beach. Invert it, float it, and swim under into the airspace below the upside-down boat. Use a waterproof marker to mark the spots where the sun shines through the bottom. You might have a chum put the marks on the outside when you press up on the trouble spots from inside. Then take her ashore, dry her out, and set about repairing.

SUPER SEAL

(Paul Sentsey) I have been plagued with leaks around the Plexiglas windows on several of my boats. The windows in question come screwed or bolted to the cabin sides. My observation has been that, though manufacturers use several systems for sealing the windows, none is long-lasting or works well. I, too, tried all of the common fixatives: silicone, 3M 5200, and Sikaflex, all to no avail.

My solution to this problem is to remove the window, clean off all the old caulking, and apply butyl tape around the edges. We use this tape in the construction industry in applying thermopane windows to window frames. It comes in ⅛-inch and ³⁄₁₆-inch thicknesses. I use the thinner of the two, a roll of which costs about $8.00 for 25 feet. After I've created a tape gasket, I screw the windows on firmly and caulk outside the seal with silicone. The tape is very dense and screws won't displace it. The installation is *mega* strong, so removal will take some time. You won't have to remove the windows, though. The tape works!

TORTURED HINGE

If a brass pin in a brass hinge has become seized, you have some chance of freeing it if you remove it and boil the whole in engine oil for five minutes. [Speaking of torture, through the ages boiling oil has caused more than a little discomfort. Proceed intelligently and with caution.—eds.]

SIX POINTS

(Will Robinson) For hex-head fastenings, six-point sockets and box wrenches are much less likely to damage bolt heads than the more common 12-point wrenches! Six-pointers have far more bearing surface in contact with the head.

SOLDERING STAINLESS

Many think soldering stainless steel is impossible, but a special acid-core flux is available for this purpose. Also, polished sheets of stainless steel are known to be incredibly hard and difficult to cut, but stainless can easily be softened by putting it in a fire to become red hot, then leaving it there to cool in the ashes until next morning. Do this job outside, keep a bucket of water handy, and be sure the metal is completely cool before you work with it. Also be wary of changes to the metal due to heat-treating.

TOOLS

(George Buehler) I was reading a book on wooden-boat repair and I came across the tool list. I've been building boats for 20 years, and I still don't own all the tools that the book says are essential. I've worked with and watched boatbuilders in third-world countries who haven't many more tools than those found in the average kitchen drawer. The difference between "essential" and "handy-to-have" is considerable.

LIGHTEN UP

(Peter Vanadia) When will boatbuilders learn not to use super-powerful adhesives where simple "bedding" is all that's required? Stuff like the infamous 5200 is great unless it's holding something onto a boat that has to come off. Heating can help loosen a fitting, but in general 5200 is much too strong for things such as hardware, rubrails, and toerails. When you choose the adhesive/sealant for your next job, beware of over-gluing it.

KEEPING WINCHES WORKING

Winches tend to be classic examples of curiosity waiting in a spot to ambush the cat. "Let's just see how this little thing works" may be the deadliest eight words known to ship husbandry. If there is a manual (which isn't that likely), *read* it. If not, proceed cautiously and systematically. It's true that winches need care, but "playing doctor" with them has yet to produce brilliant results.

It is best to work on your winches with the ship as immobile as she can be persuaded to be. Plug scuppers and tape up cockpit drains to make sure any bits and pieces that slip away won't be gone for good. Scrub the part of deck where you'll be working, then spread an old piece of canvas or sailcloth over it. When you're through, slosh the moist deck again and you won't have any problem with grease stains or oil spots setting up.

"Reassemble in reverse order" it may say in the manual, but ofttimes that's much harder to do than to say. It's not such a bad idea to take a Polaroid picture of each stage of the disassembly. Keep the photos so that anyone will have a guide to the job.

Clean small parts with a small paintbrush and kerosene, or use whatever the manual suggests (but never gasoline—too dangerous). Drain the cleaned winch parts and dry them on white, absorbent paper—with every component visible. It's nice if a winch has standardized roller bearings rather than calling for different sizes. That simplifies the spare-parts list, too. High on that list should come springs. Lose one of these devils over the side and it's not such a tragedy if you've got another.

Racers often use light oil and lubricate winches quite often. Cruisers should favor lubricants that hang on longer and won't easily wash off. Marine Lubriplate A is a good choice. Work grease into the bearing spindles with clean fingers, making sure it penetrates between the rollers. There's no need to slather the whole neighborhood with grease. Use non-detergent oil (30-weight is fine) on the gear bearings, pawl axles, and ratchet. Try to clean up as you go. Keep oil from areas that need grease (and vice versa). Keep everything that is slippery away from drum and brake surfaces. Reassemble in reverse order.

BRIGHT TOPSIDES

(*Eric Goetz*) There's nothing quite so pretty as a bright-finished wooden boat. I've built several cold-molded boats over the years, and I think I've found a good way to get today's coatings to protect and enhance the eternal beauties of wood. First, after smoothing and preparing the hull, we undercoat it with clear epoxy. An application of clear Awlgrip follows (which takes very well to the epoxy), then we apply whatever graphics will be used. We finish off the mix with another coat of clear Awlgrip.

CLEANING BRONZE PORTS

For bronze cleaner, some sailors eschew the chandlery in favor of their local Amway representative. Amway Metal Cleaner is a soft white paste that rinses off with water. Devotees claim it is the only product that will really clean bronze ports, and after the initial cleaning, almost no effort is reportedly required to keep them looking great. It also cleans chrome.

BRUSHABLY HAPPY

We recently saw a testimonial letter from someone who had painted the topsides of his Bristol 40 yawl himself. He selected Interthane Plus and was "amazed at the results," having restored the topsides to near factory condition with $200 worth of linear polyurethane paint. He encouraged anyone to try it. Not bad advice. Thin the paint just right and watch the air temperature, and you can get the same amazing results.

CREDO

(*Richard Dey*) A boat is not an ornament that's supposed to sit looking pretty at anchor all day, all season. A boat is a living thing that appreciates use. It is better to use her than to work endlessly on maintaining her beauty. It is better to use her even if it means not having her look great.

NOBLE NAMES

A ROSE . . .

(Jonathan Lewis) Naming a boat is as challenging as naming a child. Those of you who are *Jr.'s* and *IIIs* may not appreciate it, but filling the space on a birth certificate takes care and consideration. A blank transom can be equally intimidating.

I got my first boat when I was nine. She looked just like all of the other wooden prams in our Cape Cod harbor until we graced her backside with the self-sticking words *Jolly Jonch*. The name was a combination of a ho-ho-ho pirate ship and my childhood nickname. Not only did my boat "have a soul," her personality was captured in her name. It was no longer "the boat"; it was definitely *Jolly Jonch*. Bigger and tougher, the 9'2" Boston Whaler Squall that I got at 13 marked new independence and extended our adventures. It seemed only fair to call her *Jolly Jonch,* too.

Years later my wife and I bought a 37-foot fractionally rigged French ultra-light. She was not a *Jolly Jonch*. Besides, one of the two original *JJs* was still in the family and going strong. Our new boat was *Rambunctious,* but not to us. Did we dare risk Poseidon's wrath and change that name? With suitable libations poured, we risked it.

The Apollo 11 landing on the moon July 20, 1969 was a great step. "Houston, Tranquillity Base here. The Eagle has landed" was trully memorable. My wife and I shared a fascination with the exploration of space, a fascination that thankfully extends to discovering new outposts on our watery planet. For that world of adventures, for our home no matter how alien the environment—*Tranquillity Base!*

Whether a boat bobs on her mooring or rounds the Cape, her name is part of her magic. The pulse that you perceive in her helm is put there by your heart. The poet and I disagree; it would not be sweet for our high-flying home to travel under any other name. We christened the inflatable *Eagle,* but when her fabric proved faulty, we named the new one *Houston*. Now when one of us goes ashore with the handheld VHF, we gift the airwaves with "*Houston, Tranquillity Base* here."

TALEISIN

(Lin and Larry Pardey) Two and a half years while the boat was building we listened in frustration as just about everyone called her *Seraffyn II*. We said no.

We tried many names.

Brion Toss, a soft-spoken rigger we'd met, wrote in some detail about naming his dog, who responded to "Saul" as if by magic. There is some similar magic, intentional or not, in naming important things.

Tristan Jones is gone now, but when we met him we hit it off immediately. Later we learned that the Welsh adventurer had lost a leg. It seemed natural to say "we can rough out a peg leg for you if you want." He did, so Larry got a baulk of teak which he worked at and worked at until it was far from rough.

"Tristan wants to do something in return," Larry said as he sent the varnished artifact off to our friend. "Ask him to think of a name."

Dear Lin and Larry,

Taleisin

Welsh bard from pre-Christian era. He was found in the bull-rushes as a babe. He sang so sweetly that he cast a spell over the birds, and they flew away in the winter when he slept. He sailed himself over the looking-glass sea and lives in a magic land far away to the west of Ireland. He told the original tales of the Mabinogion. Therefore he is the originator of the tale of fantasy. A lovely, honorable name for a boat.

Tristan Jones

We already had a name-board carved by the time Tristan wrote to add that *Taleisin* in Welsh means "happy wanderer."

A Rhodes by Any Other name

(Robert de Gast) What's in a name? Consider Bubby Egan. He came from last place to win the 1979 Flying Scot Midwinters in *The Opera Isn't Over Until the Fat Lady Sings.*

Recently, having traded my great riches for a new used yacht, I was sitting at the dock pondering good names. Silently a sleek sloop sailed by. As the transom came into view her name was revealed: *So Long.* Then the dinghy trailed past: *So Short.* But our documentation papers were about to be filed. *How Long?* And we hadn't even bought a dinghy . . . .

I looked at *Lloyd's Register of American Yachts*—from *Abaco* to *Zulu Warrior.* Fifty-nine names

began with *Lady;* more than 200 used *sea* in their names; 10 *Dolphins,* 11 *Skylarks,* 12 *Puffins,* 15 *Spindrifts,* 22 *Windsongs.* . . . All the good names were taken. I pored over charts. I used the telephone books. Finally I resorted to the *Oxford Unabridged.* . . ; well, how about reading just the four shortest letters—X, Y, Z & Q?

That's what I did, and there, in the middle of the Qs, between "quiver" and "quiz," I found *"Qui Vive."*

QUI VIVE [FR. LIT. WHO LIVES? WHO GOES THERE? ON THE ALERT.]

And I can see the dinghy now: *C'est moi.*

SIZZLE

(Doug Terman) There was a restaurant I used to frequent back when Hector was a pup and I had all my hair. He didn't make a big deal out of it, but Bar-B Billy, prop. since 1937, only bought beef from the port side of Kansas City cows, aged the meat for 15 days, cut the prime stuff into 1¾-inch slabs, and marinated it in soy sauce for a day.

Once you ordered (no preparation instructions, please), Billy seared your steak on either side for three minutes and then mesquite-smoked it for another 20. If you had other ideas, Billy would point to a place over on the other side of town. Just thinking of Billy's steaks sets my glands aquiver. The real pleasure came when the waitress set that slab of beef bubbling hot in front of you—pure, unadulterated sizzle. Nowadays I order what's supposed to be good for me, get a tab to generate sticker shock, and pine for what's missing.

Was invited to go "yachting" with friends recently. The "yacht" was 39 feet overall with 16 feet of beam and a Malibu-townhouse superstructure. Bare-bones equipment included microwave, electric range, freezer, refrigerator, wet bar, blender, ice maker, water maker, pasta maker, chart scanner. . . to name just a few. The cockpit looked like something out of *Goldfinger.* Freddie used words like "database" and "interface" a lot. Our weekend afloat was short-circuited by a passel of house-calls from micro-chip medicos; we discovered several systems down. We had to eat dinner ashore but were bound to enjoy a drink in the cockpit. However, the pall of smoke from the anchorage's generators and the insane whine from acres of roller-furling mainsail gear in the marina drove us below.

Next weekend I'm headed out with Mac and Annie. Some years ago they bought a 20-year-old Columbia 50. They sail almost every weekend. Twice they've cruised to the West Indies. They're planning to cross to Europe when he retires. The sloop was sound when they bought her, but she needed cosmetics. John took the time and learned to varnish, paint, and splice—even took the course in diesels at the local community college.

Over the first two winters he rebuilt the interior. Annie sewed up new upholstery and sail covers. Their entertainment center is a car stereo and a large rack of books. They haul out in a little North Carolina yard where the rates are good and they can do most of their own work. The boat is Spartan, but the varnish gleams and the machinery sparkles. Mac and Annie love their boat, and it shows. On her transom is painted *Sizzle*.

ROZINANTE

(*L. Francis Herreshoff*) In the first pause in the conversation, Miss Prim inquired the meaning of *Rozinante* and *Sancho Panza*. Weldon explained, "Rozinante was the name of Don Quixote's steed. She was a long, thin animal, but every time the Don mounted her he had remarkable adventures. Perhaps seven-eighths of the romance of these adventures took place in Quixote's mind, for he was a great reader of romance who rather looked down on the times in which he lived. Like Don Quixote, every time I venture out on this Rozinante, I meet with great adventure and romance. Perhaps, also, seven-eighths of it takes place in my mind . . . As for my tender [*Sancho Panza*], she is named after Don Quixote's squire, or companion, who followed him faithfully in his exploits and often saved him from disaster at the last moment."
—*adapted from* The Compleat Cruiser

JUST ANOTHER WORD

(*Francis Stokes*) I don't consider myself any more of a philosopher than the next guy, but through my life there have surfaced propositions and sophisms that, almost in spite of themselves, have taken on a special life. I don't know where it comes from, but "Freedom, being relative, is probably best taken in small bites" is a phrase that came to loom large in my early life. Like a knife blade, it seemed to stick, quivering, into the center of what I was about.

For some reason that made me look at myself. Who am I?

Francis.

Not Francis Drake—too roguish.

Not Francis of Assisi—out of the question.

Francis? Francis Chichester? Sir Francis at that. Taken to traveling alone in small boats and planes. *Francis.*

Elizabethan navigator John Davis explored the west coast of Greenland in 1585 with two barques, the *Sunneshine* and the *Mooneshine*. Aboard the latter he introduced the Eskimos to "the playing of pipes and merrye dancing."

Even though, as I tell my wife, "I've danced my last dance," my boat became *Mooneshine*.

TRESBELLE

(*Arne Brun Lie*) *Tresbelle* is a near-perfect seaboat, if I do say so. She's 37 feet long. Sigurd Herbern designed her as a 36-footer. He and I fought about adding a foot. She was handsome before, but now that I won and added a foot and angled her stem, she's beautiful. *Tresbelle.*

JENNY'S RUN

(*Steve Rubin*) Our daughter had done a fair amount of sailing with us before her death—Nova Scotia, Newfoundland, Quebec, on down the East Coast. While we were sailing to the Bahamas, she was sailing to Cuba and back aboard *Young America*. In June she was graduated from college and joined the Peace Corps. For a year she lived in Togo, West Africa, teaching village women how to extend their dwindling supply of firewood by building simple stoves with local materials.

The following June, at the age of 23, in a village of truly warm and gentle people, she was beaten to death. Jenny wanted to do what she could for others. The progression from adventure at sea to the adventure of the Peace Corps was a natural. At sea she began to learn that in the world of a small boat at sea, everything we are and do matters. Clearly what Gail and I think of as her virtues were acquired ashore as well, but it is impossible not to believe sailing shaped her profoundly.

While she was away, Gail and I bought a larger boat. We named her *Jenny's Run* and sent pictures. The last words she wrote were: "Tell me more about *Jenny's Run.*"

After her death, vulnerable as never before, I thought that having Jenny's name on the boat would be unbearable. The more Gail and I talked, the more we realized it would be a joy to live with that name. So Jenny's name on our new boat has become a measure of solace, a reminder that decency and sanity are possible. We loved her and approved of her and were proud of her. I would have the lettering even higher and more bold, proclaiming our daughter to the world.

SCRATCH BOAT

(MB) As all of you undoubtedly know, "The wicked flee when no man pursueth" (Proverbs 28:1). So we call our frisky miniature motorsailer (a 19-foot Rowley skiff with a 75-hp Merc) *Wicked Flea.*

ATARAXIA

(Philip C. Bolger) "Ataraxia" is "calmness untroubled by mental or emotional excitement." It is one fair way to sum up the goal of a "career" designing boats. This one's proportions are compact; excrescences beyond the main envelope were kept to a minimum. The deck is a segment of a cylinder from bow to stern. Ends are upright—to use all available waterline—and she has sharp forebody sections for a smooth head-sea action. She is shallow-bodied and high-sided for initial and reserve stability (with a minimum of ballast). She is shallow draft and straight-keeled for obvious convenience.

Cedar carvel planking on steam-bent oak frames allows a complex shape with reliable quality control. The frames carry cedar sheathing inside. Air circulation is excellent and, as insulation, the "ceiling" works well. There is no paint or coating below. The copper fastening nails give a pleasing glint. Her planked bottom is tarred and sheathed with 16-oz. copper sheeting. I estimate it will last seven years of hard use. Premium grade marine plywood makes up the deck, and

Ataraxia's sail plan.

anchors fiberglass epoxy sheathing.

The boat's exterior is painted with flat acrylic house paint. It is good for sun reflection, a moderately non-slip surface, and it never has to be removed. The dipping lug sail (53 sq. m) is flown from a tabernacle mast. Dipping the lug is "no worse than tacking a big genoa," but I foresee most maneuvers taking place under power. The rig is starkly simple and eliminates chafe. A small trysail can be flown as a steadying or heavy-weather sail. The mast is fully counterweighted and swings down for bridges. Two small air-cooled Deutz diesels provide power. The lee-side propeller should always be free of air ingestion. The open stern lets engine-room air circulate well and dissipates noise. You can reach the props by hand from the endplate of the rudder. The sauna minimizes gray-water discharge. The portable toilet with one or more spare base tanks obviates all plumbing. The galley stove and cabin heater each use diesel from the main tanks. *Ataraxia* is a scaled-down re-finement of *Resolution* aboard which I have lived and worked for the past 10 years.

GOOD TIMES

(*Eric Hiscock*) "I name this ship *Wanderer V.*" Susan's voice, crisp and clear, rang out across the yard. "May God bless her and all who sail in her." The christening bottle shattered on the anchor at the stemhead, pale wine sprayed over the bows, and 11 months after her lines had been laid down in the mould loft, and six weeks ahead of schedule, our new cruising home glided down the ways. Looking back on those 11 months of building, with the countless decisions to be made, the compromises, the changes, as day by day a graceful yacht materialized from a pile of sweet-smelling timber and gallons of pungent glue, I realized I had enjoyed them as much as any period in my life. What a lot of interest, excitement, and satisfaction is missed by those who buy a boat "off the shelf."

TUGBOAT HITCH

(*Keith Taylor*)

It can be useful to use a winch like a bollard and lead a dockline directly to it. The tugboat hitch lets you belay without having to use the bitter end of the line. To tie it, take turns on the winch, then pass a bight of the tail under the standing part and drop it over the winch. Pass a bight from the opposite direction and do the same thing. Repeat from each side and finish the knot with two half-hitches to lock the turns in place.

Paul and Arthur Snyder (from *Nautical Knots and Lines Illustrated*)

STAY IN POWER

Power.

Without it we're but castaways.

With it, the seas are our highways.

Sails, engines, electrics, and the systems that make them work are at the heart of the power structure. Few are the sailors who are masters of all three; fewer still can pass stewardship for these vitals to someone else.

So it's live and learn. What's new? What works? What are the priorities? What can we troubleshoot? What can we fix? What should we carry aboard? What do we need to know?

Stay in power.

More Power to You

—*Mel Crook's column through five decades of* Yachting *magazine.*

SAILS

BEAT THE BAG   *(Tom Linskey)* One blemish on the perfection of roller-furling headsails is roller-reefing. When you need a small, flat, tough sail, you roll down and get a bloated, billowing bag. The years of sailmaker expertise devoted to this question, though, have borne some fruit. Remember to move sheet leads forward as you roll a jib down.

The traditional problem of stretchy sailcloth can be attacked through stepped-up constructions that increase the percentage of heavy cloth and reinforce critical locations (like head and tack) of the reefed sail. Scotch-cut and stepped-up vertical panel designs take this approach.

A solution that works for older sails is the foam wedge. This tapered piece is sewn into the luff (retrofittable to existing sails) and pulls slack out of the middle of the sail when the jib rolls up around it. At any rate, for consistency, durability, and improved performance, consider head and tack patches at your favorite reef positions, and the ultraviolet shields that cover leech and foot of your rolled-up sail will start to pull their weight if you replace the acrylic sunshield with ultraviolet-resistant Dacron.

SHAPING SAILS
(Dennis Conner) A sailmaker uses three techniques to put shape into a sail. First, the luff of the sail is not a straight line, but a curve. Second, the foot of the sail is also curved. When these two curved edges are forced into a straight mast and boom, the resultant shape is an airfoil. The third technique, *broadseaming*, is a similar, but somewhat more sophisticated approach. The sail is made of panels, and the panels are joined at seams. If one seam is straight and the other curved, when they are joined, shape is once again built into the sail.

OPEN OR CLOSED?
(Jeff Johnstone) Once you have achieved the desired fullness or flatness in your sails and have located the draft where it should be, what about the leech? The outer edges of sails act like doors. The door is closed when the edge of the sail is parallel to your boom (or the boat's centerline with a headsail). As the edge swings out (and your battens point more to leeward), the door opens. With the door closed, the area presented to the wind is high; therefore so is the wind force. Open the door and the wind escapes. This permits the power level to go down. As a helmsman you know you can have too much power (increased heeling, weather helm, and aggravation from your crew) or too little (the dead slows). In heavy air your sails should be shaped flat, with your leeches open. As the air lightens, tighten your leeches and make the sails fuller.

GENOA TRIM
(Mike Toppa) Even if you've bought the fastest genoa shape in the world from your sailmaker, it's still up to you to make it perform. You must first decide which size headsail is best. Normally you start reducing the size of your boat's jib when she begins to heel more than 20 to 25 degrees. Tension the halyard so that the sail's maximum draft is about 45 percent the total girth distance back from the luff. With a Mylar or Kevlar headsail, the shape won't change much so set it *hand tight* and check the draft. It should be about right. For waves or in heavier air you will want to round the leading edge of the sail by moving the draft farther forward. Depower the sail by moving the lead aft and letting the upper part of the leech twist off. When you straighten the headstay, the genoa becomes flatter. When

you need speed, let the sail deepen; to point higher, take the curve out of the luff. Likewise, trimming the sheet lets you point higher but reduces chord depth and reduces power. Sheet tension should be changed with changes in direction and velocity.

FORESTAY FATIGUE

(Ian Hannay) Fatigue to shrouds and fasteners comes from repeated changes in load. The actual changes are often only a small proportion of the total breaking strain. The worst effect is when the load is repeatedly reversed (such as breaking a wire by bending it back and forth). It is almost as bad, however, when the load is reduced to near-zero and then re-applied. Stainless steel is susceptible to this sort of fatigue.

Loads should be kept fair and straight on rigging. However, a forestay with a headsail set on a boat punching into seas is subject to cycling loads (up to 1,000 cycles per hour) and the damage that they cause. It makes sense to consider the forestay, and especially the forestay turnbuckle, as perhaps the weakest link in your rig and single it out for particular examination and periodic testing.

CUT INTO CHAFE

(Don Street) Chafe has always been a problem, and prior to World War II, baggywrinkle was seen in great balls all over the rigging of cruising yachts. Today chafe is mostly limited to the stitching on Dacron sails, which can be restitched time and again.

The worst chafe problem occurs where the main contacts the lee shrouds. Baggywrinkle will minimize this, but the windage of baggywrinkle is so great and it is such a tedious job to rig correctly—don't do it! Instead, well before your departure on any long cruise, spend a day sailing broad off with a full main and with one and two reefs tied in. Bring your sail to your sailmaker. He will be able to see the fresh chafe marks. Instead of using large, ugly, difficult-to-fit chafing patches, just have him cover the stitching in the chafe areas with a thin strip of light (say 3 oz. on an 8-oz. main) Dacron. These strips won't last forever, but they'll increase the life of the seams they protect. At the same time, be sure to cover the spreader tips in soft felt.

—adapted from the Ocean Sailing Yacht

IT'S IN THE BAG

(Dave Seidman) For centuries sailors have kept their own special tools in canvas drawstring ditty bags. Mine came from Albury Sailmakers, Man O' War Cay, Bahamas. It was made 20 years ago and looks like it's got at least another 20 good years. Here's what's in it:

- *Monel or stainless steel wire.* Shackle pins should be secured with wire seizing.
- *Anhydrous lanolin.* Lanolin is useful for leather maintenance, screw-pin lubrication, and waterproofing.
- *Sailmaker's needles.* Include at least three sizes. The lowest number is the largest needle.
- *Palm.* To make a commercial roping palm usable, soak it for days in leather conditioner, adjust it so the strap just touches the back of your hand, and develop calluses.
- *Thread.* For whipping and sail repair, use only nylon or Dacron. I sometimes substitute dental floss (peppermint preferred).
- *Beeswax.* The finest is deep amber, soft, and resinous. If all you can find is hard and flaky, use a candle.
- *Hot knife.* Butane-powered Portasol can be used on deck, as a torch, soldering iron, you name it.
- *Fid.* A fid is the proper tool for rope work. This is not a marlinspike, which comes with every sailor's knife but is meant for working wire. A fid is hardwood, egg-shaped, tapering over 8 inches or so to a point, and ideal for holding rope strands apart without damaging them.
- *Knife.* I prefer a sheath knife.
- *Sharpening stone.* Mine is of silicone carbide (Carborundum) with smooth and coarse sides.
- *Grommet kit.* Kit should include a base, punch, set of grommets, and carrying bag.

- *Pliers.* Rigging kits used to come with multi-functional pliers that combined wire cutters, adjustable wrench, and screw driver. They're still around.
- *Masking tape.* Half-inch is best.

LONG HORSE

(MB) In *Westering* we had a forestaysail sheet horse [a traveler]. The sail was boomed and self-tending, which was a Godsend, but the horse should have been longer. As Weston Martyr writes in *Southseaman*:

> If I ever own another schooner, I shall risk tripping over the horse and have it run right across the ship. Because if it does not, the sheet is unable to prevent the sail from lifting and letting its head fall off to leeward.

PULLING THE STRINGS

(Dave Franzel) You can alter the shape of your sail to increase power in light air or decrease it in a blow. The depth of the pocket in the sail is its *draft*. The deeper the curve, the more draft, and the more power. You can flatten a mainsail using halyard tension, downhaul, the Cunningham, and the flattening reef, as well as mast bend. With headsails you have only halyard tension and the position of the jib leads. (Move the lead forward, draft increases, and vice versa.)

MAKING SAILS LAST

(Larry Pardey) We've learned the hard way: it's better to practice prevention than pay for cure where sails are concerned. Flogging is enemy number one. When sailcloth is bent or flogged repeatedly, concentration of bending at the creases weakens the fiber prematurely and causes it to tear. We try to allow only a minimum of flogging in our sail handling. (We take the time to dry sails on deck after washing rather than hanging them aloft.)

Leeches are a common source of cloth fatigue.

Snug up leech lines gradually until you eliminate all but the briefest flutter. A 24-hour beat with a flogging leech can take six months of life out of a Dacron sail.

We prefer soft Dacron (about the texture of new work jeans) to the stabilized (filled with resin and tempered) cloth because the flexible soft cloth is less susceptible to work-hardening through flogging. It is stretchier, which means it holds its shape slightly less well, but that resilience and "shock absorber" effect add strength and durability to the softer cloth.

Haven Collins, a sailmaker we met in New Zealand, maintains that eliminating battens (short or full-length) can increase your sail's life by 50 percent. Even if you only focus on the inboard-end crease or boltrope area where sail meets batten, by eliminating the batten you've eliminated a troublesome hardspot.

Large reinforcing patches at head, tack, clew, and reef points; dark-colored thread to better resist ultraviolet degradation; over-size bags; chafe guards (made from light hose) on shrouds; spreader-end patches made of shag carpet remnants; use of a boom vang/preventer tackle (see pp. 199-200 of *Capable Cruiser*) to limit boom movement and virtually eliminate mainsail chafe; and replacement of freestanding luff wires with Kevlar-cored or Spectra braided luff rope are more things we do to get more miles from our sails.

STILL STANDING

(David Siemens) When we think about our rigs at all, it's most likely to congratulate ourselves: still standing! To keep it that way, know:

- Because they "cup" moisture, bottom-end swages are the most common fail-point of stays and shrouds.
- The tropics are hardest on swages—and the rest of the rig. Temperate, then colder, then freshwater regions follow in lessening degrees of unfriendliness.

Some surveyors carry a small 25x microscope and look for staining, pitting, and hairline cracks in the swages. They inspect shroud wire for a deformed strand in the cluster. These anomalies suggest that either a wire has slipped in a swage or is under severe tension.

Testing with dye-penetrants and pull testing are options, too. Since stainless relies on a thin oxide of its own for protection, barrier-coat lubrications may be counterproductive.

SAFE WAY

(Will Robinson) Rerigging a 45-footer recently, I found that the VHF antenna and the masthead-light wire had been sawn right through by the wire halyards running beside them inside the mast. There is a simple cure: install a wiring conduit inside your mast.

- Use plastic conduit or PVC water pipe (Schedule 40). For small boats, ½ ID is generally adequate, but install a larger size if your mast contains a lot of wiring.
- Mark the tube to length—from just below the sheave box to just above the exit port—along the forward side of the mast. Run the tube as high as possible to extend protection. It's best to run the conduit right to the mast cap and have the wires exit through the top, because any exposed wire inside the mast will be subject to chafe.
- Remove the tube and tape it in place along the exterior of the mast. Drill holes (through conduit and mast together) for rivets (I use # 10 or ³⁄₁₆-inch). The fewer holes the better, but also avoid over-long runs of unfastened pipe.
- Spreader light and steaming light hookups should be considered. For ease of alignment and maximum chafe protection, it is usually better to drill these exit holes after the conduit is in place.
- Realign the tube inside the mast (you can hold it in place with wire bent into 90-degree angle hooks).
- Daub the mast holes with zinc-chromate putty, then, starting at the bottom, pop-rivet the tube to the mast. Alignment is critical
- Drill exit holes for the external leads through the mast and conduit—on the rivet line. Snake the wire top-down through the conduit. You might also pull several small-diameter cords

through as messengers for future wiring.
- Seal the top and intermediate exit holes with silicone caulking.

MILES PER DOLLAR

(Annie Hill) Old China hand G. R. G. Worcester wrote, "Nobody could have *designed* the Chinese sail, if only for fear of being laughed at." You'll laugh when I say this, but there is no other rig that can beat it. Pete (my husband) and I have sailed our junk-rigged 34-foot *Badger,* a Jay Benford design, more than 70,000 miles.

Sailing the boat is simplicity itself, with only four running lines to each sail and nothing to touch while tacking. Reefing can be either down or up. Mostly it's down, but for maneuverability and visibility, up works well. As many reefs as you want can be put in at one time, stacking the battens together. Jibing is quite painless because you can sail well by-the-lee, so the sail is virtually feathered and its swing depowered.

Free-standing spars demand less upkeep, offer less wind resistance, and are cheap to build. Hoisting sail, there's no flogging. The battens tame the sail so you can let sheets run and stop the boat anytime with no problem. There's a lot to be said for doing all of the sail handling from the cockpit, even the companionway. *Badger* has a couple of small sheet winches—which we never use. It's certainly preferable to reef sails that are already set rather than change to new ones.

The cost of sails can be considerable. It's worth having a rig that doesn't need an extensive wardrobe of them taking up space that could better be occupied by strings of onions and bottles of wine. Because they're "low-tech" sails with no shape built in, you can make them yourself. Believe it or not, when we bought *Badger* in 1975, we rigged her—masts, sails, and running rigging—for $450.

The junk rig's performance is vastly underrated. William A. Robinson, in *Svaap,* learned that, "with sails consisting of various pieces of vegetable matter, old clothing, or what have you, give them a little breeze and they sail like witches. We were passed by one one day as we plowed at top speed, power and sail, trying to make port before dark. She lumbered awkwardly, to all appearances standing still, but she must have been doing about 8 knots."

Bermudan rigs are, indeed, closer-winded, but they also induce more heel than the low-aspect junk. For tacking up a narrow channel, the junk is the best! Remember, too, that in a seaway it's not always fastest to be hard on the wind. Also, if you motorsail, you will heel less with a junk rig and pick up comfort, speed, and a better-lubricated engine.

We may not sail as fast as other yachts. We may not point as high, but if you make comparisons on a cost-per-mile basis, I think you'll find that last 5 percent of efficiency comes very expensive. At the end of the day, a low-tech rig is cheap to set up, cheap to run, and cheap to maintain. As far as I can see, this means you can sail more miles for less money with fewer worries.

—*adapted from* Voyaging on a Small Income

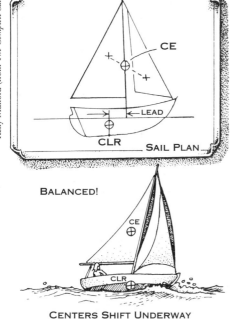

BALANCED!

CENTERS SHIFT UNDERWAY

Center of Effort

CENTER OF EFFORT

(C.A. Marchaj) The conventional method of finding the geometrical *center of effort* of a sail plan yields a point which does not correspond to the true *center of pressure*. The CP changes within wide limits, and is generally in front of the geometrically computed CE. Still, the CE is practical in assessing the balance of a sail plan and comparing one rig to another.

To find the center of effort: First determine the geometrical centers of the mainsail and the foretriangle. (Find the center of a triangle by drawing a straight line from each corner to the midpoint of the side opposite—the lines cross at the geometrical center.) Connect the two centers, then break that connecting line in proportion to the ratio of the areas of main and FT (i.e., if the foretriangle area is 35 percent of the mainsail area, find a point 35 percent aft of the center of FT). That dividing point is the CE for the sail plan as a whole.

The easiest way to find the *center of lateral resistance* for the underbody of a given hull is to balance a cardboard cutout of the boat's underwater profile (minus the rudder) on a knife-edge, the balance point being the longitudinal center.

In general, CE should be forward of CLR for the rig to balance. A rule of thumb (from *Skene's Elements of Yacht Design*) expresses the distance forward of the CLR for the following rigs in terms of percentage of design waterline: sloops—14%; yawls—15%; schooners—5%; ketches—20%.

—*adapted from* Sailing Theory and Practice

WIND FORCE

(Karl Burkhardt) An increase from 5 knots to 7 knots of wind speed nearly doubles the wind force. (Force varies as the square of the velocity.) Winter wind has more force than summer wind because the molecules in cold air are closer together. Twenty-five degrees of temperature change makes a difference of about 5 percent in wind force. Sailing in the Great Lakes (at an average of 600 feet above sea level), wind force will be about 2 percent less than at sea level because the air is slightly thinner. Humid air is lighter than dry air because water vapor is lighter than air. From dry air to saturated fog, the difference is about 2.6 percent.

NOT SO WARPED

First seen in the heavy-air '87 America's Cup series in Perth, Australia, *warp insert threads* were little things that had a big impact. The axiom in sailmaking has always been: "Suit the cloth to the load." Whether sculpting Egyptian cotton into elegant 19th-century sails or custom-weaving "stretchless" Dacron for modern racers, sailmakers have long sought materials that better resist sailing strains. Going into Perth, lamination was the prevailing technique—counter sail loads by building up layers of cloth to add strength. Under a world of competitive pressure, Dimension sailcloth went farther. Made possible by improved adhesives, their innovation (further developed by Bainbridge & Co.) was to add threads alone (in the direction of maximum strain) where sails needed extra strength.

Like tiny reinforcing rods, the threads added materially to stretch resistance; because they were only "a passel of thread," they added almost nothing in terms of weight. One-way threads made sails so strong that two-ply constructions became outmoded, "delamination" a forgotten word and, just like they're supposed to in the wonderful world of the America's Cup, sails got lighter, stronger, and faster.

POLYNESIAN SAILS

(Dr. David Lewis) It is far from easy to sort out Polynesian sails. There were three kinds: simple lateens, apex-down triangular sails, and claw-shaped sails. The lateen was certainly Austronesian, and probably the oldest. The triangular sail, as seen on the Samoan *soatau*, is probably a simplified version of the claw. The claw seems to have been the invention of the Polynesians themselves. The shape, which at first sight appears fanciful, is, in reality, highly functional. The sail tapers upward to the claw tips, which evenly reduces sail area to be supported by the marginal spars. It allows for lighter spars, less bracing, and much less weight and stress aloft than any other conceivable shape. Among

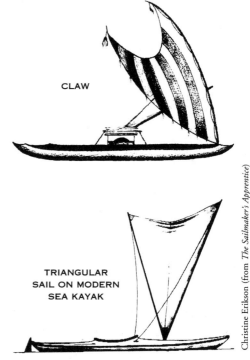

CLAW

TRIANGULAR
SAIL ON MODERN
SEA KAYAK

Christine Erikson (from *The Sailmaker's Apprentice*)

Polynesian Sails

the sail shapes depicted in pre-Christian petroglyphs on cave walls in Hawaii are three unmistakable Tahitian claws, mute testimony to voyagers gone but hardly forgotten.

—adapted from We the Navigators

SAILS IN NATURE

(Manfred Curry) Take the soaring bird and the sailing boat; both move at a given angle to the wind by means of a certain power. As nature has endowed the bird with a form to create the up-drive to hold itself in the air, we must make a sail that has the same maximum lifting component with a similarly small retarding action. Soaring and free flight—these are the qualities to study.

The albatross, the gull, and the buzzard all build forward speed without a stroke of their wings. The requisite air pressure that lets a bird or airplane float freely is not obtained until the wing is struck with air at a certain critical speed. The up-drive increases as the square of the velocity and directly with the area of the wing. If we observe gulls against the sun, their wings as they soar are being continually pulled and turned, seeking to catch and utilize every puff of wind, "tuning " themselves to achieve the best shape for soaring. Among the soaring birds, we see that those with arched wings soar more freely than those with flat wings of the same area. A properly arched surface will, in a sufficiently strong wind, both rise and move against the wind!

The next important factor is the relation of length to breadth in the wing. The longer wing creates fewer resistance eddies than the same wing presented breadth-first; longer, narrower wings make the best soarers. Birds also, I have ascertained, are able to control their feathers to suit their wings better for soaring. They possess pockets of feathers which, upon the stimulus of airflow or, it seems, at the bird's own muscle control, increase the thickness of the wing to better bend the wind and increase the up-drive.

There are reasons, however, why sails cannot conform strictly to the form of soaring wings.

First, the wing tips are not only made to soar but to move in beating flight. This has led to the fallacy among sailors that the tip of the mast should bend outward. This is a gross error. While the wing is flexible for any number of natural reasons, the sail can and should be of a permanent form. Spars that flex and bend sidewards will not achieve maximum efficiency.

Finally, we should not attempt to follow those lines which play important roles for the bird, but not for the boat. The fore edge of the bird's wing, for example, is inclined "aft." This appears to have led yacht designers, especially the Swedes, to rake masts well aft. While backward inclination assures the bird stability, it robs power from the sail.

—adapted from Yacht Racing,
The Aerodynamics of Sails *(1935)*

SET IN STOPS

(H. A. Calahan) The spinnaker (genoa, storm trysail, etc.) is first laid out on deck very carefully, with the luff and leech laid alongside one another. The middle of the sail is then rolled up very small and tight so that we get a long, thin roll from head to foot, with the luff and leech side by side on the outside of the roll, and the clew and tack together at the bottom. In this position the tube of sail is tied by ordinary cotton thread. Do not use anything heavier than cotton thread for stops. Never use string or fish[ing] line. A single turn of the thread tied at intervals of about 2½ feet is sufficient, except near the foot of the sail where two or three turns are advisable.

—adapted from The Yachtsman's Omnibus

FLYING DUCK

(Eric Tabarly) Up to *Pen Duick V,* all of my boats were named, as my father's was, for the same small black Brittany waterfowl. This boat was meant for the Transpacific race in 1969. She was experimental in terms of her water ballast and 3-to-1 length to beam ratio. What sort of sail plan did I want? I went to Paris to discuss it with Daniel Duvergie, and all the time I kept thinking that I wanted more sail. The boat's stability and the downwind nature of the race—you can carry a lot of sail off

the wind—made me sure that I wanted as much sail as I could get. With a boat so small (only 35 feet overall) I knew that handling the sails wouldn't be a big problem.

In order to carry lots of sail before the wind, I was going to have 15-foot spinnaker booms that telescoped to 25 feet—two of them. The largest spinnaker would be 1,290 square feet—quite big in comparison to my 268 sq. ft. mainsail. It is unusual to see a spinnaker set on two booms because it is illegal under the racing rules, but we often did this when cruising, especially in Sweden in *Pen Duick III*. With a following wind we sailed among the archipelagoes, jibing every five minutes or so. It's a great rig, and because the usual racing rules did not apply for the Transpac, I intended to use it.

—*adapted from* Pen Duick

UP THE MAST

(Rod Stephens, Jr.) At the masthead are the sheaves, which need to be inspected, polished, and lubricated. Between them, though, are divider plates. These are frequently made of aluminum and receive a good deal of wear. A most durable solution is to fashion a simple stainless mast guard to cover the worn edges of the divider plate. It will prevent future chafe on the plates and prevent halyard damage as well (see drawing).

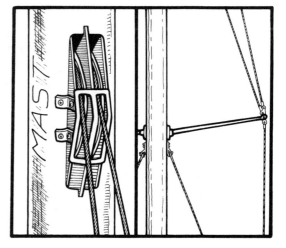

Spreader plate, left, and spreader link plates, right.

The next items to check are the tangs. Of the many attachment systems I've seen, the one that worries me most is the method of using a bent hook to make the attachment. Experience has shown the depth of the hook to be a significant weak point and not trustworthy. Even through-bolted fittings (which I like) should have exactly the right bevel or they will flex and fatigue. Sight them carefully to see that they are in line with the loaded shroud. Many tangs have inboard plates that are flatter and thinner than the outboard. This allows the outboard plate to deform under load and transfers dangerous strains to the clevis pin holding the shroud.

All rigging pins should be well-lubricated (I have never found anything better than anhydrous lanolin). Tighten screws and treat them with Loctite. And check the spreaders. Be sure the mast holds the spreader at the correct angle fore and aft. Also the spreader should more-or-less bisect the angle made by the shroud it supports.

For attaching shrouds to the spreader, I prefer link plates. If there are none, some other seamanlike solution is necessary. If more than one shroud is supported by the spreader, attach the heaviest and let the other remain free to slide.

If you don't have a forestay, think seriously about installing one, usually with running backstays. Don't secure turnbuckles with lock nuts. I much prefer open-barrel turnbuckles that let you see what you've got. If you can anticipate problems you will go a long way toward solving them. The sea is never really predictable, but the fact that it will challenge boats and sailors is.

GETTING IT STRAIGHT

(Roger Marshall) If you start with a mast that's straight in your boat, whatever you do to "tune the rig" will have a much better chance of success. The fundamental goal when you position and wedge a mast at the outset is to have it rise straight from the centerline and be fixed firmly at the deck. Lower the mast into the boat. Connect the shrouds and tighten them by hand. Hoist a tape measure to the masthead (on the centerline sheave) and measure down to the two aft lower chainplates. Adjust the upper shrouds until the measurements are the same on both sides of the boat. With the masthead thus fixed on the centerline, sight up the mast (the sail track is useful) and adjust the remaining shrouds so it is straight.

Now wedge the mast at the deck. I prefer to wedge the mast transversely rather than fore and aft. This lets the mast move fore and aft as it is bent by shroud tension and sail forces. I also recommend using Spartite, a two-part polymer product that you pour between the mast and deck. This stuff sets up solid between hull and spar and makes a good wedge/seal.

Next, heel the boat under sail. Tighten the leeward shroud so that slack all but disappears. Change tacks and repeat the process. Measure the mast again and, if it's not straight, adjust what you need to make it straight. You've begun to approach a well-tuned spar when there is no slackness in the lee shrouds, no fall-off at the masthead, and sighting reveals no lateral bend.

—*adapted from* Marshall's Marine Review

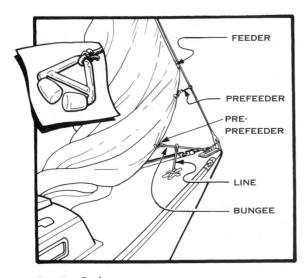

Pre-Prefeeder

PRE-PREFEEDER

(Bill Biwenga) Normally on a grooved-headstay system there is a feeder on the headstay extrusion itself and a "prefeeder" attached with a line about 18 inches to 2 feet down from the feeder. To avoid tearing sails, install a second prefeeder (about 2 feet aft of the first one). It should be secured with bungee cord. The bungee serves two purposes: (1) it absorbs shock loads as the sail is being "jerked" aloft by the halyard; (2) it rebounds rhythmically and thus serves to pull the sail forward, which lines it up for smoother hoisting. To get the best results from the second prefeeder, tie it in place with a short line aft of the tack. This keeps it from going up with the hoist but allows it to travel aft and "gather" sail.

RUNNERS AWAY

(Bruce Kirby) When Bruce Farr "re-invented" the fractional rig with his Quarter-Tonner *45 Degrees South* more than 20 years ago, he changed the skyline. Fractional spars now outnumber mastheads in many an anchorage. With the fractionals has come a whole new technology built around the use of running backstays to control headstay tension, mast bend, and mast compression. Not all fractionals have runners, but they all would be better off if they did. It's easier to sail a boat without runners, but it's easier to sail a boat well if you have them. Running backs should be led as far aft as possible (for maximum tension on the headstay), and they should be as close to the centerline as possible (for optimal angle of pull on the headstay). The best way to set up the system is with a tension meter so that you can mark the runner tails and know that each stay is cranked equally tight.

FREE POWER   *(Robbie Doyle)*

If you're headed somewhere under power, why not try motorsailing? Leave the main up. Trim it in tight, maybe even bring the traveler to weather, and the flow of air over the sail will produce drive that will add significantly to your speed. The steadying effect of the main will make the passage more comfortable, it's true, but you should see at least a quarter knot added to your speed, depending on how fast you normally power. The savings in fuel and time are real, and as long as you don't let the sail flog, they come for free.

ENGINES

TALE OF THE SCALE   *(John Vigor)*

Gasoline weighs about 6.1 pounds per gallon. Diesel fuel averages 7.1 pounds per gallon.

—Practical Mariner's Book of Knowledge

AIRSPACE   *(Dave Gerr)*   Inboard engines need more air

than you'd think. The vent area (in square inches—without blowers) the average inboard requires is at least 3.3 times engine horsepower.

BEAT THE HEAT   A heat-activated fire extin-

guisher system is an excellent safeguard in the engine room. Opening the compartment yourself to set off a manual extinguisher admits oxygen that fuels the flames. Naval architect Jay Paris reports a neat variation—a nozzle-sized port in the engine room bulkhead through which you may, from outside the compartment, insert an extinguisher and fight the fire.

MANUALLY GIFTED   The owner's manual

comes, hopefully, with the engine. To do much in the way of service or repair, though, you need a service manual. The dealer is the best place to go; try the manufacturer in a pinch. If you can't obtain a service manual "through channels," there's still hope. Depending on what sort of engine you have, it might be included in one of the commercially

The truth is that I hate motors on a sailing ship. I resent them and therefore I neglect them.

—Sir Francis Chichester

prepared tune-up guides or repair handbooks available at newsstands, by mail, or in the library.

Chilton's Outboard Motors Under 30 Horsepower is representative. Beyond its general "Troubleshooting and Maintenance Introduction," the book has specific sections on all American-made outboards, complete with exploded drawings, part specification numbers, and wiring diagrams. *Chilton's* is well-known for automotive manuals, and its selection of marine manuals is extensive, too.

Clymer's Johnson Service and Repair Handbook (9.5 to 35 Horsepower) is one step more specific. It contains factory illustrations, exploded parts drawings, specification sheets—everything you'd expect from an OMC service manual. It also addresses changes in the same model from year to year.

Intertec's Inboard Engines Manual runs from BMW to Yanmar with schematic and repair information on current models. These are just a sampling of the marine service manuals in circulation.

- Chilton Book Co., 201 King of Prussia Rd., Radnor, PA 19089
- Intertec Publishing Corp., PO Box 12901, Overland Park, KS 66282

CRUISE KIT

(Jay Coyle) Caterpillar is just one of a number of engine makers who offer packaged spares for those intending to head into the field. Cat's "Cruise Kit" is sensible and relatively affordable, certainly better than chasing down a water-pump impeller in Belize.

OUTBOARD REVIVAL

(John Vigor) If you feel sand has been drawn into your doused outboard, hose it off as completely as possible and get it to a mechanic for disassembly and cleaning fast! Otherwise:

1. Fog the cylinder(s) with fogging oil.
2. Remove and dry spark plugs.
3. Remove, clean, and dry the carburetor.

4. With plug hole down, turn engine over several times to force water out of cylinders.
5. Squirt light engine oil into the cylinders.
6. Replace plugs and carburetor.
7. Start engine. If it won't start remove and dry plugs and carburetor again. Check for spark. When it starts, let it run awhile to dry out internal moisture. If it doesn't start, seek expert help.

—adapted from Practical Mariner's Book of Knowledge

TAKING IT APART

Whether it works when you put it together, whatever *it* is, has very much to do with how you take it apart. Strive for a detached (dare we say "Zen"?) combination of focus and calm. "The work dictates the pace."

As you acquire component parts, group them; envelopes, holes poked in a cardboard, separate boxes and jars. "Lump" them and you will add to the problem. Make sketches of complex assemblies. Monitor shapes. How many pieces came from a particular assembly? From a single hole? Wires! How many? Where connected? What order? The work will teach you how it works if you let it. Don't dive so quickly into getting to the bottom of it that you can't get back.

DIESELING

(Tim Banse) If it hasn't happened in your boat or your car, you're lucky. Dieseling is the annoying phenomenon of an engine continuing to turn over after (sometimes well after) the ignition has been turned off. It's an indication of carbon build-up in the tops of the cylinders. The carbon is heated when the engine is running and continues to glow red-hot after the key is switched off, prolonging combustion. Low-octane fuel (87) is the culprit. Medium-grade (89) is the answer. Don't go to high-test because the additives used to boost octane can actually aid the carbon build-up. If a tankful of good gas doesn't seem to help, use one of the many fuel additives that bills itself as an "internal engine cleaner."

Hear the Heat

In addition to monitoring the gauges and keeping an eye and a nose open to monitor engine temperature when you're underway, consider fitting an *audible* "overheat alarm."

Smoke Signals

When a diesel starts to run, whitish exhaust is normal because the engine is not yet hot enough to vaporize its cooling water. If the exhaust remains white, though, it might indicate water in the fuel or getting into the cylinder. Blue exhaust indicates combustion of lube oil. This can come from leaks around rings, valve guides, or oil seals. An overfilled filter or excess oil in the crankcase might also be the culprit. Black smoke comes from incomplete combustion. The "smoke" is unburned fuel and comes from overloading, air starvation, or a faulty injector.

Maintain Your Post

(Chandler Bates, Jr.) Twice recently the Perkins diesel in my trawler would not start. The battery was well charged, oil and temperature alarms went off, but the starter simply clicked. Ever happen to you? I found a quick and (very) simple culprit—the positive battery post. Most boats still have collars secured to the positive post by a 2-inch square-headed bolt. Corrosion here weakens the bolt and loosens the collar, breaking this connection or making it weak and intermittent. The answer is to maintain your battery terminals, carry spare bolts (20 cents each), have spare battery cables aboard, and lift the positive collar well clear from the battery for the winter.

Reflected Truth

(Jimmy O'Cain) I found it almost impossible to get at the dipstick aboard my Cape Dory 30. The engine is mounted facing the stern, with the V-drive unit mounted at the rear of the engine. You have to find the dipstick by feel. I found a mirror taped to the engine-room bulkhead, though. There's no mystery why it's there! It's a metal camping-type mirror, and looking into it is the only way I can see where to put the dipstick back.

Bleed No More

(Jonathan Lewis) Typical of a series of products and systems designed to make managing diesel fuel flow more elegant is the Grove anti-airlock device. Sized to suit most pleasure boats, the devices look something like a filter. They let diesels run even with quantities of air in the lines, they offer "self-contained" air-venting rather than venting fuel into the boat, and they promise that "no bleeding will be necessary between filter changes."

Sludge Slayer

BioGuard is a significant new weapon in the war on sludge. It's a biocide targeted to eliminate bacterial fuel clogs, and it works in just 2 to 3 hours. Most alternatives take a day at least. It comes in self-measuring 16-oz. bottles as well as 5- and 55-gallon drums. Valvtect, 3400 Dundee Rd., Northbrook, IL 60062.

Snuff Out Radio Noise

(Paul Franson) Radio "noise" can be atmospheric, static, or an over-powerful nearby signal, but by far the commonest culprit is your own electrical system—electricity jumping through the air. Eliminate the loudest noises and the ones masked behind them will surface. Use a cheap AM portable as your noise detector. Noise can originate in one spot and be distributed to others by wiring, machinery, etc., but play "hot" and "cold" until you've localized a source.

The most likely noise villain is your engine. Diesels are quieter than gasoline, but they're harder to quiet. You can combat engine "noise" with a tune-up. Adjusting the points, spraying the wires—that should help. Your next step is installing resistive spark plugs and changing to magnetic suppressive wire. Check that the ignition coil is well-grounded to the block, too.

Bypass capacitors bleed noise quietly to ground. You might install a 0.5 or 1.0 microfarad capacitor to the positive ignition coil terminal. Feed-through capacitors modulate signals by letting current run through them. The two have the same effect.

You might also:

- Replace plastic shielding around the ignition coil with metal.
- Beware of lifeline/shroud chafe as a source of noise.
- Watch out for the prop turning in its stuffing box.
- Shut down the gen-set; its brushes are noisier than the slip rings in the alternator.

Try to meet big noises head-on while you handle little noises with a bypass capacitor.

MASTER BELT

Nordic Marine International offers the Emergency Master Belt which should, perhaps, be in your spares kit. Winner of the Chicago Marine Trades Exposition Award for innovation, it is adjustable and designed to work where awkwardly positioned one-piece belts prove a problem. The belt is made up of joints connected by snaps and will open to bypass just about any obstacle.

TRINITY

(Don Sharp) If your gas engine spins merrily but refuses to start, it means failure in one (or more) of these three essential areas: a supply of air and fuel; a means of igniting the air/fuel mixture; a means of containing the initial compression of the fuel-air charge. These are the enginemaster's magic triad. Invoked and applied, the triad virtually always induces action in an engine.

GOT A MATCH?

(Don Sharp) Sailboat engines run fairly cool, so their spark plug gaps don't tend to get wider with normal use, but check those gaps anyway. The plug gap should be about 0.035 inch. A match book cover is from 0.012 inch to 0.015 inch thick, and the match itself is about 0.037 inch. Set your plugs to fit tight on a match and, when appropriate, the distributor points to a loose fit on the cover.

NATURE'S SPONGE

(Don Sharp) A strong spark won't guarantee a start if the spark plugs are fouled at the electrode inside the engine. Soft carbon, which builds up during long periods of idling speeds, is a wonderful sponge for sopping up moisture in the air or excess gasoline from the carburetor. Once it is damp, the carbon allows the spark to go to ground without jumping across the gap between the spark plug electrodes. Hard carbon, which is accumulated over time, especially in engines that run at low operating temperatures as sailboat engines do, is an electrical conductor that also allows the spark to bypass the gap. Clean soft carbon with a toothbrush and a solvent, such as stove alcohol. Dig hard carbon out with a crochet hook or similar device. Better yet, replace the plugs.

DIESEL CLANG

(Dave Gerr) Since diesel engines spray fuel into the cylinders at fantastically high pressure through slim points (injectors), any contamination in the fuel will stop your diesel quickly! Ordinary air is a common culprit. Even a fairly small air bubble in the fuel line will shut your engine down. Worse still is the really tiny air bubble that works its way through the line. You'll know this has happened because the injectors make a loud, metallic banging for a second, like someone knocking a metal wrench hard against a bench vise. Your engine may, indeed, keep going, but you don't want this to happen often. The fuel passing through the injectors is what lubricates them. When air goes through, the banging you'll hear is the injector components crashing together (at 18,000 psi) without lubrication. Stop and look for the air leak! The usual culprit is a loose or leaky connection in the fuel line from the tank to the injectors. Air-vent the system before you start again. If clanging persists, shut down until you've fixed the air leak.

Spark Plug Tips

By examining spark plugs, you can learn a lot about what's going on in a gas engine. Monitoring the look and smell of your exhaust and paying attention to the sounds you hear underway are the best everyday barometers, but the state of your plugs when you change them is revealing.

• **Oily plugs.** These are your best indicators that something deserves attention. If the plugs are wet with oil it means that oil is entering the combustion chamber. The "blow-by" could come from worn piston rings, valve seats, or perhaps the head gasket. It might also point the finger at faulty timing. In a two-stroke engine, "oily" residue can indicate a fuel mixture that contains too much oil. An oily plug is a sign to heed.

• **Carbonized plugs.** They are tipped with dry, gritty carbon deposits. They tell you that either the fuel mixture is too rich or that the plug is too cold for the engine. If you need a rich mixture, switch to a hotter plug.

• **Burned, pitted plugs.** The insulator tip is gray, and you may see other signs of heat deformation. The engine has been running too hot due, perhaps, to a too-lean fuel mixture. Also check your cooling system, especially the thermostat.

• **Normal plugs.** If the plugs before you are dry and free from carbon deposits, and if the insulator tips are tinged with tan or slightly brown and there is very little pitting of the electrodes, it is a sign that your engine is running well.

Prime Time

(Doug Terman) If you have the embarrassing bad fortune to suck a diesel engine dry, there can be, according to the manual you have in front of you, up to 14 steps necessary before you get the engine going again. I recommend an instant fix:

1. Permanently install a neoprene squeeze bulb (like the ones in most outboard tanks) in the fuel line upstream of all the filters.

2. Locate and place in position a wrench to fit the injection-pump drain-plug fitting.

Once you've run out of fuel:

1. Add fuel to the tank, or switch to a tank containing fuel.
2. Open the drain on the injection pump with the pre-positioned wrench.
3. Place a container beneath the drain to catch the fuel.
4. Squeeze the neoprene bulb until a clear, bubble-free flow of fuel appears.
5. Shut the drain and start the engine.

Checking Sticks

(Bob Anderson) Many transmission dipsticks are screwed into the transmission body and need a wrench to loosen them. A standard socket will usually fit the assembly. Why not buy a socket to fit the dipstick nut? Fashion a hardwood handle and epoxy it to the socket to make a tool that will do the job instantly. Find a convenient place to stow your "transmission wrench," and you've taken the hassle out of checking the transmission fluid.

Carburetor Adjustment

(Will Robinson) If the engine is not idling smoothly it could be due to poor fuel mixture; there's a simple test you can make. With the engine idling I pass my hand slowly across the carburetor throat closing off a little of the opening at a time. If the engine is getting a good mix of gas and air it will die out slowly as the air is reduced (just as it would if you were running with the choke on). If it suddenly pops up with increasing revs at some point, however, that means that it must be getting extra air due to faulty adjustment or a leak. I track down the leak by spraying starter fluid around the edges of the intake manifold and carburetor base. If I get an rpm increase from the spray at any particular point, I've found the leak.

METHUSELAH, METHUSELAH

(Jeannine Herron) In the afternoon Matt and Bill tried to start Methuselah for our daily battery charging. No luck! After messing about for about 30 minutes, they discovered considerable water in the gas tank; evidently it had leaked in around or through the filler cap during rough weather. For three hours they worked to flush out the fuel system. By six o'clock we were ready for a try.

Unfortunately they had also run the batteries down to almost nothing by then. Matt calculated that we had juice enough for just two tries. We had no hand crank. Without Methuselah, we'd be without lights, without radio, and without an engine to help negotiate the unfamiliar channel to St. George's. On the second and final attempt, Methuselah coughed twice and began running. Lovely old beast.

—*adapted from* The Voyage of Aquarius

MIX WELL FOR WINTER

(Horst Klaus) To assure that you get an effective antifreeze/water solution throughout your raw-water cooling system to protect your inboard engine block for the winter:

1. Place 2 to 3 gallons (depending on engine size) of antifreeze in a bucket large enough to hold the additional 2 or 3 gallons of water still in the engine block.
2. Place the bucket beneath your exhaust outlet. You may have to use a temporary elbow at the outlet to make sure the antifreeze/water mixture coming from the exhaust will end up back in the bucket.
3. Disconnect the intake hose at the water pump and substitute a hose of similar diameter and long enough to reach into the bottom of the bucket. (For large engines, swimming-pool vacuum hose is often the right diameter.)
4. Holding the free end of the hose above horizontal, prime it with water/antifreeze and quickly (without losing the prime) stick it into the bucket. This is a two-person job! Start the engine and make sure you get circulation. Run the engine up to maximum temperature to assure that the thermostat is fully open and antifreeze reaches all parts of the engine block. When maximum temperature has been reached, simply shut off the engine and leave the system intact to allow occasional mid-winter start-ups.
5. For dewinterizing in the spring, flush the engine with fresh water and catch the antifreeze mixture in a bucket. Saving it (in the original antifreeze containers) allows you to use it again next winter, perhaps boosted with a fresh gallon.

Winterizing your engine this way avoids condensation and rust build-up commonly found in blocks that are drained and left empty all winter.

FLEX AND DIP

(MB) The fuel fill pipes in my boat have curves in them, so I made a dipstick "gas gauge" using a plastic batten. All I did was taper the ends so that they negotiate the curves.

WHOM DO YOU TRUST?

(Don Street) One cup of salt water in 100 gallons of fresh water will only serve to make the coffee a little better. A cup of water in a tank of gasoline, however, will bring you to a standstill. A cup of water in a tank of diesel, and you will have problems enough to last a month. Draw fuel from the top of the tank when you can so water and sludge from the bottom will have a tougher time getting into the system.

Fuel tanks must be vented. All too often vent pipes are 1/8-inch copper tubing (though current ABYC standards mandate a minimum of 9/16 inch). These are too small to permit convenient fueling and they are actually harmful in tanks where they allow pressure to build up and cause flexing that taxes the welds, rivets, etc. Much better is 1/2-inch or 3/4-inch plastic hose, brought up on deck as high as possible. Engineers say a vent pipe should be 75 percent the diameter of the fill pipe, but I've never seen a vent close to that size on a yacht.

ATTRACTIVE!

(Richard T. Evans) If you buy a magnetic tool-holder at your local hardware store, you can mount it (with electrical ties, in a bulkhead bracket, on a block of wood made "non-slip" with sandpaper, etc.) to hold your ferrous tools and minimize the amount of time spent hunting those tiny pieces that go missing at reassembly time. [Don't mount it anywhere near compass or autopilot.—eds.]

TAKING THE HEAT

(Nigel Calder) You might think that fuel injection on gasoline engines could be made to serve the same function as fuel injection on diesel engines, allowing much higher compression ratios to be used and thereby considerably improving the efficiency of the engine. Gasoline, however, is far more volatile than diesel fuel, and if injected into the super-pressurized and heated air found in a high compression engine, it would explode forcefully enough to damage the engine.

—adapted from Marine Diesel Engines

IMPROVE DIESEL FUEL FLOW

(Eric Forsyth and Erik Nelson) One thing you might want to do to your fuel system is insert a small external pump to help circulate, purge, and bleed the lines. A second good thing is a vacuum gauge. It will read the pressure in the line and provide reliable early warning about fuel blockages in your filters. To make these modifications, it's easiest to work with ABYC A-1 rubber diesel fuel line. We chose a Dupree type 840 pump and a Bourdon-type vacuum gauge. When you operate the engine, turn the electric pump off and bypass it with the selector valves in the line.

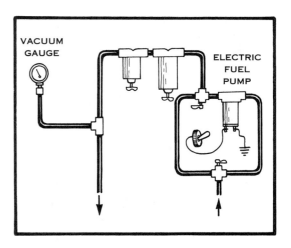

Improve Diesel Fuel Flow

GET THE POINT

(Paul Dempsey) Point gap has considerable influence on ignition timing, particularly when the points are driven at half engine speed by a camshaft. Making the gap wider allows the points to remain open and advances the spark. Narrowing the gap retards ignition. Any engine with external timing marks visible when the engine is running can be timed with a strobe light. Many mechanics favor Xenon lights, but they require an external power source. Gap the points to factory specs and connect the strobe to the spark-plug wire. Twin cylinder engines are normally set up to fire alternately, 90 degrees apart for two-strokes, 180 degrees for four-strokes. Illuminated by a strobe, timing marks appear stationary, and it is simple to bring them into alignment by rotating the magneto or solid-state module.

—adapted from Small Marine Engines

IN AND OUT

Diesel overflow from the injector pump flows back into the fuel tank at a slight pressure. Check to make sure return lines as well as feed lines are high quality.

WINTERIZING AN OUTBOARD

(Warren C. Graumann) Taking your outboard in for the winter, you should:

1. Run the motor in fresh water to help remove some of the accumulated salt deposits.
2. "Run-choke" the engine to a stop by letting it "breathe" fogging oil until it stops.
3. Drain *all* water from the cooling system.
4. Clean the exterior of grease and grime.
5. Apply a coat or two of auto polish to the casings.
6. Lubricate the controls with white grease.
7. Spray ignition parts with auto-ignition moisture-proofer.
8. Drain the lube oil from the lower unit.
9. Clean and gap the plugs. After start-up in the spring you may want to put new plugs in.

SMOOTH EXCHANGE

(Dr. Elliot Storm) The heat exchanger on my Universal diesel sat on a bracket bolted to the bell housing. Two (garden variety) hose clamps held the unit in place. As design flaws go, this set-up should take some prizes. The vibrations of the engine would cause micro-fractures in the clamps and they would break (every two or three months).

To eliminate this problem, I lined the bed of the bracket with red rainbow rubber (from a plumbing supply) secured with Sikaflex 241. I lined the holes in the bracket for the holding straps with windshield-washer hose (also affixed with Sikaflex). Then I tied the exchanger down with four long nylon cable ties (heavy duty). With the rubber cushioning the vibrations and the windshield-washer hose acting like chafe-guard for the nylon, this set-up has worked beautifully for more than a year.

THE FORGOTTEN FACTOR

(Dave Gerr) People have been specifying propellers by diameter and pitch since the *Monitor* bested the *Merrimac*. Everyone who has a screw turning below the water should make a point to begin to recognize the forgotten factor—blade area. Blade area really should come before the other factors. It has to be sufficient to absorb the power of the engine. Insufficient blade area guarantees premature and excessive cavitation. As area increases, it signals a proportional decrease in shaft RPM. An area-first formula for sizing propellers:

$$\text{REQUIRED BLADE AREA} = \frac{100 \times \text{SHAFT HP}}{\text{KNOTS} \times \sqrt{\text{KNOTS}}}$$
$$(\text{SQ. IN.})$$

An auxiliary driven at 9.6 knots by a 60 hp diesel "sees" a maximum of 57.6 shaft horsepower. The "Bigger Blade" Formula above calls for 193 square inches of blade area.

—*adapted from* The Propeller Handbook

COOL SWITCH

(Eliot H. Brown) Caught off the coast of Florida with a dying breeze and an engine overheating due to a failed seawater pump, I disconnected the hose between the pump and heat exchanger and inserted the hose from our deck-wash in its place. Once the engine was started, the deck-wash pump could be turned on, and we were able to power quite coolly (at about 80 percent throttle) out of the Gulf Stream and back to port.

WHERE THERE'S SMOKE

(John Zarella) An automatic, heat-activated fire extinguisher is a boat's best protection against engine fire. If you have to open the engine room to manually activate your fire-fighting gear, you will admit fresh air that will (often dramatically) fuel the fire. Also, make sure the mechanism that activates the fire extinguisher *de-activates* the blower —it makes no sense to have clouds of fire-retardant gas sucked *out of* the engine area. Neither does it

make sense to suck fresh air in.

CARDINAL RULE

(Tom Gross) Machines are more than just metal and magic; they are unreliable only when needed repairs exceed the mechanical ability of the operator. The cardinal principle of outboard repair, the key to all troubleshooting, is that a flammable vapor under compression will *inevitably* ignite in the presence of a hot electrical spark. You must have absolute faith in the inevitability of this reaction. Otherwise you are left with an unreliable piece of junk and a long row home.

BABYING YOUR BATTERY TERMINALS

(Dave Gerr) Even though it's common practice, *don't* grease your battery terminals. Grease of any type, even the ever-popular Vaseline, can give you more problems than it prevents. High current means high temperature. Under these conditions grease will heat up, liquefy, and trickle down onto the battery top. Salt, condensation, and dirt collect on the melted grease and, believe it or not, form a path for slow electrical discharge (a "mild short"). Even if your charging system is working perfectly, a greasy, salty, dirty battery top can silently and insidiously drain battery life during a one- or two-week layover.

Clean the battery top with a solution of baking soda mixed with warm water. It should bubble the grease and grime loose. Then wipe clean and reconnect. To protect your terminals use *polyurethane varnish.* Just brush some on over the terminal connection after it's been tightened properly.

OIL ANALYSIS

(Will Robinson) It's becoming more and more common to have spectroscopic analyses done on lubricating oil. Make your own survey, though, during an oil change. Once you've emptied the crankcase, take the drippings from the last of your oil and catch them in a glass. Swirl it, then empty it. In the film that you have left, how much metal is there? Go over the film with a magnet. Any ferrous metal that you find comes from wear inside the engine. There will be some; there should not be "a lot." Get a reading on how your engine is doing from your oil.

Originally devised to monitor million-dollar mega-engines, spectroscopic analysis has filtered down into pleasure boats. This will tell you much more than a swirl in a jar. From the lab's chemical breakdown you'll learn about sulfur content, carbon content, bearing wear, and a good deal more. [Caterpillar diesel dealers are good contacts for lab work.—eds.]

You can learn a lot through modern chemistry (some companies now supply heat exchanger dip strips that give a reading on coolant density), but you should also develop a seat-of-the-pants feel for oil smears and the metal in them.

THE SMALL OUTBOARD

(Louis Linden) The average 2½ horsepower outboard weighs just 25 to 30 pounds. If you plan to plane your dinghy, though, you'll need to horse around five times that much weight. I give you the little outboard. Virtually all the "minis" are two-strokes. Many are Japanese (like Yamaha, Mariner, Nissan, and Honda) while some are American (Johnson, Evinrude, Mercury). And there is the British Seagull (which, critics say, has but one moving part—the rower).

Apparently engines this small are intended solely for lakes. It makes sense, though, to suit them to the more corrosive atmosphere of the sea—and to the impurities of real-life fuel. Most small outboards rely on gravity to get fuel to the carburetor. Water and dirt, however, often gather in the carb bowl. In the short run this blocks fuel flow; in the long run it means corrosion of the carb bowl. An in-line filter is one solution. (The biggest problem is suiting the lines [tiny] to the filter ports.) The second weapon is a sediment bowl. Once upon a time all gas engines had these. They are casualties of "improved fuel technology," but you can find them around. Typically they will have to be mounted outside the engine housing. To work properly they should be mounted lower than the carburetor float bowl. Impurities now collect in the glass bowl—where you can see them.

To get the upper hand on corrosion, paint the engine. Paint the lower unit with good epoxy paint. Don't block the water intake holes. Add a zinc anode if you can find one small enough and have a place on the shaft housing to mount it. Strip away the engine shrouds and housings; remove the carb. Clean it. Paint it (with several coats of heat-proof paint). Seek exterior nuts; replace them with stainless. Use cap nuts to protect the ends of studs where you can.

A water-cooled engine is ripe for fogging with lay-up spray oil. (An air-cooled engine gets too hot for this "goo," but use it liberally in places like the throttle plate arm and throttle cable.) Your exhaust should get a couple of coats of high-temp paint, too. To make sure the starter comes off when it has to, paint the recoil housing, especially the tabs for the fixing bolts. Coat the ignition wire with silicone spray.

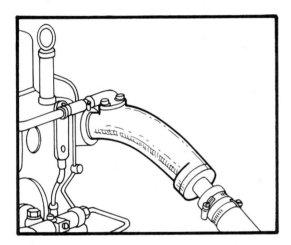

Mixing Elbow

ACHILLES' ELBOW

(Erik Nelson) The "mixing elbow," a lozenge-shaped casting in the exhaust lines of most diesels, is where cooling water mixes with the exhaust gases. Sometimes water sits in the casting. Always there is a build-up of salt inside. Sooner or later the passages narrow or the casting rots out—or both. Check the elbow every season. Depending on the design, you may have to replace it as often as every three years.

DE-BUG   *(Peter Thomas)* Fungal

growth in diesel fuel is no small problem. Minute organisms that may be airborne but live in water— fungi, yeasts, and bacteria—can turn filters gelatinous and clog injectors. Infestations are commonly caused by organisms living in water that has accumulated at the bottom of the tank. They concentrate at the fuel/water interface where they live in the water and feed off the fuel.

There are two ways to fight: attack the bugs themselves or remove the water in which they live and breed. Full tanks (which limit condensation) are good protection. Still, the moist atmosphere and the long periods of fuel stagnation interspersed with violent motion seem to be ideal for the critters. Keep tanks topped up, dose fresh fuel with biocide (most of which are at least as toxic to humans as they might be to diesel viruses), and drain water from the bottom of the tank weekly.

A further weapon against water is called Aquasolve. It's an additive, quite similar to Dri-gas, which absorbs water (as does alcohol) and is then burnt itself. Or you might try the Water Eliminator from Bowmonk (Diamond Road, St. Faith's Industrial Estate, Norwich, Norfolk,

NR6 6AW, England, UK, Tel. 1603 485153. It's a 7-by-1¼-inch nylon cage filled with water-absorbent crystals to be suspended in the tank.

There is a magnetic De-Bug that goes between the tank and the first filter. It is based on the premise that the magnetic field returns the spores to a single-celled state. This allows them to pass through the filters, which kill them. De-Bug is available under the brand name Fuelmag through Separ Distribution, UK, Tel. 923 819041.

MEGASYSTEM

(H. T. Gates) We want our fuel system to:

- give maximum protection to the injectors from receiving bad fuel
- provide the capability for us to transfer fuel from anywhere to anywhere else—in the boat, on the boat, off the boat
- completely disable fuel flow to prevent theft of the boat
- maximize delivery of "healthy" fuel during engine operation

To do this we assembled:

- dual Racor fuel filters
- filter-mounted fuel/water alarm
- vacuum gauge
- bypass valve (to bypass the engine fuel pump)
- Grove anti-airlock device
- bulkhead-mounted fuel pump (Stewart Warner 235A)

Megasystem

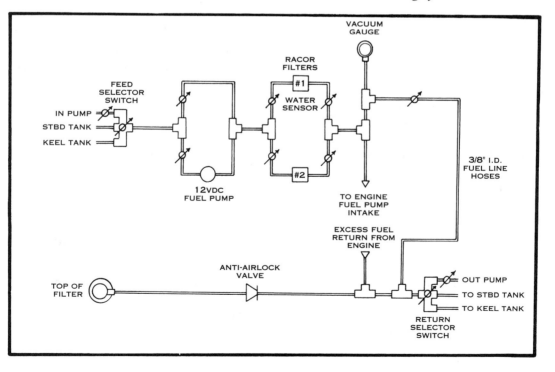

We run the filters with the alarm on the primary. When it goes off we switch to the secondary. Vacuum gauge readings help tell you what's going on. To clear the primary we open the drain valve, activate the system fuel pump, and force fuel through the filter until the water is out. Then we shut down the fuel pump and put the primary filter back on line because it has the alarm.

We have had times when the whole filter was so covered with sludge that we've had to take it apart and replace the filter before putting it back. The Grove device makes it so that we don't have to remove every bit of air from the filters during a change. It is a check valve mounted at the high end of the two engine-mounted series filters. When it opens it also bleeds off air from the line.

We're working to make *Scallasa's* fuel system simpler, tougher, and more efficient. I would like to isolate the engine fuel pump with a check valve, both for redundancy and flexibility of fuel handling. Though the SW 235A pump contains seals that will not withstand diesel for more than a couple of seasons, it's the best damn pump on the market. I just keep rebuilding them.

CRITICAL CAM

(Eric Forsyth) Everyone knows (well, almost everyone) how critical it is to replace your water pump impeller at the beginning of the season, to keep a spare impeller on board, and to routinely check for water flow through the engine by eyeballing the exhaust when you start. However, there's a less-known component in the cooling system that's pretty important, too. It's the cam against which the impeller wipes as it rotates in the pump housing. It works to deform the impeller, which creates the pumping action. When the cam is worn, the pump pumps less, so next time you change an impeller, check it out.

SURVEY YOUR ENGINE

(Henry Mustin) Obviously the surveyor can't dismantle your machinery and poke about the innards. What I try to do is take good note of the condition of what I see. Here's what I look for.

I begin with the "fixed" items—engine beds, mounts, coupling, hose clamps, wiring connections, etc. Extraordinary wear is almost always visible if you just focus and be aware. Next comes inspection of the oil pan (condition), and engine and gear seals (for leaks). Heat spots on the block, manifold, or head covers indicate overheating. Integrity of the fuel lines is important. Examine all of the connections, especially at lift pumps and injector nozzles. Test the belt tension (thumb pressure depresses ¼ inch). Examine the seawater pump impeller. Inspect the length of the control cables and brackets.

Uncomplicated visuals like the sump-oil and gear-fluid dipsticks also yield understanding. Gear fluids get milky when water gets in; engine oil gets bubbly and browner. Is there metal in the lube oil? Does it smell burnt? These signs are not good. Traces of oil around the heat exchanger suggest head-gasket trouble. Cooling passages should open wide. One key is the zinc "pencil" in the exchanger; change it yearly. Diesel problems are very often cooling problems.

Usually sea trials are part of a survey. Running an engine under load lets you tell:

- if the engine is turning its rated rpm
- how much oil pressure fluctuates between cold and hot
- if fuel flow changes as power demands increase
- if shaft alignment is sufficiently smooth
- if the fuel system stays tight underway

Tired water pump bearings might not make a tell-tale noise until they get hot. A pin-hole leak in the exhaust may open up underway. The heat exchanger is either doing its job or not. You can tell. Do a survey. Do sea trials. Know your engine better.

TROUBLESHOOTING DIESELS

(Nigel Calder) It doesn't start? Ask three questions: Checked the fuel? Checked the compression? Battery OK? If an engine has adequate air, adequately timed and metered fuel, and adequate compression, it more or less has to start.

A problem with the air supply—paper bag in the vent, emergency shut-down flap closed, clogged air cleaner, etc.—is most unlikely, but it doesn't take long to check.

Cranking speed may seem adequate to you without creating sufficient compression. Cold weather may thicken the crankcase oil, slowing cranking and lowering compression. Check for blow-by past piston rings by injecting a little oil into each cylinder. If compression improves dramatically, that cylinder is bad.

If the cranking speed is good and the compression is too, the place to look now is the fuel system. The fuel shut-off at the throttle? A fuel-system solenoid closed? No flow through the filter? Does the fuel system need bleeding? Weighing each of these symptoms, it's still nice to have a few tricks up your sleeve to get her going:

• Heat (hair dryer, blowtorch) the incoming air. Warning: Applying excessive heat to cold metal surfaces could cause them to crack.

• Drain engine oil and coolant. Warm it and replace it. Once again, be careful: excessive heat could lead to a cracked cylinder head or block.

• Oil squirted into the inlet manifold will be drawn into the cylinders and increase compression appreciably.

• Turn the motor with decompression levers open to achieve momentum before closing them.

• To boost cranking speed you can temporarily disconnect the belts for refrigerator, auxiliary pump, etc.

Starting fluid is more volatile than diesel fuel, so it ignites in the chamber when the piston is in mid-stoke. This is not good. Starting fluid has *no* place around diesels.

Do everything you can before the first crank draws down your battery. Troubleshooting doesn't take as long as waiting for your battery to recharge.

—*adapted from* Marine Diesel Engines

ELECTRICS

MAGIC NUMBERS

Battery capacity is rated in *ampere-hours*. A 100 ampere-hour battery theoretically can supply 100 amperes for 1 hour, 25 amps for 4 hours, 1 amp for 100 hours, etc.

The power consumption of electrical appliances is rated in watts *(see right)*.

Thus a 36-watt depthsounder in a 12-volt system draws 3 amps (36 / 12 = 3). A battery rated at 90 amp-hours could theoretically keep this depthsounder working for 30 hours. In practice, however, discharging (repeatedly) even deep-cycle batteries deeper than 50 percent of capacity will drastically shorten their lives.

$$AMPS = \frac{WATTS}{VOLTS}$$

FRIEND TO THE ELECTRON

(Bob Anderson) All on-board electrical connections have to survive the moisture in the marine atmosphere. Those that are topsides have it particularly rough. Liquid Tape by MDR (there are similar concoctions with other brand names) is a help in a boat's unfriendly atmosphere. It is black and gooey when you paint it on. It dries on just about anything

to form an insulating and (evidently) waterproof barrier. To make any electrical connection better and more permanent, paint this stuff on it.

DISTURBING FORCE

Unsettling as it is to contemplate, the flow of electrons that constitutes electric current also creates a magnetic field. An onboard magnetic field that is strong enough may deflect your compass and cause deviation. DC circuits are the primary culprit; AC curcuits are comparatively insignificant. The strength of the field is proportional to current flow; 8 amps produces twice the deflection of 4. Twisting the leads before installing wire so that positive and negative produce opposing fields has been the traditional defense. Leading separate positive and negative wires from the same circuit on opposite sides of the binnacle only doubles the error. The better you isolate your compass from electric circuits, the less the force will be with you.

DEEP CYCLE

(*Robert W. Merriam*) A marine battery is different from an automotive battery because it is used differently. Batteries on boats must often supply substantial loads for a long time between infrequent charging. The deep-cycle marine battery was created to meet these needs. It has thicker plates and a larger capacity for electrolyte beneath the plates. It can thus be discharged to 50 percent (80 percent *in extremis*) of capacity without damage. It also maintains a high voltage throughout most of its discharge. These batteries have a much greater ampere-hour capacity and are considerably more rugged than automotive batteries.

NICE DRIVE

Golf shoes aren't good on deck, golf bags don't stow well below, golf yarns don't sell at the yacht-club bar, but there is at least one cross-pollination between links and brink—golf-cart batteries are great in a boat. If you have two 12-volt marine batteries and one cell fails in each one, you've got

nothing. If you have four 6-volt golf-cart batteries, you can lose three cells and you'll still have juice. And they're easier to lift.

OUT OF THE HAT

Jack Rabbit Marine is in Stamford, Connecticut, and specializes in the design and sizing of 12-volt DC and 115-volt AC systems for boats. Their selling point is *free* advice. They work with handy boatowners all over the world. "If you get in a bind, call. Our ears may be furry, but we listen!"

PARK YOUR BATTERIES

Don't put batteries in the warmest place aboard because distillate evaporates faster the warmer it gets. A direct airflow isn't good because it, too, hastens evaporation. You also want your batteries secure from spray. You need some ventilation, though, because lead-acid batteries can create gas if they're overcharged [as can gel-cell batteries—eds.].

For a lead-acid battery keep a hydrometer aboard. Economy models may simply present you with red (top it up) and green (it's set to go) floats, but the actual specific gravity of your electrolyte is worth knowing.

SPECIFIC VARIATIONS

(*Nigel Calder*) The electrolyte in a battery is a solution of sulphuric acid, which is denser than water. As a battery discharges, this acid weakens progressively, becoming less dense. Samples of the electrolyte can be withdrawn from each cell in a wet-cell battery using a *hydrometer*. A hydrometer contains a floating indicator that comes to rest at a certain level in pure water, this level being calibrated for a *specific gravity* of 1.000. The denser the acid solution, the higher the indicator will float, giving a higher specific gravity reading. As the solution weakens, the indicator will sink. Since specific gravity varies with temperature, better hydrometers incorporate a thermometer that allows any reading to be corrected for nonstandard temperatures. In the USA the standard temperature is 80°F (26.7°C); in the UK it is 60°F (15.6°C). If the electrolyte is at a nonstandard temperature, conversion charts are used to correct the specific gravity reading. The corrected specific gravity can then, in theory, be correlated accurately with a battery's state of charge.

It should be noted, however, that if a battery is rapidly discharged or recharged, the chemical reactions will take place between the active material on the surfaces of the battery plates and the immediately accessible electrolyte, but not in the inner plate areas. Following the discharge or charge, if the battery is left alone the acid and water will diffuse in and out of the plates, the battery will equalize internally, and the electrolyte will reach a homogeneous state. *The only time a specific gravity reading will correlate accurately with a battery's state of charge is when the electrolyte is in this homogeneous state.* At all other times, depending on how recently the battery was used and the magnitude of the current in relation to the battery's capacity, specific gravity readings will be off by a certain margin, indicating a more discharged state than is in fact the case during discharges, and a less charged state than is the case during recharges. If the battery has been used vigorously, it can take up to 24 hours for the electrolyte to reach a stable state.

There is another phenomenon that affects specific gravity readings, called *stratification*. When recharging, the heavier acid forming in the electrolyte tends to sink to the bottom of the battery, out of reach of the hydrometer. It is not until the battery begins to reach gassing voltages, and the bubbles stir up the electrolyte, that the electrolyte reaches a more homogeneous state. Stratification exaggerates the lag between state of charge and hydrometer readings on recharge.

Once the electrolyte is in a homogeneous state, and specific gravity readings have been corrected for temperature, there is a correlation between the specific gravity and the battery's state of charge, which is given in the table below.

The figures in the table are for *industry-standard* batteries. In real life the specific gravity of fully charged batteries varies considerably, from 1.230 to 1.300. The lower figure may be found on some deep-cycle batteries sold in the tropics, where the higher prevailing temperatures

ELECTROLYTE SPECIFIC GRAVITY AS A FUNCTION OF TEMPERATURE AND BATTERY STATE OF CHARGE

SPECIFIC GRAVITY:	80°F (26.7°C)	60°F (15°C)	STATE OF CHARGE (100%)
	1.265	1.273	100
	1.225	1.233	75
	1.190	1.198	50
	1.155	1.163	25
	1.120	1.128	0

TYPICAL SPECIFIC GRAVITY VARIATIONS BY REGION

REGION	FULLY CHARGED SPECIFIC GRAVITY
NORTH OF FLORIDA AND NORTHERN EUROPE	1.265–1.280
FLORIDA TO SAN JUAN (PUERTO RICO)	1.250–1.265
SOUTH OF SAN JUAN	1.235–1.250

promote more efficient battery operation, requiring a less concentrated acid solution. The higher figure may be found on cranking batteries sold in cold climates, where more concentrated acid solutions are needed to boost output.

—*adapted from* Boatowner's Mechanical and Electrical Manual

CHARGE IT

(Richard B. Allen) Battery chargers can pour amps into a battery at a high rate.

- Don't force more amperage into a battery than it is rated for.
- Never allow individual cell voltages to go higher than 2.3 volts.
- Don't boil the electrolyte. The gas is explosive.
- Don't let the battery temperature get above 125°F.
- Keep the plates covered with distilled water. The manganese and other impurities in tap water shorten battery life.
- Battery additives are relatively close to snake-oil. The money is better spent towards a new battery.

WHAT'S UP, DOC?

(Will Robinson) To specify a power system, you need to determine the average electrical usage on your boat. List all the electrically powered items aboard. Get their electrical draw in amps from manuals, nameplates, etc. If a nameplate specifies ohms (resistance), divide your power source (most probably 12 volts) by that number to get amperes. Multiply the amps each item requires by the hours per day you anticipate using it to get daily amp-hours. Total amp-hours for all the items aboard gives you a good idea of your daily electrical requirements and thus the size and type of system that will suit you.

POWER SURVEY

(Henry Mustin) Assessing a generator is pretty simple. Is it adequate to meet the power demands that will be made on it? Total the amps that all of the boat's AC accessories draw; a generator should still have about 20 percent reserve capacity.

GEL-CELLS

The advantages of the gel-cell battery are numerous.

- It doesn't have to be filled with water.
- It's spillproof.
- It will operate from any position, even upside down.
- It recharges faster.
- It can survive dunking.
- It doesn't give off chlorine gas.

On the negative side, they cost a lot and they cannot be charged beyond 14.1 volts.

MARINE BATTERIES

(Nigel Calder) Automobile batteries are called upon to start the engine, and then they are immediately recharged by the car's alternator. Rarely, if ever, does the entire DC system (lights, horn, radio, defroster, et al.) run from the uncharged battery. In powerboats the system is somewhat similar. In cruising sailboats, however, "house" electricity is regularly required when the engine is not running. As a result, the working environment in a cruising sailboat for all DC components (battery, alternator, and regulator) is quite different from the automotive model. Yet, for reasons of convenience and economy, most of the electrical components on boats today are automotive equipment that has been transplanted with little or no modification.

Since automotive batteries are designed to deliver their burst of starting power and then be recharged, they have relatively thin plates and low-density active material. This makes them incapable of responding well to repeated deep discharges and recharges. Deep-cycle batteries are designed for these applications. With thicker plates, stronger grids, and denser active material, they can tolerate repeated discharges in a way no automotive battery can.

The differences between automotive and deep-cycle batteries are matters of degree rather than design. There is no clear dividing line; a cheap deep-cycle may not be as durable in service as a well-made automotive battery. Manufacturers' classifications for their products are not a good guide, either. To stack one battery up against another, you must compare *life cycles*: the number of times that each can be pulled down to a certain level of discharge and then recharged before it fails.

If a battery is to be used solely for engine-cranking and *immediately* recharged by an engine-driven alternator, an automotive battery is perfectly adequate. *For all other applications, you should assume the batteries will be cycled at some time.* In that case, choose a good-quality deep-cycle battery.

—*adapted from* Boatowner's Mechanical and Electrical Manual

One, Two, Three

(Dave MacLean) Most electrical problems come from three conditions:

An open circuit. A switch in the OFF position is an open circuit; the contacts are open, therefore current cannot flow. You have the same result if the switch is ON and a wire has broken its normal connection somewhere else in the circuit.

A short circuit. When load has been removed and, for some reason, current rushes through the circuit without limitation, that is a short circuit. Fuses that limit the current flow protect against short circuits.

A high-resistance circuit. This happens when resistance becomes high enough to make some part of the circuit non-conductive. The crystalline corrosion that often forms on battery terminals is an example of a high-resistance circuit that will keep the starting circuit from working. A loose connection can create the same sort of condition.

—*adapted from* Small Craft Electronic Equipment Care & Repair

24-Volt Jolt

If you need to replace a 24-volt battery, wire two 12-volt batteries in series (plus to minus). You will have the same amperage capability as a single battery, but at twice the voltage. If you need twice the current, wire the batteries in parallel (plus to plus and minus to minus). If one of the terminals proves defective, though, all of the amperage will come from a single battery and draw it down very quickly.

Top Off

(Nigel Calder) Bring a battery to full charge any time it is going to be left unused for more than a few days. All batteries discharge slowly when standing idle. The rate of discharge depends to a great extent on temperature and on certain features of internal construction. A wet-cell lead/antimony battery will run down faster than a gel-cell with no antimony in the plate grids. Lead/antimony batteries lose approximately 0.7 percent of their charge per day at 80°F, rising to 1.75 percent per day at 100°. The higher the temperature, the higher the rate of discharge. Gel-cells have a rate of discharge at 80° as low as 0.1 percent per day.

If a wet-cell battery is left uncharged for more than a month, especially over the summer months, self-discharge will lead to sulfation, the sulfates will harden, and the battery will be damaged permanently. During any extended lay-up, be sure to put wet-cell batteries on charge at least once a month. A fully charged gel-cell can be left alone for several months.

In cold climates a full charge is also essential to prevent freezing of the electrolyte, which will cause irreparable damage. Batteries in storage should be kept as cool as possible without freezing.

—*adapted from* Boatowner's Mechanical and Electrical Manual

Stellar Solar

(Capt. Michael Penney RNR) More electrical gear + more current requirement = solar panels. Because they reduce the need for engine charging, they have become the logical next step for most boatowners. Three forms of solar panel are currently available:

- monocrystalline (approximately 13 percent efficient) with cells cut from a bar of pure silicon

- polycrystalline (11 percent) with cells made up of silicon crystals
- thin-film silicon (7 percent) being silicon arrayed on ordinary glass

You measure solar output in watts peak (WP). Panels of 5, 10, and 12 WP will keep batteries of from 50 to 200 ampere-hours topped up in an owner's absence. Panels producing 100 WP, on the other hand, can power life and systems aboard a 40-footer for as much as three days before recharging.

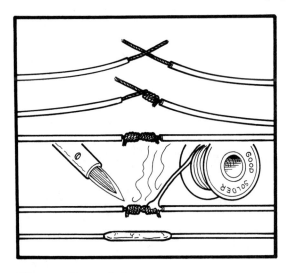

Western Union Splice

WESTERN UNION!

The Western Union splice is made as shown. When soldering, use rosin core solder, not acid core. Get the *wires* so hot that the solder melts when it touches them. Melting the solder against the iron and dropping a bead onto the wire results in what is known as a "cold joint." It is useless. Insulate the properly made joint by using a heat shrink tube, or to be more uniform and aggressive about sealing the work, use Liquid Electrical Tape.

OVEN-FRESH ELECTRONICS

(MB) No manufacturer that I know likes this recipe much, but I have a friend who, during her circumnavigation, restored the life in a myriad of things "electric," from the loran to her cordless drill, by "slow-baking" them in the oven. Salt dosing is fatal, but humidity and condensation, she claimed, can be baked away (repeatedly). The key, she says, is that you must keep the oven temperature low enough to be able to touch the racks with bare hands.

That must be the secret. I once threw my portable tape recorder in the oven and pulled out a pudding of plastic. I guess timing is important, too. Aboard a submarine in the Arctic, I tried a stint of oven heat to rehabilitate my sheepskin-lined bridge gloves. When I remembered them an hour later, they were sized to fit a baby marmoset.

WORKING WITH THE WIND

(Nigel Calder) A wind generator is a simple device that uses a propeller or turbine to convert wind energy to a rotating force that is used to spin a generating device. There are a couple of interesting relationships that hold in this conversion process: all other things being equal, a doubling of the propeller diameter produces a theoretical fourfold increase in generator output, and a doubling of the wind speed produces a theoretical eightfold increase in output.

In practical terms, at wind speeds of less than 5 knots the wind has insufficient energy to produce output from any wind generator. At 5 knots the more efficient generators will begin to trickle-charge a battery, whereas less efficient designs may not "kick in" until 7 knots or so.

Once the kick-in speed has been reached, the output of the various devices on the market picks up slowly at first, then with increasing rapidity as the wind speed rises. Above 10 knots or so, output for any given wind speed is broadly determined by blade diameter. The wind itself, in conjunction with an appropriately sized propeller, contains sufficient energy to meet the electrical needs of just about any cruising sailor.

—*adapted from* Boatowner's Mechanical and Electrical Manual

SIMPLE TIMES TWO

Joel White designs and builds instant classic boats and ran (until his recent retirement) the Brooklin Boat Yard in Brooklin, Maine. He knows something about electricity, too. "We like completely separate systems for engine starting and 'house' service. To make our system as foolproof as possible, we specify two complete alternators/regulators, one for each battery bank. This offers redundancy in charging and, while it would seem that the house alternator needs to have larger output than the one for the cranking battery, we use identical alternators to allow for easy substitution in case of breakdown. For offshore or long distance cruisers, we recommend carrying a third alternator as a spare.

To parallel the battery banks for emergency power, we include heavy-duty jumper cables long enough to join the two banks. This eliminates the worry that sooner or later the emergency switch will be activated by mistake and left ON, thus mingling the two separate battery and charging systems and risking possible trouble with the two alternators."

[More convenient and nearly as foolproof as jumper cables for making the house batteries available for starting would be the installation of a momentary (hold in contact) switch.—eds.]

THE WHITE STUFF

(Robert W. Merriam) Joel White has the right idea when it comes to boat electrics: dual alternators, dual batteries, a common negative ground, and a single jumper cable for bridging in case of emergency. The safe way to do DC wiring is the simple way. Here are a few things to keep in mind to make it truly trouble-free:

- Be sure to ground the negative side. Avoid floating grounds. With a good negative ground connection, a fault will cause a breaker to trip.
- Use tinned, stranded, color-coded duplex wire of adequate gauge covered with an oil-resistant, heat-tolerating, waterproof jacket. Going and returning conductors should be in a common sheath.
- Use a single circuit-breaker in the positive side of each circuit.
- Choose black and red in your duplex wire, and keep the black negative.
- With an aluminum alloy outboard, use a negative ground and be careful not to bond the motor to overboard bronze for fear of galvanic action.
- Before you bond hardware and large metal masses, make sure they are relatively compatible galvanically.
- Install zincs, but in moderation. They affect planks, fasteners, and some hardware.
- Porous bronze makes a poor ground plate. Solid bronze is fine.

SHRINK BIG

(Bill Biwenga) Heat-shrink tubing is the familiar plastic stuff that comes in many colors and grips onto electrical wires when it's heated. The tight, moisture-resistant cover it forms makes it convenient and popular, but electrical connections are not all it can handle. Prior to nicopressing an eye and shackle onto the end of a halyard, slip several lengths of heat-shrink tubing in alternating colors over the wire and past the location of the nicopress sleeve. After you press the thimble into place, slide a piece of heat-shrink tubing over the

sleeve, leaving at least an inch over the wire halyard, and heat the tubing until it fits. Slide the next piece over the first, applying several layers—one over the other—to build up chafe protection and seal the sharp edges of the nicopress sleeve. Alternating colors lets you easily monitor chafe as the exterior layer is abraded to reveal a different color beneath.

WIRED RIGHT

(Nigel Calder) Selecting the proper wire size for a given application is critical, especially when electric motors are concerned. Undersized cables introduce unwanted resistance, resulting in voltage drop at appliances, reduced performance, and premature failure.

In the USA, two tables developed by the ABYC are commonly used to determine wire sizes in the marine field. The first assumes that a 10 percent voltage drop at the appliance is acceptable; the second is based on a 3 percent voltage drop. The tables are entered on one side by the total length of the wiring in a circuit (which includes both the hot and the ground wire) and on the other side by the maximum current draw (amps) of the appliance on the circuit. The required wire size, in American Wire Gauge (AWG), for the given voltage drop is then read in the body of the table. Note that the larger the AWG number, the smaller the wire size.

If more than one appliance is to be operated from common cables, *the cables must be rated for the total load of all the appliances. The ground cables to all fixtures must be sized the same as the hot cables, since they carry an equal load.*

Many appliances, particularly lights, will work with a 10% voltage drop, but nevertheless I recommend that you use the 3% voltage drop tables at all times. Given the harshness of the marine environment, it just does not pay to start out by trying to cut calculations as fine as possible.

—*adapted from* Boatowner's Mechanical and Electrical Manual

Wired Right

Conductor Sizes for 10% Drop in Voltage

(Total current on circuit in amps)	10	15	20	25	30	40	50	60	70	80	90	100	110	120	130	140	150	160	170
12 volts																			
5	18	18	18	18	18	16	16	14	14	14	12	12	12	12	12	10	10	10	10
10	18	18	16	16	14	14	12	12	10	10	10	10	8	8	8	8	8	8	6
15	18	16	14	14	12	12	10	10	8	8	8	8	6	6	6	6	6	6	4
20	16	14	14	12	12	10	10	8	8	8	6	6	6	6	6	6	4	4	4
25	16	14	12	12	10	10	8	8	6	6	6	6	6	4	4	4	4	4	2
30	14	12	12	10	10	8	8	6	6	6	6	4	4	4	4	2	2	2	2
40	14	12	10	10	8	8	6	6	4	4	4	2	2	2	2	2	2	2	1
50	12	10	10	8	8	6	6	4	4	4	2	2	2	2	2	1	1	1	1
60	12	10	8	8	6	6	4	4	2	2	2	2	1	1	1	0	0	0	0
70	10	8	8	6	6	6	4	2	2	2	2	1	1	1	0	0	0	2/0	2/0
80	10	8	8	6	6	4	4	2	2	2	1	1	0	0	0	2/0	2/0	2/0	2/0
90	10	8	6	6	6	4	2	2	2	1	1	0	0	0	2/0	2/0	2/0	3/0	3/0
100	10	8	6	6	4	4	2	2	1	1	0	0	0	2/0	2/0	2/0	3/0	3/0	3/0
24 volts																			
5	18	18	18	18	18	18	18	18	16	16	16	16	14	14	14	14	14	14	12
10	18	18	18	18	16	16	14	14	12	12	12	12	12	10	10	10	10	10	8
15	18	18	18	16	16	14	14	12	12	12	10	10	10	10	8	8	8	8	6
20	18	18	16	16	14	14	12	12	10	10	10	8	8	8	8	8	8	6	6
25	18	16	16	14	14	12	12	10	10	10	8	8	8	8	6	6	6	6	4
30	18	16	14	14	12	12	10	10	8	8	8	8	6	6	6	6	4	4	4
40	16	14	14	12	12	10	10	8	8	8	6	6	6	6	6	4	4	4	2
50	16	14	12	12	10	10	8	8	6	6	6	6	6	4	4	4	2	2	2
60	14	12	12	10	10	8	8	6	6	6	6	4	4	4	4	2	2	2	2
70	14	12	10	10	8	8	6	6	6	6	4	4	4	2	2	2	2	2	2
80	14	12	10	10	8	8	6	6	6	4	4	4	2	2	2	2	2	2	1
90	12	10	10	8	8	6	6	6	4	4	4	2	2	2	2	2	1	1	1
100	12	10	10	8	8	6	6	4	4	4	2	2	2	2	2	1	1	1	1

(Length of conductor from source of current to device and back to source—feet)

Conductor Sizes for 3% Drop in Voltage

(Total current on circuit in amps)	(Length of conductor from source of current to device and back to source—feet)																		
	10	15	20	25	30	40	50	60	70	80	90	100	110	120	130	140	150	160	170
12 volts																			
5	18	16	14	12	12	10	10	10	8	8	8	6	6	6	6	6	6	6	6
10	14	12	10	10	10	8	6	6	6	6	4	4	4	4	2	2	2	2	2
15	12	10	10	8	8	6	6	6	4	4	2	2	2	2	2	1	1	1	1
20	10	10	8	6	6	6	4	4	2	2	2	1	1	1	0	0	0	0	2/0
25	10	8	6	6	6	4	4	2	2	2	1	1	0	0	0	2/0	2/0	2/0	3/0
30	10	8	6	6	4	4	2	2	1	1	0	0	0	2/0	2/0	3/0	3/0	3/0	3/0
40	8	6	6	4	4	2	2	1	0	0	2/0	2/0	3/0	3/0	3/0	4/0	4/0	4/0	4/0
50	6	6	4	4	2	2	1	0	2/0	2/0	3/0	3/0	4/0	4/0	4/0				
60	6	4	4	2	2	1	0	2/0	3/0	3/0	4/0	4/0	4/0						
70	6	4	2	2	1	0	2/0	3/0	3/0	4/0	4/0								
80	6	4	2	2	1	0	3/0	3/0	4/0	4/0									
90	4	2	2	1	0	2/0	3/0	4/0	4/0										
100	4	2	2	1	0	2/0	3/0	4/0											
24 volts																			
5	18	18	18	16	16	14	12	12	12	10	10	10	10	10	8	8	8	8	8
10	18	16	14	12	12	10	10	10	8	8	8	6	6	6	6	6	6	6	6
15	16	14	12	12	10	10	8	8	6	6	6	6	6	4	4	4	4	4	2
20	14	12	10	10	10	8	6	6	6	6	4	4	4	4	2	2	2	2	2
25	12	12	10	10	8	6	6	6	4	4	4	2	2	2	2	2	1	1	1
30	12	10	10	8	8	6	6	6	4	4	2	2	2	2	2	1	1	1	1
40	10	10	8	6	6	6	4	4	2	2	2	1	1	1	0	0	0	0	2/0
50	10	8	6	6	6	4	4	2	2	2	1	1	0	0	0	2/0	2/0	2/0	3/0
60	10	8	6	6	4	4	2	2	1	1	0	0	0	2/0	2/0	3/0	3/0	3/0	3/0
70	8	6	6	4	4	2	2	1	1	0	0	0	2/0	3/0	3/0	3/0	4/0	4/0	4/0
80	8	6	6	4	4	2	2	1	0	0	2/0	2/0	3/0	3/0	3/0	4/0	4/0	4/0	4/0
90	8	6	4	4	2	2	1	0	0	2/0	2/0	3/0	4/0	4/0	4/0	4/0			
100	6	6	4	4	2	2	1	0	2/0	2/0	3/0	3/0	4/0	4/0	4/0				

Notes: These tables are based on SAE wiring sizes. SAE-rated cables are typically 10% to 12% smaller than AWG-rated cables of the same nominal size (see Table 3-6, columns 2 and 3). Consequently, if a cable is sized by reference to these tables, and then AWG-rated wire of the same nominal size is substituted for SAE, the cable will be somewhat oversized for the application, which is all to the good. Although SAE-rated wiring can be used in DC circuits, *AWG-rated wiring must be used in AC circuits* (If you find this confusing, blame the ABYC and not me!).

GO HYDRO

Your boat's forward motion can bring you more than miles. If you investigate the hydro generator, close relative to the wind turbine, you may well find that "in movement is power." It takes a myriad of forms: spinners, trollers, and bracket-mounted units. At displacement speeds expect 5 to 15 amps at 14 volts or so. Even at the mooring, units like the Aquair water turbine can turn a 1.5 knot current into trickle-charging electricity.

Free-wheeling is another attractive way to take power from the water. In addition to the requisite alternator belted to your shaft, you must have a transmission that can take free-wheeling. For information on their "Velvet Drive," write: Regal-Bloit Corp., 200 Theodore Rice Blvd., New Bedford, MA 02745.

FREE WHEELIN'

(Don Street) Lang Syne sailed around the world with no electrical-generating problem, the matter having been taken care of in a very unusual fashion. A low-rpm generator was belted directly off the propeller shaft, which was allowed to turn when the boat was under sail. This gave electrical power for both refrigeration and the autopilot. The rig is not often seen, but it obviously works. It has been on *Lang Syne* for the better part of 20 years.

—*adapted from* The Ocean Sailing Yacht

JOINING SOURCES

The search for the source of the planet's energy requirements for the next millenia is wide and intense. Californian Ronald Weintraub suggests that we *all* might be headed in the right direction. He suggests that *combining* energy sources might turn out to be the *one* way to go. Energy supplies are intermittent. Energy sources come in different forms. By using the appropriate forms at the appropriate times, we get more from them.

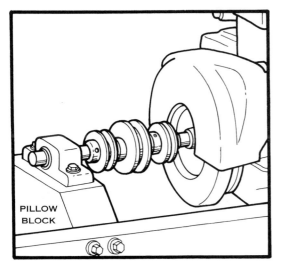

Pillow block supporting an extension shaft.

ENERGY BELT   *(Don Street)*

With modern boats and their electrical requirements, the first question for many is, "can power be obtained by belting off the main engine?" Economy and economy of space make this a workable solution, but there are disadvantages.

A big, heavy-duty compressor is likely to draw as much as 1 hp; a 60-amp alternator consumes engine power, and sometimes two alternators are belted off the engine. An anchor windlass (belted through a mechanical linkage), a hydraulic pump, a bilge pump all draw power. The result is that an engine rated at, say 40 hp, will wind up delivering considerably less.

This problem can be managed. Albina and several other manufacturers make power take-offs that can be mounted on the front of the engine. Each has a built-in clutch, so if maximum power to the shaft is required, all the auxiliary equipment can be disconnected.

The second disadvantage is less easily dealt with. Smaller diesels, of 30 to 40 hp, usually are quite sensitive to side loading. If equipment is belted off the front end of the engine, the side loading may be enough to burn out the front-end bearings in a relatively short time. The cure here is to install a short extension shaft with its forward end supported by a pillow block. This will relieve the side loading on the engine shaft.

—adapted from The Ocean Sailing Yacht

DO IT RIGHT   *(Don Street)*

Basically electricity and salt water are incompatible. On a boat you are never free from corrosion. Remember, too, that even the minimal standards and codes for electrical work that apply to buildings don't extend to the sea; you never know who did marine wiring—or how. Combine this truth with the undeniable need of today's boats for electric power, and lots of it, and you have, as they say in the islands, "predictable heartache."

A 110-volt AC generator can be run either off the main engine or as an auxiliary generator with its own motor. The latter arrangement is much the best one for daily use. This generator will operate the 110-volt sealed-unit refrigeration compressor by running one to two hours a day. At the same time it will also charge (through a 12-volt converter) the batteries. All lighting, pumps, and other 12-volt equipment will run from the batteries. Radar and loran can be run from the generator or from the batteries through an inverter. Further, this 110-volt system can be plugged into shore power.

For ultimate reliability there can be the independent diesel generator backed up by a 110-volt AC generator belted off the engine. The refrigeration unit can consist of two separate 110-volt motor-driven compressors, each with its own holding plate. Similarly two 110-volt—12-volt converters can be installed so that one will always function. The expense of putting such a redundant system in place is considerable, but if you have to depend on electric power, it should provide power that you can depend on.

—*adapted from* The Ocean Sailing Yacht

PLANTED POWER

(Tim Banse) Gen-set engines are easy to forget. Remember these few tips: Pick a gen-set rated at 10 to 20 percent more than your average draw. If you have too big a cushion between your needs and your engine's capability, your generator will run with such a light load that it will tend to carbonize its lube oil and generally cause premature wear. Fog gen-set cylinders and tune gen-set ignition just like you would a "real engine." If your diesel gen-set is turbocharged, don't forget to run it for five minutes at idle before you shut it down. That assures good oil circulation.

CATSPAW

A catspaw is a twisting hitch made in the bight of a rope to form two eyes through which the hook of a tackle is passed for hoisting.

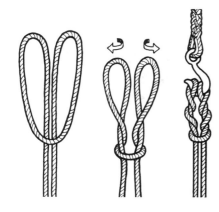

5

ENJOY LIFE AFLOAT

Making your boat a home is an instinct, a skill, and a mission. Enrich, simplify, and afford your life afloat. You'll enjoy it.

The Owl and the Pussycat went to sea

In a beautiful pea-green boat.

They took some honey and plenty of money,

And they enjoyed their life afloat.

—*with apologies to Edward Lear, "The Owl and the Pussycat"*

There aren't many "living skills" that don't come into play on a boat. Many are transportable from land. Some come only with salt-caked miles. In this chapter we've tried to tap not just the solutions of sailors who have mastered those skills but also their zest for improving the quality of shipboard life.

Some parts of life afloat are harder than others to smelt into nuggets of wisdom. To deal with the complexity, controversy, and human variety involved in some of the basics of living on a boat, we've gone beyond individual perspectives. In addition to sections on bread and water, we have examined in depth the elements of heat, security, and insurance. May the inclusion of these "surveys," along with individual tips and solutions we've assembled, help you more fully enjoy your time aboard.

BEST INVESTMENT   *(Erni Bennett)*

The most important factor for me in assuring safe, efficient, wonderful results from my boat is not about "nuts and bolts," nor is it a tactical matter. The people that I enlist to help me with my boat are my "secret."

The things I do I couldn't do without them. I try to make them feel that the boat is part theirs. I have found that they in turn are of *unlimited* value to her upkeep, operation, and safety. Sometimes I make a mystery out of who is older, *Adventuress* or me. She was launched in 1913. Both of us have nothing to complain about in terms of the excitement, adventure, and friendship we've had. Some sailors complain that it's hard to find people to crew. That's never been a problem aboard *Adventuress*.

BOAT WASTE

(RR) I read recently that the garbage deposited in the sea by boats is triple the weight of fish taken from the sea. Even small things are good things if they begin to reverse that ratio. Unpack your stores ashore. "Decant" cereals, staples, and processed foods into Tupperware and the like. Rip the plastic necklaces from your 6-packs before you take them to sea. Unbox your bottles. Crush cans flat. Package trash to last. Hang onto garbage, don't heave it!

ODOR PROBLEMS

(Allen Barry) Rare is the boat whose head is not, to a greater or lesser degree, the source of unpleasant odors. While the human users play a part, most bad smells from the head come from the seawater in the system; organisms come into the head in the water, they sit there, they die, and they smell. Two things that have helped us combat this are a disinfectant mixed by pumping action with the water intake, and coating the hoses, which are permeable and therefore allow odors to escape, with saran wrap. It works in your refrigerator to lock odors in; it seals the smell inside hoses just as well.

AFFORDABLE AC

(Doug Terman) Although commercial air conditioning is nice on a yacht, it is hardly necessary. There are, however, two situations where it's worth its cost: going to weather when everything must be buttoned up, and on those rare nights in a quiet anchorage filled with mosquitoes. Gordon Stout, who has driven a whole series of *Shango*'s, showed me how to air-condition my own *Encantada* without going broke.

Gordon's solution is to tap into the high-pressure Freon line that leads to the freezer and put an electric solenoid valve on it so the output can be redirected to just one sleeping cabin by an insulated copper line. In that cabin he installed a Fiat radiator (about 12 by 12 by 2 inches) housed in an attractive teak box with louvers in it. When he needs cooling in the cabin, he starts the refrigerator compressor and flips the solenoid switch. The Fiat fan has a rheostat by which he can adjust the airflow. Installation time was about 8 hours. Materials cost $120.

OUT-OF-THE-ORDINARY ORGANIZER

Keeping usable records helps you get maximum enjoyment and your money's worth from your boat. A 1991 book by Bob Payne and Nick Elison snappily titled *The International Marine Boat Manager: Your Vessel's Custom Handbook of Operating and Service Procedures* has bid fair to replace the old chart-table catch-all as a place to keep your most vital info. It is a:

- repository for such necessaries as model numbers, maintenance histories, warranty information, and manufacturer and dealer addresses
- coach to help you through half-remembered procedures
- prompter to keep you on top of maintenance schedules, confront you with pre-voyage and post-voyage checklists, and record important "anniversaries"
- safety guide containing well-articulated procedures for emergencies you might face
- complete record of your boat's maintenance and equipment life (for insurance purposes or for selling her)

Built from fill-in-the-blank spaces and sound information, the book is an instant reference that saves time and aggravation. As they said in *Practical Sailor*, "If you want a lot of book for the money and can use valuable information, checklists, and thousands of little spaces in which to record practically everything, this is the book for you." The book is, alas, out of print in 1996; if you see a copy for sale, snap it up.

PAN PLAN

(Allison Barry) When we took delivery of our Caliber 33, we asked the builder not to put shelves in the galley area. I then took my seagoing pots and pans and laid them out on a brown-paper sheet cut to the size of the galley space. I traced the outlines of the pots and pans (arranged as space-efficiently and conveniently as possible). From that "template" we cut holes in the piece of plywood that we fitted to the bottom of our cupboard. Our utensils sit securely in cut-out "niches" custom-made to keep them from banging or sliding.

CUT-RATE CONTROLS

(Peter Harken) Would you fly an airplane if the altimeter had a sticker on it saying, "Buy one, get three free"? But sailors do it all the time—they put bargain-basement controls on their high-flying machines. The average lawnmower has a place in the garage, gets the oil changed twice a year, and probably gets a new spark plug for Christmas. The average deck gear on a sailboat sits outside in the weather all season, is dunked in salt water on a regular basis, gets baked and chilled and doused. Why do we baby our crabgrass cutters and ignore the stuff that makes our sailboats go?

Your deck gear connects your well-made sails to your well-chosen hull. Without it, neither of them will do a damn thing. You *know* your deck gear is going to get zero care. You *know* it's critical. Doesn't it make sense to get the best gear you can? This is a commercial, I admit it, but the marine environment is really tough; it's like dipping something in acid to put it through just one sailing season. To be reliable in that environment season after season it takes the best—the best design, the best construction, the best materials, and the best engineering. If you take such good care of a machine that clips the weeds along your walkway, doesn't it make sense to invest a little something in gear to brighten your sailing life—and maybe save it?

NAUTICALLY CHALLENGED

(Sheila McCurdy) A perfect boat is one that is ideally suited to the experience and intentions of the crew who sail that boat. The breadth of the quest for the right match between boat and sailor helps explain why there is such a range of boats available, yet most owners and prospective buyers don't consciously tailor their boats to their personal strengths and weaknesses.

In the last few years I have observed how people with physical disabilities approach sailing. They expect to have to alter the status quo to a condition or manner that is manageable to them—whether a companionway needs more secure steps or the gate in the lifeline needs moving. On the other hand, able-bodied sailors assume a boat is *one big package* that is the way it is for some good reason, and they must learn to live with it. A short person continues to complain about the depth of the icebox, and the person in charge of the anchor curses the bow roller season after season. Instead, the first sailor should install a step to help reach over the counter. In the second case, a modified bow roller or a different shape anchor could ease the chore. Why work harder than you have to? Why open yourself to frustration when you are trying to have fun?

BAKSHEESH BACKLASH

(Frank McCallum) Owners of large yachts visiting Mediterranean ports with no marina facilities often rely on fishermen and dockstanders to take their lines. In gratitude for the assistance, I have always dispensed American cigarettes. On one cruise from Malta to France, one of my guests brought aboard a dozen bottles of wine from Gozo (Malta's tiny satellite island). This wine proved so unpalatable that we still had 11 and ¾ bottles left by the time we reached Anzio in Italy. Thinking to conserve a few of the smokes that we'd brought, I offered the fishermen who helped us warp alongside bottles of wine instead of the usual. They seemed quite happy, and I lit up, quite pleased with myself. When the cold light of dawn came, however, I rose to find us drift-

(continued on page 116)

HEAT

Not everyone needs heat; Don Street doesn't even mention heaters in *The Ocean Sailing Yacht*. Steve Dashew says, "Carrying a heater on most small boats is a nuisance." When Dr. David Lewis circumnavigated Antarctica in *Ice Bird*, he didn't bother to bring one along. Still, some skippers never look quite so rhapsodic as when they're describing their Tiny Tot "just drawing away as we crashed into the mountainous seas."

Even in the summer months some means of heating the accommodation and drying wet clothes is desirable, but for autumn, winter, or early spring cruising it is essential. Paraffin stoves, although they give out great heat, are not suitable as they use up much of the oxygen in the atmosphere and cause condensation. A solid-fuel-burning stove will ventilate and dry as well as heat.

—*Eric Hiscock, adapted from* Cruising Under Sail

You can figure the amount of Btus you need to heat your boat. Calculate the volume of the space or spaces you want to heat. Let us say the volume of your cabin is 700 cubic feet. Multiply that number by a factor of 10 for a living space (7,000 Btu, etc.), 12 for a stateroom, and 15 for a wheelhouse or pilot house with a big expanse of windows. The answer is the number of Btus necessary to heat that space to 70° if the outside temperature is 20° (F). It makes sense, of course, to give yourself a "heating cushion." Multiply the volume by a factor of 20 in recognition of the fact that you can always turn the heat down, but it's nice to be able to turn it up when you feel the need.

—*Jan and Bill Moeller, adapted from* Living Aboard: The Cruising Sailboat as a Home

Keeping warm below in a boat is just like keeping warm in a house, primarily a matter of insulation. Wooden boats can draw on the natural insulating properties of their hulls and, to a lesser degree, upon the airspace created when parts of the interior are sheathed with wooden ceiling. Metal and fiberglass, however, are not as good at insulating. Glass and metal hulls permit rapid interaction between exterior and interior...and they sweat. Liners improve interior comfort to some degree, but few work to solve the basic outside-in penetration. Cored fiberglass, on the other hand, is a big step forward. Airex or balsa coring not only provides space between exterior and interior surfaces but fills those spaces with relatively heat-resistant material. Honeycomb works much less well as insulation. To a large degree you're stuck with the heat-transfer properties of the boat that you've got (or are going to buy), but you can make most interiors much cozier by lining exposed areas with composite cork or foam-backed insulating patches.

—*Ron Richard*

One of the major distinctions to make in heating is between vented and unvented

(continued on page 116)

systems. Space heaters, catalytic propane heaters, even the old clay flowerpots upended over the stove burners all produce heat, but they produce exhaust, too. You need fresh oxygen and you need to vent the exhaust. We almost died one night from carbon-monoxide poisoning because we buttoned the boat up too tight. Unvented stoves MUST receive an adequate supply of fresh air.

—*Katy Burke*

Probably the biggest advantage of a diesel furnace on a boat is that it distributes heat evenly throughout. The "hot head, frozen feet" syndrome is addressed, too, because the heat is piped in at a level close to the cabin sole. Most furnaces run automatically without the constant tending that stoves demand. Some use your main diesel tank as their reservoir. Most draw upon ship's batteries for a small fuel pump and a blower fan.

Furnaces, though, have special needs. Each has very particular exhaust requirements; when you read the installation and service information the word "MUST" leaps out at you early and often. How do these hard and fast requirements fit your sailing and cruising style? Check closely to make sure you're willing to meet the demands of "heat on demand."

—*Elizabeth McCullough*

Several years ago I came aboard my schooner on the first really cold night of the winter. I went to fire up the diesel cabin heater. It didn't work! Now there's not much that can go wrong with something whose only moving part is a float valve, and after a brief disassembly I found the trouble: the burner bowl and float chamber had ice in them. To prevent this, I made Charlie Noble a sou'wester. I bought a short section of PVC pipe that fit over the chimney and bonded the suitable cap end fitting to it. Charlie now wears his lid all the time except when the heater is going. In fact I had to make myself a "Remove cover before lighting" sign to hang on the diesel petcock to keep myself from filling the cabin again with exhaust fumes.

—*Don Launer*

ing in mid-harbor. Our lines had been slipped! We powered slowly back to the quay. Beside each bollard was an opened but barely consumed bottle of Gozo wine.

SOCKS

(John Rousmaniere) Do I wear socks? In one of his books Alan Villiers recounts: "The boy Christiansen—tall and strong and blue-eyes—has no socks. He says his feet freeze only when his feet are dry." In the 50 years since Villiers and Christiansen rounded the Horn in the *Parma,* the wetsuit has been invented along the same principle. While I recognize the validity of the bare-foot theory, I like to have a soft layer between my skin and the hard rubber boot. So I wear socks—thick wool socks, the kind with 15 percent nylon and 85 percent wool. I hate cold squishy feet. Most of all I hate that maddening little crease that always forms just under the sole of my foot when a lightweight sock gets wet.

Seen in a Flash

(*Jim Brown*) We were sitting at a waterfront bistro in Costa Rica with a bunch of other gringos. I was talking with one and somehow the conversation got around to a mutual friend from California, Bud Holmes. Just then, so help me, a guy with binoculars pronounced, " and here he comes." No fooling, he and his trimaran were booming down the bay.

After they anchored we went aboard for what turned out to be *mahi-mahi* washed down with *guarro*, the local "white lightning," and Tang. This was years ago, and even from behind the *guarro* I was amazed by *Rising Sun*. She was stark, superlight, and efficient. Below were a few dry stores, some jerry jugs of water, one kerosene farmer's lantern, and two galvanized buckets, one marked "head," the other "galley."

I don't know whether he realized it, but Bud was a pioneer of seasteading. For me he was the first modern mariner I'd met who made the break, not just geographically, but psychologically. He had sailed away from the complex accouterments of terrestrial existence into true geographical and psychological *mobility*.

Ciguatera

(*Bill Robinson*) Fish poisoning is a fact of life in the tropics. Ciguatera is a disease which comes from a reef fungus. Reef-darting smaller fish ingest the fungus, and when bigger fish ingest the little fish, the toxins become concentrated. Higher up the food chain, the doses begin to present problems (acute nausea, violent pain, general disability, and the sensation that water is burning your flesh).

—*adapted from* South to the Caribbean

Nine Lives

(*Dr. Barbara Gabert*) The hooker with ciguatera is that you can't tell the difference; the fish you ate for breakfast and enjoyed might have, in the same bay, a brother that would poison you for supper. When I lived in the Marshall Islands, we had some cats who got to try the snapper in the morning. If they were still purring by supper, we ate it. Actually, the mortality is about 2 percent for this sort of poisoning.

We listened to our cats, and we developed some guidelines, too: We won't eat a fish with a leathery or warty skin, a brightly colored fish, a fish with a bony exoskeleton, or one that locals won't eat. There, by the grace of continued purring, we go well-fed.

Eat It All Now

(*Jim Brown*) On a 3-year family cruise of Central America (both sides) aboard a 31-foot trimaran, we were four aboard. Fresh food was a main concern. We caught lots of fish, and we finally realized that their goodness has about 50 percent to do with freshness—and freshness has everything to do with *eating them NOW*.

"Nothing new," you say. Wait a minute—don't even wait a minute. That's my point. If you want to taste your catch at its best, eat it when you catch it. Fish jump aboard at all times, and this isn't always convenient, but whenever you can, stop the boat—midmorning or midnight —and put on the pot. Enjoy the finny creatures before they *rigor mort*.

We tried about 50 ways of cooking fish and settled on two: frying and poaching (we didn't have a broiler). The secret of both methods appears to be don't "cook" fresh fish, just get it warm all the way through. When water boils it expands (about 1,700 times). Don't boil the "life" out of your fish and leave dried muscle behind.

To poach, dress fish no more than an inch thick. Cover the bottom of a large fry pan (that has a lid) with onions. Just cover the whole with water. If the fish is strong or oily use milk or, best-yet, the milk of a half-ripe coconut. Season if you must. Try pepper alone or a few seeds of fennel. Simmer for a little while until (using the thickest chunk as a gauge) the fish pulls away from its backbone. A squirt of lemon or lime on each bit keeps scurvy at bay.

To fry, dress as for poaching. Dip in egg, then in cracker crumbs. Corn meal or flour will work but they are slower to brown and therefore induce over-cooking. Popping fat means too much heat. *Warm* in a bit of vegetable oil (not butter).

KEEPING THE CHILL

(Bob Anderson) Anything that decreases the rate at which your ice melts is worth the effort. Check the insulation. Is it the best it can be? Replacing the old with modern, high R-factor foam can make a major difference. If the engine is close enough to heat the area where your box is, make a reflective panel (best with an air space behind) to place between the engine and the icebox. Straight drains mean the cold runs out with the water; drains need traps in them so icebox water will collect and effectively seal cold in. An insulated cover (like a hinged hard-foam panel or a space blanket) that you can put inside the box to seal off the top of the chest will also pay big dividends.

JOLIE BRISE ONION SOUP

(Hal Roth) Seventy-five years ago when the French pilot cutter *Jolie Brise* was making long sea passages, her English owner, Cdr. E. C. Martin, found that his greatest triumph was onion soup. We have made *Jolie Brise* onion soup aboard *Whisper* and think highly of it. Here is Cdr. Martin's recipe:

Get the largest and finest onions available. Peel about two for each man. Cut them into quarters. Add enough cold water to make plenty of soup. Add two full tablespoons of Bovril (an English yeast paste for which we substitute beef stock); about a quarter pound of butter; a dessert spoon full of Worcestershire sauce; black pepper, with caution; and a wine glass full of sherry, or rather more white wine, when the cooking is nearly finished. It seems best not to add salt. Allow the mixture to boil gently, and stir occasionally until the onions have all fallen to pieces and are perfectly soft. I recommend the recipe because it is easy to make whenever cooking is possible, and everyone seems to like it.

—*from* Yachting *magazine*

CHILLING TRICKS

(Martha Bliss) We used to freeze bottled water at home and take it aboard to use first as ice and then as drinking water. We've changed the routine a bit. Now we use the bladders full of wine that come in boxes (which disintegrate in the ice chest). I freeze the wine bladders (sans box) and use them to keep food cold in the chest. It's nothing new, but I also roast, say, a turkey breast and freeze it. It chills its weight in the box until tetrazzini time.

MINI-CHILL

One of the most practical approaches to on-board refrigeration we've seen came from a sailor who had returned from a cruise through the Bahamas. Not wanting to chase ice nor make the necessary modifications (and incur the expense) to install mechanical refrigeration for this single month-long cruise, he purchased a chest-type, top-opening camp refrigerator (Camping World RC 1600) designed to operate on 12 volts, 110 volts, or propane. At $375 plus the cost of a single 20-pound tank of propane—which ran the refrigerator continuously throughout his month cruise—he found this alternative "a superb value." However, propane refrigeration aboard a boat comes with serious risks that should never be taken lightly.

COLD CUT

(Allison Barry) Direct airflow is the enemy of tight insulation. I wanted the convenience of double tops on our icebox, but I knew that a seam between the lids would make the box much harder to keep cold. By insulating the top half of one cover edge and the bottom half of the other, however, we closed the seam with a lap-joint of ½-inch-thick insulation and eliminated the direct path for cold to escape or heat to enter. The box works beautifully.

FRIGID AIR

In the absence of a refrigerator or freezer, an effective method of cooling food and drink is by water evaporation. The water can be fresh, salt, or even dishwater, and all that is needed is a towel, sock, or cloth to soak it in. To cool bottles simply soak a sock, slide it on the bottle, and place it in the shade. A phenomenon known for centuries to

Arab desert-dwellers takes over: as the water evaporates it conducts heat away from objects in contact with it.

PASSAGING PRODUCE

(Cathy Hollis) Fruits and vegetables vary widely in their speed of deterioration. The most durable are cabbage (the harder and denser the better), pumpkins, turnips, carrots, potatoes, and onions. You can never have enough onions aboard. The late Bill Snaith (who, among other claims to fame, designed his own ocean racer and took Sir Francis Chichester aboard as navigator) used to say, "when you go to cook, sauté an onion and then decide what you're going to have with it."

Barry and I grow bean sprouts on ocean passages because they liven up our meals when other fresh items are beginning to run low. The mung bean seems to grow the fastest—in about three days. You'll need a jar with holes in the cover. Soak the beans in the jar, drain them, and leave them in a dark dry place; check twice a day and make sure they stay moist.

As for fruit, green apples and oranges have the longest shelf life. Green bananas last up to a week or so without refrigeration, but once they start to ripen, plan on eating a lot of them in a hurry.

Sunlight, airflow, temperature, and the pressure of items packed alongside have a major effect on the shelf life of produce. Wrapping items in newspaper before you stow them shields the produce from light and heat, absorbs moisture, and provides something of a cushion between items. Putting fruit and vegetables in plastic bags encourages harmful condensation. Similarly, try not to wash vegetables until just before you use them. Vegetable lockers, incidentally, should be well ventilated. A good alternative is a fruit hammock that swings freely.

Inspect for damage carefully when you buy fruit. Dispose of all packing material, especially cardboard, before you bring produce aboard. Roaches often make elaborate homes in packing material, so leave them ashore.

COCKPIT LIGHTS

(Art Loya) For $3.99 each I bought two automotive sidelights, one red, the other white. I flush-mounted them in the cockpit aft of the wheel, about 12 inches apart. They are wired into my "nav lights" circuit and controlled by a single-pole, double-throw toggle switch. This allows me to select red light while we're underway and white while we're relaxing in the cockpit or cleaning up.

SHOW ME THE WAY

(Allison Barry) It's not uncommon for us to go ashore in daylight, then return after dark to face the perplexing problem of picking out our boat from among the many riding in a crowded anchorage. We read one good trick in a magazine and put reflective tape on all four sides of our mast as high as we could reach. The tape makes a great "target" for our flashlight beam, and we know from a distance which boat is home.

A less energy-efficient but quite effective alternative is leaving the red nav-table light on when we leave. There aren't many other boats "showing red" through their ports, and that makes home easy to find.

WITHOUT A FLICKER

(Annie Hill) We have always used oil lamps on our boats and been delighted with them. A lot of people seem to think they are no use for reading, but after more than 15 years of living with oil lamps—and both of us are avid readers—we still have A-1 vision. Another advantage of oil lamps is that they are excellent underway. They are less bright than blue-white incandescent light, so their yellow glow does much less to impair one's night vision than an electric light.

—*adapted from* Voyaging on a Small Income

DOLPHIN DIJON

(Jeremy Thompson) Prepare a marinade of 2 parts real mayonnaise to 1 part Dijon mustard. Add a dash of Worcestershire sauce and chopped onion.

Spread over dolphin filets, sprinkle with paprika, and grill or bake. Allow 10 minutes for each inch of thickness.

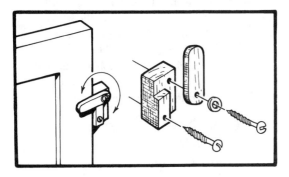

Block Latches

A divided Tupperware dish with a lid is perfect for stowing both soap and a washcloth.

BLOCK LATCHES

(Ron Gray) Finger-pull latches are standard on many boats, and they are certainly to be preferred over friction catches as a way of fixing locker fronts, drawers, and doors. Still, if you are trying to work one in a seaway and the boat falls off a wave, you might do some damage to your finger. That's happened. Turn buttons are safer because they are external. They can be made of wood or metal. Depending on their design, construction, and installation, they can be very satisfactory. Still, they can be knocked or jarred loose.

Block latches are bulkier, but they are safe, external, and relatively secure. Engine vibration, boat motion, and inadvertent elbows won't open them, yet they're simple and positive to operate. Make the pivoting piece from sheet plastic, metal, or an elegant African hardwood.

SQUEEZED TIGHT

(Allen Barry) Building a frame to fit our overhead hatch and covering it with screening wasn't really the hard part. Getting the screen to stay overhead was more of a challenge. My solution is simple, quick, unobtrusive, and it didn't cost much. I attached a length of clear plastic hose to one side of the hatch frame. It creates just the right tension when I pop the screen into place to fix it firmly, and the screen is just as easy to remove again. No fasteners are necessary.

COPING WITH COLD

(Elizabeth Loutrel) You may feel pretty toasty walking in a winter wonderland when it's in the mid 30s and a bit windy. Sit behind the helm for a while in the same conditions, however, and you'll feel much colder. Enforced inactivity accentuates cold aboard a boat; so does the high level of moisture in the air.

We've been guided in our own northern cruising by those who went before. For instance, Wright Britton cruised to Iceland and Greenland in the late '60s aboard his 40-foot yawl *Delight*. He wrote: "My normal dress from the skin out was two pairs of wool socks, Norwegian fishnet suit, set of Duofold underwear, set of wool long johns, pair of ice-man pants, CPO [heavy flannel] shirt, and foul-weather gear over everything. At night I added a pilot parka which, even when soggy, broke the wind. Plastic fish-cleaning gloves with wool inserts kept our hands relatively dry and warm. . . . I would advise taking at least two pairs of the highest boots you can find." [In intervening years sailors have learnt much about wicking moisture from the skin, trapping a thickness of dead air via fleece for insulation, and making foul-weather gear more

(continued on page 124)

GUNS?

Headed from Cebu across the Sulu sea to Brunei . . .

On February 20, 1979, Lydia was killed by pirates. It was 10 o'clock in the morning and we were belowdecks when we became aware that a motorboat was overhauling us quickly with the apparent intention to come alongside. Being apprehensive with this part of the world, Lydia suggested that we fire a warning shot so as to discourage them about coming closer. I disagreed with her, saying that it was too late. By the time we got the gun from its stowage place and got it loaded, they would be alongside. It would not be a warning shot but a declaration of war, and we were sure to be the losers.

She did not argue but went quietly down, leaving me at the tiller. I expected that they would be fishermen trying to trade some fish for cigarettes or whiskey, but at worst if they were pirates I wanted only to let them take what they wanted without resistance, and hopefully they would do us no harm. To my dismay, Lydia came up a little later through the forehatch with the gun in her hand. By then the boat was pulling alongside. Lydia shouted something to them in English and then raised the gun and fired just above them. Almost immediately I heard a shot from their wheelhouse and Lydia fell in the water splashing blood all over the foredeck and tainting the sea red as she slid off, the boat passing by.

Turning back towards the boat, I sighted straight into the gun of the man who had just killed my wife and expected to be shot also, but he hesitated and finally lowered the gun from his shoulder and gave the order for two of his men to jump across. Only then did I become aware of little Thomas who had come on deck and clung to my leg. No doubt the unexpected sight of that beautiful and innocent boy gave scruples to the bandit. They took my cash and the gun which had fallen on the foredeck, but nothing else, and seemed in a hurry to get away.

After their departure I turned around to try and find Lydia but saw nothing but the empty sea.

—Peer Tangvald, adapted from Spray,
the Journal of the Slocum Society

Think twice before taking a gun aboard.

1. Almost all customs arrival forms ask if a gun is carried aboard. If the answer is "Yes", they will usually be confiscated while you are in harbor.
2. Unless skipper and crew are familiar with firearms, they are probably as dangerous to the defender as to the intruder.
3. Firearms do not like the marine environment. They need to be kept greased and wrapped in oilcloth. No gun should be stored loaded. Few intruders are going to give enough warning to permit unwrapping, wiping, and loading.
4. Producing a gun turns a potentially dangerous situation into a potentially lethal one. There's absolutely no point in carrying or producing a gun unless you are prepared to use it first and ask questions afterward.

—Anne Hammick

A gun, like a chain saw, can be useful as well as dangerous and can be a resource contributing to self-reliance.

—Herb Payson

(continued on page 122)

When I cruised in northern waters on Steve and Liz Loutrel's Concordia yawl *Lacerta*, a rifle was part of their survival gear. This gun was suitable for shooting game or deterring polar bears on what might have been a long hike out to a settlement. In the future, in the same waters, I would carry a modern rifle designed to be easily maintained in the marine environment, one that fires (with minimum recoil) a lightweight, high-velocity bullet—a rifle something like the AR-15. Paramilitary appearance and semiautomatic operation might be a drawback in dealing with customs but would be useful in deterring an aggressor, animal or otherwise.

The difficult philosophical question for me is that if you carry a weapon for self-defense, you must be willing to shoot to kill. And when to display your weapon is a difficult matter of judgment. Confronting a trespasser with a gun may induce precisely the reaction you wish to avoid—an attacker may fire as soon as he sees your gun.

—*Jay Paris*

Families that would never consider a gun at home are putting guns aboard. Some boating publications run almost as many articles on guns and pirates as they do on anchors and weather. The likelihood of encountering a situation meriting deadly force is very remote. With a firearm aboard, the likelihood of inappropriate use of deadly force is much greater. I'm not challenging the right to arm, merely the hysteria that makes it seem imperative for prudent cruising.

—*Don Casey*

If you're going to carry a gun, you should know:

- Pistols are discouraged. You may never see them again if customs takes them. You can be jailed for refusal to surrender them, and you may still have them taken away.
- A weapon capable of chambering a military cartridge is also a prime target for confiscation. This includes the .38 revolver, .45 and 9 mm handguns, plus the .308 Winchester, 30-06, 7.65 mm, .223 Parabellum, 380 auto, and even the 12-gauge shotgun (used for riot control). Actually, though, shotguns are most often classified as sporting pieces. I've personally never had any trouble with my 12-gauge.
- A shotgun is the best deterrent. It puts as many "bullets" in the air as a light submachine gun and you don't have to be a particularly good shot to be effective.

—*Chuck Phillips*

In the US a gun is considered a sporting instrument, at worst a weapon. In many countries, though, it is perceived as a *threat to the state*. Dealing with customs over firearms is a hassle. Getting caught with undeclared firearms is a catastrophe.

Our best reason for carrying a gun aboard is for survival, i.e., capsize or remote shipwreck leading to being cast away. For that purpose (and for plinking at garbage) we like the Armalite AR-7. This .22 pistol is cheap, simple, reliable, and is the survival weapon supplied to many units of the armed forces around the world. It is lightweight and breaks down so that its barrel and receiver assemblies store in its stock. And it floats! Our plan of action if we hear boarders on deck at night is to fire—through a designated and prepared ventilator—our flare gun, at the same time sounding our horn repeatedly. We agree that we will never engage in a shoot-out with an armed assailant.

—*Jack and Charlotte Clementson*

Carol and I were asleep. On her side of the bed I heard uncharacteristic rustling and woke to find an intruder on hands and knees by the night table. After an inane "Who are you?" I bellowed and he fled. I chased him until Carol stopped me half-way down the stairs with a shout. Had there been a gun in our night table the story, and perhaps the rest of our lives, would have been very different. *Shere Khan* has been to Turkey, Tunisia, and South Street Seaport, and we don't carry firearms aboard.

—*Robby Robinson*

Many years ago when I was as naive as I was strong, I went off on a weekend regatta in Long Island Sound. It blew hard, and many of the racers were chipped up or worse by the time they limped in to anchor Saturday night. One 40-footer tore her tiller loose from her rudderhead and was engaged in fashioning the time-honored Hornblower repair of running steering lines (port and starboard) from the after corner of the rudder so that she might sail home on the morrow. The crew hoisted a dinghy onto her foredeck, filled it with water, and accompanied it with several of their beefier members to lift the rudder clear back aft. The most aquatic or perhaps the soberest among them was wrestling with the slippery blade, attempting to bring a brace and bit to bear when a cold-eyed gentleman in a perfectly handled Whitehall rowed up. "You're wasting your time," he said calmly. "Get out of there." Then he rowed away. He returned in five minutes with a 12-gauge, took aim from 10 feet away, blew a neat ¾-inch hole in the rudder, and rowed away as crisply as he had come.

—*Steve Hammond*

If I had a boat big enough for a cat, a dog, and a fireplace, she still wouldn't be big enough for a gun. My father was an FBI agent and I learned to shoot when I was seven. I know guns but I still don't want one . . . except maybe for something to plink with on those glassy days offshore. Besides shooting at garbage, what are you going to *do* with the goddam thing? plug the scrounge who's stealing your dinghy? sink the Cuban gunboat? whip it from under your pillow and win the situation back from the armed thugs who've come aboard in search of your sextant? your whiskey? your wife? Just who is that slipping aboard late at night? If you haven't pulled the trigger yet, go check. It might be your son. But even if you *are* a sitting duck, don't look like one. We always pull the dinghy aboard at night, and (effective against boarding, I think) I enjoy showing off my spotlight. If we're isolated, I'll flash it around two or three times, minimum, per evening. When Nature's call comes later in the night, I combine that visit to the rail with another spotlight display.

—*Jim Brown*

Before setting off from England with my young family in our 57-year-old lifeboat, a friend presented me with a fine Purdy shotgun, complete with tooled leather carrying case and engraved brass nameplates. I personally have not the slightest interest in guns, but also I am not inclined to look such a fine gift horse in the mouth. At the country police station where I went to register my new possession, I was asked, "What are you going to use it for?"

"To shoot sharks in the Pacific ocean," I replied, unhesitatingly.

"Aha," the constable nodded and wrote down my reply verbatim. As it turned out, I never shot a shark or anything else with the Purdy, but when I sold it some years later, it helped pay for my daughter's wedding reception.

—*Mike Badham*

effective. Nonetheless, the "layering" principle that Britton exemplifies remains the key in suiting people to meet cold.—eds.]

When we have people coming aboard, we send them a list similar to Britton's and top it with a wool hat and scarf. These two relatively small items are remarkably effective in reducing heat loss. (Everyone knows—or do they?—that the major source of body-heat loss is through the exposed head.) We try to alternate a layer of deep-loft or dead-air space (like a sweater) with another that blocks airflow. On our legs we use fewer layers to allow for flexing and movement.

We also have on board a pair of overlarge "Mickey Mouse," or Korea, boots. These military surplus items don't have non-skid soles, but they were developed to prevent frostbite, and they work. The other piece of community clothing is an out-size hooded parka with huge, hand-warmer pockets.

MAGIC BAG

(Tink Martin) It's not heavy. It's never in the way. It doesn't match my shoes or my eyes, but time and again I'm glad that I brought it: my Magic Bag. It's 5 x 9 x 5, medium-blue nylon, and it has top and side zippers plus a shoulder strap. Inside are: a zip-seal plastic bag containing waterproof matches, pins, paper clips, rubber bands, emery board, hard candies, needles, Dacron thread, and waxed seizing; gloves, rigging knife, and marlin-spike; headband (Velcro fastener) and dark glasses; glow-in-the-dark watch with second hand and bezel ring; compass; dividers, protractor, and 10-inch flexible ruler; pencils, pencil sharpener, colored markers, and red fluorescent marker; insect sting kit, mini first-aid supplies, sunscreen, and wet pads; nylon-net shopping bag (fine mesh), plastic bags, and ties; nylon line (stored with double bowlines to serve as instant safety harness), whistle, mini air horn, signal mirror, and a pocket pack of aerial pen flares; red wool (for tell-tales); and sometimes bottles of red and green nail polish.

EGGS TO GO

(Bob And Nancy Griffith) Preserving eggs for a long voyage? No need to go to the messy lengths of smearing them with grease or using water glass; just immerse them briefly in boiling water in a wire basket (for about five seconds). This seals the permeable shell by cooking a thin layer of the white. It also sterilizes the shell. Farm-fresh eggs that have never been refrigerated are the best. We carried a 30-dozen case aboard *Ahwahnee.* Even after two months, finding a bad one was rare.

—*adapted from* Blue Water

HOME MAKING

(Virginia McCullough) We thought we might be doing things a bit backwards when we moved aboard our 34-footer before we'd done any extensive cruising. Instead we learned a lot about how to make the most of our home afloat, and that's helped our cruising to work out well.

It became clear quite quickly that you don't change yourself when you change where you live. We still had the same interests and enjoyed the same activities as we had living ashore; we just had to fit them into a different space and a different lifestyle. We thought we'd pare down to the essentials, but I was amazed at how many *essentials* we had. We've had to find space for more aboard than we'd planned.

You'll be a lot happier if you can do without the services marinas have to offer. We use a giant canning pot for a bathtub rather than relying on shoreside showers, and our kerosene heater means we don't have to seek out shore power when the temperature drops. The more that you are truly on your own, the better value you'll get from your budget and the more pleasure you can take carving out your own lifestyle.

Interior plans on small and medium-size boats call for a fair amount of "two-way" space. A stove that slides out over the sink may be fine for a short cruise, but for three meals a day plus snacks, making the conversion gets tiresome. The same is true of berths that convert from tables. Privacy is not just an idle concept; the more of it you can achieve in your set-up, the better.

Keep maintenance simple. Pay as much attention to systematic stowage as you can. Be flexible. And learn to treat the uncertainties as adventures rather than ordeals.

TABLE TALK

(Allen Barry) A high table fiddle is a wonderful thing in a seaway, but think about it—aren't you most likely to be reading, writing, or eating on the level? Isn't a fiddle edge a nuisance then?

Some tables have a "fiddled-in" area in the middle where you can perch things when the table is on the gimbal or where you can stick things when you're underway. We don't eat underway very often so we took the fiddle off along the edge where we work or eat.

Table space is very nice, especially firm, trustworthy table space. We took our very small cockpit table and used it as the base for a much larger table, which we stow beneath a bunk cushion when we're underway. There are lots of types and sizes of cockpit tables, but when you want one you almost always want a big one. Therefore we made ours as big as would fit, yet we took pains to make sure it was sturdy and secure. When we want a cockpit table, we have a real one.

GOOD BOOKS

Many long-distance cruisers depend on their libraries for entertainment. Swapping paperbacks with other sailors is one of the pleasures of being in port, but now there's another—*The Good Book Guide* (91 Great Russell St., London, WC1, England). Issued seven times a year, it not only reviews new books but will send you any book on its list for the published UK price plus postage. For a dollar surcharge, the group will purchase and mail requested books not on their list.

A good book to have if you're cruising overseas is *Elsevier's Nautical Dictionary*—covering English, French, Spanish, Italian, Dutch, and German.

An alternative is the *Yachtsman's Ten Language Dictionary* by Barbara Webb and Michael Manton, which adds Danish, Portuguese, Turkish, and Greek to the six languages *Elsevier's* covers. (John de Graff, Inc., Clinton Corners, NY.)

FLYING FISH

Once you've completed a port-to-port passage not less than 1,000 miles in a boat under 70 feet overall, you are eligible to join the Ocean Cruising Club. In addition to a twice-a-year newsletter, the club runs rallies, races, and dinners wherever there are sailors, but most often in the UK, USA, and Australia. Membership includes club privileges at the Royal Thames Yacht Club in London, including its world-covering "chart chest." Add to that the OCC's *Cruising Information Service,* which is detailed (18 listings on Christmas Island, for example) and accessible (copies of requested materials are available at 15 cents each). The US representative of the OCC is Emily Morse, 43 Siscowit Rd., Pound Ridge, NY 10576.

BREAD ON THE WATER

(Lin Pardey) Baking bread fits the offshore rhythm and time schedule perfectly, but it's nice to have fresh bread anytime. The ingredients for bread are available worldwide and, with a bit of care, keep quite well. Dried yeast, in either individual packets or 1-pound cans, will keep up to two years, especially if "decanted" into plastic containers with tight lids. Flour is more difficult to keep, especially if you are voyaging in warm waters. I've found it pays to buy enriched flour and put each 5-pound sack in a plastic bag, which is then wrapped inside another plastic bag. If you suspect weevils in the flour you buy, repack it into gallon containers and add an egg-size lump of dry ice. Leave the lid ajar until the ice dissipates, then seal the top and tape it for extra security. The chemicals in dry ice kill weevils. If you miss some, simply run your flour through a strainer. The critters you miss will add protein to the final mix.

The first thing I learned about most bread recipes printed in US and English cookbooks is that they tell you to knead the bread much more than necessary. Kneading is a way to make the texture of your bread approach that of the store-bought article, so why not knead less and enjoy the more cake-like coarseness of unkneaded bread.

Pour into a large salad bowl:

⅔ cups salt water
1⅓ cup fresh water

Heat to 90°–100°F—hot but comfortable to the touch. Then add:

2 heaping tbsp. dry yeast (or two packets)

Stir until yeast dissolves, then add:

¼ cup sugar (honey, molasses, etc.)
5 or 6 cups flour

Keep working flour in until the dough no longer sticks to your fingers. Form the dough into a ball, cover the bowl, and put the mix in a warm

place to rise, someplace between 80° and 110°F. Check in half an hour. If the dough hasn't risen the place is too cool. If the mix has a crust, it's too hot. Dough will rise to twice its size in less than an hour. Punch it down and let it rise again if you want a smoother texture to your loaf.

Place risen loaves in 350° oven and bake until golden. Turn the pans at least once if you want a uniform color. Rap your bread with your knuckles. When it sounds hollow, it's ready. Let loaves cool five minutes before removing them from the pans. Set them on their sides or on a cake-cooling rack to let the steam dissipate from the bottom. Wait 15 minutes before you cut into them.

PAN-FRIED BREADS   *(Gretchen Martin)*

My family likes the taste of fresh baked bread, biscuits, and cornbread, but this is hard to arrange sometimes on a cruising sailboat with barely 3 feet of counter space and no oven. Store-bought breads don't keep. Prepared mixes are expensive and contain preservatives, so I make my own mixes.

For stovetop baking I recommend a heavy aluminum "chicken fryer" with straight sides, or a heavy black-iron fry pan with high sides, and a tight lid. Thin pans don't distribute or hold the heat well enough for a minimum of 30 minutes baking at low, *low* temperature. Preheat the pan and lid, grease well with oil or margarine, place loaf or biscuits inside, and replace the lid. Adjust the flame to ultra low; you may need a

---

MASTER MIX

8 cups unbleached flour
⅓ cup baking powder
1 tbsp. salt
2 tbsp. sugar
2 cups instant non-fat dry milk
2 cups shortening

BISCUITS

2 cups Master Mix
½ to ¾ cup milk (reconstituted dry milk works
    fine)

Mix to make a soft dough; turn out onto a floured surface and knead a dozen or so times; pat out to ⅜-inch thickness; cut with glass or biscuit cutter; and cook in pre-heated, greased pan.

flame tamer. I put a folded moist dishtowel on top of the lid to keep the heat in. Turn biscuits once to brown both sides. Breads are done when the top springs back when you touch it.

SHIPBOARD SLICES   *(Dianne Taylor)*

I remember sitting at anchor in the beautiful, calm, isolated bay at Little Harbor on Long Island in the Bahamas; the idea leapt into my mind—PIZZA! Suddenly it was the only thing that mattered. No one would deliver. We didn't even have an oven, but I would not be denied.

Frying-pan pizza: Roll the dough, laying it in the pan about half an inch thick; smear on spiced-up tomato paste, chopped onions, salami, etc. to taste; top with cheese; "bake" over a medium flame (I have a flame tamer) for about 20 minutes. It was a craving well worth pursuing.

COOKING WITH GAS   *(Allen Barry)* We like

cooking with propane. There is a problem, of course, in determining how your supply is lasting after you've been cooking for a while. Our answer is a simple fish scale. We can weigh the propane bottle virtually any time to find out how much gas is left. The McCreary brothers, builders of our Caliber 33, long ago took a thoughtful step and began to include a spare 2-pound bottle (compatible with the main stove and stowable in a tidy case) to eliminate the need to carry a full-size spare aboard.

A STEP UP   A knotted ladder is

salty, stows neatly, can be used for getting aboard, and is blessedly quiet and easy on the side of the hull. Use thick rope—about 1 inch in diameter or larger. Make a trial step so you can see how much rope it takes, then double the length you judge it will take to do the whole ladder.

Seize an eye in the middle of the double length and begin the first step about a foot below the eye. Take care that the steps come level. Four turns around a step are usually enough, but more can be taken according to the size of rope or feet in question. Work with alternate parts, keeping the ladder and all parts hauled taut so it will not stretch unevenly in use.

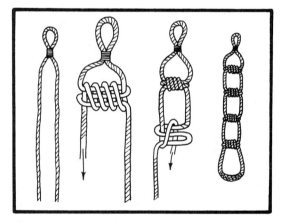

A Step Up

Finish off by splicing the ends together. You can work a headstick into the top rung, if you wish, to ensure that the ladder is fully spread.

SCRATCH BOAT   *(George Trautman)* When I

bought *Gannet,* my 57-year-old wooden Rhodes 27, I knew nothing about wooden boats. I undertook to make her the kind of boat that I could cruise aboard for good distances and long times, but without taking anything away from her classic good looks and wood-boat feel.

I've had the hull fiberglassed to the waterline (using mechanical fastenings à la Alan Vaitses). I had the icebox and coal stove replaced with modern units. I had the deck painted with epoxy paint and the doghouse glassed. I also put radar, KVH compass, and Trimble (GPS/Loran) navigational systems aboard. I had a considerable amount of work done, but I was able to keep from spending the kind of money that sailboat restoration is legendary for. All of the changes work well together, and I now have the sort of boat that I wanted. I think there are three principal reasons for this:

- I went out of my way to find knowledgeable people. Reputation, recommendations, and legwork yielded good results.
- I read voraciously.
- I thought long and hard about what I wanted to do. Because I wasn't in a rush to get things done, the things I got done continue to be easy and fun to live with.

SUPER SCOOP   *(Don Street)*

The best windscoop I've ever seen is on *Maverick*. It merely needs to be hoisted. It works no matter what the direction of the wind, which makes it excellent for ventilating while you're tied to a dock or in a slip. The device is simply an X of cloth with each of four panels joined along the center seam and attached to hoops of equal size top and bottom. The panels on *Maverick* taper from 21 inches at the top to 9 inches where they enter the tube that ducts air below.

—*adapted from* The Ocean Sailing Yacht

WATER   *(Lin Pardey)* The average island-hopping onshore voyager needs about 1½ gallons of fresh water per day per person. The offshore passagemaker uses less, about 3 quarts per person. It's not necessarily a simple matter to take care of these basic needs.

Tankage is positive in terms of comfort but often a negative in terms of performance, living space, and economy. Intelligently sited (low, balanced, close to the centers of gravity and lateral resistance), isolatable, connnectable, inspectable, cleanable, taste-free tanks are what you're after. They can be made from any number of materials, and we prefer stainless steel. Aluminum, though recommended by some, is one material I'd avoid because calcium build-up can lead to taste problems. Good baffles make tanks easier to live with and add to their life. Try not to keep your entire water supply

Super Scoop. General dimensions: Each of the four panels should be ⅜ the circumference of the hoop at the top edge, and ½ the diameter of the hoop at the bottom edge.

⅜ (HOOP CIRCUMFERENCE)

3 FEET

½ (HOOP DIAMETER)

in the same tank so that if there is contamination, you will have a potable reserve.

Sailors cruising overseas face a constant concern with water quality. Though it is the trace minerals and differing elements in "foreign" water that more often than bacteria cause stomach problems, "don't drink the water" is a warning not without foundation. You can drink it, though, if you purify it:

- Use liquid chlorine laundry bleach. Read the label to determine the percentage of chlorine in the solution.

% Chlorine in Bleach	No. of Drops/Qt.	
	Clear Water	Cloudy Water
1	10	20
4-6	2	4
7-10	1	2

1. Mix thoroughly.
2. Let stand for 30 minutes with maximum ventilation.
3. If you cannot detect a slight chlorine odor at the end of 30 minutes, repeat process and let stand for 15 minutes.
4. Water is safe to use.

- Use Tincture of Iodine

% of Iodine	No. of Drops/Qt.	
	Clear Water	Cloudy Water
2	5	10

Let stand for 30 min., after which time water is safe to use. The figures were obtained from the US Department of Health, Education, and Welfare, and I was interested to learn from the Orange County (CA) Health Department that purification of this kind has the same effect as boiling all of the water for five minutes.

Sailors' Survey

INSURANCE

We insure lives, cars, houses, health, even prize pets and airplane travelers. What could be so tough about boat insurance? Surveys, salvor rights, lay-ups, acts of God, cruising zones, limited warranties, market value vs. replacement cost, etc, etc.—*that's* what's so tough about boat insurance. In search of trails to take through the thicket, I spent a morning asking friends about their boat-insurance programs and experiences: [RR]

- "I've got a 15-foot daysailer. I laugh at the thought of insurance."

- "The premium for my 41-footer went up $200 this season while my zone for cruising coverage shrank to ⅓ of what it was. When I took my boat to Europe, I self-insured because standard coverages were prohibitive. I took out liability insurance and covered the boat myself. I'm thinking of doing that now in home waters."

- "We went with Boat/U.S. because a friend worked with them. When Hurricane Bob trashed our boat, they set up claims depots right nearby and handled everything very efficiently. They offered me $16,000 and our much-maligned hull as settlement on our $20,000 coverage. My friend intervened

(continued on page 130)

and we got $19,000 worth of work (and a virtually new boat cosmetically)."

- "I got a fairly reasonable quote for a policy on my 19-foot cruising catboat from the company that insures my house. When I got the bill it was nearly twice what I'd been quoted. They added a surcharge, not mentioned to me in the original contract, of 75 percent because my boat is over 25 years old. I paid what I had contracted and then canceled. I now insure my $12,000 boat on my own."

- "The only claim I've made in 30 years was for a lost dinghy. Even though I was towing it in weather when I shouldn't have been, and it was not specifically mentioned in the policy, my company paid me enough to replace it. Insurance firms hardly make me feel warm and cuddly, but I'd be lying if I said that I didn't get good value for my premiums."

THE PRICE IS RIGHT   *(Tom Shaw)*
The cheapest insurance available is a US Coast Guard Auxiliary Courtesy Inspection. It's free! The inspection team will examine your PFDs, lights, ground tackle, engine systems and ventilation, safety equipment, communications gear, liferaft, emergency gear, and more to make sure you meet USCG standards and are well prepared. Contact the USCG Auxiliary flotilla closest to you.

MOTIVATION   *(MB) Westering* was everything to us.
Close calls like a near-collision with a drifting, unlighted fishing boat off the mouth of the River Tagus made us realize how close to the edge we were sailing. We were uninsured. Our boat was 57 years old. Every broker I approached responded with a seemingly prohibitive quote. But: "If a marine-insurance agent pronounces you a bad risk, he's probably right. He's the one with the experience." That thought kept us sufficiently on our toes to survive.

PROTECT YOURSELF   *(David Siemens)*
Accidents happen. They produce loss. Loss produces litigation. Even the finest boats and the best skippers need protection. In that light, adequate boat insurance is a very wise investment.

Unfortunately not all states regulate boat insurance uniformly. Insurance is available from general agencies (such as those that insure houses and cars), specialized marine houses, and through various consumer and membership groups. The forms themselves are not standardized.

Rates and coverages vary significantly by locale. (One company's Florida quote was twice as high as its California quote for the same boat and owner.) Further, an individual company's quoted rate on the same boat may vary significantly from month to month. The marine insurance marketplace cries out, "SHOP AROUND."

We solicited quotations on three different boat/owner packages from companies in Maryland, Florida, and California:

- *Boat 1:* A 1984 25-foot O'Day w/ 9.9 outboard; $10,000 hull coverage, $300,000 liability, $5,000 medical, $100 deductible. Owners: married, first boat, mid 20s, limited experience.
- *Boat 2:* A 1982 Tartan 37-foot sloop, 41-hp Westerbeke, day-sailing with two-week cruising window. $60,000 hull value, $300,000 liability, $5,000 medical, $500 deductible. Owners: married couple, mid 30s, two children, second boat, completed USCG Safe Boating Courses.
- *Boat 3:* A 1985 Pearson 53-foot ketch, 85-hp Perkins diesel. Complete electronics. Vacation retreat and offshore passagemaking. $250,000 hull coverage, $500,000 liability, $10,000 medical, $2,500 deductible. Owners: married, mid 40s, third boat, completed USCG Safe Boating Courses; he holds USCG 100-ton license.

Almost every responding company attached some form of disclaimer or exclusion. Comparison of the numbers is instructive, though, even without that "fine print:"

ANNUAL PREMIUMS

AGENCY	ANNUAL PREMIUM (BY BOAT LENGTH IN FEET)		
	25'	37'	53'
CHESAPEAKE BAY MARINE AGENCY	$200	$760	$2,570
NATIONAL DIRECT UNDERWRITER	$200	$370	$1,940
NATIONAL BOATING ORGANIZATION	$123	$320	$2,111
SOUTHERN CALIFORNIA MARINE AGENCY	$329	$591	$1,865
NATIONAL DIRECT UNDERWRITER	$245	$543	UNAVAIL.
NATIONAL BOATING ORGANIZATION	$110	$369	UNAVAIL.
WESTERN FLORIDA MARINE AGENCY	$280	$638	$1,661
NATIONAL DIRECT UNDERWRITER	$288	$662	UNAVAIL.
NATIONAL BOATING ORGANIZATION	$204	$532	$2,613

Shop Around!

INSURE YOURSELF
(Jim Brown) Jack and Charlotte Clementson are self-insured. Charlotte has a teacher's retirement and Jack a military pension. They invested Charlotte's lump-sum benefit as their "insurance." The interest on the sum is re-invested, and they can draw upon it and the principal *for any expense*, such as health care, travel, major repairs, etc. That versatility is something no insurance policy can match. They hope they can cover most everything except great liability expense, but liability insurance is cheap.

DECLARE YOURSELF

(Annie Hill) Remember to hoist an anchor light by night and the black anchor ball by day. Without them you will not be recognized as properly anchored, and no matter who runs into you at no matter what the speed, *you* will be held in violation of the Collision Regulations and have precious little chance of collecting recompense for damages.

—*adapted from* Voyaging on a Small Income

WHO'S ON YOUR SIDE?

(Don Street) Many experienced sailors believe that they don't need hull insurance. After all, they may have been sailing 30 years, never been in a jam they couldn't get out of, and never damaged dock or hull. Self-insurance is, in my opinion, a serious mistake. You might assume that if someone runs into you at your mooring, all you'd have to do was contact the offending party's insurer. Well, I know of four cases just like that, and in three the companies refused to pay. Private lawyers were an option, but not a low-priced one. In all three cases the owners failed to collect a cent. In the fourth case the owner had insurance. His company got the offending party's company to settle within 48 hours.

FINE PRINT

(Tom Shaw) Federal law requires you to report to state boating authorities, in writing, within 10 days, any accident where more than $500 damage was done to any vessel (including your own). If there was loss of life or even medical treatment in excess of first aid, notification must come within 48 hours.

SAILOR'S SOLUTION

(Tom Service) In preparation for our four-year circumnavigation back in 1987, the Service family spent our "insurance" money on heavy ground tackle and the best navigation system we could buy. Now we've developed, through Seven Seas

Cruising Association, a program affordable enough so that people can (as we couldn't) afford good gear and insurance, too. Our group has found an underwriter to provide worldwide, two-person-crew, agreed-value, hull insurance. It's not about cheap rates. It's about reasonable, targeted, hard-to-get coverage for liveaboard cruisers. It has taken five years of work to be able to bring this opportunity to Seven Seas members, but we hope many who might have gone without can now enjoy over-the-horizon, mom-and-pop hull insurance.

DEALING WITH DEDUCTIBLES

(Howard E. Candage) A rule of thumb for deductibles: you should be able to amortize the deductible amount into savings in premiums over three years. For example, if you select a $1,500 deductible instead of a $500 deductible, unless you reduce your premium by $333 per year, the larger deductible is unlikely to be financially advantageous.

TOWING TARIFFS

(Seaworthy, Boat/U.S.) Commercial towing is filling the vacuum left by the Coast Guard. Many insurers include towing coverage, but it's not at all rare for owners to be presented bills for towing services that vastly outstrip their protection. Start with the basic $100 an hour running time established by TOWBOAT/US and it's easy to see where the money goes. Typically, towboat rates increase if a vessel is aground ($5 - $10/foot), and surcharges are common for bad weather and heavy sea conditions. Nighttime tows are an added $25 an hour. Where you might in the past have cast off the towline and waved the Coasties thanks and good-bye, what's waving now is a hefty invoice.

PEACE OF MIND

(Annie Hill) Even before they consider taking on your boat, insurers will start to influence your decisions and, therefore, your freedom. Having told you what type of boat to sail and whom to take with you, insurers hedge *their* bets by telling you what time of year to go and how far away you can

head. When you think of it, the underwriters, far from giving you the peace of mind for which you've paid, provide instead the constant niggling worry that you might somehow be straying from the bounds of your agreement with them. The freedom for which you've worked so hard is swept away by them at a single stroke. Freedom is never safe. If you need so much security, are you doing the right thing by yourself in going voyaging in the first place?

—*adapted from* Voyaging on a Small Income

ALPINE BUTTERFLY KNOT
(David Seidman)

The *alpine butterfly knot* puts a loop in the standing part of a line that will take a pull parallel to the rope. It won't slip or jam; mountain climbers trust their lives to it. Use it to make a rope ladder. Fishermen use it to rig sinkers or a series of leaders. And I have used it to add a second anchor rode to the first when there was only one cleat. Of all the mid-line loop knots, this is probably the best on land or sea, and it's easy to tie:

1. Make a 360-degree twist in the standing part. Fold the lower loop up.
2. Bring this loop over the top and down the center.
3. Finish the knot by "dressing" (smoothing and orienting all of the parts) and "setting" (tightening all of the parts so that they achieve maximum internal friction).

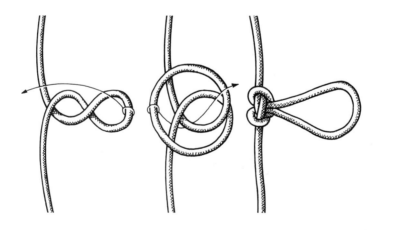

6 STUDY THE WEATHER

Fickle, awesome, intricate, mundane—the weather is always with us. Like farmers, astronauts, lifeguards, and ski resorts, sailors have an especially close connection with it. Fair wind or foul, big waves or small, sunglasses or slicker—it all depends on the weather.

Out of the sun comes rain.

—*Rig-Veda (circa 1100 B.C.)*

Real-time weather information has never been more accurate and complete, weatherfaxes and onboard computers have never been more sophisticated, forecasts have never been more detailed and authoritative. Sailors today have a better handle on the weather than sailors ever have. Yet, reliance on electronic observations and *official* conclusions can blunt the sensitivity to "glass and sky" sailors once enjoyed. To fill the holes in today's forecasts, to bridge the gap between regional predictions and local realities, to make weather-wise decisions, we need to reawaken that *feel*.

We talked with Bob Rice about weather. He is a "special projects" meteorologist (weather router) who's been involved in the highs and lows of transatlantic crossings by hot-air balloon (*Double Eagle II*, 1978), singlehanded transatlantic racing (*Moxie*, 1980, the first American win), record solo circumnavigations (*American Promise*, 1985-86), Cape Horn record runs (*Great American*, 1993), and America's Cup challenges (*Kiwi Magic*, victorious in 1995).

"I started doing weather in the Air Force in 1960, so I've got some time in. I've been pleased with all of my projects, what they've meant related to history. Nowadays in weather work you begin with computer models. They are fabulous, but they only take you so far. I think you've got to develop a feel for it. ESPN was kind enough to say that *Kiwi Magic* 'through a whole season of racing, was never on the wrong side of a shift.'

"Predicting the wind in the short term is tough. You can't depend on numbers. The wind isn't periodic—it doesn't follow set rules. You just have to look down the course and ask yourself, 'If I were the wind, what would I do now?'"

Rice obviously provided the Kiwis with some pretty good answers. From time in the business, a familiarity with the atmospheric "facts," and an ability to get beyond the pieces of the puzzle to a feel for the big picture, Rice has become a prophet much respected in his own time.

Getting clearer about the weather means mastering a host of puzzle pieces. We've tried to help arrange them below in alphabetical order.

*Lord this is
a huge rayn!
This were weder
for to slepen inne!*

—*Geoffrey Chaucer,*
Troilus and Criseyde
(circa 1385)

Adiabatic Process   The temperature of an air mass cools as it rises and warms as it descends, even though there is no change in the actual heat content of the air itself. This is due to changes in pressure. The rate is 1 degree Fahrenheit for every 150 feet of altitude change.

Aeolus   King of the winds in Greek mythology, he gave Odysseus the famous bag of the winds (which the hero's crew opened while he slept and set loose a whirlwind). Said the late transatlantic race champion Phil Weld, "Please, aboard this vessel, never speak ill of the wind. Better to spend your energy figuring what Aeolus will come up with than to cuss him."

Africo   The southwesterly in ancient Rome.

Air Mass   Parcels of air having uniform temperature, moisture content, and density, air masses take their character (and their names) from where they come from—arctic maritime, tropical continental, etc. They can cover whole continents but average about a third that size. Influenced by both pressure gradients and the earth's rotation, they can move at up to 30 mph.

Altocumulus   Cumulus clouds are "lumped up" or "'cumulated."(Stratus clouds are "stratified" or laid out in layers.) "Alto" designates the middle deck of the atmosphere. Altocumulus, then, are puffy clouds in the middle tier of the sky.

Anticyclone   An area of high pressure. A high.

Arctic Air Mass   Air masses are identified by where they come from. The coldest are called arctic. As soon as air masses leave their regions of origin they begin to modify, but for five days or more, air masses generally retain their characteristics of origin.

Arctic Sea Smoke   This type of fog appears over open water in cold weather when frigid air causes vapor rising from the surface to condense virtually immediately. Dramatic as it is, sea smoke has little weather significance.

Aristotle   He wrote *Meteorologica* in the fourth century (B.C.) and propounded a world composed of four elements (earth, air, water, and fire) in which atmospheric movement occurred due to "the tendency of each to return to its rightful place." He deduced that air cools as it rises. He placed "logical deduction" and "pure reason" above detailed scientific observation. His logical (but largely false) picture of the atmosphere persisted until the Renaissance.

Atmosphere   A gaseous mass retained by the gravitational force of the planet, the earth's atmosphere is roughly 900 miles thick and layered like a cosmic onion.

Atmospheric Charge   The ancients worshipped Zeus and Thor for their thunderbolts. Ben Franklin caught sky-bolts on his kite string. We have long known that electricity lives in the air above. Research suggests that the violent contact of seawater with molten lava fuels the atmosphere's charge. Even garden-variety evaporation may, in fact, give off sparks.

Atmospheric Circulation   We know the movement within the "ocean of air" surrounding the planet as wind and weather. This movement comes from temperature and pressure differences (the tilt of the planet relative to its plane of orbit around the sun exposes the surface to uneven amounts of radiation, and cold air weighs more in column than hot) plus the earth's rotation and the effects of its varied terrain.

Atmospheric Pressure   Measured in inches of mercury, millibars, or kilopascals, atmospheric pressure readings are corrected to sea level and denote the weight of the column of air stretching from ground level to the stratosphere.

Atmospheric Stability   A crucial weather variable, atmospheric stability depends on temperatures at differing altitudes. Because hot air rises, an air column that is warm at the bottom and cold at the top is unstable. Convection will cause the temperature layers to mix. Air is stable when temperature increases (or decreases very slowly) with altitude. A good index of stability is visibility. When clear, cold air is held low, you can see for miles and the atmosphere is stable. Warm, hazy air at the surface, though, means instability and the prospect of volatile weather change.

Aurora Borealis   Over 2,000 years ago Seneca of Rome described them as "gaping displays, flitting, shining, yellow without eruptions or rays." This phenomenon occurs when atmospheric gases are agitated (in the way that the gas in a fluorescent-light tube is agitated) by particles discharged from the sun. Were these particles not deflected at a high altitude by earth's "magnetic shield," life on the planet would quickly come to an end.

Azores High   Varying in size and shape, this high-pressure cell is in near-permanent residence over the Atlantic Ocean between the islands of Bermuda and the Azores. Known alternately as the *Bermuda High*, it affects much of the weather in the Atlantic Basin. In winter it is relatively tight and small, which allows turbulent weather to breed between polar and equatorial air masses. In summer it strengthens and expands, effectively blocking much of the westerly transoceanic flow and creating mild and relatively settled weather on both sides of the ocean.

Aztec Anemometer   You can see in a Mexico City museum a model of perhaps the first known device for measuring wind speed. It consists of a tripod supporting a central platform. Inside the tripod's legs are concentric circles of boxes, or pigeonholes. A ball dropped from the center will be blown from the vertical and land in one of the boxes. The farther out toward the legs the ball is blown, the faster the wind is blowing.

Babylonian Weather   Babylonian weather lore was quite sophisticated. Well before 2,000 B.C. they engaged in weather forecasts. Predictions were based on many sources, including planetary motions and the appearance of the evening sky. Babylonians paid attention to haloes around the sun and moon, looked for recurrent cycles in natural phenomena, and undertook to predict harvests by counting thunderclaps. Their beliefs—observational, scientific, and devoid of supernatural elements —were honored in many places well into the modern era.

Back   The wind backs when it changes direction *against* the clock.

Bamboo   The changes in climate over the past 5,000 years may be seen in bamboo growth; the northernmost evidence of bamboo in China has receded southward nearly 600 miles.

Barometer   The "glass" has long been the sailor's bellwether. Invented by Evangelista Torricelli (a pupil of Galileo), the first instrument used mercury to balance the weight of the atmosphere pressing upon the surface of the planet. See chart on page 138.

Barometric Tendency   The best information comes from a barometer only after you are able to establish its *tendency*. Take readings hourly for three hours and you can tell if the glass is *falling*, *rising*, or *steady*. The direction is important; falling indicates deterioration in the weather, rising forecasts clearing. However, pronounced change in the barometer, *up* or *down*, means pronounced change in the weather.

Bermuda High   See "Azores High."

Vilhelm and Jacob Bjerknes
These Norwegian weather pioneers discovered during World War I that air moves in masses that are homogeneous in temperature and humidity. Air masses do not intermix easily. The brothers termed the boundaries between air masses "fronts."

The Book of Signs   A pupil to Aristotle, Theophrastus compiled, around 300 B.C., the most exhaustive weather text of the classical era. The behavior of sheep, the crawling patterns of centipedes, the flickering of lamp wicks, and a host of other natural indicators were seen as keys to the weather. Theophrastus was the first to note that a red sun in the evening was a good sign.

WEATHER FORECASTER

Using the wind as you observe it, and the trend of the barometer for the preceding three hours, you can arrive at a reasonable estimate of the coming weather. This chart is intended for use in continental North America between 30 and 50 degrees north latitudes. Barometric readings are in inches of mercury.

WIND	BAROMETER	FORECAST
SW to NW	30.1 to 30.2, steady	Fair with slight temperature changes for one or two days
SW to NW	30.1 to 30.2, rising rapidly	Fair followed within two days by rain
SW to NW	30.2 and above, stationary	Continued fair with no major temperature changes
SW to NW	30.2 and above, falling slowly	Slowly rising temperature and fair for two days
S to SE	30.1 to 30.2, falling slowly	Rain within 24 hours
S to SE	30.1 to 30.2, falling rapidly	Increasing wind and rain within 12 to 24 hours
SE to NE	30.1 to 30.2, falling slowly	Rain within 12 to 18 hours
SE to NE	30.1 to 30.2, falling rapidly	Increasing wind and rain within 12 hours
E to NE	30.1 and above, falling slowly	Summer: With light winds, no rain for two days Winter: Rain in 24 hours
E to NE	30.1 and above, falling fast	Summer: Rain, probably in 12 hours Winter: Rain or snow with increasing winds
SE to NE	30.0 or below, falling slowly	Rain will continue for one or two days
SE to NE	30.0 or below, falling rapidly	Rain with high winds followed within 36 hours by clearing and colder in the winter
S to SW	30.0 or below, rising slowly	Clearing in a few hours and fair for several days
S to E	29.8 or below, falling rapidly	Severe storm imminent, followed by clearing in 24 hours and colder in winter
E to N	29.8 or below, falling rapidly	Summer: Severe NE gale and heavy rains Winter: Heavy snow and cold wave
Going to W	29.8 or below, rising rapidly	Clearing and colder in the winter

Kelly Mulford (from *The Complete Sailor*)

Bora   This dry, blustery, downdraft off the Alps sweeps over the Adriatic from the northeast year round.

Buys-Ballot's Law   Dutch meteorologist Christopher Buys-Ballot said, in 1857, "with your back to the surface wind, extend your left arm at right angles and it will point to the center of low pressure." He was right. If, while you stand back-to-the-wind, high clouds approach from your left, the weather will worsen. If from the right, expect it to brighten. [All of this is reversed south of the equator.—eds.]

Cape Doctor   The strong, cool southeaster in the Southern Hemisphere that blows the smog away from Cape Town during summer.

Chinook   To the Indians living east of the Canadian Rockies, *chinook* means "snow eater." When moisture-laden westerlies are elevated quickly by the mountains, they cool and moisture condenses. The latent heat it took to vaporize the moisture (about 600 calories per gram of water) is released. The result is warm, dry air that slides down the back side of the mountain. The chinook has been known to melt foot-deep snow fields in a day. In the Alps the wind born from a similar phenomenon is called *fohn* or "fire" wind. Destructive *Santa Anas* in Mexico and Southern California originate in much the same way.

Christmas Winds   Trade-wind veterans agree that the surprising thing about the trades is how light they are. Christmas winds are the exception. These robust easterlies harass the Caribbean during December and January. They have something to do with the wintertime contraction of the Bermuda High and the increased force commanded by denser, colder air.

"Clear Moon, Frost Soon"   Succinct and largely accurate, this rhyme is among the best of the host of weather-predicting jingles. Clear air means high pressure, cooler temperatures, and radiational cooling due to the absence of a blanket of cloud to help earth retain heat. "Frost soon" is a better than average bet.

Climate   The prevailing weather over time.

Some say the world will end in fire,
Some say in ice.
From what I've tasted of desire
I hold with those who favor fire.
But if I had to perish twice,

I think I know enough of hate
To say that for destruction ice
Is also great
And would suffice.

—Robert Frost, "Fire and Ice"

For 95 percent of the past million years the world has been very much colder than it is today. Any natural changes in our present climate are thus extremely likely to be for the colder.

—Nigel Calder,
The Weather Machine

Our comforting sense of the permanence of our natural world is a subtly warped perspective. Without realizing it we have already stepped over the threshold of change.

—Bill McKibben,
The End of Nature

Climate Change   Some climate gurus say "ice," but others see "fire": global warming, the deadly greenhouse, acid rain, a shredded ozone layer—an apocalypse. If not now, very soon.

Who can make an accurate cosmic forecast? Who's to say if it's fire or ice, or a lasting extension of the climate we know now? Will global warming reveal itself through violent aberrations in weather patterns? What do the 100-foot waves recorded twice by sea buoys off Nova Scotia portend? The monster 95-footer encountered by *QEII*? Is sea weather changing? Are forecasts of a meter rise in sea level by 2015 accurate? Who can offer a cosmic forecast? Perhaps the widest agreement is that the predictable weather patterns man has known since exiting the cave have now become unpredictable.

Climate is complex. Whether it rains or shines today depends upon what was happening in the seas off Japan last week, in the polar ice sheet centuries ago, in the earth's orbit around the sun 10,000 years ago, in the movements of the continents ten million years ago. . . . Some climate changes are clear. We can chart them by counting tree rings and sediment layers, by prospecting canyon walls and the banks of the Nile, by examining fossilized crustaceans or petrified pollen, by analyzing oxygen isotopes trapped in polar ice. By studying sunspot cycles, cloud-distribution patterns, volcanic activity, deep-water circulation, earth's solar orbit, and much more, we get some idea of what's coming next. Still, who knows? Fire? Ice? Or maybe endless spring? As it is with daily weather, so it is with climate change—we won't really know until it happens.

Clipper Way   One of the most famous optimal routes outlined in the British Admiralty's *Ocean Passages for the World*, the Clipper Way was the "road" out and home for the China clippers that raced to return to England from the Orient with the season's first tea.

Clouds   From meteorologist Alan Watts we learn that there are really just two types of clouds—heap clouds (cumulus) and layer clouds (stratus). Add to that the transparent wisps of ice-crystal cirrus that cast no shadow, and you have what you need to identify and (eventually) interpret the clouds you see. In the lower deck of the sky you find these types singly or you find them run together (stratocumulus) into a more or less continuous layer. The middle deck contains just alto-stratus or altocumulus. The upper deck contains cirrus plus cirrostratus and cirrocumulus.

Alan Watts's book *Instant Weather Forecasting* builds on these cloud types.

Courtesy Marty Baron, National Weather Service

Anvil Clouds. When a mature cumulonimbus cloud rises to the tropopause inversion boundary, the top spreads out in an anvil. This nasty-looking cloud can bring heavy rain, hail, and thunderstorms, perhaps with downbursts.

Puffy Clouds (cumulus mammatus). Spawned from cumulonimbus, mammatus clouds indicate thunderstorm activity some-where in the vicinity. If the clouds are large and headed your way, you may be in for some severe weather.

Wave Cloud. Formed by a wave-like transport of air into and out of an atmospheric layer wherein condensation occurs, these clouds, unlike roll clouds, do not augur squalls.

Cloud Tops

The top of a cloud is the key to its intentions. If the cloud is relatively flat on top, it has reached its ceiling. If there's a puffy ballooning at the top, the air in a cloud is rising. Uniform layers of cold air pin clouds beneath them. That's atmospheric stability, and it's signaled by long, thin, low and middle-level stratus (stratified) clouds. Warm air inverted over cold allows updrafts to form. That breeds turbulence and cumulus (accumulated) clouds. Lumpy and round, fair-weather cumulus clouds usually chill out at 25,000 feet or less.

Cold Front

When a wedge of arctic or polar air snowplows into a warmer region, it creates intense activity along the "front" where the two air masses meet. Warm, moist air is sprayed aloft by the intrusion of the cold. Warm air cools into thunderheads that pile up to and beyond 50,000 feet. "Line squalls," miniature whirlpools around local depressions, run up to 150 miles ahead of the cold front. A typical front will move at about 15 knots; some sweep in at up to 50 knots. As a squall line approaches, estimate its forward speed and add 20 knots; that's a good guess at the strength of its most powerful gusts.

Christopher Columbus

By his fourth voyage to the New World, the "Admiral of the Ocean Seas" knew about hurricanes. He had not only witnessed one while ashore on Santo Domingo, he'd ridden one out at sea. Thus, noting "an oily swell with light, shifting winds from the southeast," he asked for permission from the governor of Santo Domingo to put into port to shelter his ships. The governor, however, mocked Columbus's "fantastical prophecy" and not only refused sanctuary but sent his own fleet, 20 ships strong, to sea. Columbus found shelter in the mouth of the Jaina River; the Spanish squadron met the hurricane and 19 ships sank.

Among Columbus's other "discoveries" was St. Elmo's fire. He was the first European to record the eerie glow of static-charged rigging into the moist sea air. Relieved to have survived it, he named it for the third-century Italian Bishop whom he and his men took as their patron saint.

Says square-rigger master Alan Villiers, "I value Columbus most for his discovery of the Atlantic circulation of wind and water (from east to west across the bottom of the basin and from west to east across the top) that enabled centuries of regular sailings between the Old and New Worlds."

Continental Air Mass

Formed over land (or "continents"), these chunks of air, like all others, are given personality by where they come from. Continental polar and arctic masses are both colder and drier than their maritime cousins. Continental tropical air masses are a

---

Use these natural weathervanes to help you see the wind.

—*Lyall Watson,* Heaven's Breath

rarity in the North American mix because there is more water than land to our south. Dry and searing off the highlands of central Mexico, though, a "continental tropical" blast occasionally hits America's heartland.

Contrails
These artificial cirrus clouds formed by condensation of exhaust gases from high-flying airplanes are significant. They disappear rapidly into dry upper air, but if the upper air is moist, the vapor trails linger. They may be shredded by crosswinds or fluffed and thickened by a breeze that runs parallel to them. They thus make good tell-tales for the upper air.

Convection Cell
Hot air rises. This accounts for much of the circulation in earth's atmosphere; hot air rises and cooler air is drawn to replace it. This is how the sea breeze works—and the monsoon. Astronomer Edmund Halley, best known for his comet, was among the first to realize (1686) that trade winds flow to replace hot air rising above the equator. In 1735, English lawyer/scientist George Hadley wrote that hot air rising at the equator must be fed by colder polar air and argued that the process was part of a "linked chain of convection cells," an accurate model of global weather as we've come to understand it.

Coriolis Effect
In 1835, French theoretical physicist Gaspard Coriolis put forward the proposition that the swirling motion of storms was due to the earth's rotation. He was right. One of the true pioneers in exploring planetary rotation came even earlier. German Joseph Furtzenbach fired a cannon vertically in 1627 and then sat on the muzzle to prove that the projectile would not fall where it had been launched (because the earth would rotate out from under it). He survived.

Air moving from point to point on the globe moves *above* the earth's surface. It moves in a straight line but appears to "bend to the right" (in the Northern Hemisphere) because the earth is moving beneath it. Thus, wind blowing from north to south seems to move west due to the earth's rotation. This is the "effect" described by Coriolis. (Winds in the Southern Hemisphere appear to bend to the left.)

Cyclone
From the Greek *kykloesis*, meaning "to circle around," a cyclone is an area of deep low pressure around which winds converge in a counterclockwise direction. Tornadoes and waterspouts obey the same rules. In the Southern Hemisphere, rotation around a low is clockwise.

D-Day Weather
(Samuel Eliot Morison)
When the Nazis withdrew from the *Schatzgraber* weather station on Greenland at the beginning of June in 1944, they hoped submarine meteorological reports would keep them posted on the flow of weather across the North Atlantic, but when a storm hit the Normandy coast on June 4, no submarines were in position. Feldmarschal Erwin Rommel, commandant of the Fortress Europa garrison, felt certain that no invasion could be mounted due to the storm, so he went home to Germany.

From his headquarters in England, General Dwight Eisenhower postponed the invasion of Normandy, scheduled for June 5, because of high winds and breaking waves off the French coast. Tidal conditions would not be favorable again for another two weeks. Keeping the huge invasion secret for that long loomed nearly impossible. June 6, then, seemed the last good chance for success.

Rain whipped around Allied headquarters on the morning of June 5 as Ike and his staff held their final weather conference. Group Captain J. M. Stagg, RAF, the head weather officer, reported a cell of high pressure embedded in the storm. "The worst is over. It will moderate for the next two days," he predicted. On that assurance the largest amphibious action in history was set in motion.

—adapted from
The History of United States Naval
Operations in World War II

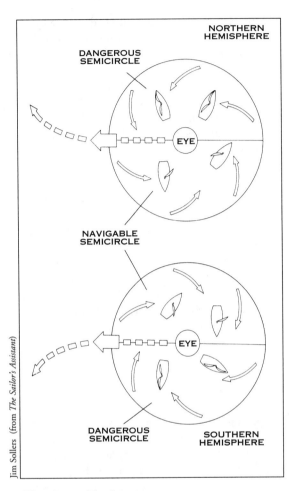

Hurricane Tactics

Dangerous Semicircle   Facing an approaching hurricane at sea, maneuver if you can to keep it to port. That puts you to the left of the storm's track and in the "navigable" semicircle, where the forward motion of the storm and its cyclonic winds to some extent cancel one another's force. In the dangerous semicircle—on the right side of the storm's track—the forward speed of the storm and the counterclockwise whirl of its winds combine. The winds in the dangerous quadrant will also tend to shove you into the path of the storm. [Because cyclones in the Southern Hemisphere rotate clockwise, the dangerous semicircle there is to *left* of the storms' track.—eds.]

Leicester was now in the right front quadrant of the cyclone. As the centre drew closer, the maelstrom of revolving wind steadily changed direction, coming ever more southerly. The helmsman fought to keep the furious wind just on the starboard bow, but the wind was veering far more rapidly than the towering seas could alter the direction of their march; as a result the ship was often broadside to their assault. Her motion was becoming wilder and wilder. Shuddering and creaking, she rolled, pitched, and yawed at one in the same time. There was no question of moving about outside—the decks were being continuously swept as great seas boarded her and churned themselves to foam against her hatch coamings and deck gear.

—*Farley Mowat,* The Serpent's Coil

Daniel Defoe   Author of *Robinson Crusoe*, the first novel written in English, Defoe was also a weather pioneer. He made the first written mention of a storm's travel. When a violent storm hit Great Britain in November of 1703, he was able to link it to a storm that lashed New England a few days earlier.

Dew Point   The temperature at which air becomes saturated and the water in it condenses.

The Doctor   A robust sea breeze off the Indian Ocean, it brings relief from the 100° days of west Australian summer.

Dew almost always predicts a southerly wind, but if the decks have been dry, expect a northerly through the day.

—*L. Francis Herreshoff*

Doldrums   From the old English *dol* for "dull," this band of flat calms and frequent squalls circles the earth near the equator between the northeast and the southeast trades. Generations of sailors have dreaded the doldrums. Beyond all storms and ice and wrack, they were "hell" to Coleridge's ancient mariner. The unflappable Francis Chichester wrote: "Calms were the very devil. Sometimes it could feel quite creepy as I sat or lay alone in the cabin. The little noises seemed to be in a deathly silence in vast space, the bulkhead at my shoulder creaking."

A more recent circumnavigator reports, however, "They can frequently be crossed in a day or two. [The band can be anywhere from 15 to 150 miles across—eds.] Pilot charts give some indication of the best longitude for crossing the various doldrums belts, but since conditions vary so much from year to year, the charts are wrong as often as they are right. Still, none of our friends, even without engine, has taken longer than a week to cross the worst stretches."

> *Do business with men when the wind is in the northwest.*
>
> *—Ben Franklin*

Dry Easterly

We were ready to leave when the wind swung right round; after a rainy spell, the westerlies that had brought us into the Baltic from Norway shifted 180 degrees. "Skoal!" toasted a Finnish friend. "You have luck! A dry easterly . . . the only good thing to come out of Russia."

—Carleton Mitchell, The Wind's Call

Earth's Aura   Aristotle conceived of the interplay of "auras"— "breaths or emanations given off by earth, moon, and sun"—as fueling the winds and controlling earthly weather. Today solar flares plume the surface of the sun, blacking out shortwave communications on earth; showers of ionized particles bombard the atmosphere causing, among other things, aurora borealis; and magnetic fields and thermal barriers deflect the charged particles. Auras?

Earth's Axis   Earth tilts at 23½ degrees relative to the plane of its orbit around the Sun. This creates irregular amounts of solar radiation and thus our seasons. The axis is pointed at Polaris. That makes Polaris the "unmoving" North Star in an otherwise revolving heavens. The axis of the planet "wobbles," though (on a 22,000-year cycle), and its tilt varies between 22 and 24 degrees (over 41,000 years).

Elephanta   A severe southerly gale on the Malabar coast of India.

El Niño   Every year a south-flowing warmer current intrudes upon the normal flow of the cool Humboldt Current to the fishing grounds off Peru. The equatorial waters usually arrive around Christmas and depart near Easter. The Peruvians call the seasonal current "El Niño" after "the child" (Christ child). That name has since been extended to the century's most destructive weather event. Every few years ocean warming extends beyond the South American Coast into the Pacific Basin and over a quarter of the way around the world. This larger "El Niño" (officially labeled the Southern Oscillation) was responsible for major disruptions from Australia to South Africa and India in 1972 and again in 1982. It saw trade winds reverse direction, monsoons fail, populations of birds and livestock die, and thousands starve. Unseasonable or "freak" floods, storms, and droughts caused property damages upwards of $7 billion. El Niño underlines the delicacy of earth's climate balance and emphasizes the interdependence of natural elements. So far it gives few clues about where it comes from or when it will appear again.

Evaporation   The process by which a liquid becomes a gas (or "vapor") involves the infusion of seven times the heat necessary to raise the liquid to the boiling point. This "latent heat of vaporization" is then given off when the vapor condenses again into liquid. One trillion tons of water per day enter the atmosphere by means of evaporation.

Eye Wall   The towering ring of cumulonimbus cloud that surrounds the eye, or center, of a tropical cyclone. Great stores of heat energy trapped in these mountains of vapor supply much of the storm's power.

Fetch   The distance wind travels over open water (or clear space) before it reaches you. Fetch affects wave height greatly and wind force slightly.

Robert Fitzroy   Master of HMS *Beagle* during the epic cruise that spawned Darwin's theory of evolution, Fitzroy was later made governor of New Zealand, then returned to the Admiralty and was given the sinecure of "Chief of Weather Researches."

Instead of fading quietly into administrative obscurity, he used his post to develop the first weather-forecasting system. Gathering meteoro-

logic observations from around Europe and the British Isles by telegraph, he published digests, which he had the nerve to call "forecasts," through Lloyd's of London and in daily newspapers. Despite listing "47 principles of weather prediction" in the widely read *Weather Book* he authored in 1862, he was roundly criticized by London's Royal Society for proceeding without sufficient scientific data.

The forecast service was canceled (at the insistence of the Society) upon his death in 1865. An outcry from sailors, farmers, and the citizens of London succeeded, however, in restoring it a year later. To many, Admiral Robert Fitzroy is the father of forecasting.

Fog   Fog comes not only on petite feline feet but in different varieties. You'll see it more in some places than others, but it is always a question of condensation. Whether it's warm air flowing over cool water, cool air over warm water, moisture "dropping in," or radiational cooling, when airborne vapor condenses into a "surface cloud," you've got fog. When an air mass reaches the *dew point*, droplets form into a mist. You can predict the dew point with a wet-dry-bulb thermometer. When air temperature is within two or three degrees of the dew point, fog is imminent.

Sightings through fog magnify distance off, and because it slows and bends sound, fog also plays tricks with your ears. A British Admiralty study once determined that when the atmosphere went from 71 to 77 percent humidity, a fog horn decreased in range by 2 miles.

Fohn   From *fon*, which is Gothic for "fire." See "Chinook."

Frankenstein   The summer of 1816 ("the year without a summer") was so dismal and drizzly that Lord Byron and his houseguests (he had left his wife and rented a villa in "sunny" Italy) could hardly go outdoors. They resorted to writing stories to amuse one another. Mary Shelley began her famous novel about the creation of a monster then, on a dare from her host.

Ben Franklin   Best-known for his clever stove and down-to-earth almanac, he was also interested in the weather. By flying his kite in a thunderstorm, he proved the presence of electricity in lightning. Reporting on storms, he derived their courses and successfully predicted them. He "discovered" the Gulf Stream in 1769. He was correct in thinking that volcanic dust and ash in the atmosphere could chill local weather. He discovered the pattern of wind shifts attending the passage of cold fronts.

"Some people are weatherwise, some are otherwise," he said.

Friction Slants   Sailing into a lee, expect the breeze to back (against the clock) as it drops. This is because wind speed is related to surface friction. The more wind is slowed by the surface, the more it seems to bend toward the center of low pressure. Wind over land is slowed by half; wind over (the smoother) water is slowed only a third.

Gaia   "Mother Earth" to the ancient Greeks and the name chosen by English naturalist James Lovelock to describe earth as a "living thing" with atmosphere "like the fur on a fox," which the planet controls for its own protection.

Galileo Galilei   A Renaissance physicist and astronomer, Galileo helped replace Aristotelian "metaphysics" with experiment and observation. He was the first to see that the period of a pendulum is a constant; he employed the newly invented telescope to discover the Milky Way and Saturn's moons. He accurately estimated the size of the mountains on our own moon using their shadows. He also invented a "thermoscope" to reveal temperature change. He proved that air has weight and that a vacuum can exist in nature. His assistant, Evangelista Torricelli, developed the first barometer three years after the master's death in 1641.

GARP   Administered through the United Nations' 145-member World Meteorological Organization, the Global Atmospheric Research Programme (GARP) was the most ambitious effort to date to study world weather. Experiments came first in 1974 off Japan and West Africa. The larger *Global Weather Experiment* of 1978 followed, an attempt to understand the entire world's weather throughout a single day. Global collaboration has shifted now to a focus on long-term climate changes and prediction, but intense scrutiny of the world according to GARP has made today's daily weathermen wiser.

Geomagnetic Field   Generated by the slow rotation of the planet's solid inner core with respect to its liquid outer core, the earth's magnetism protects the globe from infusions of solar wind and has been the key to maritime navigation for centuries. Observed to be growing weaker, it may not last another 3,000 years.

Geostrophic Wind   Air flowing out of high pressure to fill low pressure creates wind. The Coriolis effect makes the wind bend. Instead of following the "fall line" from high to low, wind blows perpendicular to it—along isobar contours instead of across them. This "earth-turned" wind is called *geostrophic*.

Good Night Moon   Remember the bedtime story that goes: "Good night cup. Good night spoon. Good night chair. Good night moon." That punch line takes on new poignancy when you learn that the earth and its moon are diverging by 2 inches per year. "Good-bye moon!"

Gradient Wind   A wind more than 2,000 feet above the surface of the earth is a *gradient wind*. At this level, wind speed is the result of the pressure gradient (the slope from high to low pressure) alone. The term is often used to identify a large-scale system of airflow inside which local winds form.

Green Flash   The startlingly bright, elusive, and momentary burst of green light (lasting from ½ to 10 seconds) seen by some initiates when the upper limb of the sun dips the horizon at sunset. Jules Verne wrote a science fiction novel called *Le Rayon Vert*, popularizing the phenomenon, but even then a number of skeptics put sightings to eye fatigue or imagination. However, clear air lets you look to the horizon. There refraction of the sun's rays into the slim green band of the spectrum produces a flash that is (they say) not only real, but an accurate harbinger of fine weather.

Greenhouse Effect   The relatively short-wave energy from the sun passes through earth's atmosphere with little problem, but the longer-wave energy "exhausted" by earth has great trouble penetrating carbon dioxide and water vapor to abandon the planet. The result is a one-way "greenhouse" that keeps the heat lid on.

Gregale   The "Greek wind," a cold northeaster that sweeps over the Central Mediterranean from the Balkans.

Groundhog Day   February 2 was originally *Candlemas* in the calendar of Christian feasts. Set to mark the Christ-child's presentation at temple, it was observed by a parade of candles in honor of Simeon's prophecy that Jesus had come "as a light unto the Gentiles." This "day of prophecy" became, itself, prophetic:

Somehow in the minds of Pennsylvania Germans, the rustlings of hibernating rodents were added to the predictive mix. Had not seven citizens of Punxsutawney, Pennsylvania formed a club in 1898 to drink beer and eat groundhog every February 2, that tradition might have stayed underground. Today, although "Punxsutawney Phil" proves right only one time in three, he and his shadow have a worldwide following.

Gulf Stream   Seeming to originate in the Gulf of Mexico, this most famous of ocean currents actually makes up just outside the Gulf, where remnants of west-running (across the trade-wind belt) and north-flowing (up the coast of South America) streams combine. The Gulf Stream then becomes the western and northern sides of a current "whorl" that spins clockwise across the Atlantic Basin.

Deep blue and as much as 10°F warmer than the waters it traverses, the Gulf Stream has been called a "river in the ocean." It trends northward from the Florida Straits past Hatteras and just south of the Grand Banks. There it brushes the much-colder south-flowing Labrador Current (making the Banks the foggiest place in the New World) before continuing transatlantic (now known to oceanographers as the North Atlantic Current) to split and warm the British Isles and Norway with its northern arm, the Mediterranean approaches and the Canaries with its southern branch.

The Gulf Stream is really less a river than a giant cable. Small filaments of hot and cooler water splice together to form its axis. Near its edges, eddies spin off and meander. These circles surround both hot and cold centers and can spin in either direction. They can be as much as 50 miles in diameter and make crossing the Stream a navigational challenge. Its weather significance includes warming the coasts of northern Europe and "feeding" rejuvenating warm water to hurricanes.

Thor Heyerdahl   Having drifted the Pacific on the balsa raft *Kon-Tiki* and sailed from Egypt to the New World on the papyrus-reed boat *Ra,* explorer anthropologist Heyerdahl knows something of the old days. "Man hoisted sail long before he tamed the horse; he navigated the seas long before he set wheels to the road," he says.

High Pressure   Under high pressure the atmosphere is squeezed dry, systemic breezes are stirred up, and you can see tomorrow. Low tide is lower when the pressure is high.

Hollow Winds   "Hollow winds presage a storm." Makes sense! In clear, dry weather, sound travels unimpeded. Under moisture or clouds, sound "bounces back" from a low ceiling, causing an echo—or "hollow"sound.

Horse Latitudes   Similar to the doldrums, these bands of calm are on the *poleward side* of the trade-wind belts. Though the weather is generally fine, weak pressure gradients mean little air circulation. Are they called "horse" latitudes because, as Lemar Reiter *(Jet Streams)* suggests, "the winds are fickle as an old mare"; because, as Captain Alan Villiers *(Wild Ocean)* observes, "there the ocean is stagnant, panting quietly like a heat-tormented beast"; or perhaps, as tradition has it, because mariners were forced to share the same sea with dead livestock they dumped overboard. The conquistadors, bound for the adventure of the New World, sometimes had instead to dine on their steeds in these waters.

The World's Prevailing Winds

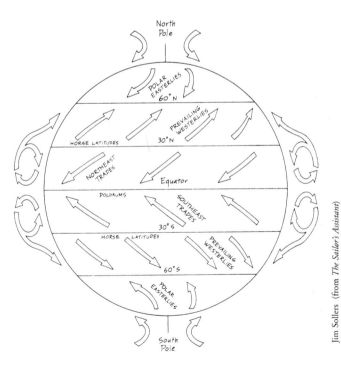

Jim Sollers (from *The Sailor's Assistant*)

Luke Howard   An English chemist and Quaker, he devised the first classification of clouds in 1803. His training in classical science explains their Latin names (see "Clouds").

Hurricane   The Spanish *huracán*, or "evil wind," came from the Mayan storm-god Hunrakan. Hurricanes, like typhoons in the Pacific, "Bengal cyclones" in the Indian Ocean, and "Willy Willies" off Australia, are tropical cyclones—inward-whirling wind systems around centers of extreme low pressure. It's a hurricane once the winds top 64 mph, and they have been clocked at 210 mph. Wind force, of course, varies with the *square* of velocity! The pressure typically sinks to 28 inches or below; the lowest barometer reading ever recorded was 26.18 at the center of a typhoon in 1926.

The average 'cane has a life span of nine days. Year-in and year-out, hurricanes annually do an average of $50 million worth of damage in the United States. They contain 100 times the energy of the average thunderstorm. It would take 13 Nagasaki-vintage A-bombs to equal the

Hurricane paths.

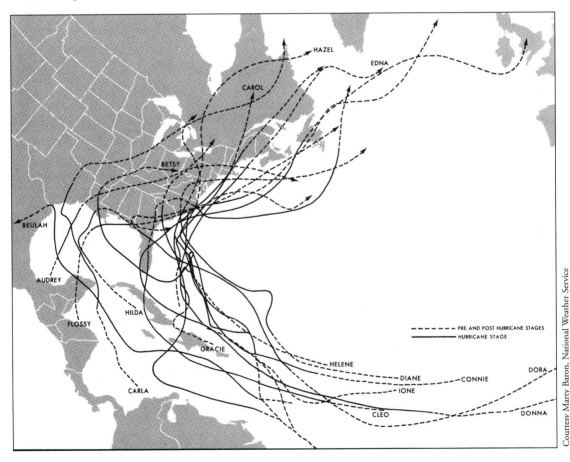

PRE AND POST HURRICANE STAGES
HURRICANE STAGE

Courtesy Marty Baron, National Weather Service

power of a small hurricane. They can drop a foot of rain in an hour, so even after they cross over land they can cause serious floods.

Hurricanes average about 130 miles from edge to eye, making the normal-size storm about 300 miles in diameter. The eye might measure 12 to 15 miles across. Hurricanes often blanket 10,000 square miles. They are fueled by heat and need water temperatures of 80°F or better to breed. They also must have a constant supply of water; they don't often last long over land.

Hurricanes form in the lower portion of the trade-wind belts, just poleward of the equatorial zone(s), and move along the trades. "Breeding" season in the Northern Hemisphere is between the beginning of June and the end of November, but rogues have appeared before and after those dates.

What makes a hurricane isn't clear, but they seem to be triggered by troughs of low pressure embedded in the trade-wind flow. If a low slows enough, it can become enveloped; isobars close around it, turning the trough into a cell. Winds begin to eddy around the center and a chain of cyclonic phenomena starts up. If the air at the center is relatively cool, the cell may stay a mere storm. If it is warm enough, though, it grows into a hurricane. Warm water starts the updraft that sucks in moist air that fuels the convection cycle that builds to megastorm proportions.

'Canes give off warnings. If you were a seaman, like Horatio Hornblower, of the Napoleonic era, you might feel them in your bones: "He felt restless and disturbed. There was something heavy in the breathing of the air and something unusual about the swell. A gale before morning, he decided." (*Admiral Hornblower in the West Indies*, C. S. Forester.)

If you are the master of a modern container ship, like Capt. Paul Washburn, you might still say, "When you get close to a big storm you can feel it. For some reason the ship takes on almost a palpable uncertainty. It's hard to define. It's just a tiny little different motion, a little hesitancy, a little tremble from time to time." (*Looking for a Ship*, John McPhee.)

Low pressure at the center of a tropical cyclone lifts seawater (about a foot of rise for every inch the barometer drops). This lengthens the period of swells, making waves that radiate out from the center bigger and slower than normal. Suction at the center of a hurricane pulls air in, and that creates a signature trail of cirrus at upper altitudes, a thickening "tracer" moving across the upper sky toward the storm center. Lower in the sky, tell-tale blood-red and green streaks will appear if the storm is between you and the sun. Especially in the trades a hurricane may cause wind to blow from an unusual or abnormal direction. A falling barometer is also a good indicator, but most often the glass won't fall to alarming depths until the storm is actually there.

In the tropics, storm speed is normally about 10 knots. Typically hurricanes approach the lower US from the Caribbean, curve northward, then recurve into the northeast and out to sea. The jet stream and blocking high-pressure ridges over the continent have a lot to do with

I cannot imagine anyone looking at the sky and denying God.

—*Abraham Lincoln*

determining these tracks. Sometimes storms enter the Gulf of Mexico or come ashore in Florida.

One of the strangest things about hurricanes is their eyes. Oases of clear air with relatively calm winds and puffy-clouded blue skies overhead, these "navels" are surrounded by doomsday coils of towering black cloud and shrieking winds. Typically, northerlies or easterlies attend the storm's arrival; the eye will pass, providing a lull of not even an hour; then winds set in again from the opposite direction—generally the west or southwest.

If clouds all look scratched by a hen,

Stand by to take your topsails in.

—traditional rhyme

Hurricane Flower   A close relative of ginger, this edible root supports a pale white flower wherever it grows throughout the Pacific. During hurricane season, though, its blossom turns crimson.

Hurricane Frequency   Hurricanes strike or closely approach regions of the eastern United States on the average of 10 per year. In the northern Pacific, typhoons form at a rate of about 20 per year.

Hurricane Modification   The most famous effort to tame hurricanes began in 1962. Project Stormfury sought to seed the eye wall of a storm with crystals of silver iodide. The mechanics of storm-busting need refining, but the biggest stumbling block for Project Stormfury proved liability: once you alter a storm, aren't you responsible for what it does?

Hurricane Names   Early in the history of the New World, survivors called hurricanes by the name of the feast day closest to when it struck. The St. James Day Storm of July 25 on Antigua became the St. Anne's Day Hurricane when it struck Puerto Rico on July 26, etc. In the more secular world, storms became attached to the places where they struck (à la the Johnstown Flood). The storm that devastated New England in 1938 is still known as the hurricane of '38. Hurricanes weren't given women's names until just prior to World War II. At that time (1941) George Stewart's best-selling novel *Storm* centered around hurricane fighters in the Miami office of the US Weather Bureau whose private joke was naming storms for their girlfriends. It only took until 1953 for the Bureau to make the practice official and christen a string of beauties like *Carol, Donna, Camille, Hazel,* et al. Sexism was addressed in 1979 and storm names now include both genders.

In Nature's infinite book of secrecy a little I can read.

—Shakespeare

In the Hurricane's Wake   *(Peter Matthiessen)* Sea birds are aloft again, a tattered few. The white terns look dirtied in the somber light, and they fly stiffly, feeling out an element they no longer trust. Unable to locate the storm-lost minnows, they wander the thick waters with sad, muted cries. In the hurricane's wake the labyrinthine coast where the Everglades deltas meet the Gulf of Mexico lies broken, stunned, flattened to mud by the wild tread of God. Day after day a gray and brooding wind nags the mangroves, hurrying the unruly tides, leaving behind brown spume and matted salt grass, driftwood. On the bay shores and down the coastal rivers a far gray sun picks up dead glints from windrows of rotted mullet heaped a foot high.

—*adapted from* Killing Mr. Watson

Ice Age Winds
Sediments from deep ocean beds reveal that winds in glacial times were stronger than they are now. For millennia easterlies have been carrying red sand from the Sahara out to sea. The layers of sand can be dated; those farthest to sea are the oldest. The Ice Age atmosphere was probably fueled by greater temperature differences than those we have now.

Ice Caps
It is only in the past 2 million years that the planet has had two permanent ice caps. Today they hold 3 percent of the planet's water and cover 7 percent of its area.

Ice Sheets
Study of the oxygen composition of cores taken from deep ice sheets and of the effects of ice upon our geological world suggest that "Ice Ages" have been more frequent and more severe than previously thought.

Islamic Weather Science
The fall of the Roman Empire (completed in 476 A.D.) was followed by a millennium of church-dominated orthodoxy now known as the Dark Ages. In Europe, scientific observation in general and weather science in particular stood still or stepped backward. During this same time (beginning with the death of Mohammed in 632 A.D.), Islam spread to much of the Mediterranean basin and beyond. Somewhat ironically, much of the classical thought "rediscovered" in the time of the Renaissance was in fact preserved and handed on, along with some significant discoveries of their own, by Muslim scholars.

Isobars
Isobars are lines on a weather map that connect areas of equal barometric pressure. They help create a sort of "contour map" of the weather. The closer together they are, the steeper the grade between high and low pressure, thus the stronger the wind.

Isotachs
Lines connecting points experiencing equal wind speed.

In quietness the universe can be observed, the inner moods felt, and real truth obtained.

—*Yeh Ming-Te, 1156 A.D.*

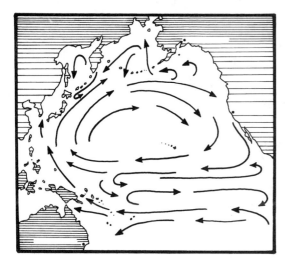

Japan Current

Japan Current

The "Gulf Stream of the Pacific", this "black stream" (called *Kuroshio* in Japan) brings equatorial waters north to warm the southern Japanese islands. Further north it encounters the colder, west-running *Oyashio* Current and stirs up fog over northern Japan. Spinning across the Pacific and past the Hawaiian Islands, it broadens and slows but retains warmth enough to mist the Aleutian Islands before fueling the California Current along the west coast of North America. Near Baja California the stream joins the North Equatorial Current and heads westward to the Orient and ultimately completes its circle off Japan.

Thomas Jefferson

Thomas Jefferson had a number of interests, high among them the weather. After he installed a weathervane on the cupola of his library at Monticello, he connected the vane via a long rod to an indoor "repeater" in his study.

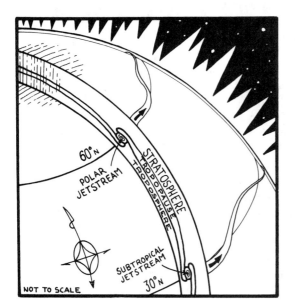

Jet Stream

Jet Stream

A jet stream is a river of fast-moving air, like a stream shot from a nozzle, that circles the planet at high altitudes. Many upper-level jets have been charted, but the one that affects North American weather (*the* jet stream) surges west to east. It marks the southern boundary between polar air and the warm air to its southward. Jammed between the troposphere and the tropopause (between 5 and 10 miles above the earth), squeezed between air masses, and fueled by big temperature and pressure differentials, the stream moves fast—more than 300 mph. It herds highs and channels lows: the jet goes inland of the Himalayas and moist monsoons burst onto the Indian subcontinent; it bends down to the mid-Atlantic and hurricanes recurve out to sea.

Kamikaze

Kamikaze is Japanese for "divine wind." To most Westerners, the word identifies the "do and die" efforts of one-flight aviators who hoped their *hari-kari* would save Hirohito's Empire. *Kamikaze*, however, first referred to the miraculous storm that sank 700 of the 1,000 ships in the Mongol invasion fleet of 1274 A.D.

A second *kamikaze* came close to saving Japan during World War II. On December 17, 1944, Admiral Bull Halsey's Third Fleet of the US Navy was engaged in mid-ocean refueling and became trapped by a powerful typhoon. The damages—three destroyers sunk, nine ships crippled, 200 planes destroyed, and 800 men killed—qualify the storm as "one of the worst disasters in US naval history."

During the first Allied bombing raids of World War II, divine winds seemed still to be protecting Japan: at high altitude, aviators encountered mysterious tailwinds of up to 200 mph that sped them and their bombs harmlessly past their targets. This was the first we knew of the jet stream.

Lenticular Clouds
Ice-crystal clouds like cirrus cast no shadow and, because you can see through them, are called "lenticular."

Libecchio
Milton mentioned this perky sou'wester in *Paradise Lost.* It kicks up a chop on the Bay of Naples and momentarily relieves the summertime swelter of southern Italy.

Lightning
Separation of electric charge within a cloud begins when raindrops are whipped into smaller droplets by updrafts. Electrical potential increases as the top droplets (positive particles) and bottom ones (negative particles) are blown apart. Flashes from positive to negative occur within the cloud or among neighboring clouds. Ground strokes come when a negative jolt from the base of the cloud is attracted by a stream of positively charged ions from the ground. Tall and pointed objects like trees and steeples tend to concentrate and "give off" positive ions. So does a mast. You might sit at sea for 100 years and never be hit, but having a good grounding system (see Chapter 10, "Be Safe") adds peace of mind to statistical comfort.

Thunder comes from the expansion and contraction of the air that a lightning bolt passes through. Count the seconds from when you see the flash until you hear the thunderclap, then divide by five to find how far away in miles the flash was.

Little Ice Age
Beginning almost 500 years ago, Europe and North America began to experience markedly colder weather. Greenland, once verdant and a magnet for Viking colonization, was abandoned. The last graves there were less than a third as deep as the earliest because the permafrost had grown that much closer to the surface. Polar bears were seen in the Faroe Islands. The River Thames froze six times as often as ever before. The "Great Snow" of 1717 buried New England. Long Island Sound froze across. Records of wine harvests, ships' logs, patterns of tree rings, and layers of sediment all confirm the cooling.

There was gradual warming beginning in the mid 1800s, but not until 1850, when several Alpine glaciers began receding, was the "ice age" over. Best guesses about the cause of the cold include irregular sunspot activity. Between 1645 and 1715, at the heart of the deep freeze, no sunspots were observed.

Local Wind
When the pressure gradient is strong, it creates a gradient wind—a howling northeaster, for instance. When the gradient is weak, i.e., high and low pressure centers are either far apart on the planet or close together in pressure, it allows local winds to develop. The classic "local" is the sea breeze.

Local topography also affects local wind. The height, shape, and attitude of land affects the air passing over it. A valley between hills will increase wind speed through it but diminish a wind across it. Mountains and high islands create a wind shadow seven times their height, and eddying turbulence—analogous to the backwind off a sail— trails well to leeward of terrain that breaks the wind flow. If slopes are smooth and angled to accelerate wind flow, however, they can foster downdrafts, or *williwaws*, that come down off their heights into what would appear to be a protected lee. On the other hand, a steep windward shore can "bounce" an onshore wind, leaving a pocket of calm along what ordinarily would be a lee shore.

Local winds give rise to "local knowledge," but the laws the wind obeys are universal.

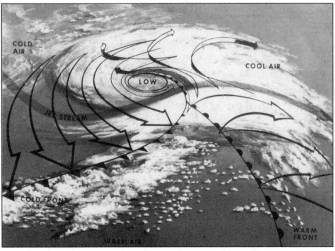

Courtesy Marty Baron, National Weather Service

Low Pressure. In the scenario shown here, a cold polar air mass moves southeastward over North America, preceded by a cold front, ahead of which a warm front forms as a wave in the isobars. A low pressure cell forms at the peak of the wave. As the fast-moving cold front overtakes the warm front, it forces warm air aloft, and thunderstorms develop.

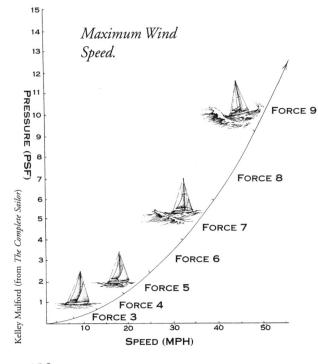

Maximum Wind Speed.

Kelley Mulford (from *The Complete Sailor*)

Low Pressure
Depressions increase cloud and wind as they suck air in.

Fingers of cirrus wisping across the eastern sky (mare's tails) mean wind is whipping moisture from the top of a storm. High-level globules of cloud ranged in lines (mackerel sky) mean the air mass is losing stability. Take in your topsails.

Maraamu
The fresh southerly that occasionally displaces the trades in the vicinity of Tahiti and the Society Islands.

Maritime Air Masses
Just as an easterly comes out of the east, a maritime air mass originates over water. North American weather includes polar maritime and tropical maritime air masses.

Matthew Maury
Kept from sea duty because of a leg injury, Lt. Maury took charge of the US Navy's Depot of Charts and Instruments. From a broom-closet office with a staff of one, he compiled America's first pilot chart. He divided the North Atlantic into sectors, collated log reports and historical sources, and collected observations to determine prevailing wind speeds and directions for each sector during each month of the year. His information is still used today. He wrote, "There is a river in the ocean; in the severest droughts it never fails, and in the mightiest floods it never overflows. . . . It is the Gulf Stream."

Maximum Wind Speed
The greatest recorded gust (outside of a tornado) was April 12, 1934, atop Mt. Washington (New England's tallest mountain): 371 kilometers per hour (or 222 mph).

Meltemi   Out of a clear sky it whips the Aegean to a froth. Down from the north it can screech for days. The wind is called *meltemi*—evil-tempered. Move at first light when it's not around if you want to cross wine-dark seas; meltemi blows hard enough by breakfast to ruin your whole day.

Meteorologica   One of the first weather texts, written by Aristotle circa 350 B.C. (See "Aristotle.")

Middle Cloud Deck   The layer from 6,500 to 20,000 feet, the "middle deck" is the most useful of the three cloud decks in forecasting. It tends to be "where the action is." Altostratus says the atmosphere is stratified by temperature, colder over warmer, and thus is "stable." Altocumulus indicates vertical air currents, which suggest mixing and instability.

Mistral   This dry, cantankerous northwester shoots down year-round over Provence, Corsica, and Sardinia from the Rhone Valley, though less frequently in summer. Strabo complained that it "strips men of their clothes and weapons." Today it is said to knock down chimneys and overturn railroad cars. Whole villages in its path are filled with houses with no windows in their *mistral*-facing walls.

Monsoon   The largest sea breeze on the planet. *Monsoon* means "seasonal," and the system splits the year just about in half. During six months it blows cold from the Himalayas. High pressure and fine, dry weather are the norm over most of the Indian subcontinent. Then, in summer (about the middle of June), low pressure moves in, the wind changes, sometimes 180 degrees within an hour, and the breeze comes warm, moist, and laden with rain off the Arabian Sea. The summer breeze is a lot like a daily sea breeze. The temperature difference between the land and the sea provides convection to pump warm, moist air ashore. Clouds of moisture climb the slopes of the Ghat Mountains and the precipitation starts.

This seasonal weather trick has profound effects. It reverses, for instance, the current gyre that governs the circulation of the Indian Ocean. It brings rainfall amounts that measure over 30 feet in places. Without it, Indian agriculture would shrivel. When the monsoon was late by three weeks in 1972, the national harvest was reduced by a third.

National Oceanic and Atmospheric Administration
NOAA is Uncle Sam's weatherman.

Natural Forecasters   Legend has it that as he strolled the pasture, Sir Isaac Newton came upon a shepherd. "Nice evening," remarked the Father of Modern Science.

Mackerel sky and mare's tails

Make tall ships carry low sails.

—*sailor's saying*

"Might be, but t'will soon rain," remarked his simple companion.

"Oh?" queried the scientist.

"Sheep there don't turn that way 'less it's going to rain."

Not much later drops fell on the field, Newton, and all.

From the beginning, man has looked to nature's signs for forecasts, and he still does. Sentient mammals like Newton's sheep have good credibility. The wild goats on Mt. Nebo (Oregon) go high in fine weather but stay low when the barometer drops. The cats aboard a British man-of-war in the Persian Gulf forecast a storm 10 hours before it arrived by "going quite mad, rushing about and biting peoples' feet." After dismissing much animal lore as superstition, naturalist Hal Borlund couldn't help but remark how often muskrats dig new holes higher in the bank before an approaching storm. "When the ass begins to bray, there will come a rainy day."

"Worth more than all the barometers in Christendom," remarked renowned composer William Cowper ("Amazing Grace"), especially when linked, as they were at the London Exhibition of 1851, so their combined wrigglings could activate a "storm alarm." He was referring to the lowly leech.

Some snails turn from yellow to blue as rain approaches. The spider, supposedly, spins fine threads for fine weather. Ants march in straight lines to meet the challenge of an approaching storm. Crickets not only chirp the temperature but lengthen chirps with warming weather. Cicadas will cease their song if humidity increases. A rapid pressure drop will bring a butterfly out of its cocoon, sometimes prematurely. Able to circulate with sophisticated navigation gear, bees buzz close to home when the atmosphere might throw their instruments off.

What do they know? All, evidently, know the atmospheric pressure. Fish, too. The cod grovels for bottom gravel; is it "ballasting" for an upcoming blow? The mullet deserts its bank; wind change? The logy loach suddenly starts to fidget;

storm within two hours? Shark liver oil in the glass clouds; storm approaching? (Bear grease clouds as predictively as shark oil in Native American barometers.)

Bird flight was monitored long before millibars. Geese honk low, we understand, because in low pressure airflow that's where the "thickest" air is. Pressure-sensitive bats fly low to clear their ears in falling pressure. Sensitized to sound, even to feeling vibrations through their hollow feather stems, birds can "hear" far-off turbulence. Birds roost rather than battle the unstable air that breeds storms.

All of these reactions tell us things about the weather that we can use and rely on, but animals are sensitive to changes in weather rather than capable of predicting it. The bushy tail on the squirrel tells you about last winter, not the one to come.

Navigable Semicircle
When facing a cyclonic storm in the northern hemisphere (hurricane), keep the eye to your left and you will remain in the navigable semicircle.

Nephology
The science of clouds, from the Greek *nephos,* cloud.

Nimbus
A cloudy radiance surrounding a deity.

Norther
When the smudge pots are out and there's skim ice on your *Hatuey* beer at Sloppy Joe's in Key West, it's a norther. The incursion of arctic or polar air south of Hatteras can bring to the Southland and Islands high pressure, virile winds out of the northern quadrant, and temperatures well below average.

Northern Lights
See "Aurora Borealis."

Occluded Front
When a warm air mass is overtaken by a cold front and the two merge, the result is an occluded ("pinched off") front. The cold air slides in and forces the warm air aloft. Atmospheric instability and big pressure differentials then cause potentially violent frontal activity.

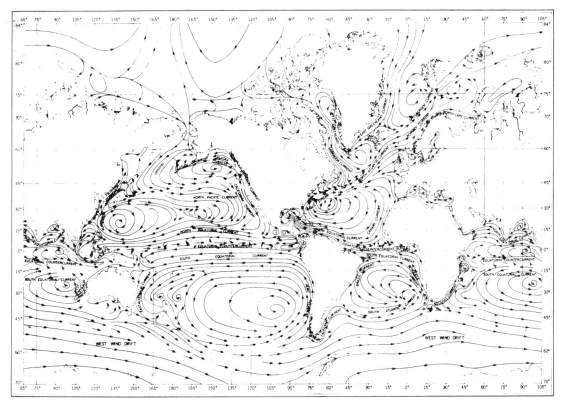

Ocean Currents

Ocean Currents
Pundit Nigel Calder writes, "Ocean currents are important enough to merit half of this book (*The Weather Machine*). They are more important in distributing heat worldwide than anyone yet suspects; they may arise, not from the winds, but from differences in temperature and salinity in the ocean itself; pressure whirlpools or eddies (similar to depressions in the atmosphere) travel for months in the ocean and feed the major currents just the way eddies of air fuel the jet stream."

Ocean Floor
Only one twentieth as old as the dry-land crust, the sea floor is cut by canyons deeper than the Grand Canyon and sends up peaks nearly as tall as Everest.

Ocean Passage Weather (Louis Linden)
Eight times a day on its high-powered stations, the Coast Guard broadcasts weather forecasts prepared by the National Weather Service. Station NMN is in Portsmouth, VA. Its West Coast counterpart is NMC in San Francisco. You can get either offshore (coastwise out to 200 miles) or high-seas forecasts. Both are broadcast four times a day on three of five designated frequencies in the shortwave band.

Your shortwave receiver must cover frequencies from 2 to 30 MHz and copy single-sideband signals. Sets like this begin at about $200. Because radio waves bounce off the ionosphere, the best frequency may change during the day as conditions change, which is why the broadcasts are made on three frequencies at once.

Use the two-minute introductory period of schedule and frequency descriptions that precedes the forecast to select the best frequency. Sector by sector forecasts make up the broadcast. Gulf Stream information is included twice a day. Take notes or record the broadcasts.

The National Weather Service prints charts of the offshore forecast sectors that are very useful. With a clear overlay and grease pencil, you can make your own weather map.

—adapted from "Pennywise Weather"

Ocean Weather Routing

I've raced around the world and "sprinted" to a record from San Francisco to Boston. Weather impacts sailors' enjoyment of our sport whether we're sailing on lakes or across oceans. Our own observations are a necessary beginning, but the bigger our overall picture, the more we can get from them. Aboard Great American *racing the clipper-ship record around Cape Horn to Boston, Rich Wilson and I were in constant touch with weather consultant Bob Rice. Time and again his analysis of our local observations plus the systemic information at his fingertips provided us with an edge.*

—Bill Biwenga

Working with Dodge Morgan, Rice broke Morgan's circumnavigation into 5,000- to 6,000-mile legs, matched the route against the calendar, and issued a round-the-world weather route:

- On the passage south from Newport, the dominant elements are the Azores High, migratory mid-latitude highs and lows, and the possibility of subtropical cyclones in October. There is little to be gained here by any marked deviation from the traditional sailing routes. Cut across the equatorial regions as directly as possible to gain access to the South Atlantic southeasterly trades.

- In November the trades will be easterly with chances of occasional northeast. They should average 10–20 knots but can fall off to less than 10. This is both the most stable leg of the trip and (due to the doldrums) the most frustrating.

- About the latitude of the Cape of Good Hope in the mid-Atlantic is the center of the South Atlantic High. High/low-pressure couples break from it and trend east. Pay particular attention to a graceful transition from these marching waves to the polar westerlies (and polar ice) as you round the Cape of Good Hope.

- Across the Indian Ocean toward Australia, sail eastward on the northern side of 40° S. Frequency of gale force winds is 15–25 percent, but that increases markedly (as does ice danger) if you stray south. Heading at all above 35° S will increase the chance of both tropical cyclones and calms.

- The Pacific High tends to break in two in summer. Rounding New Zealand and heading across the Pacific, gale frequency along the route is 15–30 percent, 25–30 percent approaching Cape Horn. Cloudiness will be dominant. Icebergs will again become a threat after you reach 130° W.

- The Cape Horn passage will be under prevailing winds that continue to reflect the merging of polar low pressure with subtropical high pressure—north to west winds will be dominant. The Falkland current and the West Wind Drift current move icebergs well to the north of the Cape.

- The encountered weather between Cape Horn and Newport is the reciprocal of weather experienced on the outward legs. The return route farther west in the Atlantic, though, will be less susceptible to light and variable wind conditions. Typical conditions will be similar in spring to those in fall.

Later Rice critiqued his plan for *American Promise,* comparing his predictions with what actually happened:

In general it would seem that the study has held up pretty well. However, several conditions are better understood now.

- *The first is the frequency of light air and calms that can be encountered to the south and east of Australia and New Zealand. They come when blocking high-pressure systems make a mockery of the "roaring forties" and last surprisingly long.*

- *The second is the frequency of winds to the east side of north. They are much more prevalent than we would have suspected. A high percentage of cold fronts swing through a wind sequence that backs from the northeast to the northwest as the front passes. As the next front approaches, the wind clocks back through northwest into the northeast. When fronts come close together, the wind is very often northeast.*

- A quick comment on tropical cyclones. Atlantic subtropical cyclones have a low probability in November, but are not an impossibility. Dodge had to skirt Hurricane Kate after he left Bermuda in November.

Oceanic Credo   (*William F. Buckley, Jr.*) The day we arrived after our crossing we learned that a yacht had capsized off Bermuda essentially because she had received no warning of a hurricane. We had a Weatherfax aboard *Sealestial*, but, despite 25 hours of trying, we couldn't make it work. Voice radio and Morse code let us down, too.

Moral? Teddy Tucker's is simple. *Go where you want to go and take your chance with the weather.*

My own position is down the middle. Forget trying to tease out of the weather the sort of information that might prove critical to a racing sailor. Take what comes, but try to make certain that you and a man-eating hurricane are not headed on converging courses.

—*adapted from* Atlantic High

Pampero   Southwesterly squalls that bring moisture and heat relief to the Argentinean *pampas.*

Blaise Pascal   A Renaissance thinker, Pascal had his brother-in-law take a barometer up a mountain while he monitored an identical one on the flat, discovering that barometric pressure changed with altitude. A kilopascal is 100 millibars.

Peru Current   This cold-water stream flows from Antarctica toward the equator along the west coast of South America.

He draweth up the drops of water which distill as rain to the streams. The clouds pour down their moisture and abundant showers fall on mankind. Who can understand how He spreads out the clouds, how He thunders from his pavilion?

Job 36: 27-29

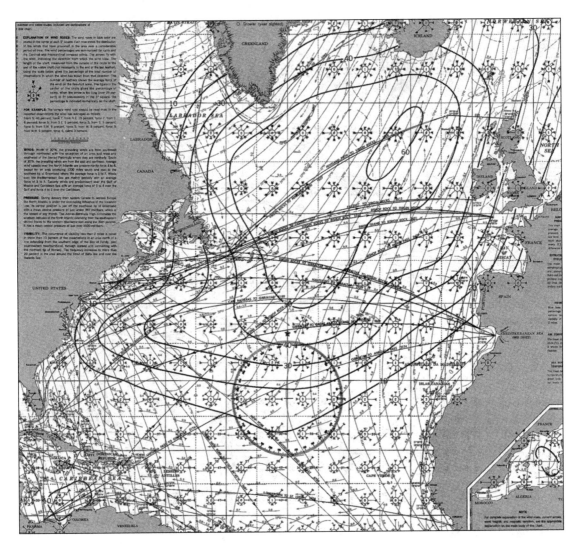

Pilot Charts. This portion of the Defense Mapping Agency's pilot chart for the North Atlantic in the month of June includes shorthand notations for currents, wind speeds and frequencies, ice sightings, and more.

Pilot Charts   For local knowledge, take a pilot; for global knowledge, study a pilot chart. Cape Bojador, where the Sahara comes down to the sea and shoals break out of sight offshore, was "The Bottom of the World" to Portuguese explorers, but once Gil Eannes rounded it in 1434, other navigators followed easily and the route to Cathay was opened. Encyclopedic pilot charts, such as the one above, issued by the Admiralty (one chart for each month) were nearly as critical to Britannia's rule of the waves.

Today pilot charts from the US Defense Mapping Agency Hydrographic Center contain local wind roses and current vectors, temperature tables, ice zones, shipping patterns, atmospheric records, and an amazing amount of additional information.

Plate Tectonics

First articulated by German Alfred Wegener in 1912, the theory of plate tectonics states simply that the landmasses we know today were once part of a single landmass (a megacontinent which Wegener christened *Pangaea*, or *All Land*), which began its breakup over 200 million years ago. In terms of weather study, the main significance of Wegener's view—since substantiated by plant and animal fossils and other evidence—is that the climate, based as it is upon the relationships of land and water, has always been in flux. Said Charles Darwin, "Daily it is forced home on the geologist that nothing, not even the wind that blows, is so unstable as the level of the crust of this earth."

Polar Air Masses

Air masses that originate in the vicinity of the North Pole are called arctic. *Polar* air masses come, somewhat arbitrarily and confusingly, from central Canada or the open water reaches of the North Pacific and North Atlantic. They are cold, but arctic air is colder.

Poor Richard's Almanac

Though best known for homilies like "Early to bed and early to rise makes a man healthy, wealthy, and wise," Ben Franklin's little book also included words to make one weatherwise.

Probability Forecasts

The old "partly cloudy" became, about 1965, "the probability of rain is 30 percent." As carried out by NOAA, probability forecasts have proven more specific and flexible than their forerunners, but they still have shortcomings. "Southwest 10 to 20" is forecast routinely over much of the East Coast in summertime. Ten knots is delightful; 20 is formidable. Greater precision would make NOAA's forecasts more useful. "Weather wisdom" can help.

Prognostica

The first weather almanacs, published in Europe during the medieval period, were called *prognostica*. Based on astrology, observable events in nature, or just hunches, they contained predictions ranging from the coming of floods and disastrous freezes to forecasts for abundant harvests. Though they were seldom accurate, they were among the most popular offerings of their time.

Robin Quartpot

Leader of the aborigine band summoned to do a rain dance in downtown Sydney in summer of 1965, Quartpot and his mates danced and danced. The temperature stood right about 100 and not a cloud came into the sky. Finally the dance was abandoned.

"What went wrong?" a reporter asked.

Sipping on his beer, Quartpot replied, "God knows how to make rain. We just dance to ask him to do it."

Quaternary Period

During this relatively brief span (quaternary is the geological term for the past 1.8 million years), ice has reached to middle latitudes over the sea repeated times and glaciation has far exceeded the norm (based on the past 100 million years).

Radiational Cooling

When not being heated by the sun, earth cools off. The atmosphere affects this process, low pressure holding heat in like a blanket, high pressure allowing it to escape rapidly. Radiational cooling actually refers to the cold that is deepened as heat radiates freely outward from the planet.

Rain Shadow

In the lee of a mountain range is an area where the wind is almost always dry because moisture has been "squeezed out" and fallen on the other side. Most land within rain shadows is arid, if not desert.

Rain Shaft

Rain Shaft   Rain hurled earthward by the explosive downdrafts—microbursts—that grow from convection in storms. Without the signature rain shaft, microbursts can sneak up as "invisible" *white squalls*.

Rainbows   A rainbow to leeward looks prettier than one to windward. Light passing through falling rain is refracted into a spectrum of colors in either case, but showers to windward will soon be falling on you. Those to leeward are headed for the horizon.

Raindrops   Wind tunnel work has revealed that the popular image of a tear-shaped raindrop doesn't exist in nature. Time-lapse photos show that water takes a teardrop shape when a large drop breaks into droplets. The droplets, though, go on to take a shape something like a flat-bottomed jellybean or a hamburger bun. As they fall to earth, individual drops of rain look like nothing more than miniature rain clouds: flat on the bottom, puffed on top, almost as deep as they are wide.

USS Ramapo   Aboard this 478-foot naval tanker, the champion of waves was triangulated and certified. In mid-Pacific at the edge of a gargantuan storm system in 1933, *Ramapo* ran before 60-knot winds and gigantic waves that had a fetch of over 3,000 miles. Sighting aft, Lt. (jg) Frederick C. Marggraff used the known heights of *Ramapo*'s aftermast and bridge to size up a roller that measured 112 feet in height.

Red Sky at Morning   Perhaps man's oldest nugget of weather wisdom is: "Red sky at morning, sailor take warning; red sky at night, sailor's delight." Theophrastus wrote around 300 B.C. in his *Book of Signs* that a red sunrise means rain while a red sunset portends good weather. The same idea is enshrined in French, Italian, and Chinese proverbs and is mentioned by St. Matthew in the New Testament.

Modern meteorology has proven the weather rhyme to be true at least 70 percent of the time. Clear air refracts sunlight primarily into the red band of the color spectrum. A "red sky at morning" means the atmosphere stretching 500 to 700 miles *to the east* is predominantly clear and dry, i.e., fine weather has already passed and deteriorating conditions will follow ("sailor take warning"). "Red sky at night" indicates clear, dry air *to the west*, which means there is an equally wide band of fine weather lying that way, and that it approacheth ("sailor's delight").

Relative Humidity   The ratio (expressed as a percent) of the amount of moisture in a parcel of air to the amount it can hold before it becomes saturated. Because warmer air has a greater capacity to hold moisture, *relative* humidity increases as air cools. This helps explain both clouds and fog.

Rising Barometer   *(Newbold Smith)* Preparing to take *Reindeer* to Labrador and beyond, I relied heavily on the logs of Paul Sheldon (Dr. Paul of *First Aid Afloat* and a veteran high latitude cruiser): "Winds blow hard and are from the north and west much of the time. Radio weather broadcasts are not to be depended upon. The lowly barometer again becomes important, and one tends to venture cautiously once the glass starts up." I'd always thought a rising barometer was a fair weather sign!

[Sheldon was right. The prevailing westerlies near the top of the globe are fueled by *rising* pressure. Remember, too, the amount of change in the glass is more meaningful than whether it rises or falls.—eds.]

—*adapted from* Down Denmark Strait

Roaring Forties   Toward the bottom of the globe there is precious little land. Forty north cuts Madrid and New York; forty south runs through New Zealand and lots of waves. "Roaring forties" describes the screech of unimpeded westerlies chasing themselves round and round down under.

Roll Clouds   Like tight-rolled black cigars or elongated steam rollers, roll clouds ride the leading edge of squalls. Formed on eddies between the forward edge of the downdraft and hot air rising from the surface, these clouds roll backwards against the storm's direction. They look fierce but they don't pack either wind or rain.

Sahel   Arabic for "shore," this "coastline" along the southern border of the Sahara used to be arable land supporting farms and herds. During the late '70s the area became increasingly dry until in the '80s drought and famine made it a disaster area. This drastic climate change happened because the subpolar jet stream dipped south and blocked the monsoon flow that normally sprinkled the *Sahel*, sending the rains southward deeper into sub-Saharan Africa.

Roll Cloud. A roll cloud precedes a squall line, which in turn may precede a cold front by a hundred miles or more.

Mt. St. Helens   Once 9,677 feet high, this peak in the state of Washington erupted in 1980. While this was the most intense volcanic activity in the US in memory, the eruption was small by world standards. Mt. Tambora in Indonesia, for instance, ejected 100 times as much volcanic ash into the atmosphere as Mt. St. Helens. While the Indonesian eruption in 1815 has been blamed for "the year without summer"(1816), the Mt. St. Helens eruption produced no measurable atmospheric cooling, but it did chop the mountain's height to 8,364 feet.

St. Swithun's Day   Bishop of Winchester and trusted advisor of King Ethelbert, Swithun died in 862 A.D. and was canonized in 940. Legend has it that removal of the saint's body to the cathedral in 971 was delayed for 40 days by very heavy rains, hence the lore that rain on St. Swithun's Day (July 15) would bring 40 days more. Further, if fair, it would continue so.

Santa Ana   When high pressure builds up over the Mojave Desert and low pressure deepens along the Pacific coast, *Santa Ana* comes riding. Drawn through mountain passes by the pressure differential, a hot, dry wind approaching 50 knots can bang down onto the Pacific and extend out to sea for 15 to 20 miles.

Sargasso Weed   The Sargasso Sea is the region virtually at the center of the Atlantic Current Gyre. Near the "eye" of this continent-size eddy beneath the Bermuda/Azores High, a super-saline, highly refined pool of seawater supports a uniquely evolved seaweed. Without the "suckers" that let its rock-hugging cousins stay put on shore, Sargasso weed has developed a system of floating gas bladders to make the most of its perpetual drift. It is biological proof of the relative permanence of fine weather at the center of the North Atlantic weather system.

Screaming Fifties   Wave heights in this high-latitude band of open water above Antarctica show little change twelve months of the year, unlike the polar regions in the Northern Hemisphere where summer provides a break in the action.

Sea Breeze   The convection cycle that brings sea air in to replace the air that rises over heated land (see "Convection Cell").

Sea Ice   Ice on the surface of polar oceans prevents the heat transfer from atmosphere to water and back again that is an essential element in global climatic self-regulation. Once the ice sets in, insulating the water below and reflecting the solar radiation above, it "takes over" as a dominant factor, influencing climate well below the poles.

Seagull, seagull, sitting in the sand,

It's always foul weather when you sit on land.

—*anonymous*

Seiche A continuation of a water level disturbance after the external forces causing the disturbance cease to act. For example, if onshore winds pile water above normal height and push it into a bay, when the winds abate, the water will surge back to sea. That seaward surge is a seiche. The National Marine Weather Service issues seiche warnings on its regular radio broadcasts.

Shamal "The plague" is what they call this dry easterly in Iraq. Appearing in the Middle East in spring, with humidity as low as zero, the *shamal* elevates the temperature and pushes up the blood pressure. Crackling with static electricity and whirling with dust, it earns its name; in a University of Jerusalem study, one third of the population queried reported the onset of physical and/or psychosomatic ailments during the *sharav*, the Israeli version of the same wind.

Shear Edge Between air masses of differing density is a border zone of clear air turbulence.

Simplified Assumptions In pursuit of the competitive edge, Dennis Conner has weather records that go back 20 years on some race courses, uses the best meteorology available, and ferrets out local knowledge, but to evaluate the interaction of all of the weather information that comes in before a race, he uses a methodology of "simplified assumptions." Considering the wind, for example, he looks at three components:

- gradient wind—the wind generated by a major weather system
- thermal wind—the wind created by temperature differences in the immediate vicinity of the course
- geographic winds—winds that result from the effect of topography on local airflow

"The wind will come from the interplay of these three factors," Conner says. "By analyzing the wind in terms of these variables you can narrow your focus and better your odds of knowing what's happening in time to do something about it."

—adapted from Sail Like A Champion

Sky Waves Radio waves that bounce back to earth off the ionosphere are called sky waves and they carry great distances. In the daytime the ionosphere tends to absorb low frequencies and reflect high. At night that reverses.

Eric Sloan's Weather Book
Written in 1949 by a well-respected author, weather expert, and architect (the Hall of Atmosphere at the American Museum of Natural History), this whimsically illustrated volume is chock full of weather concepts and pictures. "The sky is my re-

The sharper the blast,

The sooner 'tis past.

—old English proverb

ligion and philosophy" Sloan said. Nearly 50 years later his insights and images remain remarkable.

Captain John Smith

In the New World he encountered more than Pocahontas: "The winde and water so much increased with thunder, lightning, and raine, that our mast and sayle blew overbord and it was by great labour we kept from sinking by freeing out the water." This is the first written description of a Chesapeake Bay line squall.

Smoky Sou'wester

Thick with salt haze (like sea breezes the world over), best known east of Long Island and west of Cape Cod, and drawing power from the shapes of Buzzards and Narragansett Bays (both funnel-like), the smoky sou'wester is a summertime fixture.

> As the sun lifted, the breeze freshened, part of a local phenomenon called the Buzzards Bay sou'wester, a sea breeze so regular you can set your watch by it. Rarely in these waters is there a golden day after the sea breeze appears. Instead, the sun takes on a frosty look. Land and buoys and other boats are seen as through a gauzy curtain. The sea turns a cold gray, and the sun path is silver. So it was as Finisterre *neared the entrance to Buzzards Bay.*
> —*Carlton Mitchell,* The Wind's Call

Solar Energy

The sun is central to life on earth, yet earth receives only $\frac{1}{2,000,000}$ of the energy generated by "our" sun.

South Atlantic

(Noel Mostert) The South Atlantic is a sea, not sinister, but where nothing is as it seems; its perversity begins with the deceptive serenity of its surface, where dead calm is placed on the backs of massive swells, which roll smooth and crestless under it. These swells are known as Cape rollers and they gain their size and momentum from their long journey up from the seas of Antarctica. The Southern Ocean not only sends rollers into the South Atlantic but folds into it its own icy currents, making it a cold sea under a hot sun.

—*adapted from* Supership

Southerly Buster

In the South Atlantic, sailing ships were sometimes taken aback by sharp blasts coming up from the south—gear-busters that snuck in amid the gentler northeast trades.

Sputnik

Launched by the USSR in October of 1957, this beeping spheroid was earth's first artificial satellite. Rushing to respond, NASA launched *Explorer* four months later. NASA's first meteorological satellite followed a year later—to assess the radiation balance of the earth. The first dedicated weather satellite, *TIROS*, came in 1960.

Squall

According to *Webster's*, a "brief, violent windstorm." According to racing guru Buddy Melges, "sail for the squall. That's where the wind is."

Squall Line

A shoulder-to-shoulder formation of squalls, probably detonated by the pressure shock wave in advance of an advancing body of cold air, often precedes the front by 100 to 150 miles. Typically, squalls advance at around 25 knots, and they generally pack winds almost twice that.

Starlight

The twinkling of stars is due not so much to atmospheric moisture as it is to turbulence in the upper air, the sort of mixing that permits convection, the sort of wind shear that means a jet stream is playing across the upper sky. Still, "twinkle, twinkle" means bad weather.

Stonehenge

Begun near the beginning of earth's most recent warming period and constructed from stones transported on sledges over ice (perhaps) or, in one version, embedded in and transported by glaciers, the stone jumble on the plain near Salisbury has awed and puzzled people for millennia. Temple? Fortress? Mead hall?

Both archaeology and computer analysis now suggest that Stonehenge was, if not a computer, at least a megalithic calculator by which druid priests could predict and measure heavenly events. The sun at midsummer solstice, when seen from the central "altar" stone at Stonehenge, rises over the "bowing" stone. Beginning with that alignment,

Gerald Hawkins, Chairman of the Astronomy Department at Boston University, computer-tested hundreds of alignments between Stonehenge axes and the sun and stars. The overwhelming majority were both "precise and significant." The monument may thus have been a calendar for planting and harvesting, an observatory predicting eclipses, and a "cathedral" for sharing in "sacred" times like the return of the sun at the winter solstice. Stonehenge seems not only the "eighth wonder of the world" but proof of early man's weather wisdom.

Storm

We know storms as destructive and dangerous, but they are also a valued release for energy in the atmosphere. "Letting off steam" around local temperature imbalances keeps big, explosive inequities from developing.

Storm Surge

At the center of a cyclonic storm, the core of deep low pressure not only sucks in air but lifts the surface of the sea into a bulge. The storm is likely to raise water a foot for every inch the barometer falls below normal. When a hurricane (or even a lesser storm) passes, that bulge produces abnormally high tides.

Stratosphere

Around 1900, French meteorologist Teisserenc de Bort named the parts of the atmosphere. As a driving force in balloon-born exploration of the upper reaches, he more or less earned the right. Above the troposphere (from the Greek *tropos*, "to mix") he expected strata of gasses—so came the name stratosphere.

Stratus Clouds

The family of horizontally layered, flattish (stratified) clouds.

Sun Dog

A bright spot or "false sun" sometimes appears to either side of the sun and usually presages unsettled weather.

Sunlight

Unlike most solar systems, we have but one sun. It is 73 percent hydrogen, 25 percent helium, with a remainder of sundry gasses. The sun is 100 times the diameter of the earth. It was about 70 percent as bright in its youth as it is today.

Supercooling

When moisture in clouds is very pure, it can remain in droplet form even when chilled below the nominal freezing point. Droplets formed around particles of dust or clay freeze earlier. Cloud modification is often directed at supercooled clouds because they are "ripe" for change. Supercooled fog, for instance, is sometimes cleared by seeding it with dry ice. Crystals grow in the cloud until they fall and leave the atmosphere clear.

Surface Wind

The wind along the sea and ground is distinct from the wind aloft. Surface wind is slowed by friction, which makes it bend (30 degrees over land, about half that over water) toward the local low-pressure center. When surface winds and winds aloft are relatively closely aligned, that means stable conditions. Should the two cross, look for rapid change.

Synoptic Weather Map

Observations taken from widely separated stations are gathered and displayed at once in a single "snapshot" of the weather.

Tai Fung

Chinese for "great wind."

Tehauntepecer

When a "norther" heads south over the Gulf of Mexico, it may cross the hilly isthmus of Tehauntepec and be drawn down on the Pacific side. A "Tehauntepecer."

Thales of Miletus

In 585 B.C. he successfully predicted a solar eclipse. He accurately described the atmospheric mechanics of evaporation and cloud formation. He used systematic analysis and exhaustive record-keeping to predict the future based upon the past. Legend has it that his studies led him to anticipate one of the most bountiful olive harvests ever in Greece, so he cornered the market on oil presses and made a fortune.

Tornadoes

When the prophet Ezekiel warned of a "whirlwind out of the north," he was talking about a tornado. These turning (*tornare* in Latin) windstorms are among nature's most deadly. The pressure inside a twister's funnel can be 150 millibars (almost 6 inches of mercury) lower than the ambient atmosphere, which creates powerful suction. Tornadoes average about 50 knots over the ground, but their circular winds reach upwards of 150 knots.

Thunderstorms spin out tornadoes only under very specific conditions: most occur in spring and fall when temperature differentials are large; most require lift from a cold front to supercharge convection; most need strong upper-level winds to further fuel the updraft; and all require the air in the updraft to begin to rotate. This latter happens when wind shear (the increase of wind speed with altitude) drags lower-level wind toward the upper-level direction. The vortex then spirals down toward the ground.

While electrical storms produce intermittent static at the low end of the AM radio frequency band, the static generated by a tornado is constant.

Trade Winds

Steady enough to "trade" upon? Crucial to sailborne trade? A trade-off to bandit-dominated overland routes to the Orient? *Webster's* says these regular winds got their name from the phrase "to blow trade." Trade, archaically speaking, meant "course"; trade winds are winds that *hold their course*. Carlton Mitchell writes, "Curved sails overhead, a wake creaming astern; the world offers no better cruising conditions. Almost constantly there is a breeze from the east. Rare is the day when it does not come up with the sun."

World wind pattern, July through September.

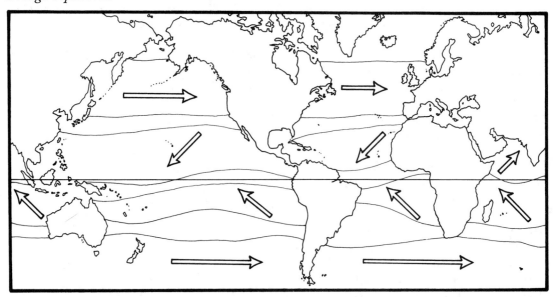

The trades, north and south, result from circulation around relatively stationary high-pressure systems. Many passagemakers have found the trades "surprisingly light" for making miles. Sailing closer to the center of the high reduces their velocity.

When the central high changes shape, pressure, or station, the winds change. Joshua Slocum observed, "nothing could be easier or more restful than my voyage in the trade winds, but even here the phenomena of ocean meteorology were interesting studies. About every seven days the wind freshened and drew several points farther than usual from the direction of the pole, while at the same time a heavy swell rolled up from the sou'west. All this indicated that gales were going on in the anti-trades. The wind then hauled as it moderated 'til it stood again at the normal point, east-southeast. From Juan Fernandez to the Marquesas I experienced six changes of these great palpitations of the sea itself, the effect of far off gales. To know the laws that govern the winds, and to know that you know them, will give you an easy mind on your voyage 'round the world. Otherwise you may tremble at the appearance of every cloud."

Tropopause   At the top of the troposphere, earth's skin of atmospheric gas, the tropopause is a "ceiling" of constant temperature. Air parcels rising by virtue of convection rise no farther. Ten miles high near the equator, about five at the poles, the tropopause is the "pitched roof" on the greenhouse.

Troposphere   From the Greek root *tropo*, "to turn over." French meteorologist Teisserenc de Bort designated the area where gases mix the troposphere—a 5-to-10-mile-deep band above the earth's surface that contains all atmospheric moisture and virtually all of earth's weather.

Tsunami   Japanese for "great wave in harbor," *tsunami* are seismic sea waves. Should the sea recede and expose its floor, should it return at up to 500 mph, should unparalleled destruction result—that's *tsunami*. Loosely known over the ages as tidal waves, seismic waves may not be over-

whelming at sea—some are as slight as 2 feet tall. Their incredible power comes both from their mass (wavelengths approach an unbelievable 600 miles) and because, as "shallow-water waves," their velocity is proportional to the square root of the depth. As depths shelve, the wave slows but piles up. Wind-generated breakers may rise to impressive heights, but there is a trough behind them. Behind the *tsunami* is simply more *tsunami*.

Updrafts   Hot air rises. Most updrafts are "thermals," heated from above, below, or the latent heat of condensation. Air can also be lifted by a slope or by convergence with another airstream.

Variable Westerlies   Earth's most variable surface winds are the prevailing westerlies that blow between 40 and 55 degrees of latitude North and South.

Veer   The wind veers when its direction changes with ("runs with") the clock. [Both *veer* and *back* are used in both hemispheres, but the significance of clockwise—or counterclockwise—motion differs. When the wind veers in the Northern Hemisphere, it presages an increase in atmospheric pressure. The opposite is true for the Southern Hemisphere.—eds.]

Venturi Effect   When airflow is constricted, it increases in velocity.

Virga   Moisture in the form of ice crystals or vapor that trails from clouds in the middle deck yet evaporates long before it reaches the ground.

Voyager's Moon   "I once met a man," writes Eric Hiscock, "who told me that he always planned passages so as to have the benefit of the moon at any difficult point when making a landfall. I don't know how he managed unless he used his engine a great deal."

Warm Front   When a warm air mass moves into an area occupied by a colder body of air, the warm air rides up over the cold air. The slope is about $\frac{1}{90}$ in a "classic" front. This produces drizzle and clouds. High overcast proceeds to thicker overcast, clouds, and eventually rain as the warm air infiltrates the area.

Water Is Weather   Raindrops, snowflakes, cloud droplets, ice crystals—these are all "weather" and they are all water. Like fish, we are surrounded by water. That water takes many forms. When it changes from one to another, we have weather.

Waterspout

Courtesy Marty Baron, National Weather Service

Waterspout   Waterspouts are tornadoes that develop over water. They are weaker than tornadoes, with winds that rarely exceed 50 knots. It seems to be a myth that you can get a water column to collapse by firing a gun near it. It is also an exaggeration to think fully found vessels can disappear "without a trace" due to waterspouts. The velocities and effects of waterspouts are akin to other squalls.

Common waterspouts form out of local thermal differences. Dark, ragged cumuli with serrated lower edges generally accompany them. Tornadic waterspouts accompany fully developed storm systems (either in advance of or embedded in the storm front). Both types are localized, with low pressure at their centers. Most waterspouts can be avoided by maneuvering.

Weather Analysis   Thanks to offshore races like the Whitbread Round-the-World Race and the BOC Challenge, optimal passage routes can be improved. Weather consultants like Bob Rice (see "Ocean Weather Routing") have played big roles in these advances. Weather information is no longer limited to pilot chart prediction. Real-time pictures of clouds, sea, and even the (Doppler-dissected) wind are available onboard (see "Weatherfax" and "Ocean Passage Weather").

Weatherfax   Facsimile machines create current weather maps on the high seas. Onboard weatherfax machines provide for worldwide reception of scheduled weather map transmissions provided by a number of countries. Some weatherfaxes are stand-alone units and some must interface with the ship's HF or SSB radio. Some can be pre-programmed to receive scheduled broadcasts without an operator. Computer software is also available to transform an onboard PC to a weatherfax receiver.

Surface analyses are prepared by the World Meteorological Organization and are the backbone of fax service to sailors. They offer weather maps; isobars are plotted and give a topographical picture of the atmosphere. Compiling observations creates a 5 to 6 hour lag for the map behind real-time conditions. Surface analysis includes, however, 12-, 24-, 36-, and 48-hour predictions.

Nephanalysis is also available. It is a "map" of cloud cover, and yields information on weather essentials like pressure systems and fronts. Gulf Stream analysis provides temperature and direction for the various current strands that make up the Gulf Stream. Sea-ice analysis is a less-than-perfect census of berg-size ice (with coordinates). Wave height analysis can also be helpful.

Broadcast schedules are listed in *Admiralty List of Radio Signals, Vol. 3.; Worldwide Marine Radio-facsimile Broadcast Schedule* by Alden Electronics; and by broadcast stations 0000Z Norfolk, 1014Z Halifax, 2020Z San Francisco, etc.

With the right equipment you can supplement weather maps with the latest infrared and visible light satellite photographs. The great advantage with these is that the conditions are current. You may also:

- Multitask your instrument package and completely integrate weather forecasting, navigation, course management, and communication.
- Acquire automatically and unattended all pertinent data.
- Store at full resolution *all* images received and zoom onto selected picture segments.
- Draw on incoming map and picture material via cursor or digital vector.

D. F. Crane Associates sells software that will turn a laptop into a weatherfax for $99. At the other end of the range, for $1,700 you can buy Furuno's Dfax, a dedicated stand-alone machine (with its own HF receiver) that makes maps unattended and needs no additional equipment.

Working with weather maps takes time and study; the symbols are important and the subtleties within images are crucial. Still, as a passport to understanding, the weatherfax truly beats wetting your finger and sticking it in the wind.

Wind Cell

The closed "updraft/downdraft" system at the heart of a thunder squall. Fueled by pressure and temperature differentials, warm winds blow into a central depression. This forces surface air upward where its moisture eventually changes to liquid, which releases the latent heat of vaporization, fueling convection.

The updraft that generated the cloud's growth is overcome by the downdraft born of precipitation, and the surface is visited by strong gusts. If the initial downblast is drastically cooler than the ambient air, tuck in another reef.

Wind Rose

The Tower of the Winds on the slopes of the Acropolis in Athens has eight faces sculpted with likenesses of the eight deities of the principal winds. A huge bronze figure of sea-god Poseidon stood atop the tower and rotated to point with his trident at the wind that was blowing.

A modern-day wind rose in an almanac or on a pilot chart points the cardinal directions like a compass rose, but it also gives a picture of wind activity for a given period via a system of feathered arrows. The longer the arrow pointing northwest, for instance, the greater the percentage of northwest wind for the month. The number of feathers on the arrow indicates the prevailing strength of those winds by indicating their average force on the Beaufort Scale.

Wind Shadow

To leeward of anything the wind blows across is an area of lessened and turbulent wind. Boats, houses, buildings, and islands create these "lees" where the wind strength is diminished. A building blocks the wind for a distance downwind of seven times its height. A sailboat's wind shadow extends up to seven mast lengths downwind (but is weak toward its outer edges).

Wind Shear   Contiguous air masses moving at different speeds is a form of wind shear. Upper air, for instance, moves faster than surface air, which is impeded by surface friction. The "clear air turbulence" airplanes experience is also a form of wind shear. When air masses rub past one another relatively smoothly, that is wind shear, but when they swirl and mix, it becomes turbulence. The airplane drops 200 feet because it passes from a fast airflow into a slower one. The passage of a jet stream though the surrounding atmosphere creates wind shear. Updrafts and downdrafts are "vertical wind shear."

Wind Shifts   No wind blows in a purely constant direction. Every wind is made up of shifts in direction and changes in speed. Each wind has a character of its own. Winds in the daylight are different from winds at night. Winds off land are different from winds off the water. Winds from the east are different from winds form the west. Gradient winds are different from thermals. All gradient winds are generated by pressure differences and shaped by the earth's rotation.

On the East Coast, easterlies produce extreme shifts, often from one side of east to the other. The wind's movement seems sluggish. Westerlies, on the other hand, jump about and gust with sharp, darting movement. The former comes across the regularity of the flat, open sea. Westerlies dance across varied terrain through varying temperatures. Winds on the West Coast have almost opposite characters. Each wind's character is determined by where it came from and shows up in its shift pattern.

Wind Witch   Sir Walter Scott told of meeting a wind witch at Kirkwall in the Orkneys circa 1800: "We clumb by steep and dirty lanes, an eminence rising above the town. An old hag lives in a wretched cabin upon this height. She subsists by selling winds. Each captain of a merchantman, between jest and earnest, gives to the old woman sixpence. She, in return, boils her kettle to procure a favorable gale." It seems small price. Agamemnon sacrificed Iphigenia, his daughter, to get a fair wind for Troy.

Worldwide Marine Weather Broadcasts   A resource for bluewater cruising, this NOAA publication lists a myriad of sources for weather information around the world.

Xerxes   Son of Persian emperor Darius, Xerxes continued his father's campaign to punish the Greeks, mounting a mammoth invasion force and building a bridge for them into Attica across the Hellespont in 480 B.C. When storm waves threatened to break up his floating bridge, Xerxes whipped the water (300 lashes) so that it might obey him. His invasion might well have succeeded had not his fleet been scattered and fragmented in a storm within days. Themistocles and his Athenian mariners outsmarted the remainder of the fleet at Salamis,

Yea though slimy things did crawl upon a slimy sea, he blessed them unaware.

—*Samuel Taylor Coleridge, "The Rime of the Ancient Mariner"* where Xerxes had to flee the throne he'd built to watch the battle. Even emperors cannot make the sea obey.

Yokut Indians To aid the harvest, the Yokut burned grass from their fields before planting. Then they hired a rainmaker. In 1870, the Indian agent at Fort Tejon (CA) promised a rainmaker named Hopodno a large sum of goods if he could deliver rain to the drought-stricken tribe. That he did. The downpour became so fierce that the agent offered a further sum if Hopodno could stop the rain. That he did.

Zeus Most powerful of the Greek Immortals, Zeus was sky-god. While Apollo drove the chariot of the sun and Aeolus managed the winds, when trouble came sudden and severe from out the sky, it came from Zeus.

ANCHOR BOWLINE

A normal bowline has a tendency to saw back and forth under strain and rub against the ring or eye that it's tied into. To cut down on (but, unfortunately, not eliminate) chafe, tie an anchor bowline: simply take a turn around the ring, eye, etc., then complete the knot as normal. [In the old navy we were taught to secure a line to the anchor ring with "a round turn and two 'alf 'itches (or a fisherman's bend; see page 218). Drawn taut, there'd be no chafe.—MB]

The anchor bowline here is augmented with a fisherman's hitch through the round turn.

Hervey Garrett Smith (from *The Arts of the Sailor*)

7

HANDLE HEAVY WEATHER

Blow, wind!
Come, wrack!

At least we'll die with
harness on our back.

—*Shakespeare,*
Macbeth, *V, 5, 51-52*

In grammar school we had air-raid drills: "Sit on the floor, backs to the wall, heads on your knees. Let's all get ready for the nuclear fireball!" Most of us are not much better prepared to meet heavy weather. Until you've met a storm at sea, you can only imagine its force. Even after you've met one, how much do you truly understand? What we all understand, though, is the need for heavy-weather tactics that can prove more effective than sitting still with our heads on our knees.

Don Street has weathered more gales than most of us have seen sun showers. He equates heavy-weather tactics to the early days of flying, when any landing a pilot could walk away from was a good one. Likewise, if a sailor sails through a gale successfully, he must have done something right.

In erecting the pillars of heavy-weather "wisdom," we began with our experiences, surveyed seagoing lore, then consulted others who have "walked away." For this topic, we tend to put words like "expert," "master," and "wisdom" in quotes because having the last word and saying your last word are not that far apart where storms are concerned. The beginning of heavy-weather wisdom is to distrust heavy-weather "rules."

Get your head off your knees.

A FRIGHTENED BOY WITH A BUCKET

(RR) My first storm at sea was a surprise. I'd never heard of a hurricane during the Bermuda Race, but then I was 16; what did I know? Aboard *Mistral*, a 40-year-old Off Soundings yawl, we were slicing along on starboard tack hard on the wind. Cocooned in the forward lee berth, I felt us slamming into waves and was aware of water dripping, but a warm berth is a warm berth.

"We're sinking, we're fucking sinking," Tommy Kelly said as he shook me in my bag.

"Right . . . ," I moaned as I swung out of the covers. I hit chilly water that was already crotch deep. Seas were coming aboard and our house and deck were leaking; it seemed, indeed, that we *were* sinking.

We switched on the bilge pump and almost instantly labels from the (foolishly unwaterproofed) cans we'd stowed in the bilge schlurpped into the strainer and clogged it. There wasn't much to do but join the bucket brigade. Once we got the flood under control, I repaired to the bilge pump and picked out *Dinty Moore* labels for an hour or so until we got it working.

Our navigator, a former submarine officer (all due respect, Mike), faced the storm, held out his arm at right angles, and sent us running off to the east. By the time we straggled south and west again to Bermuda we were 134th boat (out of 136) to finish. On the dock we heard about *Finisterre* and her veteran crew feathering through 80-knot puffs to win while we floundered toward Spain trying to survive.

Knowing what you're doing has a lot to do with what you make of a storm at sea. My memories include shock, frustration, and quavery doubts whether I'd still be there bailing when the sun came up. I remember the glazed intensity of skipper and crew. Am I seeing men at their best? I remember, too, the incredible crystal-blue clarity of the backs of the combers that swept beneath us when the morning came and the sun broke through. I walked away, but I felt about as "expert" on storms as a passenger on the Concorde might on breaking the sound barrier.

DIPPED IN THE WATERS

(MB) Despite all the heavy weather at sea I've since survived, it surprises me that I remember so vividly a storm that struck us in the submarine HMS *Thorough* in the eastern Mediterranean on a passage to Australia. But maybe it's because that's when I discovered Christianity.

I was officer-of-the-watch on the bridge, with one able seaman lookout. It started to blow from the east, and soon we were shipping water over the bridge in deluges, to the extent I had to send for safety harnesses from below. Before long we were taking such a pounding that I was forced to reduce revs to the minimum. Ducking and weaving behind the bridge superstructure to avoid being pummeled by each successive wall of water, it occurred to me suddenly that I was very frightened. It also struck me that it was quite ridiculous for this mere mortal to assume he had much, if any, control over his own destiny.

I had gone to church and sung in the choir at Windlesham and Dartmouth, learned the catechism and been confirmed, attended matins with my parents when on leave, but it wasn't until I'd had the shit (pardon the expression) scared out of me in that easterly blow that I cottoned to what humility was all about. This specific sinner, I now learned, had to acknowledge he'd always be hopelessly up the creek without a divine insurance-policy paddle unless he paid his premiums regularly, graciously, and willingly.

The storm abated eventually, and the lookout and I were relieved. We went below to tussle ourselves out of our sodden Ursula suits and to have a hot cup of "kay." Rubbing a dry towel over his head and neck, my bridge companion glanced at me and said, hesitantly: "Sir, d'you think you might approach the skipper and ask him if we might have a short church service in the fore ends each Sunday forenoon, at least until we arrive?"

The skipper readily agreed.

HANDLE IT

Learning lessons from the sea is a lifelong proposition. Learning heavy weather wisdom can be a life-and-death proposition. Some pillars:

PREPARE TO THE LIMIT

"Gale conditions should be considered all part of the game and dealt with by careful thought and preparation," says offshore legend Captain John Illingworth. Heavy weather comes with the territory. It's not bad luck or the wrath of God that brings heavy weather our way. It's out there; if you are, too, it *will* come!

Says Lin Pardey, "There is a feeling among modern sailors that you can avoid storms by careful planning, by consultation with radio nets and meteorologists, by waiting for a perfect weather window, by making faster passages to spend less time at sea, but if you will cross oceans, you *will* meet heavy weather."

Sailing offshore needn't be suicide; just be prepared to get yourself out of what you get into. "Have a seaworthy yacht, sound and strong, that carries spares for every contingency," says circumnavigator *par excellence* Eric Hiscock. Good gear is basic to offshore safety, but perhaps even world-girdling wizards like Hiscock put too much emphasis on equipment: "A study of disasters shows that the majority of them can be traced to failure not of the yachts or their crews, but some part of their gear or, more commonly, that there was no spare gear with which to make the necessary repairs," Hiscock wrote in the introduction to his heavy-weather chapter in *Cruising Under Sail* (1950).

There are dangers in Hiscock's pronouncement. First of all, it's tough to "trace the roots of disaster" to any specific cause. Says Steve Callahan, author of *Adrift* and survivor of 79 days in a liferaft, "there is a real danger of using anecdotal evidence and presenting it as scientific proof. Everyone's situation is unique, and how does one know about the ones that failed, that never lived to tell the tale?" How do we know what really happened? How, then, can we pinpoint lack of gear?

Hiscock also points out, with great perception, that fear of bad weather is mostly fear for yourself and how *you* will stand the strains. Stockpiling back-up widgets hardly addresses that concern; in fact, don't some of us "hide" behind our gear? Spares, then, are a good measure of readiness, but "seaworthy," "sound," and "strong" are better measures.

A boat can never be *too* seaworthy, *too* sound, or *too* strong. Recut sails, change a sheeting angle, rebed a fitting, enlarge a backing plate, improve all-weather ventilation. The better a boat works—period—the better she will stand by you in a storm. Jackass rigs may cut it when it's nice; they'll bite you in the ass when it's not.

PREPARE YOUR BOAT

To prepare your boat for heavy weather:

- Enlarge scuppers so the cockpit drains fast. Remember that high cockpit coamings are good protection but they add to the volume of water a cockpit well will retain.
- Fit removable strainers so you can open scuppers completely at sea. Don Street suggests, "fill your cockpit some afternoon and see where the water goes and how long it takes." [A lot will go below through the blower vent and around locker lids unless you have ways to seal them.—eds.]
- Erect a boom gallows to take the main boom while sailing under trysail.
- Fix a permanent or demountable forestay halfway between the mast

Ready!

and stem to let you use stormsail combinations where jib and reefed main are roughly the same size and "centered."

- Beef up your steering system. Highly stressed and super critical, steering is a weak link that can be strengthened in advance.
- Try your emergency steering. Most boats have emergency tillers but they are often too short. Test for steering leverage by steering with the emergency gear at 5 to 6 knots in reverse. Can you swing the emergency tiller from side to side? It may need to be longer.
- Disconnect your self-steerer. When it starts to blow over 30 knots, vanes and even autopilots get busted up. Worse, if you let them steer, they'll bust you up.
- Rig permanent messengers for halyards, lifts, and preventers. "I rigged a permanent main-boom preventer tensioned by shockcord," says Dodge Morgan. "When things are easy to use, you use them."
- Prefabricate strongbacks, or stout timbers (2 x 4 at least), to fit behind hatches, companionway boards, etc. When you bolt them in place, they temporarily reinforce those critical closures.
- Beef-up or modify stanchions. "Lifelines are critical offshore, especially in heavy weather, but stanchions in general are weak points," says round-the-world racer Sir Peter Blake.

CONFIDENCE

Confidence separates salts from rookies in heavy weather, but it's tough to be calm and confident when it's your first storm. Experience is valuable, but no amount of experience will redeem carelessness.

"I have yet to meet anyone who has gone through a hurricane who can talk of it lightly," says bluewater veteran Dennis Puleston. No one is beyond the need for deeper, better experience; Joshua Slocum himself was lost in a storm at sea. The face of a wave can cut short the learning curve. Short of courting Hurricane Amy as Phil Weld did to shake down *Gulfstreamer,* or heading out when you should stay in, how do you build confidence?

Prepare to the limit. Weld talks about tying that extra stopper knot in his jib sheets. "Belt and braces" is the way to keep your pants up. Knowing you've done your best to be ready is almost like being ready.

Practice. How many of us have hove to, even in 20 knots? Or set a sea anchor? A trysail? Take the trouble to practice heavy-weather evolutions and you will put yourself way ahead of the crowd.

Study the lore. Bernard Moitessier carried the logs of Cape Horn clipper masters aboard *Joshua*—and read them. It's inspiring to see how many recognized "masters" had mentors. Noah, Columbus, Cook, Chichester, et al.; they're all in the library, and all speak wisely of heavy weather.

See the progression. Storm tactics change as the wind and waves change. Be clear in general, though, about what moves to make when; it will bring order to your mind.

Read the weather. Every day offers a weather lesson. You needn't ride out storms at sea to know how storms work. The better you see and understand the weather, the better able you'll be to act instead of reacting. Get ahead of your boat.

NOISE

I honestly do not know what I would have given for a moment's peace from the howling squalls.

—Kathryn Lasky Knight,
adapted from Atlantic Circle

Prepare yourself in advance for the devilish caterwauling of the wind in the rigging that will try to unnerve you.

—Adlard Coles,
adapted from Heavy Weather Sailing

My experience is that in these gales you cannot set sail again until the sound in the rigging, a mild roar one might call it, eases.

—Sir Francis Chichester,
adapted from Gipsy Moth Circles the World

Noise is probably the most unnerving aspect of a storm at sea.

—Lin Pardey, adapted from Storm Tactic Handbook

Noiseproof your boat as much as possible when she's at rest. It will make dealing with sounds underway much easier.

PUMPS

Most bilge pumps are undersized, unreliable, and awkward. The more of them you have, the better chances are that one will work when you need it. Hand pumps both topside and below as backups are a great idea. "The Offshore Racing Council specifies that you've got to carry them," notes Don Street, "but it never says how big they need to be. Bigger, believe me, BIGGER."

STOWAGE

- Don't stow jugs of fuel or water on deck. They can break loose.
- The more sound and secure the arrangement for keeping your dinghy on deck, the better (rightside-up is an obvious problem once waves start coming aboard).
- Spray shields, dodgers, and weather cloths need to be extraordinarily sturdy to withstand an average storm. It's a good idea to take them off.
- Have sturdy shutters to fit any glass larger than a porthole.
- Clear what you can from the deck; double lash what you can't.
- Batteries and ballast must be strapped down.
- Positive catches on lockers, deep drops on drawers, tall fiddles, and easy gimbals—these are a beginning.
- Fuel and water are good ballast; fill your tanks. Shift movable ballast to put the boat in trim; the more closely she rides on her lines, the better she will ride out heavy weather.
- Early sailors (like Conor O'Brien in *Saorise*) and late (like Steve Dashew in *Intermezzo*) hold to the same ideal: "Turn her upside down and shake her; nothing should come loose."

Harriet and Tom Linskey tried to make *Freelance* 360-proof before crossing the Tasman Sea from New Zealand to Australia: "We through-bolted twist-lock hold-downs on all 13 bunk-top lockers, screwed down the cabin sole, made sailcloth containment covers for galley and bookshelves, installed an automatic latch on the chart table, added barrel bolts to the companionway hatch and drop boards, devised shock-cord hold-downs for everything from the compass to coffee cups, and just as we were finished, a friend pointed out to us that our kerosene lamps would go flying, as would the burners on our stove, and the companionway ladder." They made it without rolling over. Be prepared.

To say that we rounded Cape Horn would be presumptuous and inaccurate. We merely continued to be blown ahead of the gale that came up suddenly at midnight. But, the water that I bailed into the Atlantic this morning came from the Pacific last night. Being notably the most experienced bailer in the world today, I can attest that you can move as much water with a bucket as a pump. The secret is to adopt a steady pace and brace yourself while your vessel careens sporadically down the face of waves.

—Webb Chiles, adapted from
Storm Passage

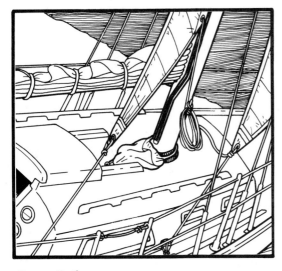
Storm Sails

STORM SAILS
Prepare your storm sails. Having a separate track for the trysail is a good idea. So is stowing it somewhere vaguely retrievable: "you can't set it if you can't find it." Street suggests a large trysail with reef points (Scotch-cut to minimize stretch, and with heavily reinforced grommets and corners). The Pardeys think trysails should be day-glow orange. An alternative to the track for putting the sail on the mast is to lash it with cross-laced loops of line. In either case, set the sail in stops to avoid unwanted flogging and strains on the rig. Storm jibs work better and last longer if you fit them with tack pendants to lift them clear of the waves. Street says "you can run off quite nicely if you get a small jib wung out on a pole," but you can't do that if you don't carry a suitable pole, lift, tackle, and guys.

BEFORE A STORM HITS
Before a storm hits you can track the weather, lay out gear (a sea anchor?) you'll need, rig jacklines, and batten and lash last-minute loose ends. Also tend to items you've forgotten, like plugging the hawse; closing—or blocking—engine-room vents; dogging cockpit lockers; hoisting a radar reflector; lining up matches, flares, and first-aid supplies; closing sink-drain seacocks and perhaps those for the toilet. Should you shut off the engine fuel line? Will you need a safety line down the cockpit centerline?

Next prepare your crew. Street says, "very few people ever got seasick when they were well fed and settled into a warm, dry bunk." A big pot of bland, hearty fare—such as a stew—is a good foundation and should probably be kept simmering. Alcohol is not a good idea, but coffee, tea, and bouillon are good to drink. Seasick remedies in suppository form are best because you don't throw them up. Neck towels, watch caps, rubber-band closures at wrists and boot cuffs of your foul-weather gear, a billed cap, ski goggles? You're ready!

It's common to feel marked exhilaration when the storm finally hits. It's likely, however, that the struggle plus the noise and discomfort will sap your strength before too long. Lethargy most likely will take the upper hand as the storm wears on. It can become much harder to get things done or even make decisions than you'd thought possible. Be prepared on both counts. Good luck.

SPARES FOR EVERYTHING? *(RR)*
Roughly 1,000 miles from the Eddystone Light finish of the 1963 Transatlantic Race, our 57-foot yawl *Dyna*, carrying storm chute and reefed mainsail, broached in 50 knots of wind. When we righted her, got sail off, and straightened up, we discovered we had lost our rudder.

You can get a bearing on an approaching hurricane by adding 115 degrees to the direction of the surface wind.

—*Coleen O'Leary*

Where's the spare? I wondered. Well prepared and well campaigned as Clayton Ewing's race boat was, she had none. Throughout the morning we tried various sail combinations to get *Dyna* moving again toward England. Trimming the staysail to one side and the storm jib to the other worked as a sort of mini-twins, but it was slow. At 1420 we tied a double reef in the main and set it opposite a wung-out working jib. Both sails had to be hoisted simultaneously to keep us on course, and the whole setup depended on a small staysail set and trimmed to weather in the foretriangle. The staysail kept us heading virtually downwind while the larger sails supplied a balance of power.

The speed went up to 7 knots and rose often above 10 as we surfed, without a helmsman, down the face of the steep, quartering seas. Our major fear was that one of the waves would throw our stern around and jibe us. Instead of standing wheel tricks, we took turns poised by the main halyard brake to release it in case we were taken aback, but though she was pushed as much as 20 or 25 degrees off course by the waves, *Dyna* never jibed.

The next day, in 35 to 40 knot westerlies, we made a noon-to-noon run of 184 miles—with no rudder. Weaving under jury rigs through Channel traffic, we made it to Eddystone, where we finished fourth (of 14) in the Transatlantic race.

There is a limit to preparation. Rudderless in mid-ocean, we used sails, a gerry-built sweep oar, and memorable amounts of trial and error to steer *Dyna*. Preparation is not a protective rampart. "No boat truly knows protection from the sea," as Naomi James asserts. Preparation, however, can be a springboard from which to rise and meet Neptune's challenges.

HEAVY-WEATHER TACTICS

Heavy weather rarely comes without warning. The barometer; sea, sky, and natural signs; weather bulletins—they all let you know something is up. What do you do?

Port is appealing, but running for shelter isn't always the best or safest option. Get in or stay out? Sea-wise as the fishermen of Brittany are, the majority of their losses, says Adlard Coles, come from trying to make port ahead of a storm. Reckon that a frontal storm packs its most violent conditions in its leading edge and that shoaling waves gather steepness and tower in height, so if you get hit before you get in, you'll get truly hit. Running off to leeward can also put you on a lee shore.

A wide-mouthed, deep-water, easy-access port still might not be a bad risk. Figure, however, what backwash from the

Figureheads were often given bare breasts in the belief that it gave them the power to calm storms.

—Linda G. dePauw, Seafaring Women

shore can do to a mounting sea, what havoc current can wreak on wave shapes, and how a straightforward channel might become very tricky in big waves and low visibility. If the channel is tricky and/or has a bar at its mouth, or if the tide is strongly ebbing, don't even think about it.

"The beginning skipper," Hiscock says, "should be mentally on his guard against any feeling of panic that might arise. Just as the inexperienced man may reduce sail too much, putting his boat at risk, so fear of the storm can prompt a rash response like running for an ill-chosen harbor." *Land creates problems; sea room solves them.* That is a pillar of heavy-weather wisdom!

"A modern, well-found yacht," says circumnavigator Steve Dashew, "properly secured for heavy weather, at worst, can expect a rollover and perhaps a dismasting. Providing you are well-secured below, that's certainly no more dangerous than a moderate fender-bender on your local highway."

Power or sail, *suit your speed to the seas.* (Another pillar!) Banging into storm seas is not good for men or boats. Taking them on the beam can work, but not without heavy rolling. Whether it's running with the storm or feathering into the wind under power to simply maintain station, respond to the storm in the way that gives you the most control— of your boat and of your situation.

RUNNING OFF

When you have the room and the choice, run with the storm. Open-sea waves undulate like a flag. Surface walls of water (crests) move down the wave faces at speeds of up to 25 knots. Match your speed to the crests' and their impact is minimal. Semi-planing and displacement boats, though, have to manage by riding out each wave and letting the crests foam beneath them. Added speed increases control, but pitchpoling comes with too much speed; a displacement boat reaches hull speed (the point where her resistance curve becomes almost vertical) but the wave keeps pushing. The resultant "trip" means dire loss of control at the least. Powerboat hulls are generally fine forward; that means ease off on the throttle rather than back off abruptly to avoid being pooped and "pronging" deep into the back of the next wave. Broaching, i.e., swinging beam to the wave, can happen if you go too slowly and allow the wave to grab your stern and run it forward.

Roger Vaughan, who crewed aboard *Kialoa* during the 1979 Fastnet storm, tells what it's like to surf a 79-foot sailboat: "With her bow hanging out of a wave as she took off, *Kialoa* felt light as a feather and in full control. The crew sat on the deck in stone silence, marveling at her performance. In tense concentration the helmsman would spin the big chrome wheel with quick hands, settling her in the groove as her stern rose on a wave, then break into a grin as she took off on her own,

Never ever sail at night.

Always keep the land in sight.

—visitor's log entry from
Humphrey Barton,
veteran of 25 transatlantic
passages and founder of the
Ocean Cruising Club

roaring and trembling as the speed gauge rose toward 20."

Minimizing the danger from broaching, pooping, and pitchpoling is a question of helmsmanship and boathandling. Automatic steering is not often the best way to run off. You know your boat's abilities; help her handle herself. If you are too short-handed, seasick, tired, or frightened to steer well, running off makes less sense. Sea room is essential, as are people to steer. Do you have enough of both? Will you run out of room if the storm changes course? Shoal depths and strong currents cause waves to break, so they become hazards that limit your range and course. Will you "attach yourself" to the storm by moving along with it (instead of escaping it)? Unless you get good answers to these questions, consider a different heavy-weather tactic.

As winds build, storm waves get steeper and crests become less stable. For most boats, bare poles provide speed enough to match these waves. Keeping your boat pointed where you want her becomes tougher as waves grow steeper, though. You might set a postage stamp of sail as far forward as possible to provide directional stability, but any tight-leeched sail, even set in the foretriangle, can produce weather helm through twist and heeling moment. "I have seen boats run off successfully just by tying sailbags to the bow pulpit," Street says.

Make sure you have the horsepower to climb the waves. "Don't wallow," cautions Dennis Conner.

"Keep enough sail on so that you don't get ambushed in the troughs," agrees Kiwi offshore veteran Chris Bouzaid.

Running off is a simple response; since it was "rediscovered" by today's sailors, it has become an orthodoxy.

- Bernard Moitessier was in the midst of one of his worst Pacific gales when it came to him. After a long, weary stint at the helm dragging warps, he realized his *Joshua* was essentially a trade-winds vessel, born to run. He tried to recall what Vito Dumas had said about running off. "It's in the book," he shouted below to his wife Françoise. As she read aloud it came to him—Dumas had circled the world at high latitudes by carrying sail and running with the seas. He said to take the seas at an angle of 15 to 20 degrees. That was it! Moitessier cut loose his warps and let *Joshua* run.

- BOC class-winner David Adams has sailed 250,000 miles and never hove to.

- "Taking speed off the boat to save her has become a thing of the past," says Bruce Farr.

- Still, "I feel that you get a false sense of security running off," says multihull racer/builder Walter Greene. "When we ran off in *Gonzo* (in 65 knots of wind), we were on edge. Our jury-drogue kept us from surfing, but what I'd do next time is ride to a parachute on a bridle off the bow. You need something to handle each and every wave. One slip running off and you're in trouble."

"With each wave the vessel would heel over sharply but respond perfectly to the rudder, and the comber would break harmlessly alongside."

—adapted from
Sailing to the Reefs

- Trimaran designer Jim Brown agrees. "Multihull or monohull, the key is not to go too fast. Pitchpoling comes when a boat 'trips' over her underbody resistance. Even BOC and Whitbread racers can reach that edge. Rudders cavitate and, more severely, the water flow down the top of a wave can match boat speed so that you have no steering control. When your steering starts to mush out, that's when you need to tie to something to keep you from surfing, to pull you through the waves."
- Dominique Eustache credits his $20 drogue with saving him and his family (aboard Morgan 43 *Hippo Camp*) from the 1994 Queen's Day "storm of the century" off New Zealand. "At times the boat would feel so 'heavy' that I thought the cockpit was full of water. It was only the drag created by the drogue."
- William A. Robinson's *Varua* eased through a Gulf Stream gale by streaming coils of heavy manila.
- *Warrior Shamal*'s crew used her engine to position her stern to the storm seas, and 300 feet of warp to hold her there. [Warps in the water and the engine running could be a dangerous combination.—eds.]
- The first ocean-going gauloses (fourth century B.C.) did "stream coils of rope in big bights" to keep sterns to the wind in gales.
- Karl Kirkman, chairman of the Smallboat Committee of the Society of Naval Architects and Engineers, determined through model testing that a boat left to run off on her own might be broached by a wave the equivalent height of 35 percent of her waterline length. "Steadied" by a drogue, however, yachts withstood waves as tall as 55 percent waterline length.
- Chuck Tobias's heavy-displacement ketch *Mar* had a large reel on the after side of her cabin from which she streamed 600 feet of heavy line.
- Gordon Stuermer's 40-foot heavy-displacement ketch *Starbound* runs well and has no tendency to surf streaming 300 feet of 1-inch-diameter anchor warp in a bight from the quarter hawses.
- Roger Wood, aboard the 40-foot trimaran *Triad*, streamed warps and chained an automobile tire to the end of the heaviest. The tire skipped out of the waves at times, and the bucking, jerking motion was a concern.
- Blondie Hasler often towed a Bruce anchor astern on 75 feet of warp, with good results.
- Bob Griffith aboard *Ahwanee* towed a drogue to limit his speed sailing through ice off Antarctica.
- Multihull designer/builder Chris White recommends a series drogue: "two or three small 'anchors' in tandem. I use motorcycle tires. You can handle the loads in this setup with a normal sheet winch."
- Today's boats are capable, even under bare poles, of speeds that previous sailboats never achieved. There is an edge to the envelope; today's boats can overrun it. Whatever your tether, multihull *guru* Walter Greene says, "tie yourself to something that will break you through the waves."

Or lie a-hull.

LYING A-HULL

- Halfway into his first crossing, Malcolm McConnell realized that "lying a-hull may not be the best response to a storm, but it's the easiest."
- "Pressing on was wearing thin," remembers circumnavigator Jim Moore, "and lying a-hull was all that we'd practiced."
- Thomas Fleming Day said, "in heavy weather a good boat is best left alone."

That's what lying a-hull is about. Should the wind build so that even storm sails are flogging and overstrained, or if your boat becomes difficult or impossible to control under the sail she has up, take the sails off! Fix the helm and just let the boat self-tend. From the sublime to the terrifying, lying a-hull can produce a variety of results:

- Phil Weld pronounced his trimaran *Moxie* "a dream" as she lay a-hull in Force 11.
- The dragger *Ellen Marie* with 25,000 pounds of ice and 30,000 pounds of fish aboard "could lie broadside to the seas in a full gale with no real danger, like a small iceberg."

- Moore's Cascade 36 *Swan* lay elegantly a-hull "because of her low center of gravity and sufficient ballast to recover from being rolled down."
- *Robertson's Golly* lay a-hull for Clare Francis "quite happy with no sail up, beam-to in 40 foot seas, rising to each wave as its crest passed noisily by."
- In *Gipsy Moth V*, Sir Francis Chichester found riding beam-to in Force 10 seas created a motion "albeit natural but by no means comfortable."
- John Guzzwell's light-displacement *Trekka* "lay 75 degrees off the wind and had a most violent motion."
- Will Corry's *Sea Lion* was thrown on her beam ends.
- "Lying a-hull won't work for *Whisper*," says Hal Roth. "Too much windage aft."

Lying a-hull, whether by design or out of desperation, has some positive benefits. So long as the boat is drifting with wind and waves abeam, she will leave a wake, a "slick," of quiet water to weather. This can and does calm the crests of approaching waves and discourages them from breaking. The force of the wind in her rigging will dampen her tendency to roll. Fix the helm to help her maintain beam-on orientation but beware of making sternway, which can damage the rudder.

The more regular and rounded the wave pattern, the easier it is to lie a-hull, so it's a good tactic in the open ocean, a bad one where there's current or cross-chop. The vulnerable cockpit/companionway areas are somewhat sheltered when you lie a-hull, but be prepared for "an ungodly din" as the waves slap against the side of your boat.

"On several occasions *Wanderer III* has lain a-hull safely in winds of Force 8-9," reports Hiscock in *Cruising Under Sail*, "drifting to leeward at half a knot or so, but I would not consider lying a-hull in stronger winds, for in a severe gale a mass of broken water may pour down the advancing face of a sea and, with the vessel's keel held still in the water beneath, could throw her on her beam ends or roll her right over. I am convinced the only safe procedure in such weather is to get the vessel end-on to the seas and keep her so."

SEA ANCHORS

Sea anchors were once the time-honored tool for bringing a boat end-on to the conditions, but things have changed. Except when there is a need to slow a boat's drift to an absolute minimum, sea anchors are no longer as popular as they once were. "No modern yacht we have met cruising actually carried the gear," Steve Dashew reports.

Modern boats sail around their anchors enough to make streaming a sea anchor from the bow less than effective and a jerky ride. Even the most massive sea anchor won't hold today's boats head-to-wind. The weight of the gear, the strains, the stowage problems, and the exhausting chore of retrieval are also strikes against sea anchors. Chafe is a huge hassle. Sea anchors also become liabilities by "holding boats down" and robbing them of natural buoyancy.

Riding stern-to to a sea anchor has advantages. For one, it keeps tension on the rode more even. A good quantity of water will come aboard, so keep scuppers clear and companionways closed (with dropboards secured). Elementary as it sounds, have a system of communication between those topside and those below so the companionway isn't opened as a wave is breaking aboard.

"I have used sea anchors and found them unsatisfactory. I think the wisdom of restraining the boat so firmly against the advancing seas is debatable," Hiscock says [adapted from *Cruising Under Sail*]. "Still, I once used a sea anchor near the Tonga Islands, and it so reduced our speed that it was safe to steer a little across the wind and thus go clear of a small island that lay under our lee. That we could never have done in safety traveling at 5½ knots under bare poles—even with all the ropes we had aboard dragging astern. I have also been glad of a sea anchor when conditions were too wild to permit lying a-hull and I had suffered an injury, leaving my wife to manage alone. The sea anchor kept us stern-on to the seas without any need for a helmsman. Only in situations such as these would I now contemplate its use." He found floats and trip lines to be "unnecessary, annoying, even unsafe."

Whether you see them as salvation or a necessary evil, you may want to stream a sea anchor or a drogue. If you make more than 3 knots with the drogue streamed astern, get a bigger one.

Walter Greene, builder/racer of the first rank, was sailing *Gonzo* in 65-knot winds and (by Coast Guard measure) 53-foot seas. "I thought

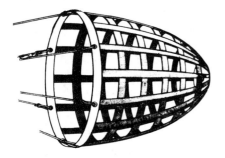

Gailrider Drogue

I'd run before the storm just to see what it was like. We cobbled together a drogue from sailbags, chain, and stuff, and it kept us from surfing. Next time, though, I'd be tempted to ride to a parachute anchor on a bridle from the bow. The big thing is to break through a breaking wave without being thrown by it. You need to be physically pulled through the wave, and that takes a sea anchor." [Hiscock describes a sea anchor consisting of two planks bolted to 90-degree angle irons, with a 2-inch gap between their inner edges. The angle irons project a little beyond the outer edges of the planks, and four metal rods to form a bridal are bolted to them. Such a sea anchor is immensely strong, is proof against chafe, and will stow compactly when dismantled. After two Biscay blows, I can testify to it.—MB]

Doug Terman says, "secure the end of a warp to one quarter, run a sturdy block with a length of chain or other drag-making material (like fenders or floorboards) attached to it into the bight in the line. Lead the other end to a cockpit winch. By giving the weight in the bight more scope, you add to its bite and slow the boat down. Winch in to speed up." Doug says that 0.6 times hull speed while running off 150 degrees from the wind worked for him.

There's understandable confusion surrounding sea anchors, drogues, and what's the difference. A vessel "rides" to a sea anchor much as it would to ground tackle. A drogue—almost always smaller—is a device to create sufficient drag to slow the boat. Warps are a poor man's drogue.

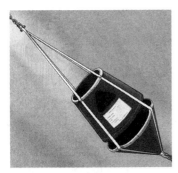

Seabrake Drogue

Dan Shewmon, whose company makes sea anchors from 5 to 40 feet in diameter with rated holding powers from 1,500 pounds to 3,000 *tons*, says, "our sea anchors are equivalent in pull to suitable jibs or ground tackle, and they are comparable in cost. Sea anchor or drogue? We make both. The question is something like 'Phillips head or standard screw driver?' Each does its job. Each should be in the toolbox."

The drag created by drogues can be varied. "Lengthen the tether to increase drag. The tether should be about 250 to 300 feet in the average open-ocean storm. The idea is to have the boat and the drogue crest waves at the same time," says sailmaker Skip Raymond, who makes Galeriders. "Use braided nylon because three-strand can unlay (and weaken). Have a stout thimble and strong splice where the tether attaches to the drogue."

Conceived by Australian John Abernathy and tested in the Bass Strait, Seabrake is designed to provide drag that increases with the amount of water flowing through it. This makes it work well not only for displacement vessels but for high-speed boats, too. Seabrake's tether is geared to minimum stretch, so use (expensive) Kevlar or braided Dacron.

Control of any drogue is better if you use a bridle. That lets you put seas on a chosen quarter and helps prevent seas from tugging your stern around. If the strong points for the bridle are forward of the rudder you will have significantly better steering control because the stern is not being "dragged" by the drogue. But in most cases you are better off with the drogue attached completely aft because you *want* the stern held into the waves.

Jon Sanders' seven circumnavigations give his voice some weight. "I've run before a number of storms, trailing a bight of anchor rode and just about every other piece of rope I could find. I've used the Seabrake with excellent results, but running before a storm, you're always on the line between too fast and too slow. I prefer to heave to rather than to run before storms."

HEAVING TO

"Heaving to is really best when one no longer knows what to do," Bernard Moitessier admits. Pick a flat spot in the waves. Come about without touching sheets, put the helm alee, voilà! Stretch out in the cockpit, eyes closed, and then see things as they are.

"Heaving to is tougher than it looks," wrote Richard Maury. Indeed, once the wind gets up over force 7, sails start to flog, and waves start to break, it may be time to consider another tactic. Still, with reefed main or trysail trimmed tight amidships and a suitably small headsail trimmed aback in the foretriangle, most boats will self-tend—virtually "parked"—about 60 degrees or so off the wind. Heaving to is simple and allows you to take control of your situation rather than letting the elements continue to dictate to you. Long-keeled boats heave to most mannerly, but generations of fin-keelers have learned to park nicely with just a bit of tweaking. You drift with your wake broad on your quarter. You bob on the waves as they sweep beneath you. You don't need to steer or to go anywhere.

"If you are making headway, you are not hove-to," decreed Capt. John Claus Voss. The consummate seaman (like Hiscock) will remember also to show a riding light when he's hove-to at night. Don't tie your rudder all the way onto the stop or lash your tiller hard alee; you want the helm to be somewhat resilient and flexible if the boat makes sternway in the waves.

"I've hove to at sea three times," reports William F. Buckley, Jr., "each time with total success."

HEAVING TO
SEA ANCHORS

Out of their 28 years of cruising and delivering both modern and classic boats (averaging more than a month offshore every year), Lin and Larry Pardey have come to swear by a "final defense" of heaving to *to a sea anchor*. Says Lin, "Before I went cruising, my imagination made me quake with visions of running before gales. Finally I spoke to Larry. 'We can stop the boat and lie still just like a resting bird,' he said. The only time we were ever capsized occurred in *Seraffyn* running before a Baltic gale. Before that we'd usually chosen to heave to. After that we always did."

Normally a moderate-air, first response to heavy weather, heaving to (in the form they've perfected) is a tactic the Pardeys prefer to all others and through all foreseeable conditions.

"If you are considering taking off all sail to lie a-hull or to run under bare poles, heave to instead. If you are shorthanded or have a tired crew, heave to sooner," Lin says. "When running in rough weather, if the boat begins to feel 'squishy' on the helm, it's time to heave to." The object is to get your boat to make good a "square drift" 90 degrees to the waves. That places your "slick" to weather and affords good protection from breaking waves.

"We used a 12-foot para-anchor together with our storm trysail to ride out the worst blow of our careers, a three-day cyclonic depression off the Great Barrier Reef, where it blew 85 knots hours on end. Now we use an 8-foot-diameter para-anchor, an army Bureau of Ordnance munitions-dropping chute, that we purchased secondhand.

"To heave to with a sea anchor, we use an adjustable pendant (from our primary winch through a snatchblock on the quarter to a snatchblock that rides the anchor rode). We adjust it so that we ride with our bows at about 50 degrees from the axis of the waves. Adjust the setup so that boat and parachute are cresting at the same time. We use three-strand nylon for its shock-absorbing properties."

Chafe is a major enemy. Strain is considerable.

Use large-sheaved, smooth-running snatchblocks, your strongest strong points, and attention and gear to minimize chafe. Use paper towels floated to weather to judge your relative movement. When you have fine-tuned your setup, you should not be moving forward but drifting downwind in the protection of your slick. To retrieve the sea anchor, winch it in when it is in the troughs.

—*adapted from* Storm Tactic Handbook

DESIGN FOR HEAVY WEATHER

Thor Heyerdahl found the drawings for *Ra,* his Transatlantic reed boat, on the wall of an Egyptian tomb. Though the crypt was near the banks of the Nile, Heyerdahl felt ships from 3,000 B.C. and before "were designed not for river navigation, but for riding surf and huge waves." He built *Ra* to the lines he found. When he met his first ocean storm, *Ra'*s bundled reeds "rode like a submerged submarine, tons of water frothing over her but dropping straight through her sieve-like bottom. . . ."

Designing for heavy weather is an ancient (and honorable) practice. Here is what some of today's prominent designers and sailors are doing.

FASTNET LEGACY

(Jim Taylor) The Fastnet hurricane and the studies that came out of it showed that boats that rely primarily on beam for stability are not much good in heavy weather. The International Offshore Rule (IOR) fostered most of the '79 Fastnet entries. It rewarded boats that were made artificially tender by moving ballast inside, and encouraged shapes that were somewhat distorted and hard to drive. That affected broaches and tripping (but

there's nothing more stable than a fat boat . . . upside down).

The International Measurement System [IMS—to which Taylor has designed winners from maxi to mini] governs most of today's offshore racing. We are building boats now with centers of gravity materially lower than those from the IOR. Positive stability values are not in the rule *per se,* but many races, like the Bermuda Race, won't accept entries with numbers less than 120 degrees. Stability ratings are much higher than they were under IOR. Increased rudder efficiency and improved hull shapes make today's offshore racers easier to steer, and we've learned a bit about constructing rudders that won't fall off or break under storm loads. Hulls tend to be more balanced and easily driven, thus reducing tripping. Offshore racing boats today are better at meeting heavy weather.

However, a number of relatively flat-bottomed boats are beginning to be built to the IMS rule. That's a step backward for heavy-weather handling; they pound and are subject to structural damage because of it. Worst of the modern boats in heavy weather, though, are some of the newest full-cruising designs. With exceedingly low ballast/displacement ratios, they are heavily reliant on beam for their stability, and their centers of gravity are alarmingly high. This new wide-bodied "fun-in-the-sun" generation of cruisers looks like a bunch of bad bets to take offshore.

LIGHT HAS MIGHT

(Jim Taylor) When it comes down to "light versus heavy," the Kirkman study of the Fastnet and the US Sailing Association capsize study both say that light boats are less safe than heavy. As a designer of light boats, I will agree that a light boat should have its center of gravity lower than a comparable heavy boat. I concede that boats that rely heavily on form stability are more vulnerable to capsize by waves than narrower boats. Still, I continue to design light boats; I believe that they are best suited to heavy weather.

There are conditions that will overwhelm any boat. Light boats provide the best options for staying out of those conditions and the best responses should they overtake you. Light boats respond better to better seamanship—you can make bigger changes faster. Heavy boats can dig a big trough and hang suspended between bow and stern waves. In instances where all types of hullform have been subjected to similar conditions, like the Queen's Day storm off New Zealand in 1994, light boats survived better than heavy (though the comparison between boat types is never as material as that between crew and tactics). As far as modifying my own designs to suit them better for heavy weather, I've deepened the forefoot and increased the deadrise some with my most recent cruising boats.

OFF SHORE AND MORE

(Bob Perry) [When Bob Perry sprung the Valiant 40 prototype "performance cruiser" on the world in 1975, it responded. She was a "go-anywhere" boat AND she was still fun to sail. The Valiant 40—and Perry's folder-full of subsequent designs—have been making miles enjoyable ever since. Here he grapples with a "go-everywhere" boat—eds.]

You have to design for the worst condition, right? Say 35 knots true going-to-weather. First, cruising yachts should have relatively neutral helm. You can always dig up some weather helm from somewhere by varying sail trim. A near-neutral helm is more forgiving and allows the boat to be driven hard-pressed without overloading the steering system and rudder. The hull I have in mind I'd call "deep-chested"—a displacement/length ratio of something between 250 and 300. A cruising boat has to have substantial displacement for lots of real life reasons like tankage and stowage, but displacement here is part of performance, too; the greater the displacement the greater the righting moment. This boat will be somewhat tender initially, but that rewards you with a softer and more gentle motion. She's stiff enough to carry the sail you want as long as you want.

Pounding is not exactly the same thing as

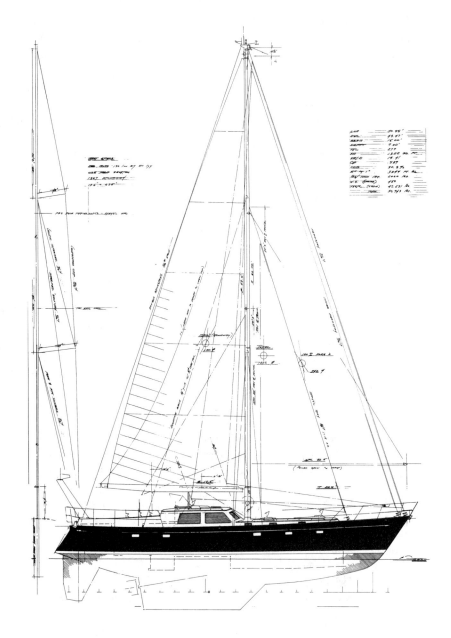

The Robert Perry —designed Eden 50, with aluminum hull and deck, was created for voyaging and illustrates her designer's thinking on rocker, overhang, and a "deep-chested" hull.

pitching, and I've come to see that pounding is not so much a question of U-sections vs. V-sections as it is a question of rocker. Rocker orchestrates contact between the hull and the wave. This boat has substantial fore and aft rocker. She will deliver you safely, quickly, and comfortably upwind in 35 knots. Apart from static stability studies, there's not as much science as there should be to designing for heavy weather.

Double-enders have long been associated with good heavy-weather performance, but that may have come from the old Colin Archer lifeboats that were designed to lie a-hull in big waves. I have never bought into the often heard Moses theory that the pointed stern "parts the waves." For safety in heavy weather running, I would prefer to see a stern with more buoyancy aft, and that's why I used the tumblehome canoe stern as seen on the Valiant yachts. With this shape the volume is pulled as far aft as possible before pinching it together. Certainly bringing the ends together can produce a "balanced" set of waterlines that may enhance a boat's helm predictability.

I've designed sterns that have "the shape you love to pat" myself, but I've put those sterns on boats whose sections were full right aft. It is an aesthetic thing, yes, but I make no claims that it makes a boat safer in heavy weather.

Some things, though, begin to look better the heavier the weather gets. Plumb stems are a modern trend. They obviously maximize waterline length, but in a cruising boat do you want to give up a foredeck and make your boat into a submarine for an extra little boost in top-end speed? Traditional elements like overhang are traditional because they work. Overhang keeps people dry and provides space to do what foredeck work you have to do. It's not all bad.

SEAKINDLINESS

(*Gary Jobson*) What is it that lets some people keep on racing while others drop out? I think that it's the motion. A boat that inflicts snaps and jerks on her crew "takes it out of them" in a hurry. My ideal is to keep racing longer than my competitors. Comfort has something to do with size, but it also has to do with speed. When the boat's moving, the crew's morale is high and that means safety. Part of "comfort" comes from sailing through tough conditions with the attitude that you will not only survive but enjoy yourself.

SHAKE, RATTLE, AND ROLL

(*Barry Peale*) We're talking about seakindliness, not seaworthiness. The distinction became tragically apparent in the Fastnet disaster when 15 lives were lost. Forced to lie a-hull, many crews made the dangerous choice of taking to liferafts because they were literally being shaken to pieces in their viciously rolling race boats. The aim is to make roll, pitch, and heave—the elements that make up a boat's motion in a seaway—each have as long a time span and as moderate an amplitude as possible *without compromising seaworthiness or performance.*

TED SAYS

(*Ted Fontaine*) Physical comfort is the key to safety. You start getting beat up and you make bad decisions, and bad decisions make bad conditions worse. The Little Harbor approach to the problem is total. Ted (Hood) has always been known for "whale-body" hulls. It's a cliché, but there's a lot to it—rounded, smooth, and substantial. It's the light weight and flat panels that'll jar your teeth. We want to make an impact on the waves instead of the other way round. Back aft the veed sections help tracking.

Steering is another heavy weather virtue. We have a main centerboard and a steering board aft on most designs. The steering board takes the load off the rudder and works very well for balancing the helm and helping to stay straight down the faces of waves.

I think Phil Weld (*Moxie*) and Dodge Morgan (*American Promise*) proved what kind of speed and control roller-furling sails can give you. Powered winches mean you can reserve your strength; sail plans are taller with narrower sails that reef very efficiently. It's a sailing system that's been proven. Dodge Morgan was 56 when he set the non-stop record for a circumnavigation.

Add an elevated, full-access engine room; accommodations that make good use of the hull's "low-motion" center section; maximum emphasis on illumination; well-engineered ventilation; insulation from temperature, sound, and condensation—did I forget anything?—and we think we've got some answers to how to handle heavy weather.

SAFER AT EVERY SPEED

(Chris White) Stability is a comfort factor as well as a safety factor. Navy studies show that a stable platform is a good antidote to seasickness and helps sailors stay functional when conditions deteriorate. Multihull stability thus makes multis safer.

Another factor is that they can sail at 20 knots *in control*. The broaches and tripping that come when monohulls exceed their speed limits are not a problem with multis. Multihulls can capsize. Street and others say that makes them *unsafe*. In 17 years of multihull sailing, I've never seen a multihull broach. When a monohull broaches, it can sink. Not so with a capsized multi! There are design advantages that make multihulls a happy choice in heavy weather.

FASTER AND TOUGHER

(Bruce Farr) When it's a question of a flat-out race boat and it comes to something that will compromise performance, the racer's decision will always be "give me the speed, I'll tough out the motion."

We know that's not always prudent, but we also know that it's human nature. With cruising boats, though, the results from the racing test bed are helping us develop more-seakindly shapes, more-durable materials, and more-efficient gear and equipment. All of this lets us design comfort and safety more completely into each new pure cruiser.

We're learning so much from concentrated results like the last BOC that we're getting a leg up at last on the old problem of obtaining reliable data about the loads involved in real conditions. I'm sure there are materials capable of meeting those stresses, but I'm not sure how affordable they might prove to be. Beyond strength, today's boats have pretty much made the act of taking headway off to save the boat a thing of the past. For one thing, you have speed available to avoid a storm track in the first place or to run away once it hits in the second. And, if the boat's top end is the same as the wave's, where's the tripping to worry about? The advice they used to give crossing the Tasman Sea was "go like hell." We're giving them boats that can do that.

RECKON WITH THE ROGUES

- A "concave wall" overwhelmed *Integrity*.
- A "monster wave" threw *Felicity Ann* on her beam ends.
- "Unexplainable freak waves continued to wrack *Kon-Tiki*'s lashings." (Thor Heyerdahl)
- *Sea Foam* was weathering 30-knot gusts and then, BAM!
- Wave tops blew away and Will Corry saw *Sea Lion* was on a collision course with a wall.
- "The wave had two crests, and both of them were breaking." (Phil Weld)
- "Two troughs opened up to leeward of us and we fell in the hole." (Steve Callahan)

Even the Little Old Lady from Pasadena knows that waves come in sets. The mystic number is seven, isn't it? Not if you talk to Bob Guza, professor of oceanography at Scripps Institute in La Jolla. Not seven, not three, not nine. "The grouping of waves is even more random than the sizing of individual waves," he says.

Next question: Aren't some waves bigger than others? Says Guza, "Not every wave in a wave train is the same height. If the average height is 10 feet, you can expect some waves to be half that tall and you will find others that are twice that tall."

Wind speed, duration, and fetch determine the height of the wave trains. This mix of creative forces accounts for the variations within a wave train. There's no discernible pattern, though, no deadly seventh wave, just a random jumble around the mean. For many, a double-the-average wave is a monster. Going from 10-foot swells to a 20 is no easy slide.

Adlard Coles says, "reef for the gusts, not the mean." That protocol also makes good sense in dealing with waves; expect the 20-footer instead of being lulled along by 10-footers.

"To me," says weather guru Bob Rice, "a rogue is when you don't know it's coming and then there are no more"—something decidedly outside the averages, in other words. "I guess it's statistically like the army marching over the bridge. It's possible for everyone to put the same foot down at once and collapse the span. Possible, yes, but. . . . Still, I've heard these monsters reported."

Brian Hancock left Cape Town aboard a Whitbread boat when he was a child and he's been soldiering around wide oceans ever since. "Rogues? You mean one of those big fellows that pops out of nowhere and swallows everything up? Bullshit. I've seen big waves, but none that came randomly out of nowhere. In the Southern Ocean the waves are good-size, some bigger than others, but if there's something down there that breaks the mold and makes dwarves of the rest, I've never seen it!"

They may not be real rogues, then, but there *are* waves prowling around out there bigger than most. That is because:

Wave of the sea, laden with suffering.

—*The Odyssey, Book V*

- Shoaling creates bigger waves. The longer the wavelength, the more a wave train will swell. The continental shelf slows and steepens long rollers because they are a product of deep-water undulation. "Chop" isn't affected by coming on soundings, though, because it is a surface phenomenon. Dodge Morgan was willing to go a longer course just to give the sea mounts off East Africa wide berth. Even in the open ocean, shallower water makes bigger waves.
- Wind against current adds size and steepness to waves. Local currents or ocean streams can pile seas up. Phil Weld flipped *Gulf-*

streamer just above the north wall of the Gulf Stream, where both current and converging weather systems stirred the pot. An adverse current of 3 knots can double wave height.

- Ship wakes are a sometime hazard when combined with big waves.
- Combinations happen. Webb Chiles writes, "The waves were not the highest I've known, but there were two sets of them, one from the southwest driven by the gale, the other from the northwest rebounding off the land. Both were breaking." The mixture of two different wave trains can add significantly to wave height. Says Tom Linskey, "The 1979 Fastnet storm was a crossroads of wave trains when swells from the southwest, south, and northwest met under storm conditions."
- Wind force increases with the square of speed, so wave size may grow by four times if the wind speed doubles.
- As Farley Mowat describes in *The Serpent's Coil*, the wind can veer far more rapidly than the towering seas can alter their march. As a result, a ship steaming head to wind can be caught broadside to the waves.

In summary, it's tough to find scientific support for the true rogue, that solitary monster that pops out of nowhere to overwhelm us, but there's little doubt that big waves abound. How to account for the 95-footer that smashed the QE II? All sailors can do is remember that what we see between us and the horizon is not all (nor even the half) of what we might get.

HEED THE LORE

When a voyager returns, he tells what it was like "out there." Those at home listen and learn. Some even follow in his wake. Nowadays charts and pilots detail most of the globe. Heavy weather, though, remains a sort of *terra incognita*. Pioneers, victims, heroes, and everymen write of storms at sea. None has the "answer," but heavy-weather accounts are still a great resource. They fill uncharted voids in our seamanship, they deepen our appreciation for each other, and they are the closest things we have to "simulators" to prepare us for Neptune's worst. Marty Luray, one of *Sailors' Secrets* original coauthors, said it well: "Sea stories, especially fact-filled ones, are eternally interesting and useful." Read these, then take them to sea.

If Sniff You Must

(Frederic A. Fenger) We were edging in along Navesink when the whip-crack came. It was not as though we hadn't been expecting something, for all afternoon we could see with half an eye that something was herming up in the northwest. But it would be a mere puff we were thinking to give us a hand around Sandy Hook. And when it rushed out from under a line of hard black cloud, we were ready for it with sheets trimmed and the fores'l already handed. For 10 minutes it blew hard enough in all conscience while we took the smell of it on the inshore tack. Then with a buffet that laid us on our beam ends, it chopped around to the north and ramped like an angry strumpet. By that shift our weather shore had gone whistling and now we were close to the beach. Our deadeyes were still in the boil, and for a moment or two it became a question as to whether the skipper could bring *Diablesse* about. Twice he failed and was on the point of lowering everything to run off, when a bit of a lull came and around she fetched. Caught napping there, the owner swore that next time he took a smell o' squalls, he'd do it on the offshore tack.

—adapted from The Cruise of the Diablesse

Master of Cape Horn

(Alan Villiers) At no time did the clipper-masters or owners make a systematic study of the best way to make use of ocean winds . . . until Robert Hilgendorf. The "Devil of Hamburg" to competitors and shipmates alike, he wanted most to avoid *calm*. What his critics called *trolling* and sailing by black magic was Hilgendorf's skillful, concerted application of natural meteorology.

Off the Horn Hilgendorf's genius was outstanding. There was one essential to his defeat of the Horn. Unlike most masters who shortened down and awaited fair wind, he *used* whatever breeze he found. He was a genius at using the violent winds of the Horn to benefit the ship. If he emerged from the Straits of Le Maire to find a violent westerly, then he did not shorten down but took the gale on his starboard beam. He would

storm across it (as close to his compass course as he could) down to 59 or 60 degrees S if he had to. Sometimes such a course was advisable, sometimes not. He seemed to know.

Wearing ship or tacking in Cape Horn seas wasted a lot of time and that was poison to Capt. Robert. Heading south he might go about and stand in toward Tierra Del Fuego, making the whole coast his lee shore. He knew by the signs, when he did such a thing, that the wind would free him up and change. This kind of sailing took nerve and knowledge. Even to think clearly in those screaming, roaring hurricanes took courage. Hilgendorf had these qualities in abundance.

—adapted from The Way of a Ship

Slick

Using oil to calm troubled waters has become less popular since Biblical times, but many are the sea stories that mention it nonetheless:

- E. G. Martin's unruffled transatlantics in his pilot cutter *Jolie Brise* were remarkable in 1926. "I cannot ever remember having torn a sail or parted a rope in a gale of wind." Part of the secret: "If you can get a film of oil even 10 yards to windward, the effect is good while heaving to."
- Jean Gau routinely hung a pierced oil drum between *Atom*'s shrouds and "the thin film would spread to weather, reducing the waves to large swells."
- Square-rig sailors as recent as Alan Villiers deployed oil bags. "They help," he wrote, "but nothing can stop the real breaking of a Cape Horn sea if a ship swings into it with speed."
- Aboard the barque *Grace Deering* bound for New Zealand, April 24, 1898: "We had a heavy southeast gale. Was layed to during the night—oil bags out. Even with oil bags over she rolled unbelievable."
- Says Eric Hiscock, "any oil other than paraffin, the thicker the better the effect, will modify breaking waves. The best way to spread it is half-gallon bags filled with oakum and pricked here and there with a sail needle. Tie them aft when running, at the shrouds reaching, on the

stem beating. Allow them line enough to float to weather."

- "Pull an oil bag along an anchor (or sea-anchor) rode to get it where it will do most good," says H. A. Calahan.
- Adlard Coles agrees: "There has never been any doubt about oil's calming effect."
- It was not such an open book, at first, to Benjamin Franklin. When on a sea trip, he observed that two ships that had just emptied greasy dinner water enjoyed smoother sailing than his own. Franklin fixed on the phenomenon and studied it. Once ashore he began carrying out experiments. Into a wind-ruffled pond he dropped oil from a cruet. Though not more than a teaspoonful, the oil produced instant calm over several square yards. Before long the whole pond was slick without ripple. After this, Franklin contrived to carry half a teaspoonful of oil in the upper hollow joint of his bamboo cane. More than once he had occasion to make passes with his "magic" cane and leave brook, pond, or stream shining mirror-smooth to the astonishment of his onlookers.
- Don Street feels whale oil or fish oil are best and that oil might be floated to weather in perforated plastic jugs.
- Richard Dey says, "Why not calm the waves from down below by flushing small doses of oil occasionally from your head discharge?"

FOR FISH OIL:

BEAUFORT
  FISHERIES, INC.
PO BOX 240
BEAUFORT, NC 28516
(919) 728-3144

MISERY LOVES MISERY   *(Tania Aebi)*

On that storm-tossed voyage to Bermuda (my first offshore passage), it was reading about Dr. David Lewis's North Atlantic crossing in a folkboat that cheered me up. Dr. Lewis, in turn, found consolation in the accounts written by Hanness Lindemann, himself a doctor, of crossing the Atlantic in a fold-up canoe.

—adapted from Maiden Voyage

Sea surface at 90 knots.

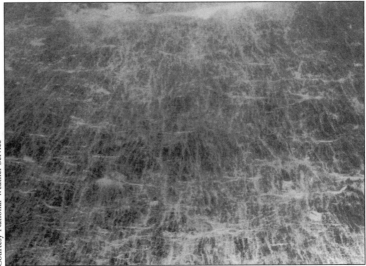

Courtesy National Weather Service

STORM NAVIGATION

Heavy weather can make you lose your bearings. As dangerous as storms themselves are, the navigational quandaries that they put us in can be worse. Positions, however, have never been surer or easier to find than they are with today's Global Positioning System (GPS). Thanks, Neptune.

In the brief space of the past 24 hours we have had four winds of gale force, each from a different direction, with the sky gloomy and threatening and the sea so ugly and confused that the bewildered ship, not knowing how to shape her motion in order to maintain her balance, threw the pots from the galley stove and the plates from the table.
—*Alan Villiers,* Cruise of the *Conrad*

We hove to, but Isjborn drifted fast downwind from the island into the most frustrating, toppling seas. We dared not drift away from Ulawa—there were reefs and islands 17 miles to leeward. We clawed our way back under the shore in the howling blackness.
—*Dr. David Lewis,* The Voyaging Stars

Oct. 1, 1748: Amsterdam came out of the storm and struck bow-on near the legendary landing spot of William the Conqueror near the tiny village of Hastings. Some of her crew drowned instantly in the boiling surf. Others sang bawdy songs as they drunkenly awaited rescue.
—*Peter Marsden,* The Wreck of the *Amsterdam*

We were 5 miles north of Suvarov. I began with the premise that the southeast wind would push us to leeward at 1 knot. From the pilot chart I figured the current to flow southwest at ½ knot, so we hove to on starboard tack with double-reefed main and staysail flat (not backed) in the foretriangle. We could get no celestial fix through the rain. The wind blew 30 and, with a few hundred rpm to help us point, we careened across 20-foot waves like a skier on a breakneck traverse. By the time we'd gone 30 miles we not only had a ripped main, I knew we were lost.
—*Herb Payson,* You Can Never Blow Home Again

I noticed the captain put his hand to his brow, as if to shade his eyes, and then turn pale. "There's land ahead! Lively there, for your lives! WEAR SHIP!" With belaying pins the captain and I went aloft to help the sailors break the ice that covered the sails.
—*Vernon Briggs,* Around Cape Horn to Honolulu on the Bark *Amy Turner*

For we knew, to the minutest contour of the shore and sounding of the waters, where we were going and exactly—in degrees, minutes, and seconds of latitude and longitude—on which of the 16,600,160,000 intersections on the screen of our earth-consciousness lay the very iron ring-bolt to which we should, by God's sweet mercy, tie.
—*Rockwell Kent,* N x E.
[Kent was the navigator of Direction, *and this was written two weeks prior to her loss on the Greenland Coast.—eds.]*

WHAT'S BEHIND THE STORM?

And where does heavy weather come from?

It must have been at least midnight when I stumbled topside to take a leak. I leaned against the stern rail gratefully, urgently, and looked down. At first I thought that it was phosphorescence. It wasn't that. I was pissing on the stars! I was well awake now. I could see. In the table-flat water beneath Tresbelle's *counter, black and deep, the stars in bright whorls, just like above, just like a mirror, just different because I was looking down at them. Halfway from Boston to Oslo, in the middle of the ocean, there wasn't a ripple. There wasn't a cloud. Just stars. All up and down it was stars, a bowl of stars!*
— *Arne Brun Lie,* Night and Fog

Profound rest and solemn peace. *That is what a hurricane is. The ocean stands, furrowed. It is a range of mountains and broad valleys as if cut in steel. On the mountain crests lie white glaciers. The valleys are streaked with molten foam. What moves is the ship.*
— *Heinrich Hauser, aboard the grain ship* Pamir

The stormy petrel was a rarity, the ones with *yellow feet, and Jack could not identify them. "If rarity and the force of the gale are in direct proportion," said he, "then we are in for a most prodigious hurricane."*
— *Patrick O'Brian,* Post Captain

Here at the edge of the world I was going to *drink a champagne toast and have some fresh bread! After weeks of solitude, lost among the towering waves, without heat or light, with no means of automatic steering, alone to face the elements, the nights on watch, the damage, I could hardly bring myself to believe that I was going to have the undiluted pleasure of drinking a toast to the dream and to the solidarity of the human race.*
— *Alain Colas,* Around the World Alone

Athrilling pulse beat high in me. I felt there *could be no turning back, and that I was engaging in adventure the meaning of which I thoroughly understood. . . .*
Looking out the companionway, to my amazement I saw a man at the helm. His rig was that of a foreign sailor, and the large red cap he wore cockbilled over his left ear, and all was set off with shaggy black whiskers. "Señor," said he, "I have come to do you no harm. I am one of Columbus's crew. I am the pilot of the Pinta *come to guide you. Lie quiet, Señor Captain, and I will guide the ship tonight."*
— *Joshua Slocum,* Sailing Alone Around the World

The gale turns the sea white. I drop the main-*sail, then the mizzen. Joshua tears along under single-reefed staysail and storm jib, surfing once in a great while. I could steer for the Galapagos now. Just a push to the right on the tiller. They are so close. But it would be too soon. I have not really found my Ganges yet. It is hard to shorten sail so long as there is no real threat and you want to get to the other side quickly. . . . I have been at the foot of the mast for hours now. One surfing run*
(continued on page 201)

MORALE MAKES THE DIFFERENCE

Morale is important. For example:

TRESBELLE COMES ON SOUNDINGS
(Arne Brun Lie) On soundings! The depthsounder used to read infinity. Now it reads 90 fathoms. Just like that. It intrigues me that they used to take soundings with weights and strings long before this beautiful echo sounder. It intrigues me, too, that you can drown in 6 inches of water or less. What does it matter how deep the water? What does it matter, once more out of the abyss, that we are back on the continent's shelf? Why should it matter? But it does.

          —*adapted from* Night and Fog

CAPTAIN BLIGH
Even before Charles Laughton's performance in the movie, a "Bligh" was a small-minded, sadistic, and tyrannical master. Of none of those things was the historical Captain William Bligh actually guilty. Instead, the logs and diaries that he and two others kept during the remarkable 3,600-mile open-boat transit he and his crew survived in 1788 show him to have been very different from what Hollywood, or even Nordhoff and Hall (authors of the best-selling trilogy based on the mutiny aboard HMS *Bounty*), might suggest.

    "Another night of gales, rain, and breaking seas," wrote Bligh at dawn 13 days after he and 18 others were cast adrift, with minimal food and water, in *Bounty*'s 23-foot launch. "The sun showed to me a poor miserable set of beings full of wants but nothing to relieve them. Some complained of a great pain in their bowels and all but little use of their limbs. I served my tea spoon of rum at day dawn as usual, and ¼ lb. of bread."

    When the odd fish or bird was taken, Bligh would dice it into equal

I wish someone had told me how dangers are most portentous on a distant sight, and how the good in man's spirit rarely or never deserts him in the hour of need.

          —*R. L. Stevenson*

(though not necessarily equally nourishing) parts. "And who shall have this?" he'd ask for each portion, kept concealed beneath his hat. "I shall" might as easily bring a breast or a beak, but the system was fair and the men knew it.

Hope is the fundamental ingredient of survival. Bligh kept his men alive not just with their ration of bread and rum, but with small rituals, songs sung in cracked voices, watch keeping, and attention to the daily record. The navy of King George was the most powerful entity—political, military, or religious—in its time. It maintained itself through precisely those orders and priorities, rights and wrongs, observances and rituals. There has perhaps never been a better example than William Bligh's command of his men against the sea of how the articles, expectations, and customs at the heart of the Royal Navy could be (and were) applied to wring high morale and incredible achievement from common men.

—with thanks to Bligh, *Sam McKinney*

Just imagine you'll drown within three weeks and go from there.

—Bill Homewood's cure for pre-OSTAR nerves.

MAGIC BEANS

(Malcolm McConnell) Mastata was lying a-hull in the North Atlantic, weathering a summer gale in the Gulf Stream. The fear of capsizing in a storm was akin to someone's fear of the wing falling off a modern jetliner. As I left the bunk, I summoned up a press picture of the DC-10 in Chicago, rolling over to port uncontrollably until it impacted in a fireball. Even my attempts at self-assurance ended in paranoia.

I swung out and groped aft. Leaning down, I dug in one of the lockers under Carol's bunk. The first object to roll into my hand was a large can of franks and beans. From the second locker two bottles of beer tumbled out as if they'd been shot out of a cockeyed vending machine. I swung back into my bunk with the can opener and a spoon. Opening the beans required two hands and both knees to grip the can, so I stuck the two squat beer bottles under the web of my safety harness as a GI hangs his hand grenades. "Those beans smell good," Carol said, sitting up. I finished my share and passed them across. I opened a bottle of beer—fizzy, warm, delicious. I might get up and check the deck in a bit. Then I'll come back here and sleep. This was the worst weather I'd ever encountered, yet I was seriously planning to go to sleep.

—adapted from First Crossing

We seem to be getting into life-threatening situations that might easily be avoided and then feeling jubilant that we haven't killed ourselves.

—Jim Moore, By Way of the Wind

GOT A MATCH?

(James Tazelaar and Jean Brussiere) Jean Gau is a legend among sailors. Before *Atom,* his 30-foot Tahiti ketch, was wrecked on the beach in Tunisia in 1973, the part-time chef and his home for 26 years made two circumnavigations, 11 transatlantics, and weathered at least seven hurricanes ("with names"). His philosophy was "between the sky and the water I am not alone. I live with the sea and the gale." Those thoughts no doubt sustained him, but said a boyhood pal, "Johnny only thinks of land when his cigarettes start to run low."

—To Challenge a Distant Sea

FIRE WHERE YOU FIND IT

(Tania Aebi) It was a storm in the Med. I decided to let *Varuna* lie a-hull. I crawled below, and it wasn't long before I was paralleling my trials and tribulations with those of Thomas Hardy's Tess of the D'Urbervilles. Suddenly the din of the wind was drowned by a huge crash. All hell broke loose. Everything from *Varuna's* starboard side catapulted down on me while hundreds of gallons broke past the protecting canvas and flooded down the companionway.

We were in the middle of a full-fledged, almost Biblical tempest; dodger ripped off, weather clothes and solar panels ripped up and gone. . . . I sat below eyeing the disaster.

A package of cigarettes, still dry in their cellophane, floated by. I lit one. Then I looked for the airplane-size nip of whiskey I'd been saving. The burning liquid settled my stomach and began to suffuse me with warmth.

As I started to bail with a bucket, the fatigue of a few minutes before dissipated and my thoughts became clear. For an hour I bailed, then I fixed the creased hose that had crippled the pump. I pulled out the kerosene heater and started drying things out. As the breeze died, I raised the mainsail only to find that it had ripped. "What else have you got?" I screamed. "Let me have it now! If I ever get to land, you won't get another chance."

—*adapted from* Maiden Voyage

THE STRONGEST KNOT

Most sailors realize that tying a knot in a line reduces its strength. Samson Cordage determined that the bowline-reeved loop bend (simply one bowline reeved through the loop of another—see illustration) retains about 60 percent of the rated strength of braided, three-strand, and double-braided line. That made it the strongest of all knots tested but placed it considerably behind the 90 percent achieved by professionally tucked and tightened eyesplices.

8

KNOW WHERE YOU ARE

We've always needed to know where we are, and we've always respected the wisdom of those who could tell us. "Navigation" comes from *navigatus*, the past participle of the Latin verb "to sail." And so it has always been—if you sail without knowing where you are, you're history.

Know where you are.

The winds and waves are always on the side of the ablest navigators.

—*Edward Gibbon,*
The History of the Decline and Fall of the Roman Empire

ALL AFLOAT   *(Eldridge Tide & Pilot Book)* It was our sincere hope to include alongside each aid to navigation its latitude and longitude in hundredths of minutes to make your piloting fit with loran and GPS usage since many sets now have the capability of using latitude and longitude in hundredths of minutes (20 yards).

However, the local Coast Guard districts have told us firmly that providing coordinates in hundredths of minutes is not advisable on the grounds that many navigational aids are buoys and that the location of floating buoys should be considered approximate; to consider locations exact is unrealistic and could lead to trouble. The latitudes and longitudes we provide (in tenths of minutes) should still give you positions within about 100 yards. [Though a tenth of a minute of latitude is about 200 yards.—eds.]

CROSS CHECK

(Ralph Naranjo) Statistics show that a bluewater sailor's biggest enemy is being off course. Blind faith in a single means of determining position is not healthy. By contrast, if you can compare two or more position-finding determiners—any combination of dead reckoning, celestial, GPS, radar, or whatever you have available—you will tend to have a far more accurate idea of your true position.

Plotting coordinates on a chart is really just the beginning of the position-finding process. Understanding clearly the strengths and weaknesses of all the navigational systems and equipment, and what that means for your data, is the second level of awareness that helps you decide how much faith you should put in each instrument's accuracy. Radar, for instance, is limited to line of sight, but it is superior at painting a detailed picture of the actual physical surroundings. That works very nicely to fill the small-scale void that is inherent with a Loran-C or GPS fix. Radar does not produce the photograph-like images our senses are used to, and targets must be tuned, but once you've mastered the machine, once you've got the knack of tuning out echoes and the feel for what different sorts of targets look like on the screen, the information you gain from your radar can act as the link between the GPS fix and the deck watch.

When we are approaching a coastline in overcast, I try to come in on a bold, shoal-free headland. I proceed to a waypoint that I have entered from GPS onto the chart. Once I have a radar picture of the coast, I take the bearings and ranges of all the distinguishing characteristics that appear on the screen and plot the resulting radar fix on the chart. I then compare this picture with my DR, and I try to build a consensus. Only after the positions have been crosschecked do I lay out an approach course to the safe harbor on the chart.

WHERE ARE THEY?

(Peter Isler) The rangefinder has been a part of match racing since the days of J-boats *Enterprise* and *Ranger*. Its earliest form was a stadimeter (or stadia, somewhat similar to a sextant) that mea-sured the angle of the opponents' mast (a known height) above the horizon. In 1983, Halsey Herreshoff, Dennis Conner's navigator on *Stars & Stripes*, was still using the same stadimeter. He added a programmable Hewlett-Packard calculator, a plotting board, and a "hockey puck" compass, but it still took him at least 35 seconds to measure a range, take a bearing, key the numbers and the wind speed into the calculator, and receive a "distance ahead" or "behind" result.

By 1987 we were still using the same rangefinder, but we'd combined it with a digital readout and KVH fluxgate compass, and connected it to our onboard computer. I got quite comfortable with the equipment, but there was still math to be done in my head, and the lag time between the need for a reading and the result was still on the order of 20 seconds.

By 1992, though, laser rangefinders had come into their own. We started in 1990 with pretty much the standard unit used by the police to check your speed on the highway, but we beefed it up, made it waterproof, and equipped it with a digital compass and a heads-up display that made it much easier to use in action. The basic premise is still "obtain the range and bearing of the enemy" and send that information to the onboard computer to look at the true wind direction and calculate the distance (or time) ahead or behind, but the shift from stadimeter to laser and the growth of onboard computer capability has made "how are we doing?" an easier question to answer.

ALARMING DEPTHS

(RR) Navigating in a big regatta (the Half-Ton North Americans) for the first time had me a bit uptight. I was worried about dragging our 5½-foot keel around Chesapeake Bay, so on the way to the starting line off Annapolis I set the depth alarm for 6.

It was a spinnaker start, and the fleet was bunched along the Eastern Shore trying to get the most from a dying norther and stay clear of the flooding current. Playing the cat's-paws off the beach and minding the curl of the chute, we were all concentration until the raucous beeping of the depth alarm cut in.

"Whazzat?"

"Shoal!"

"Let's get outta here!"

A slam-bang jibe put us on the other tack headed away from the fleet—out into the middle of the Bay. I watched for the rest to follow us, sure that they, too, wouldn't want to skim the flats. They all held on, out of the tide, on the favored jibe, in better air. But they'll run aground!

Finally I checked the chart. No flats!

The alarm?

I checked the depthsounder. It was still set to 6.

Six fathoms!

FINGER FIRST

(*Phinneas Sprague*) Develop the innate ability to know without instruments—within your personal limitations—where you are. You can develop this state of competence by practicing the "finger first" method of navigation. Constantly play the game of putting your finger on the chart where you think you are—*before* you advance your dead reckoning, *before* you plot your sight reduction or GPS position. If your guess is way off, why? Make a better-educated guess next time. On one level the "finger first" method is intuitive error-trapping, but some day a competent seat-of-the-pants assessment of where you are will prove a lifesaver.

SQUARE-RIGGED NAVIGATION

(*Alan Villiers*) Navigation in many sailing ships was not their strong point—"no sun, no fix" was the usual rule. Nor were the old-timers well-off for charts, since the masters had to buy their own. It was usual to have a very few—one for the whole South Pacific, one for the South Atlantic, one for the North Atlantic, and a general chart of the English Channel. Chronometer rates were kept as carefully as possible, but even with two or three aboard, there was an element of chance. Herman

Piening, on his first voyage to sea, was 99 days beating off the Horn in a big, full-rigged ship—the *Susanna*—partly because the master was afraid of the place (having been dismasted there on an earlier voyage), and partly because his one chronometer was so far out that when he came to run for his destination, he found he sailed 500 miles farther to the westward off Chile than he need have done.

—*adapted from* The Way of a Ship

COMPENSATE YOUR COMPASS

(*William V. Kielhorn*) Compensating your own magnetic compass isn't that difficult if you know a few basic facts and follow a few simple rules.

The compass is simply a magnetized needle, balanced on a jeweled bearing, that aligns itself with the horizontal component of the earth's weak magnetic field. It will faithfully point along the local north/south magnetic lines of force—*as long as no other magnetic field interferes*. Unfortunately, the steering compass on a boat is often mounted in proximity to items that may be magnetic—electric motors, speakers, tools, canned goods, DC wiring, eyeglass frames, even the grommets in the helmsman's cap.

Begin the compensation process by keeping magnetic items as far away from the compass as practicable. It is equally important to assure that the compass is mounted so that the "lubber's line" (the course indicator inside the compass) is exactly aligned with the fore-and-aft keel line of the boat.

Next check the bearing and pivot. Use a weak magnet (such as a steel screwdriver) held near the compass to deflect the card *no more than* 2 or 3 degrees. When you withdraw the magnet, the card should return to *exactly* where it was before. If it doesn't, send the compass to the factory or buy a new one.

Almost all modern yacht compasses come with built-in correcting magnet systems that permit correction of "semicircular" deviations of 20 degrees or more. The various systems are all analogs of fore-and-aft (for E/W correction)

and athwartships (for N/S correction) simple bar magnets. Steel ships require more complex systems, but these need not concern the average boater.

If the compass is properly aligned with the keel, if reasonable care has been taken to keep strongly magnetic material away, and if the bearing and pivot are good, then a satisfactory compensation becomes remarkably simple. Here's how:

1. Have the boat in normal cruising configuration, with all electrical equipment on that would normally be in use.
2. Find a wooden (non-magnetic) dock or piling, and tie up. Beware of using any structure that has vertical or horizontal steel members.
3. Find on your chart some clearly identified distant (couple of miles) object that bears within 10 degrees or so of MAGNETIC east or west. Point the bow of the boat exactly at that object. Turn the E/W correcting screw until the compass reads exactly the magnetic bearing you determined from the chart. Don't touch this screw again.
4. Do the same thing for an object bearing nearly north or south MAGNETIC. Make the adjustment only with the N/S screw.
5. If the correcting magnets are not strong enough to make full correction, you should then consider employing a professional compass adjuster.

One word of caution: neither loran nor GPS give you precise *heading* information. Each provides you with *track*, integrated over some time period. This track is presented as the resultant of leeway, current, and steering errors, and does not substitute for your basic and reliable magnetic compass—which indicates nothing but heading and is unaffected by power loss. [We seem to recall that adjusting one screw often takes the other out of adjustment, and the process is to reduce the error in each alternatively until it is minimized. A single pair of adjustments seems optimistic.—eds.]

—*adapted from* Basic Motorboat Seamanship

COZY COMPASS

(*Ridge White*) Wherever you store your boat for the winter, unless she's heated, take your compass home and keep it warm. Compass oil contracts significantly in the cold, and even with good gaskets, air can get pulled inside the compass. The resultant bubble is surprisingly hard to get rid of. Avoid tricky filling operations by giving your compass a warm spot to spend the winter.

FRICTION TEST

(*Ridge White*) You can test your compass to see whether its pivot and jewel are frictionless. After the card has come to rest, use a magnetic object to deflect it 3 degrees. Remove the magnet. Does the card return a full 3 degrees? Perform the "3 degrees" test clockwise and counterclockwise on several headings. Average the results. One or 2 degrees of friction probably isn't worth worrying about. Three degrees, though, and perhaps you should invest in a new pivot/jewel assembly.

VARIATIONS ON A COMPASS

Choosing a compass is a big choice. The larger the better, for visibility, durability, and steering ease. It's important not to be lured into false economy. Bargain compasses rarely are able to withstand the temperature variations that come with normal use. With a hemispherically sealed, flat-bottomed dome typical of bargain instruments, the liquid has nowhere to go when it expands. Better compasses have a phosphor bronze bellows built in to allow them to accommodate volume change. The spherical design of the higher-priced compasses reduces internal turbulence and maximizes card stability. Flush or binnacle mounts do the best job of insulating the compass from vibration; if you have to choose a bracket, pick heavy cast bronze. Check that your compass comes with good red-light illumination.

LESSEN LORAN NOISE   *(Gordon West)*

Marine loran receivers generally give us plenty of signal to work with thanks to transistor pre-amps in the antenna. Along with the signal, though, comes range-lessening noise. Better receivers have noise filters. "Notch filters" (dedicated suppressors that prowl for noise in pre-specified frequency ranges) can be automatic (expensive) or manual (medium-priced) or minimal (el cheapo). They are a big part of what you're paying for when you buy your set.

The more noise you can dampen, the cleaner the pulses your set has to work with and the better it will perform. Noise on loran is similar to AM radio static you hear if you hold a radio next to your engine or outboard. A quick way, then, to reduce noise is to turn off the engine when you're trying to pull in a weak loran signal. A radical answer to the problem is to shield the inside of the engine compartment with copper screen or foil to suppress the noise. Another step you might take *in extremis* is suppression wiring on your spark plugs. Beyond that, noise filters are available for other noise culprits (alternating system, bilge pump, fans, etc.). Snoop around with a cheap AM portable. When it is deluged with static from an appliance, your loran will be, too.

Perhaps the most effective improvement you can make, though, is to improve your set's grounding. Use copper foil or something that has *width*. Don't use round wires for a loran ground because the quality of the ground is a function of the surface area of the ground connector. Attach the foil to the back of the set and run it to something that contacts seawater—a bronze through-hull, a grounding plate, etc.

The last loran trick is to wire the set directly to the ship's battery. Bypass the instrument wiring, put a fuse in the positive end of the connection, and let the battery act as a DC line filter to further eliminate noise from your alternator system.

HOW FAR?   *(John Irving)* The following standards of

distance are approximate only—but may be of some use when recording a beam position of a yacht as she passes a buoy, beacon, or similar aid to navigation. In general, judging distances at sea is something of a disillusionment when estimates come to be compared with the correct distances as measured. Usually the estimate will exceed the correct distance—distances over water almost invariably seem greater than they really are, although on a bright, clear day, a distant object can appear to be nearer than it is. Overcast produces the opposite result. Height of eye is important, too. At 8 feet the horizon is 3¼ miles distant. At 6 feet it is but 2½ miles away.

A ship with her bow wave just below the horizon line, then, will be between 2½ and 2¾ miles away. Two miles distant (from an 8-foot height of eye), a large navigational buoy should be visible but its shape and color will not be clear to the naked eye. Smaller buoys and the details of flags and ensigns become clear at about a mile. At 400 to 500

Tis distance lends enchantment to the view

And robes the mountain in its azure hue.

—*Thomas Campbell*

yards, a walking man's legs become discernible and a rowing man's arms may be seen to work. Between 200 and 300 yards distant, a man's face becomes discernible, and the swirl of the tidal stream around a buoy or pile can be detected.

—adapted from The Yachtsman's Weekend Book

THE GREAT BEAR

For the navigators of the pre-Homeric era, almost 1,000 years B.C., the only things to rely on were knowledge of the winds and weather, a leadline, and a few signs in the sky. Principal among these was the Great Bear (also called the Plow), which we know today as the Big Dipper.

Even the earliest mariners could find north as soon as the stars came out. They knew the Great Bear "never bathes in the ocean stream." Odysseus was the first man in recorded history to make use of the stars for navigation. Calypso told him "keep the Great Bear on your port hand as you sail across the open sea, and you shall reach your home."

TIDAL LUNACY

(Capt. Bill Brogdon) Telling the height of tide by the moon begins with using the angle of the moon relative to due south. The moon will be at approximately the same angle for high tide every day. The angle the moon makes with due south will be the same at low tide, too. To tell tide by the moon, first determine the time of high tide (by observation). Note the position of the moon. If it's not visible, wait until it is. Let's say the moon bears due south at high tide. Throughout the month, whenever the moon bears due south, the tide will be high.

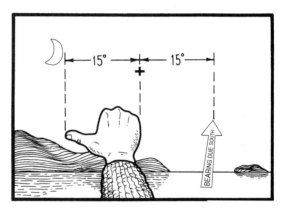

Tidal Lunacy

TIDAL TWELFTHS

This useful formula describes tidal flow across the planet where there are two high waters within a 24 hour period. Such *semidiurnal* areas include Europe and the East Coast of North America.

"One, two, three; three, two, one"—that's the way the tide goes. In the first hour of flood or ebb it changes by one twelfth of the total height of tide. In the second hour, two twelfths; third and fourth hours, three twelfths; fifth hour, two twelfths; and in the sixth hour, one twelfth. If you know the tidal range and the time of high or low water, you can pinpoint the depth throughout the entire tide cycle. If you know the depth of the water, you can figure the exact state of the tide.

TIDE CLOCK

Tidal information for where you are and where you might be headed comes now in a battery-operated unit. In the US, Marisystems, (800) 528-4337, makes a TideTracker whose information bank extends as far as 2010 and includes current height of tide, next high/low tide, current speed, next peak current, and more. It can be referenced to 1,666 locations between Eastport, Maine, and Galveston, Texas. In the UK, Proesser Scientific Instruments of Ipswich offers a similar instrument, which has the same functions but also includes the date of neap and spring tides for over 500 European ports from Norway to Gibraltar.

MARKING HIGH WATER

(Eldridge Tide & Pilot Book) Many people wonder why the times of high water and the beginning of ebb tide at the mouths of rivers and inlets giving into an ocean are not simultaneous. Picture the tide in the ocean rising. It rises until it reaches its maximum height at the inlet. At that time the water in the bay behind the river mouth or inlet is not as high as the water at the inlet. For the ebb tide to start, the water in the river must be higher than the water in the ocean. The time that it takes for the bay to "fill up" is the difference between high water at the inlet and the beginning of ebb tide through it.

SHOOTING STARS

(Rosalind Miranda) If you are going to sea, are you going to depend on your electronics? If you're like me, you want more dependability than they can provide. Take a sextant. (Don't worry about not knowing or having forgotten how to use it. My book *Miranav* walks you through with only addition and subtraction and with no theory at all to learn, remember, or digest.)

The very best sextants are remarkably accurate, but is it accuracy you can use? With practice you can become steady and accurate, but *in practice* you'll be on a rolling, pitching platform that is bound to throw in some sort of monkey wrench. In practical terms, therefore, don't spend 20 times more to get the best; you won't be able to use it to advantage. Having the cheapest sextant isn't good,

either. Your own sextant work will most likely introduce a nautical mile or two of error into your sights. Why double that by using imprecise equipment?

I recommend a sextant that is accurate to 5 minutes or less of arc. The cheapies can't do that, but the better plastic sextants fall in that range. If you prefer metal to plastic, prices now are not that different. Also, you might try a used sextant, as I have. If you know what to look for and/or have a reputable nautical shop to help you check them out, the used ones can be great values.

STAFF TRAINING

(Lt. John St. John) As I ate my porridge, I thought of the problem of navigating ships back to the prize court. The compass was the main instrument, of course, and most seamen could box the compass. The latitude a ship sailed on could be important, too. We had no extra sextants aboard *Rapid*, but I remembered that before the sextant was invented, a seaman had been able to determine the latitude by a crude device called a mariner's staff. After breakfast the men were lined up on the afterdeck in the formation reminiscent of church services. "Men," I began, "to make sure that our captures reach a port, an English port rather than a French one, we will be conducting classes in basic navigation for every seaman who wishes to learn."

At noon the next day it seemed that every seaman not on watch was trying to sight the sun with his primitive equipment.

[While Mr. Moxon's fictional hero, Lt. St. John, undoubtedly had need, we wonder about his breech of custom in educating common seamen in the art of position-finding. More than wealth, breeding, and refinement, what separated officers from seamen was the ability to navigate. Without it even the saltiest tar was "lost." How else did generations of officers retain such complete control over homeless, shanghaied, and countryless crews century after century, country after country?—eds.]

—*adapted from* Lay Her Before the Wind,
by Lloyd M. Moxon

PALU

(Dr. David Lewis) I have sailed many thousands of sea miles without instruments as the pupil of the last great natural navigators. They have shown me how to steer by horizon stars, the sun, and the swells, to find latitudes of islands by knowing their zenith stars and the height of the Pole Star. I have learned their various methods for expanding small targets into wide screens marked by cloud formations, bird zones, wave patterns broken by islands, and other signs. I have seen the mysterious *te lapa* (underwater lightning) under the Pacific waters.

—*adapted from* The Voyaging Stars

ONE GOOD TERN

(Stephen Thomas) I first met Mau where he waited for the ship to return to Satawal from Ulithi.

"Sam says hello," I said nervously, trying to establish contact through a mutual Hawaiian friend.

He shook his head, holding me in his hard gaze until I felt even more uncomfortable. "No."

"Excuse me," I stammered.

"Sam no say hello—Sam say 'Aloha,'" he said erupting into wild laughter. "You come to study with me—welcome."

Once we boarded the ship he began my instruction. He took my pencil and made a circle on the page of my notebook. Around it he painstakingly placed 32 dots. The stars keep their relation to one another and always rise and set at the same place on the horizon. He laughed at my notebook. This star map, like everything else he taught me, came from his head.

At sunset I stood with Mau at the rail. I asked the direction of the current.

"From there, weak" he said, pointing to the setting sun.

"How do you know?"

"Water is tight. You look. Water is tight."

I stared at the shimmering water until my eyes hurt. I'd delivered boats across the Atlantic and the Pacific, but I couldn't tell a thing. In the morning we anchored off Eauripik. I asked the captain about the current during the night. "There wasn't much, just a little from the west."

Before long I graduated to sailing with Mau. Pikelot is 80 miles from Satawal. If the wind increased, we decided, we would go. A light wind sprang up. Mau announced, unwinding a trolling line, that we were nearing a reef. A dolphin leapt across our bow and squeaked. Night fell and we caught no fish. Late at night the wind died and there began a maddening cycle of slatting and changing course. I wondered how Mau knew our position.

At sunrise we studied the swells. I would have been very nervous were I navigating alone. We caught two tuna during the day, but when the sun went down darkness came over our heads like an oily rag. All night wind and rain swirled around us. I shivered after baking all day. In the gray dawn, a light wind was left over and we sailed silently for an

To be a palu you must have three qualities: fierceness, strength, and wisdom. The knowledge of navigation brings all three.

—*Mau Piailug,*
from The Last Navigator,
by Stephen Thomas

hour looking for birds. Disappointed, Mau told us we would have to run down to (the much larger) West Fayu instead of continuing to Pikelot. I was disappointed but too tired to really care. Mau sat glumly by the outrigger.

Then someone spotted a lone tern. Fifteen minutes later a flock appeared. Now that we were inside Pikelot's zone of birds, we swept close-hauled back and forth hoping to sight it. Early in the afternoon one of the crew spotted swells, which mean a reef, in the east. We sighted Pikelot before sundown, but by the time we paddled the canoe through the surf to the sand, it was three in the morning.

—*adapted from* The Last Navigator

WAYFINDERS

(*Will Kyselka*) Mau was Nainoa's teacher. Never, though, was Nainoa apprenticed to Mau in the traditional master-novice sense. He was always Mau's student, an unusual one to be sure, who approached the art of wayfinding in a manner unfamiliar to Mau. Yet each found Tahiti.

Nainoa had no way to fully understand traditional navigation. He arrived by inquiry. He invented what he needed in order to discover, borrowing from Mau that which was freely given, to develop a wayfinding system uniquely his own.

Mau danced and sang at the *lu'au* celebrating the arrival of *Hokule'a* in Tahiti. Then, at the moment that was right for him, he went to Nainoa's family, greeting each and saying, "You are my sister," or "You are my brother," welcoming each into his own family.

Happy with Nainoa's success, he turned to his special student and said, "Now you know all there is to know—but it will be 20 years before you see."

—*adapted from* An Ocean in Mind

GREATER POSITION SURETY

(*Jonathan Lewis*) My first exposure to the wonders of the Global Positioning System (GPS) was during a return trip from the Virgin Islands to the States in 1989. Back then coverage was limited be-

cause the total number of satellites needed to complete the system hadn't been deployed.

Finding a flat island in a large ocean can be tough. We were looking (after our current-crossed transit from the Dominican Republic) for Great Inagua. Loran is virtually useless in that area and cloud cover made a sun sight impossible—it was the sort of situation where anxiety tends to creep into cruising. But GPS was the tonic. It made scanning the horizon not a desperate measure but a case of fulfilled expectations. The fear of missing our mark was replaced with the thrill of hitting it on the nose.

I know, of course, that all navigation systems are subject to error. Of course there must be some redundancy. Of course you should be wary of the hypnotic efficiency of GPS. Of course you should take all input as an aide to *your* navigation—don't let the silicon chips do all the thinking. However, the fact that it's not 100 percent foolproof does not negate GPS's immense value.

Its ability to provide pinpoint position-fixing is just a portion of its promise. GPS has all of the functions that Loran-C provided (without the drawbacks of storm interference, transmitter proximity, etc.). It is much more user-friendly than loran ever was: course over ground, speed over ground, cross-track error, velocity made good, just to name a few, pop up painlessly. The earlier satnavs pale by comparison. GPS provides a constant stream of accurate fixes!

Information makes you a better navigator. Whether that information comes from the tiny hairs on the back of your neck, the seat of your pants, numbers wrung from sun and stars, or an LCD, you are the one who has to decide what to do with it. This gizmo called GPS gives me information that makes that process both pleasant and rewarding.

ALLOWING FOR LEEWAY

(*Eric Hiscock*) An approximate estimate of leeway can be made by judging the angle between the wake and the fore-and-aft line of the boat. Going to windward, allow for leeway in calculating your course made good. Sailing off the wind, however, you can compensate for leeway in advance by altering course to allow for its effect.

—*adapted from* Cruising Under Sail

MAGIC COCONUT

Polynesian voyagers often took to sea a nut drilled with three holes. The voyager would fill it so the water level in it just reached two of the holes. The third hole was angled so that sighting Polaris through it would put the sailor on the latitude of his home island. Keeping the angle constant, he would thus run down his easting (or westing) until he arrived home.

Magic Coconut

WORST SIDE SCENARIO   *(Phinneas Sprague)*

Always navigate off the worst side of the triangle. Some will say to start from the center of your "cocked hat" when you get three LOPs to cross, but take the worst side. In a world of GPS positions within feet, this advice dates me, but as a place from which to take your course to the next mark, take the one that's farthest away, farthest out, farthest to leeward. Be tough, be smart, be realistic—always navigate off the worst side of the triangle.

CHIP LOG   *(R. M. "Mike" Willoughby)* When you are

almost becalmed, you still need to know your speed. We mark positions on the bulwarks, drop in a piece of wood forward, and time its passage over our measured "course." We then figure the speed.

The formula for calculating boat speed is as follows:

$$\frac{0.6 \times \text{DISTANCE IN FEET BETWEEN MARKS}}{\text{TIME IN SECONDS}} = \text{SPEED IN KNOTS}$$

KNOT LOG   *(Roger Duncan)* Our "chip" is a piece of

pie-shaped wood. I bore holes in the corners and attach the one at the point to a line on a free-wheeling drum. Bridle lines from the other two corners are clipped onto the running line with a clothespin. After a few "stray" fathoms the main running line is marked with knots at 25-foot-4-inch intervals. We drop the chip over and let the line run. After 15 seconds we stop it and count the number of knots pulled out. That number equals the boat's speed.

The distance between knots is calculated: 15 seconds is to 3,600 seconds (one hour) as X (distance between knots) is to 6,080 feet (one nautical mile). Thus,

$$\frac{15 \times 6,080}{3,600} = X = 25 \text{ FT. 4 IN.}$$

Therefore every 25 feet 4 inches traveled in 15 seconds is equivalent to a knot of boat speed.

CORAL CONFIDENCE

(RR) I've poked between reefs enough, Caribbean and South Pacific, to know that it can be done. The thought that it can be done casually, however, is false confidence of the most dangerous kind. Like most other piloting situations where mistakes can be too costly to make, the pressure mounts. Seaway, surge, and the anticipated joys of making a landfall can all push you toward getting it over with—rushing through. Combat that pressure and stay at your best. Know your boat, trust yourself, concentrate on known elements, and don't let lurid images of the snaggletoothed menace beneath the surface mess up your mind and your piloting.

It's nice to *see* what's beneath the surface. "Eyeball" navigation is something you should be continually honing and developing. It's worth it, for instance, to go out of your way to find whatever books, magazine articles, or even picture postcards are available that let you get the sort of "lay of the land" that pilots and charts don't often provide. Aerial photos are ideal, but topographical maps, sketches, perspectives, and renderings have all proven helpful from time to time. And talk to anyone who's run the pass or made the passage. Blind faith, however—in charts, markers, stakes, or advice—is the enemy of good eyeball piloting. Keep your eyes open.

You can help those eyes with polarized sunglasses to cut through reflected glare; a long-billed cap helps vision, too. Standing on the bow pulpit may provide enough elevation to extend your view, but if you need a better perspective, go aloft. Piloting from the crosstrees has advantages, and sometimes it's the only way, but it subjects you to exaggerated boat motion and isolates you from boathandling. You can minimize these drawbacks with mast steps, a clipboard for your chart, a lanyard for everything else (glasses, binoculars, etc.), and excellent communication with your driver. Hand signals (another subject) are a must.

Veteran circumnavigator Steve Dashew says, "water quality is the first factor" in piloting. Crystal clear or hopelessly cloudy are both possibilities. Since eyeball navigation is precisely that, I try not to go where I can't see well enough to "pick my way through."

The sun is another big factor in visibility. You can see with it over your shoulder but not when it's overhead or in your eyes. Low sun angles provide narrow windows that are limiting and even deceiving. Glassy calm is tough to penetrate, but overcast sets a reflective shield over the water that is impenetrable. Occasional clouds present problems by casting shadows that look just like coral heads on the bottom.

You can tell the water depth by the play of the colors:

blue = deep water
light blue = shoaling but navigable
white = shoals
brown and purple = definite bottom crunchers

Passes through barrier reefs are different from coral channels. Currents are extremely strong because the heavy volume of water from waves breaking over the whole reef into the lagoon has just the pass as a way out. Stemming a powerful ebb presents problems. Shoot for slack tide when you can.

Finally, if you're forced to close with coral in the dark, a barrier reef will show up very well under a powerful spotlight.

VIKING RADAR

(Mike Saunders) The technique is as old as the hills. Sailing through fog or mist, take the belaying pin in one hand, stopwatch in the other. Rap the belaying pin hard against something that will make a sharp sound, then listen. When the report bounces back, time it. Ten seconds equals a mile. Hopefully the echo won't be drowned out by the sound of the surf breaking at the foot of the cliff.

THE DEPTH/SPEED FIX

(Jack West) The vertical line from the bottom to your boat can be a Line of Position. Cross that with another LOP, such as the distance-run line obtained by watch and speed, and you can find your position. Your distance run is the radius of a circle. Where along that circle are there depths similar to the ones you are recording?

If your depthsounder doesn't have an offset adjustment, you will need to know the depth of your transducer below the water, and add that to your reading to get the true depth. Also keep the height of tide in mind. If you are enjoying 5 feet of tide above low water, subtract 5 feet from the depth reading to get soundings that will correspond with the data on the chart, which were taken at mean low water.

LASER TRANSITS

Entering New London harbor after dark is a unique experience. Look up! Do you see an emerald tracer, a laser light beam beckoning you down the fairway? If not, you're off course. For several years a laser beam generated by the US Coast Guard Research and Development laboratory at Avery Point has nightly traced the range into the harbor from Long Island Sound. Lasers are highly directional. Move more than ten degrees from beneath the beam and it fades into the dark and becomes invisible. Cross-sound ferries and other regular harbor users are recording the beam's effectiveness through all seasons and sorts of weather. "Beam me in, Coastie."

SHIPS OF THE DESERT

(T. E. Lawrence) Next day we left Abu Raga. Auda led us up a tributary valley which soon widened into the plain of Shegg—a sand flat. About it, scattered in confusion, sat small islands and pinnacles of red sandstone, wind-eroded at the bases until they looked very fit to fall and block the road; which wound in and out between them through narrows seeming to give no passage but always opening into another bay of blind alleys.

Through this maze Auda led unhesitatingly. There were no footmarks on the ground, for each wind swept like a great brush over the sand surface, stippling the traces of the last travelers till the surface was again a pattern of innumerable tiny virgin waves. Only the dried camel droppings, which were lighter than the sand and rounded like walnuts, escaped over its ripples. They rolled about, to be heaped in corners by the skirling winds. It was perhaps by them, as much as by his unrivaled road sense, that Auda knew the way.

—*adapted from* Seven Pillars of Wisdom

TEACH YOURSELF TO SEE

(Ralph Naranjo) One of the hallmarks of an experienced navigator is the ability to look at a two-dimensional chart and to "see" the three-dimensional reality it represents. One of the best ways to develop this ability is to work with the charts of areas that you know well. Rather than ignoring the chart in home waters, consult it:

- Are the features you see as pronounced on the chart as they are in fact?
- Does the cartographer's representation of the shoreline match what you see?
- Does the distant "background" appear closer than the chart makes it seem?
- Do the "protected pockets" that seem to provide good lees on the chart offer more or less shelter in reality? Why?

RHUMB LINE

A rhumb line is a line on the earth's surface that intersects all meridians of longitude at the same angle. The extension of the *lubber line* of the compass card fore and aft will cut all meridians crossed at a constant angle. This is the course angle. A line of constant course, therefore, is a rhumb line. On a plane surface over a relatively short distance, where the earth's curvature is negligible, a rhumb line is used for plotting a boat's course. On ocean passages, *great-circle* sailing provides a more direct course.

CIRCLES TO TRAVEL

The shortest way of connecting any two points on the face of the earth is by a *great circle* cutting through both points as well as the center of the earth. The Equator is a great circle, as are the meridians of longitude.

Standard navigational charts are Mercator projections, representing the curving earth on a flat paper. This makes it possible to draw straight lines between points on the chart. While these *rhumb lines* are adequate for coastwise work and short (under 600 miles) passages, the distance between endpoints of longer passages will be markedly less along a great-circle course than the rhumb line distance (more than 100 miles shorter for the 3,000-mile North Atlantic crossing, for instance).

Probably the easiest way to obtain a great-circle course is to plot it on a *gnomonic projection* (where great circles appear as straight lines) and then transfer points along that line onto a Mercator chart. (There are also formulas and calculator programs that let you generate a great circle from the position coordinates of your starting point and destination.) Connect the waypoints you have transferred by means of a series of rhumb lines. This will let you approximate great-circle sailing and its distance saved.

MAKESHIFT CHART

(George Roosevelt) Using any chart of the same scale as the one that you need, prick through the latitude/longitude intersections to form a position grid on the back of your old chart. Next refer to the *Light List*. It gives the position of major aids to navigation; you can fix them using the coordinates that you have pricked through. Because the lights and plotted aids to navigation are outboard of the dangers they indicate, you can steer to seaward of the marks and have safe passage. I delivered *Mistress* through the upper Chesapeake (10-foot draft and all) using just such a jerry-built chart.

EASY ENTRANCE

(Mike Saunders) Especially at night or at any time when you're entering a narrow channel and are unsure if you're making leeway, take a bearing on either side of the channel entrance. Steer so that the two entrance marks are each the same number of degrees to port or starboard, then keep the difference between your course and the two entrance bearings constant as you advance.

PAINLESS PLANNING

The Cruising Information Center was operated by the Cruising Club of America until recently. It closed its doors, but its resources were bequeathed to the Stephen Phillips Library in the Peabody Essex Museum, Salem, Massachusetts. The charts, pilots, logs, and cruise summaries gathered by the CIC are personal, pertinent, and very valuable in planning a cruise. It is good that they are still available.

FISH TRAILS

The Ocean Cruising Club operates a service similar to the CIC. Port officers and cruisers in the field have helped the O.C.C. over the past five years to build an extensive library of port and cruising facilities, much of it covering areas that are otherwise poorly documented. For a copy of current worldwide or area listings, contact Murray Kenneth, 36 Upper Gardner St., Brighton BN1 4AN, England. (Allow 14 days for copying and return. A stamped self-addressed envelope would be appreciated.)

BOWDITCH

(Rosalind Miranda) The American Practical Navigator was originally written by Nathaniel Bowditch and published in 1802. This is not just for the amateur looking for a simpler way of doing things. It is the navigator's Bible. Everything you ever wanted to know about any aspect of navigation is between its covers. I take it with me wherever I am navigating. If anything does go wrong, *Bowditch* will have the answer.

WHO ARE THOSE GUYS?

The *World Status Map* is an unrivaled resource for foreign cruising. Prepared by BRI/Pinkerton, whose International Travel Service specializes in briefings for corporations and travel agents, it shows at a glance the peculiar visitor requirements and restrictions for all countries in the world. Passports, visas, health, and currency facts . . ., but beyond that:

- Do you know which countries require you to have an AIDS test before visiting?
- Do you know where carrying binoculars is unwise?
- Which 97 countries currently report malaria?
- Which rebels have specifically targeted Americans?

The answers go on.

DIPPING A LIGHT

When you first sight a light at night, lower your height of eye. If the light disappears yet reappears when you return to your original height, the light is on the horizon.

REMOVING A COMPASS

Before removing the compass from a binnacle to work on it or store it, place four strips of tape across both compass and mount at about 90-degree intervals. Slit the tape to remove the compass. The tape will show exactly how to position the compass when you remount it.

LEADING LEADLINE

(Carlton Poulnot) A useful way of taking soundings as you approach shore is to attach a cork or float to the leadline at a depth of your draft plus 2 feet. In that way, as you swing the lead out ahead of your boat, as long as the float sinks, you have passable water. When the float floats, STOP. [Casting a weight and float with a fishing rod will let you find the depth well in front of the bow.—eds.]

CHARTS ABOARD

(Don Street) It is seldom possible to have too many charts. It is also seldom possible to find room to stow the ones you've got. A nice big chart table with 30 or 40 charts stowed inside is wonderful, but for me it's not enough.

When we delivered *Mariann* south, she had by far the best chart stowage arrangement I've ever encountered. Mrs. Gibbons, the owner's wife, folded the charts, labeled them, classified them by areas covered, and then stowed each group in a clear plastic envelope. On the inside of each envelope she taped a list of the charts inside (by number and description). Finally, she composed a master list showing exactly which chart was in which envelope.

NOTEWORTHY NOTES

(John Mellor) Offshore navigation is most often practiced from the palatial, plenipotentiary splendor of the nav station, and it quite often entails naught but the leisurely sifting of myriad strains of information to determine, without particular pressure, at what spot in the wide blue ocean you might happen to be.

Inshore navigation is, by contrast, accomplished most often at the helm while, 'midst attendant boathandling and maneuvering chores, you endeavor to steer clear of shoals and hazards as they present themselves in dizzying array at a blistering pace.

Therefore, when navigating inshore, study your books and charts well in advance, have them close at hand, and—this is my major point—digest them into a list, much as the copilot on a cross-country flight or the navigator in a sports car rally might. I list every danger and major decision, along with the scraps of info (bearings, characteristics, intervals, depths corrected for tide, distances, etc.) that will help me deal with them best. I cross each one off (along with each landmark, buoy, beacon, transit, or what-have-you that we pass) as we go. It's easy, and it works.

—*adapted from* The Art of Pilotage

MANAGED GUESSING *(Arthur Beiser)*

The problems of a sailboat navigator are too anachronistic to be considered in most textbooks. I feel that the overriding consideration is to build into every course a healthy allowance for uncertainty. The worst moment for the navigator is to complete the plotted journey and know neither where he is nor in which direction his destination lies.

The wise navigator, therefore, draws on the chart lines on either side of the rhumb line that represent his guess as to the limits of what might actually happen. Often I don't even try to make a perfect landfall but instead deliberately head over to one side, well beyond the limit of any misjudgment of leeway or poor estimates by helmsmen of courses made good. Then, when land is sighted, I know which way to turn. If you combine this fail-safe scheme with staying to windward of your destination, it's hard to see what is to be gained by sailing a direct course in any but the best circumstances.

—adapted from The Sailor's World

FISHERMAN'S BEND

A *fisherman's bend* is similar to a round turn and two half hitches, except the first of the two half-hitches is made through the round turn, and the second through the standing part. The fisherman's bend is a fine way to bend a rode to an anchor, but even then you should seize the loose end to the standing part for safety.

Fisherman's Bend.

Hervey Garrett Smith (from *Arts of the Sailor*)

Fisherman's Bend plus two half hitches and a seizing.

Jim Sollers illustration (from *The Elements of Seamanship*)

SAVE YOURSELF

Seadogs are fond of saying it, usually out the sides of their mouths. It is the glaring lesson of the 1979 Fastnet storm disaster. It came clear in the "Queen's Day Storm" of 1994. It's become as commonplace and easy to ignore as advice about taking wooden nickels or eating yellow snow.

It's "step up!" As in, "Don't get into a liferaft until you have to step up."

No matter how you slice your disaster at sea, the mother ship has better survival, navigation, and self-rescue potential than any liferaft. Stay with the boat. I can remember my father shoving me out into the backwaters of the Shrewsbury River in our 8-foot pram for my first solo sail. "Have fun. If anything happens, *stay with the boat.*"

Odysseus is the hero of one of man's first recorded sea stories. When his raft was breaking apart, the waves were building, and things looked bleakest, a nymph named Ino appeared:

Radio transmitters should not be permitted. Calling for help would bring discredit upon the race. It seems, indeed, more seemly for the entrant to drown like a gentleman.

—Blondie Hasler,
from his proposal
for the first Singlehanded
Transatlantic Race.

". . . do what I tell you.
Shed that cloak, let the gale take your craft,
and swim for it—swim hard to get ashore.

Here, make my veil your sash; it is not mortal;
you cannot now be drowned or suffer harm."

After she had bestowed her veil, the nereid
dove like a gull to windward
where a dark waveside overcame her whiteness.
But in perplexity Odysseus
said to himself, his great heart laboring:

"Oh damned confusion! Can this be a ruse
to trick me from the boat for some god's pleasure?
No, I'll not swim. With my own eyes I saw
how far the land lies she called my shelter.
Better to do the wise thing as I see it.
While this poor planking holds, I stay aboard.

—Homer, The Odyssey (Robert Fitzgerald translation)

It made good sense then and it still makes good sense
now: *Stay with the boat.*

There's more to offshore survival than this simple bit of
wisdom, but it's a good place to begin. Not only has it been
true through thousands of years, it also spotlights the truth
that no wisdom, no gear, no rescuer, nor any tactic has
proven as powerful over the generations as sailors' determination to save themselves.

Save yourself.

WRECKLESS ABANDON   *(Don Street)*

A ship is much easier to spot than a liferaft. When *Curlew*, a 72-foot
schooner, was supposedly sinking off Bermuda, a ship answered her
SOS, and the crew managed to abandon her and scramble aboard via a
cargo net. Three days later *Curlew* was found still afloat by a salvage
tug. *Integrity* going south in 1970 was abandoned in sinking condition
but found afloat weeks later and towed in by another yacht. The only
way to abandon ship is to tie the liferaft down on deck, inflate it, and

sit in it until the boat actually goes down. Then cut loose.

—*adapted from* The Ocean Sailing Yacht

SURVIVAL GUIDE

Every once in a great while a book comes along that manages to stand head and shoulders above the rest. *Survival at Sea* by Bernard Robin is such a book. The first part of the book is a thoughtful compilation (and brief analysis) of 31 true shipwreck-survival accounts. Beginning in 1431 and extending through 1973, these incidents are a rich sampling of the things survivors must face. In the second part, Robin draws on those stories (and much more) to assemble the lessons learned into practical chapters such as, "The Battle Against Thirst," "The Battle Against Hunger," ". . . Fatigue," ". . . Climate," ". . . Panic and Despair," ". . . Drowning," ". . . Illness," ". . . Not Being Spotted," and "Preparations for Survival."

Given modern knowledge, equipment, technology, and communication, those who go to sea have an excellent chance of surviving shipwreck. What they most need in order to enjoy that chance is *training*. Robin's book is a great place to start.

CANNY CREDO

(Steve Callahan) I carried Dougal Robertson's *Sea Survival* when I was adrift. Aside from chapters of invaluable advice drawn from his own ordeal in the Pacific, he gave me a helpful way of looking at my own antics: "Rescue will come as a welcome interruption to the survival routine."

—*adapted from* Adrift

[Callahan survived 76 days adrift in the Atlantic after *Napoleon Solo*—his own design—was holed and sank. He covered 1,800 miles until he came to be rescued by fishermen from the Caribbean island of Marie Galante, near Guadeloupe.—eds.]

GIFT OF LIFE

(Arne Brun Lie) The camps were certainly . . . hard—hard to survive, hard to understand, hard to get over. Maybe all I really got from the concentration camps was a sense of how sweet life is. I mean, anytime your life is threatened you appreciate life more. That's what the death camps gave me . . . life. I don't know what to tell you exactly about the camps, but a walking scarecrow like me would have walked halfway 'round the world for a meal like the one we had tonight.

Torre Hytten and I were together in Dachau and Natzweiler. To this day he still keeps tins of meat under his bed. Your body has ways of dealing with hunger. As your stomach shrinks, you feel it less. Nonetheless, we felt it. There were differing ideas on how you should deal with it mentally. One group said that you must never think, speak, or dream about food. I belonged to the other group. We composed menus incessantly, spoke of food constantly, shared and elaborated our most outlandish food fantasies. My dream was at least four helpings of meat pudding,

Although the sea was my greatest enemy, it was also my greatest ally. I know intellectually that the sea is indifferent, but her richness allowed me to survive.

—*Steve Callahan*, Adrift

green peas, boiled potatoes, and thick brown gravy. When I had dysentery attacks, I was so thirsty that I'd have traded my right hand for a pilsner beer. Meat pie and pilsner beer—simple as that.

—adapted from Night and Fog

Ghostly White

(MB) Several years ago I wrote a piece about a certain brand of European foul-weather gear that was being marketed in the US. It was lightweight, well made, and able to "breathe." Perhaps my purple prose helped sales; in any event, I received a complimentary set. Somewhat later my teenage daughter was assigned to a marine biology course aboard a Wood's Hole sail-training ship. She began a clamor for the cash to outfit herself with suitable foul-weather gear. I remembered my gift set and dragged it out of the closet.

"Daddy," she replied reproachfully, "are you trying to get me out of the way forever?"

I scratched my head.

"It's WHITE!," she cried. "Ever since I can remember, you've said that white foul-weather gear was idiotic because nothing could be harder to see in breaking white waves."

I felt meekly for my wallet.

Survival Chute

(Claudine Pare-Lescure) The keel was driven into a crevice in the coral. The next wave broke the keel off the hull with awful cracking sounds. Water flooded into the boat in minutes. I have just enough time to take out the liferaft, pull its inflation cord, and tie it to the boat. I grab a 15-liter jerry can of fresh water, a chart, a compass, a crayon, plastic bags, and the spinnaker.

The wet and bulky spinnaker takes up all the space in the bottom of the raft. To spread nearly 1,300 square feet of sail to dry on a 32-square foot canopy will take patience. I need to make my raft into a sailboat. The farther west that I travel, the more likely are a landfall or rescue.

First I dive and cut free the anti-drift pockets on the raft. Then I fashion a mast with the two paddles tied together end-to-end. Then I cut off a piece of spinnaker and tie one of the corners to the top of the mast. I get as much of this piece of sail to fill as possible. We are making 2 knots to the west! I put reinforcements cut from the spinnaker at each friction point on the rigging lines.

This sail, retrieved at the last moment, is a marvelous resource. I use a piece to make an inflated float for my fishing line. Foreseeing that the next night will be cold, I cut myself a large "blanket," a skirt, and a double-lined jacket. I fish as much as I can and keep my catch alive in a submerged bag made of spinnaker—but it attracted sharks. When the wind shifts into the north, to reduce my drift I use a sea anchor made from spinnaker cloth.

One evening the mast of a fishing boat appeared over the horizon. I waved the bright spinnaker, but the boat kept on. Finally there is an island in view. The wind dies completely. I must paddle. I wrap my hands in spinnaker. Fishermen throw themselves into the water, grasp the raft, and guide it through the reef. How good it is to see all these welcoming arms and sparkling smiles. I cry!

M'Aidez

The international MAYDAY call of distress stems from the French for "help me." If you don't use a radiotelephone often, the responsibility of making a MAYDAY call can weigh heavily. There is a procedure. Prepare yourself by reading it, and then keep it near the radio.

Speak SLOWLY—CALMLY—CLEARLY. (This is probably the hardest part.)

1. Make sure your radio is on.
2. Select the distress channel (16 on VHF, 2182 on SSB).
3. Key the microphone and say "MAYDAY" three times, slowly and firmly.
4. Say, "This is *(your boat)*, *(your boat)*, *(your boat)*."
5. Give your call sign once. (If you don't know the call sign, don't worry. You can be legally rescued without it.)

6. Say "MAYDAY" again and give your boat name again.

Then:

1. Give your position.
2. Describe your distress.
3. Give the number of people (adults and children) aboard and the condition of anyone who is injured.
4. Estimate the current seaworthiness of your boat.
5. Describe her briefly.
6. Say "I will be listening on (distress channel)."
7. End message by saying "This is (*your boat*) Over."
8. Release the microphone key. If no one responds, repeat the call.

OTHER DAYS

Mayday should be reserved for life-threatening situations, for "grave and immediate danger." For assistance when you're aground, out of fuel, or in some other need that is not grave and immediate, use the prefix *Pan-Pan* (repeated three times) to signify that yours is an urgent transmission for all ships and stations.

Securite (pronounced as in French: say-cure-e-tay) is a third level of urgency. It precedes a message having to do with urgent weather or navigational information. Though it is most often used by shore stations, use it to open communication with unidentified contacts.

YEA COASTIES!

(*Walter Greene*) When *Gonzo* capsized, we'd been running off all night towing a drogue. It kept us from surfing; we never went more than 12 knots or so. In the morning I was steering the boat downwind when a big wave broke right over me, capsizing the boat at the same time. When water breaks aboard like that, you can't really tell what's happening—can't tell which way to push the tiller. By that time you are long out of control.

Gonzo had no escape hatch fitted. Sawing a hole in the bottom worked well, but we sawed it too close to the water and took waves inside until we plugged it up. You really want that hole as close to the bilge as possible.

A portable VHF is a lot more valuable than a bunch of flares if you're in trouble. We heard a plane the next morning. I got out the VHF and raised it on Channel 16. The pilot said there was a ship about 50 miles away.

It was *Getty California*, a huge tanker. He drifted down on top of us, but we couldn't manage to get aboard. Eventually he came right upwind at us. His bulbous bow hit one of our floats and it split in two. Holding onto a long line, we jumped off the boat and swam away, trying to get away from the ship. Eventually I got on what was left of *Gonzo*. I told the tanker skipper this wasn't going to work. The plane came on and told us there was a Coast Guard cutter about four hours away. We decided we'd hold on.

The cutter was a 240-footer. We spoke on the radio, and he said he'd come upwind and lay his bow next to us. They did that, threw a sling over, and hauled us up one at a time. The tanker captain handled his ship well, but she was just too big. One of the problems is that the crewmen get running up and down 1,000 feet of deck and no one can communicate with the bridge, and vice versa, so no one really knows what's happening.

—*adapted from Chris White's* The Cruising Multihull

HELP YOURSELF

(*Tom Gross*) The joke among SAR professionals is that boats have just two color schemes: blue and white, and white and blue. Is there something you can do to increase your visibility in the blue and white world of ocean waves? A small contrasting target is twice as visible as a non-contrasting target several times its size.

Something as simple as a signaling mirror can immeasurably increase your chances of being found—especially if you use it correctly. Hold the mirror to your cheek. Extend your other hand and make a "vee" sighted on the target. Reflect the light on your fingers and your flashes will reach your rescuer.

Working with a Coast Guard rescue helicopter, either dropping you a high-capacity pump or lifting off all or part of your crew, know what to expect. Radio contact (established via Channel 16 or 2182 MHz) should allow for step-by-step instructions, but the basics are:

- Secure loose gear and furl sails tightly to withstand rotor wash.
- Prepare an area, at least 6 feet square, to which the hoist operator can deliver the equipment or litter. The pilot sits to starboard, so an area well aft on the port side maximizes his visibility.
- Bring the boat head-to-wind and then steer 30 degrees to starboard of the true wind. (This allows the helicopter to hover head-to-wind.)
- Whether the helicopter crew drops equipment, litter, or trail line, don't touch it until it hits the deck. The rotors impart static electricity to the line; before it comes to ground, it will give off a painful jolt.
- Never make any line from the helicopter fast to your boat.
- Work with all deliberate speed to complete the drop (or hoist).

NEED TO KNOW

Search-and-rescue situations are difficult at best. The Coast Guard never knows what information will prove valuable, but it has a protocol for vessels to describe themselves. If you have that information ready, it may well make a difference. Make a sheet that records the following facts and post it handy to your radio transmitter, where anyone in communication with rescuers will have it available.

Vessel Information Data Sheet
1. Description of vessel:
   commercial or pleasure
   cabin configuration
   sail or power
   inboard or outboard
   rig
   length, beam, draft
   color
   hull markings
   name
   homeport

2. Survival gear aboard:
   PFDs
   flares
   flashlight
   raft
   dinghy or tender
   spotlight
   horn
   auxiliary power

3. Electronic equipment:
   radiotelephone(s)
   radar
   depthfinder
   GPS
   loran
   RDF
   EPIRB

4. Vessel owner/operator:
   name
   address
   telephone

5. Miscellaneous:
   Be prepared to describe local weather conditions, depth of water, etc.

WILD COYOTE

Had Mike Plant registered his EPIRB, he might still be sailing. In the press to get *Coyote*, his newly launched BOC entry, across the Atlantic and tested in time, Plant neglected a critical safety step. Though he had a new 406 MHz EPIRB aboard, he found no time to register it with the NOAA data bank (NOAA, NESDESIS E/Sp3, 4401 Suitland Rd., Federal Building No. 4, Room 0160, Suitland, MD 20746). Since its inception, SARSAT (Search and Rescue Satellite Aided Tracking) has saved more than 3,000 lives.

A Halifax station of the Canadian Coast Guard received EPIRB distress signals two weeks after

Plant's departure, but they remained unidentified and no search was initiated. An overturned *Coyote* was found 300 miles west of Brest 10 days after the "mystery" EPIRB transmissions were recorded in Halifax. Her skipper has never been found.

EPIRB TEST

The new 406 EPIRBs have internal test systems. For Class A and B EPIRBs, the test used by Coast Guard inspectors on commercial vessels is also fine for private owners.

1. Test only during the International Distress Frequency Test Period: 00 to 05 minutes every hour.
2. Tune a stereo receiver to 99.5.
3. Turn the EPIRB on. If it is working, you will hear an oscillating tone on the radio.
4. Your test must not last more than 10 seconds. Turn off the EPIRB as soon as you hear the tone.
5. If you get no signal, turn off EPIRB and check the radio. Repeat the test. If there is still no sound, have the EPIRB serviced.

LOOK UP

(Steve Callahan) Something as simple as route maps from pertinent airlines or as sophisticated as a pattern of overflight available from the Federal Aviation Administration would be most helpful in knowing how and when to use your EPIRB, and even what course to chart for a survival voyage.

"TRAVEL BOOKS"

(RR) Credit most of us with making a "don't-cast-off-without-it" list and checking it twice. I call your attention to a set of items that should always make that list. Passports to power, keys to critical doors, insurers of convenience, I am referring—no, not to your credit cards—to your *owner's and service manuals.* If they remain in the drawer at home, maybe you'd better stay home, too.

CREDIT IN HEAVEN

Steve Callahan tells the story of two downed aviators. Discouraged that no rescue had come during their first day, they sat in their small raft and inventoried what they had.

First, one took from his wallet a laundry bill. The other took it, folded it once, and had a 90-degree "sighting device." Folded twice—45 degrees. Three times—22.5 degrees. They were closer now to knowing their position. Next, one of the men noticed the reflection of the moon off one of his credit cards. The next day, using the credit card as a reflector, they alerted a search plane and were rescued.

DIVIDED WE DROWN

(Givens Associates) Survival is a team effort.

- Carry a top-quality liferaft.
- Have it inspected annually.
- Provide a survival suit for everyone!
- Rehearse abandon ship procedures.

  In an emergency:

- Inflate your liferaft well in advance. Keep it tied to the boat.
- Have survival suits accessible.
- Transmit a "MAYDAY," complete with position.
- Activate your EPIRB.

  Be prepared. (Givens Associates, 3198 Main Rd., Tiverton, RI 02878.) [Manufacturers of liferafts and survival suits.—eds.]

DEATH RAFT?

(Chris White) In my opinion the liferaft ought to be called a "death raft." Given a choice between treading water or entering a raft, I'll be happy to crawl into the raft, thank you. But if the choice is between a floating boat and a liferaft, I'll take my chances with the boat.

Liferaft survival is terribly difficult. They capsize easily. They're small, wet, uncomfortable, and *fragile.* Commercially available liferafts are designed to fulfill the needs of typical cruising boats—sinkers. Multihulls with sufficient flotation present a different situation. The scenario is to tether the raft to the inverted boat, but this can present big problems. Due to the force of waves trying to pull the two apart, multihull rafts need multiple reinforced strong points if they're to remain tethered to an overturned boat for any length of time.

At the risk of heresy, *Juniper* carries no raft. She is her own raft—200 times more stable and 25 times larger, with more stowage for food, water, and critical stores than any inflatable, even when inverted.

—*adapted from* The Cruising Multihull

ALL IN ONE

(Mike Saunders) In the ordinary way, a yacht's lifeboat is an inflatable liferaft. Being constructed of flexible material and generally round in shape, they usually cannot be propelled for any distance by any means. These rafts are ideal for coastal and frequented waters, but they are less than satisfactory in the more remote seas. What is needed is a liferaft that can actually sail.

The requirements of sailing ability and toughness point to a craft made of solid material. Which means in turn that the lifeboat will have to double as a tender, for there is only space on most yachts for a single solid dinghy.

I feel that aluminum is the best material of construction, but one has to accept that after a time it will look like a saucepan. Wood or fiberglass, though, while robust, tend to be too heavy. The size should be the largest that can conveniently be carried. It should:

- have adequate buoyancy for two different functions—at high level to assist self-righting and at low level to lift the gunwales above water if the boat founders.
- have a hollow keel which could be filled with water ballast (through shut-off valves) to increase stability. Also aiding in stability would

be a detachable weight that could be clamped to the bottom of the centerboard.

- have a flexible cover, mounted on curved frames, for protection of the crew but demountable for daytime and tender use.
- employ a lug sail which provides modest all-round and fine off-wind performance with a minimum of spars and rigging.

She will be a costly little boat, but the price of building her need not exceed the combined cost of a conventional tender and a liferaft (which usually lies rotting on deck year after year at any rate).

—*adapted from* The Walkabouts

ESCAPE PODS

(Steve Callahan) At the survival lectures I give from time to time, I often get the question, "What would you choose for an emergency craft, an inflatable raft or a hard dinghy?" Well, when your boat is going down, you want to pull a rip cord and have the *QE II* inflate beside you. Emergency craft must suit a wide range of conditions, from the tropics to the Arctic and from calm to storm, and you'd like yours to be stuffed with gear—and all the while fit into your pocket like a pack of cards.

Obviously you want a high-quality liferaft, well maintained and ready to go, but customizing your tender *in addition to carrying a liferaft* will improve your chances of survival. There are many instances that prove this out: the Robertsons had to abandon their raft after 17 days but were rescued from their dinghy three weeks later. The Baileys survived for 119 days aboard a dinghy/inflatable sportboat tandem. The Aros family lashed an 8-foot inflatable and an 8-foot dinghy stern-to-stern to fashion a larger "double-ender." When the chips are going down, you want to employ as many auxiliary craft (preferably already set up for habitability offshore) as you can store aboard.

And dinghy and raft complement one another:

freeboard—Low-sided rafts are easy to board from the water, but they take on water easily. A high-sided dinghy offers just the opposite mix.

space—A raft supports more people than a dinghy, but a dinghy offers space to stretch.

Both factors are important.

stability—A raft is useless as a tender, but it's where you want to be in a mid-ocean blow.

mobility—A dinghy's mobility offers survivors strategic options. Much of the time in typical survival situations is *not* spent in storms.

You can suit your tender better for duty as an emergency pod by fitting a canopy—strong, high visibility, with windows. Supports can be inflatable or made from rod or PVC tubing; avoid materials that can shatter or splinter. Reflective patches on the hull and canopy make your boat easier for searchers to find. A fully covered dinghy not only protects survivors, it will not need to be bailed as often.

Supplement flotation and reserve stability in the dinghy with a gunwale collar (inflatable or made from large fenders). To your liferaft add an inflatable floor—thick for insulation, and removable to give access to the raft bottom.

Stability and mobility are two seemingly opposed qualities, but the ideal emergency craft should combine the two. It's hard to go far in a water-ballasted (Givens-type) liferaft, but their "stationary" stability is legendary. National Maritime Institute's test of liferafts, however, showed that retrievable sea anchors can also create significant amounts of stability. Towing half of the raft canister can work very well in this regard. You should load passengers to windward. You can also pull your canopy into a concave shape to resist aerodynamic lifting, and skirt your weather rail with cloth or tarps to prevent "kiting" (when the wind gets beneath the raft and flips it).

With small pockets of water ballast and a sea anchor, I weathered conditions that were quite heavy. But safety, for me, lay thousands of miles away. I needed to make wake, too. I wish that I'd had a parafoil kite (similar to Ed Veasey's "mastless sail") to provide propulsion, control, and visibility. To make miles, collapse the water pockets on your raft and lash them to the raft.

The best sailing rigs are those that allow the canopy to remain in place. Tinker inflatables, made in England, are probably the best-known hybrid raft/dinghy designs. They are cramped for more than two people but have acquitted themselves well in a number of tests and real-life survival situations.

WELL PROVEN

(*John Glennie*) Just before we left, one of the wives came to the boat and asked where was the liferaft. I said I didn't believe in liferafts, that they are the most dangerous things you can carry on a multihull. You should always stay with the boat. It's the largest platform and far superior to any raft. [Aboard their capsized trimaran *Rose Noelle,* Glennie and his three crewmen drifted for a (record-tying) 119 days before drifting ashore to safety.—eds.]

—*adapted from* The Spirit of Rose Noelle

CREDO

(*Alain Colas*) If a man is going to fight the elements, he has a much better chance of winning if he is in full possession of his physical and moral strength. I felt that if I was to bear the solitude, I would need some comfort. The human heart, if it is to remain firm, needs an occasional touch of tender, loving care.

—*adapted from* Around the World Alone

MAYDAY MIKE

Automating your distress is now possible. A distress call system that can be instantly activated is now available through communications standbys like ACR, Shakespeare, Furuno, and Hull SSB. Flick open the protective shield and punch the SOS button to activate the *Emergency Vessel Location System.* It turns on the radio, moves to Channel 16, takes your position from GPS or Loran-C, converts it into voice via a speech synthesizing chip, and then transmits your complete, prerecorded distress message. It seems impersonal, but it might be providential if you were disabled in a Mayday accident.

DON'T DRINK IT

"Voluntary castaway" Dr. Alain Bombard sailed his tiny inflatable *l'Heretique* from the Canaries to Barbados. His 65-day ordeal in 1952 made a number of points about how "victims" needed to become "sailors," how "foraging and hunting" were the best ways toward survival. Far and away his most revolutionary proposition, however, was the contention that castaways could and *should* drink seawater. He did it, he said, and he reported that taking small amounts of seawater early and often extended his effectiveness and helped postpone debilitating dehydration. To mariners brought up on "water, water everywhere, nor any a drop to drink," Bombard's assertions were a thunderbolt. Unfortunately, there is not much in modern science to confirm the hope or make his theories reality. Conventional wisdom remains:

> *Seafarers are reminded that if they are cast away, they should never, under any circumstances, drink seawater. A belief has arisen recently that it is possible to replace or supplement fresh-water rations by drinking seawater in small amounts. This belief is wrong and dangerous.*
> —Merchant Shipping Notice, March, 1968

Steve Callahan says, "I was able to make drinking water, so I wasn't put in the position of having to consider seawater. Everything that I've learned since I was rescued, though, says, *don't drink it.*"

Dr. Charles Pattavina chaired a recent seminar at Brown University on medicine at sea. "The concentration of salts introduced to the body by drinking seawater works to pull more fluid from the cells than seawater can replace. Drinking seawater speeds dehydration."

Surgeon Captain John Duncan Walters, Royal Navy Institute of Naval Medicine: "When water is in short supply, there appears a preoccupation with drink. Delirium sometimes occurs, but frank madness is unusual unless the castaway has been drinking seawater."

Bombard's fearlessness helped better the lot of countless castaways, but the rule remains: *Don't drink the (sea) water.*

DRINKING WATER

(Dr. Alain Bombard) First, don't keep all of your water in the tanks below. It is essential to provide some deck-stored jerry cans. These should be partly filled so that they will float. For good measure, jerry cans can be lashed to fenders.

Condensation yields water in climates where night and day temperatures are significantly different. I collected a pint almost every morning with a sponge. The problem of getting the caked salt off the collecting surface was solved by washing it off with seawater.

A *hydropic* fluid is similar in chemical composition to water. Two such are "fish juice" and turtle blood. With a decent-size fish, make an incision in the back passing about an inch from the root of the dorsal fin. Hold the fish on its side and this groove will fill with fluid. Make similar grooves over the upper portion of the fish's body. Don't cut the lower portion or you will rupture the abdominal cavity. Next, cut the fish into cubes, wrap the chunks in a cloth, and squeeze the juice from the flesh. Fish eyes sucked and munched are also an excellent source of vitamin C.

Care in maintaining your water containers is crucial. Sometimes, though, you will need to use plastic bags as vessels, or even the large intestines of big fish or turtles.

—*adapted from* Survival at Sea

OVERTURNED COLORS

(MB) Years ago I noticed a yacht in the Windward Island of Bequia with her blue ensign flying upside down. I went over to investigate and found an old submariner colleague, a diabetic, sprawled on the cabin sole in the last stages of consciousness. I ferried him to the hospital, but I couldn't help but wonder how many others in the anchorage might have responded to his *cri de coeur*—or even recognized it.

FISHING

We had seen a number of prehistoric-looking turtles. They would swim in a leisurely fashion round the raft and then disappear underneath. I mentioned to Maurice the possibility of killing one to eat it, but as we still had a thin supply of tinned food, he decided to spare them until it was absolutely necessary. . . .

At dawn we sat in the dinghy and planned the killing. Our instruments were simple: a blunt mariner's knife, a mild steel penknife honed on a leather sheath, and a pair of stainless steel scissors. I knew the only way to kill it was to cut its throat. Maurice stunned the turtle by hitting it over the head with the paddle, but it came to life again. It took a lot of effort for Maurice to keep the neck stretched. When it was half severed, I dug deep for the arteries and, as the rich blood spurted over my hands, the turtle ceased its struggle.

—Maralyn Bailey, adapted from Staying Alive

Very soon after I am set adrift, an ecosystem begins to develop around the raft. Dorado (dolphin fish) appear, body-surfing down the waves, tantalizing my, by now, volcanic stomach. After one is hooked with a lure I make and calmly bites through the line, no others are fooled. Triggerfish arrive. When I finally catch some of these untasty fish, I am ecstatic. Slowly the dorado begin to approach until I am able to spear one. (I wonder why I chanced to pack my spear gun in my emergency bag.) I wonder, for that matter, what made the dorado come closer. They followed me, I know not why, for all 1,800 miles. I eat a small one every day or two, devouring every part except the stomach, intestines, bones, and skin. The eggs of the females are delicious, as is the liver. The nuggets of liquid between the vertebrae are my "chicken soup."

—Steve Callahan, adapted from Adrift

Compared with the simplicity of hook and line, other methods may seem inferior but they can turn out to be effective. I made my first hook of a dorado bone from a fish caught on a gaff made with a bent knife blade. Survivors have used bloody seabird wings as "rigs" (hook, bait, and all) extended by the "lines" of their bare hands.

If a shark is not over-large (smaller than 5 feet), you can catch it by hand by grabbing it at the base of the tail. Drag it over the gunwale. The minute the shark opens its mouth, stick a piece of wood or wad of cloth into it. To kill it, strike it repeatedly with a club on the point of its snout.

—Dr. Alain Bombard,
Survival at Sea, *Bernard Robin, ed.*

When, because of Maurice's illness, I had taken over the fishing, I had to be extremely careful with the one hook that we had left. Maurice always let the fish swallow the hook, and used about eight pieces of bait to catch a single fish. I learned to jerk the bait away from them and, when they hit it, flip them quickly over the side. At times like these we usually contented ourselves with 20 fish or thereabouts, but there were times when we caught 50.

—Maralyn Bailey, adapted from Staying Alive

(continued on page 230)

(continued from page 229)

We began to rely more and more on the gaff as a method of catching fish. Not only did it become our main fish-catching tool, it changed Phil's pessimistic attitude. Right from the first day it became more and more difficult to convince Phil that we had a fighting chance, and that went on for three months—until he discovered that he was a dab hand with the gaff. He caught more fish than any of us. We nicknamed him "The Wand" and "The Hook." We found that if we dropped a lure about 6 meters down, the kingfish would follow it up as we hauled it in. They'd never bite, but soon we used the lure to entice them in to where we could gaff them. [Glennie and his mates were on an inverted trimaran. A gaff— even a fishhook—is a big risk around an inflated liferaft.—eds.]

—John Glennie, adapted from The Spirit of Rose Noelle

Where the Humboldt Current turned west south of the Equator, we could pour several pounds of plankton porridge out of the bag every few hours. The plankton lay packed together like cake in colored layers. When we poured them into a bucket, the squashy mess ran out like a magic gruel composed of glow worms. Our night's catch looked as nasty at close quarters as it had pretty at long range. Bad as it smelled, it tasted correspondingly good—shrimp paste, lobster or crab "soup," like caviar, and now and again oysters.

—Thor Heyerdahl, adapted from Kon-Tiki

THINK AGAIN

(Walter Lord) Within the sinking ship the heavy silence of the deserted rooms had a drama of its own. The crystal chandeliers of the *à la carte* restaurant hung at a crazy angle, but they still burned brightly, lighting the fawn panels of French walnut and the rose-colored carpet. A few of the little table lamps with their pink silk shades had fallen over, and someone was rummaging in the pantry, perhaps for something with which to fortify himself. The *Louis Quinze* lounge with its big fireplace was silent and empty.

The Palm Court was equally deserted, but the smoking room was not completely empty. When a steward looked in at 2:10, he was surprised to see Thomas Andrews, builder of the ship, standing all alone in the room. Andrews' lifebelt lay carelessly across the green cloth top of a card table. His arms were folded over his chest; his look was stunned; all his drive and energy were gone. A moment of awed silence and the steward timidly broke in, "Aren't you going to have a try for it Mr. Andrews?" There was not a trace of an answer, no signal that he had heard. The builder of the *Titanic* merely stared aft at the mahogany-paneled wall with its large painting entitled "The Approach of the New World."

—adapted from A Night to Remember

TOMORROW'S RUM

(William Bligh) Tuesday, May 19: We past this day miserably wet and cold. Covered with rain and sea, which we could only act against at intervals by pulling off our cloaths and wringing them through seawater.

In the night we had severe lightning but otherwise so dark we could scarce see each other. The morning produced to me many complaints on the severity of the weather. I would gladly have issued my allowance of rum if it had not appeared to me that we were to suffer more, and that it was necessary to preserve the little I had to give relief at a time when less able to bear such hardships. To make up, I issued about an half ounce of pork to each person, with the allowance of $1/24$ lb. of bread and a jill of water for dinner . . . which was thought a feast . . . all night and day bailing without intermission.

—*adapted from* Bligh, *Sam McKinney*

HUMAN SYSTEMS GO

(Ethan L. Welch, M.D.) For a blue-water voyage, the best kind of medicine is preventive medicine. A complete physical for all makes good sense. Some conditions, like significant cardiac disease, severe diabetes, and emphysema, preclude going on a long voyage. Beyond the physical, have your doctor contact the Center for Disease Control in Atlanta to assure that you receive the proper shots and immunizations. Also, each person aboard should have a "document of fitness" including all pertinent medical information, which the skipper should keep on file adjacent to the medical kit.

There are two ways of preparing said medical kit. The hard way is to buy a manual, drop by the drugstore, scurry around to pharmaceutical-supply places, and dump it all in a fishing-tackle box. Your chances of collecting the "right stuff" aren't great, and the kit is a confusing, intimidating hodgepodge that no one feels happy opening. The easy way, if you'll pardon the commercial note, is to buy the appropriate Medical Sea Pak. The kit is experience based and very complete. The skipper then takes it to his physician to add medications appropriate for the crew.

Beyond the tailor-made aspect of the kit, it contains an excellent manual. Good supplies without good instruction, or vice versa, make for dissatisfaction. When crunch-time comes, the courage to use the kit is best found among those

who have made the effort to prepare.

SEA SHIRT

(Alice Robinson) The first time you snorkel in any given season, chances are you won't have established a protective tan on your back and legs. Silly as it seemed, my parents made me always wear a tee-shirt to snorkel in. To protect both his back and the backs of his knees, one charter client of mine, a doctor, snorkeled in a full set of pajamas. The alternative, with the water's cooling effect keeping you from feeling damage until it's been done, is ugly at best. Nothing short of shielding yourself is proof against the tropic sun.

SEEING CLEARLY

(Gary Jobson) I have found in my lengthening sailing career that sunglasses are more and more critical. Glare and squinting breed fatigue, and long passages mean big-time exposure to radiation; sunglasses are your best weapons. It pays not to scrimp. Get a good pair. Obviously two-dollar numbers from the drugstore aren't great for your eyes. The pink-tinted designer creations don't cut it, either. I'm looking for glasses to protect my eyes from strain, fatigue, and spray, but they also help in contrasting colors and seeing into glare.

I'm not an eye-doctor, but glasses that cut out about 80 percent of the available light are a good place to start. I check to make sure they cut out both ultraviolet and infrared radiation. Polarizing to cut glare is a pretty standard feature nowadays. Your basic Vernays and Bausch and Lombs are serious glasses and worth their cost. I bring two pair aboard. It's nice to have a backup against breaking or losing them, but the main reason that I use two is to have clear vision when I need it.

Depending whether I'm racing or cruising, I'll have a clean rag (and maybe even a designated "cleaner" if I'm doing a lot of steering) and try to keep the ones on my head clear. Depth perception is much improved when the salt spots are wiped away. For eyeball piloting through coral or shoals, picking out puffs as they come downwind to you, and seeing clearly up a sunpath, sunglasses are worth their weight in diamonds. I've had sunburned eyes; that's a pain I'd just as soon avoid. I've come to like pairs with shields on the side to block light and ease eyestrain. I tie a string on them so they hang around my neck but don't fall in the drink.

UNFRIED

(Dr. Bebe Wunderlich) How you react to the sun depends on a number of things. The person most susceptible to skin cancer has a fair complexion, light hair, and blue or gray eyes. But everyone has the potential to get fried. Unusual reactions to sunlight (such as blistering, rashes, burning, etc.) may come about if you have some chemical reaction going on in your body. Expect unusual reactions if you are using some deodorants; some bacteria-inhibiting soaps; and some oils (such as oil of lime) used in cosmetics, perfumes, after shaves; dyes (used in cosmetics); and coal tar derivatives (such as those used to treat eczema and psoriasis).

Some drugs taken orally induce light-sensitivity: antibiotics (like Declomycin), some water pills, some tranquilizers, sulfonamides, some pills for diabetes, and some artificial sweeteners. There is a significant variety in reactions, but if you use maximum protection during the first few days of sailing, you dramatically reduce the chances of having problems.

Remaining in the shade won't prevent sunburn, though it reduces the intensity. You will still fry. It will just take twice as long. On hazy days, even though 70 percent of the solar radiation from a cloudless day is operating, the infrared radiation that warns of burning with heat is usually absent. Very dangerous! We often get fried going to weather because the breeze over the deck masks the heat.

OPEN WIDE

(David N. Taft, D.D.S.) Dental pain ranks right up there with childbirth and passing kidney stones as the worst most humans endure. To ocean voyagers it is not only debilitating, it can be fatal.

Prevention of dental infections that can pass to the heart or brain is the best known deterrent. If you had a dentist aboard he would want to know:

- Did the pain come gradually or appear suddenly?
- Is there swelling and/or elevated body temperature?
- Is there something specific stimulating the pain?
- Do you have a funny taste in your mouth?
- Is there any drainage?
- Does the pain awaken you?
- Has medication helped to reduce the pain?

But you don't have a dentist aboard. Using this matrix of questions, however, you can determine the symptoms for:

- Trauma: Sudden pain, swelling, fever, bad taste, bleeding, and airway problems. Get the airway open and keep it open. Try to assess the actual damage. Most likely jaw fracture; it needs to be reduced and immobilized. Pain relievers may mask a concussion so treat the patient as though he had one.
- Dental abscess: All of the previous symptoms without the airway threat. Treat with antibiotics and pain relievers as needed. Swelling may occur at any point, or a pimple-like lesion may appear. Encourage drainage with gentle "milking" and warm saltwater rinses.
- Angina: Sudden pain without swelling, normal temperature, no bad taste, bleeding, or airway problems.
- Chest pain. This is not a dental problem. Treat with cardiac vasodilator (such as nitroglycerin) if you can.
- Broken tooth: Sudden pain in a patient without swelling or fever, no bad taste nor bleeding, nor heart nor airway problem. This is usually a broken tooth, which the patient most often can pinpoint. Treat with application of zinc-eugenol mixture in the form of temporary filling material. Eugenol (oil of cloves) may be made by crushing cooking cloves. Direct application is good for pain relief.

(continued on page 234)

HYPOTHERMIA

Oblivious to the icy downpour, I sat on a log and pulled off my boots. I set them in the snow bank beside me and, in a January rain squall high in the Cascades, I proceeded to methodically wring the water from my socks. I had lost it. I had hypothermia. Without help from my friends I might never have left the mountains.

A popular medical "discovery" of the last two decades, hypothermia—the result of critically lowered core temperature—is familiar to sailors. The best defense is prevention; fight heat loss as the temperature drops. It's not a question of "toughing it out." Your mind has no control over your core temperature. You've got to prevent heat loss to prevent hypothermia. Water cools 25 times faster than air of the same temperature. Immersion is a powerful enemy.

If you're in the water, how long will you last? Longer than you think. The bigger you are and the more body fat you have, the better your chances. Unless rescue is close at hand, don't move about. If you're wearing a PFD, adopt the fetal **Heat Escape Lessening Position**. The more you disturb the layer of water around your body, the more heat you will lose.

A victim who plunges beneath the water is likely to be blue when retrieved because his organs are in oxygen debt. He needs immediate oxygen. A victim who has floated for a long time will be dusky gray; conscious victims should be re-warmed. Give unconscious victims a half-dozen breaths of forced respiration to oxygenate the heart before commencing CPR. Because of the cold-water-induced *mammalian diving reflex*, an unconscious cold-water drowning victim, though he passes all the tests for being dead, might well be alive.

—*Dr. Tom Gross, USCG*

Hypothermia is heat loss from the body core. It's not freezing to death; it's not frostbite; it can kill at temperatures well above 32 degrees (F); and victims need more than simple "first aid." One of the first signs is diminished judgment. This is a hazard that's particularly daunting for solo sailors; be alert for lethargy, slurred speech, or a slow irregular pulse (in your mates or yourself). The first prevention is to stay warm and dry. The second is regular small meals (which the body turns into heat). Wear a watch cap. Fifty percent of the body's heat loss is through the head. In hypothermia situations it is doubly prudent to wear your PFD and hook on your harness. To help the victim:

1. *Radio the Coast Guard. The faster the victim gets help, the safer.*
2. *Handle gently. Hypothermia renders victims vulnerable to rough handling. Do not rub in the mistaken attempt to restore circulation.*
3. *Strip wet clothing away. Cover victim with blankets. Consider huddling with victim, skin-to-skin, to share body heat.*
4. *Give nothing orally—not tea, coffee, and most emphatically NOT alcohol.*
5. *Treat for shock (as you would per Red Cross Guidelines).*

6. Whether or not the victim requests it, make sure that he/she receives a medical check up when you land.

—Tom Shaw, USCG Auxiliary

Regarding nutrition for a cold environment, it is important to eat a good balance of carbohydrates, protein, and yes, fat, at regular intervals to keep the muscles' fuel supply steady. Even though a Hershey bar on the dog watch may appear to provide a quick burst of energy, studies show that, in fact, it takes quite a while for sugar in the blood stream to become available as energy. If anything, the boost is more psychological than physiological. In order to provide heat by shivering or doing work, muscles need a constant source of glycogen supplied by regular meals.

—Tim Murphy

The research into the 1979 Fastnet Race loss of life indicated that hypothermia probably caused many otherwise experienced yachtsmen to act illogically, leaving sound boats by jumping into liferafts or even leaping into the sea. The most important method in preventing hypothermia is keeping the layer of air next to the skin reasonably dry, which prevents conductive heat loss. "Wicking" underwear is a good way to do this. Simple net-like material can create a dead-air space next to the skin. Polypropylene "wicks" moisture away from the skin. These principles combine to make the modern underlayer very efficient. In moderate weather it is possible to wear just underwear beneath foul-weather gear, but in colder climes another layer is needed. The critical quality of this layer is "loft," or thickness of dead air space. Almost any material can work, but polyester fleece has stolen the show, providing superior loft along with suppleness and light weight. On top of the composite underlayer should come well-chosen foul-weather gear.

—Donald Graul

Castaways are in particular peril. Rafts should be enclosed, floors insulated, and wool and mesh worn against the cold. Digestion raises the body temperature, so eat often if you can. Alcohol increases heat loss by dilating the capillaries. Toddies are bad for you. Sleep and rest help resist cold. Sharing body heat helps. Survival rations should contain fatty foods for moderate chill and sugar/glucose-based foods for severe cold.

—Dr. Alain Bombard, adapted from Survival at Sea, Bernard Robin, ed.

(continued from page 232)

- Sinus infection: Sudden pain without swelling, but encompassing a fever and bad taste without bleeding, airway, or heart problems, might, if there is concurrent stuffy nose and/or if changing head position causes pain, be a sinus problem. Treat with decongestants and antibiotics.
- Gum disease: Gradual pain, swelling, fever, bad taste, and bleeding suggest a form of "trench mouth" most likely precipitated by malnutrition and high stress. Treat it with analgesics, gentle/careful oral hygiene, and topical hydrogen peroxide. This is not contagious.
- Fractures: Treat with the basic ABCs—Airway, Bleeding, and Circulation. Listen for raspy sounds. You may have to pull the tongue clear of the airway. Dental fractures that show bleeding from the tooth or a pink color involve the pulp of the tooth and are excruciating. Protect them with zinc oxide/Eugenol putty along with anal-

gesics and direct application of Eugenol for pain relief. The temporary filling material is not adherent and must be worked into areas that will retain it. Control bleeding from lost teeth by applying moist tea bags and pressure.

Dental-care kit:

- Pain relievers: Narcotic pain relievers are difficult to bring into some countries. Keep all prescription medication properly labeled and in its original packaging. Keep the narcotic pain relievers locked away. Of the non-prescription analgesics, aspirin, acetaminophen, and ibuprofen are all useful.
- Antibiotics: Choose one of the penicillins. Begun with a loading dose of two 500-mg tablets and continued at 500 mg a day for four days, penicillin should be taken for the full dosage to prevent development of resistant bacteria.
- Equipment: a good, narrow-beam flashlight; a small mouth-mirror; silk dental sutures.
- Local anesthetic: This broaches the need for a needle. In addition to finding someone aboard to use it, it presents customs and entry explanation problems. Check with your dentist on topical alternatives.

Brush and floss energetically. Prevention is the best cure. In the absence of toothpaste, a baking soda/salt mixture provides everything but fluoride. Smile!

THE ABANDONMENT OF *TRASHMAN*

(Deborah Scaling Kiley) I crawled up the companionway behind Brad, fighting to keep my balance as the boat hurtled down a wave. We both made it to the deck. But where was the ship? Where were the people who had come to rescue us? There was nothing, only the monster seas and the freight-train wind and the ugly sky. The Coast Guard wasn't here for us. No one was here—I was dizzy with the sickening truth. *Trashman* was sinking and we were alone.

I saw Mark dive for the compartment at the stern where the liferaft was stowed in a canister the size of a suitcase. I saw Brad on top of the

cabin struggling to untie the Zodiac. It burst free. He swam . . . he pounced on it as it stalled in the leeward shoulder of a wave. In the lull between waves, I managed to swim away. I could see Mark with his arms wrapped around the canister, and Meg being lifted forward by another wave. Somehow I pulled her free of the boat.

I saw Brad holding onto the Zodiac, and I swam madly, finally grabbing onto its side; and then Meg was there. Then John appeared. The four of us clung to the overturned Zodiac. We had drifted 50 feet from *Trashman*. She was heeled so far that her masts were almost flat in the water. She seemed to bolt up in one final stab at survival, but when we came out of the next trough all that I could see were the tops of her masts. We dipped down and crested again just in time to see the tip of her mainmast vanish. The sinking had taken less than two minutes.

"We're going to fucking die!" Mark screamed.

"Shut up, Mark," I shouted back.

—*adapted from* Albatross

DITCH KITS

(Steve Callahan) To make sure you will have all you will need if you become a castaway, carry a supplemental "ditch kit," or what one friend of mine calls his "going-away bag." Liferafts come with standard equipment, but some of it is about as well thought out as the patch kit that warned, "do not apply glue unless cloth is dry." Seriously!

By all means inventory your raft and add items that make sense, but for gathering and stowing survival essentials, there's nothing like a ditch kit. It should be securely stowed but quickly accessible. I like to secure it, like the liferaft, with a quick-release shackle. Keep it in a position close to the deck (like under the companionway ladder or chart table). Don't bury it under other gear. You can keep it in its own locker or on deck, even link it to the liferaft (perhaps in a second canister), but protect it from the elements.

Fit most survival gear into Tupperware boxes, polyethylene wide-mouthed jars with screw lids and O-ring seals (as supplied with PW* flares), or waterproof (EWA*) bags. [*The full name of abbrevi-*

ated manufacturers—indicated by asterisk—are provided at the end of this section, along with telephone numbers and/or addresses.] I prefer a mix of types. Double-seal the boxes and jars with electrician's tape. Print a list of the contents outside each container in waterproof ink; hunkered down in a tossing liferaft, you'll need to know what's inside each.

Put these smaller containers into a valise or a hard box. A soft bag is easier on the crew of the raft, but the hard box can be towed. You might think of making up more than one kit. Water jugs, sealed with tape, should also be ready to go if abandonment comes.

Rory Nugent threw his vital life-support gear in his raft when his proa overturned, only to have those necessaries vanish through a split bottom. Need I EMPHASIZE!!: *anything and everything that can be secured with a painter, cord, or lanyard should be.* Add closed cell flotation to your kits if you have to, but make them float. That gives you more space and more survival payload.

I can't promise that my recommendations for what to take in *your* kit will cover everything, but I can assure you that you'll have a better ditch kit than I did when I was set adrift for 76 days in 1982. Proper equipment is sometimes missing from liferafts because most survivors spend less than 48 hours adrift. A sizable minority, though, spend much longer. In the short term, drowning, injury, or hypothermia can kill in a few minutes to a few hours. In the intermediate term, dehydration kills in a matter of days (about 10). The long-term survivor has to face starvation, which will take about 30 days. Prepare for both short and long survival stints.

Without a vessel of some sort, humans can't last more than 48 hours, even in tropical water, so take care of your platform. You must be prepared to become an aquatic caveman who can and will learn to live off the sea.

Raid the mother ship.

- PFDs and survival suits are good to have, but bulky.

- Carry the EPIRB. If the unit is too big for the kit, stow it alongside; too big for the raft, get a smaller beacon. I heartily recommend an EPIRB for the raft. In fact, I would make that priority number one.
- Very close in value and usefulness is a handheld VHF. How many stories have you heard of ships in sight that failed to respond to castaway signals? Keep the unit in a waterproof (EWA*) bag. If you match it with a small solar charger, it will serve you best.
- Any gear that is big enough should have the name of the mother ship stenciled on it so that items recovered by searchers can be linked to the rescue effort.

Short-term needs (hypothermia, drowning, first aid).

- A pneumatic lifejacket or horseshoe with heaving line to rescue people separated from the raft.
- Evac suits (typically available in the UK), Thermal Protective Aids (S*), or Survival Bags (SA*) in suit form or sealed as "mummy bags." One per crewmember. Space blankets as a second choice.
- Chemical heat packs (SA*). As many as practical; minimum four small (6-hour) or two large (20-hour) per crewmember. Can be placed inside survival bags to warm survivors.
- Self-inflating foam pad or boating air seats (V*)—second choice air mattress—for insulating raft floor.
- Minimum of one pair wool gloves, one pair rubber gloves, and one watch cap per crewmember.
- Minimal first-aid kit with sterile bandages, good first-aid manual (raft kit will lack this), sunscreen, burn cream, seasick pills (or suppositories), enema sack (for rehydration), petroleum jelly (good for a number of things, including lubricating metal), pain killers, etc. Try to retrieve the mother ship's first-aid kit.
- Raft repair kit: raft repair cymbal clamps (if not included in raft gear, add them), heavy needles and sail twine, good goop such as silicone sealant (this even cures under water), spare ma-

terial like rip-stop nylon and rubberized (or Hypalon) cloth, underwater epoxy and glass cloth (if you have a hard dinghy), plus duct tape and surgeon's tape.

- Spare line for lashings. I recommend 200 feet of ³⁄₁₆-inch and 100 feet of ¼-inch.
- Spare air pump (stow in the raft if you can). Most inflatables are impossible to inflate by mouth. Check it out during your next inspection. If you lose your only air pump, you may be lost.

Signaling and storm management. Your EPIRB and VHF cover some signaling, but also good are:

- A dozen SOLAS parachute flares (many liferafts come with six). Non-SOLAS parachutes burn half as long but cost much less. Meteor flares are, I feel, a waste of space and money. Three handheld red flares (for pinpointing the raft once it's been spotted) and two orange smoke flares should do it. If you need a gun for the parachutes, pack some gun oil, too.
- A signaling mirror.
- A parafoil kite (optional). Should be international orange.
- Sea anchor. I like the improved "Icelandic" style of tapered cone with mesh around the bridle to prevent fouling, and a strong swivel.

Moderate-term needs. Recommended survival ration = 1 to 2 pints of water per day.

- Watermaker. I think the only reasonable option is the reverse-osmosis watermaker by PUR* (Survivor 06 minimum, Survivor 35 preferred). The only solar still I would recommend is by W. L. Gore, but they are out of production.
- Drinking water (16 oz. per person, pouches or cans). [Or jugs.—eds.]
- Quart plastic biking bottle for secure water storage and rationing in view of the whole crew.
- Other water containers. (The plastic bags from solar stills are excellent and allow the crew to build a water stock.)
- Piece of tubing to siphon water. Can double as enema tube.

Long-term needs (food, navigation, etc.).

- Survival rations; Verkade or similar sweet ship's biscuits.
- Multiple vitamins.
- Dried fruits and vegetables (if making water); chocolate.
- Fishing kit: small trident spear, large Hawaiian sling (for small and large fish), at least 200 feet of 50-pound test line (I like natural cod line), assorted hooks (trout to 4") and sinkers.
- Small plankton net. You can live off plankton alone in many places, especially before your raft develops an ecosystem and attracts fish. Best trolled at night.
- Knives. At least one big sheath knife. Swiss Army knife and/or Leatherman tools are valuable.
- Cutting board. I prefer two—8-inch by 12-inch pieces of ⅛-inch plywood. They protect the raft floor and can be marked for navigation. [*Marine* plywood. Common plywood would fall apart in a week in the bottom of a raft.—eds.]
- Two sponges.
- Plastic sacks.
- Navigation kit: pilot chart for your area (preferably plasticized), small compass, waterproof watch, plastic protractor.
- Survival manual.
- Pencils, pads, paper.
- Flashlight (diver's type): Teknalight, Pelican, or similar.
- Reflective tape (you can attach it strategically to raft during its next inspection).

Miscellaneous.

- Photocopy passports, visas, and other essential documents, and have the copies on hand for when you get back to land.
- Think of items for "desert island" survival and include waterproof matches, a flint, a wire saw, etc.

Specified suppliers:

S = Stearns (800) 328-3208
EWA= EWA (609) 854-2424
V = Voyageurs (fax) (913) 764-7755

ADDENDA

Dr. Bernard Robin specifies in *Survival at Sea* a few additional survival-kit items not covered by Callahan:

- portable bilge pump
- sailing rig (". . . cannot be jury rigged. It must be provided in advance.")
- small, solid-fuel stove
- stainless steel scissors
- underwater mask and snorkel
- several large towels and/or a large sheet ("Experience shows that every scrap of cloth is valuable.")

ROCKETS' RED GLARE

(Don Street) I have seen one demonstration of the comparative effectiveness of Very flares and rockets, which was most impressive. At the celebration of the 250th anniversary of the Cork Water Club (Crosshaven, Ireland), each yacht, as she passed the original home of the club, fired a salute. Most of the American boats fired flares. They were spectacular and effective, but they were far outshone by the rockets released by the British boats. The height reached by the Very flares was only one-third that reached by the rockets. Since a rocket goes three times as high, it is visible over nine times the area—an advantage certainly worth the extra cost. [Street is talking about 25mm meteor flares compared to the forerunner of today's SOLAS parachute flares. Terms have changed in the nearly quarter of a century since this was written, but the point remains valid.—eds.]

—*adapted from* The Ocean Sailing Yacht

POCKET ROCKETS

Skyblazer red aerial flares are waterproof, need no pistol launcher, reach a height of 500 feet, burn for 10 seconds, and are rated at 10,000 candle-power. They cost 15 bucks for a pack of three, and they fit in the pocket of a float coat or foul-weather parka.

TWO FOR THE SHOW

(MB) When Robin Gardiner-Hall lost *Pentina II* anchored in a storm in the mouth of the Elbe, the lifeboat officer who rescued him told him that flares should always be set off in pairs—about 10 seconds apart is ideal—because the observer who sees the first flare often has trouble identifying it or believing that it is a distress signal. The second confirms that it was not his imagination but a genuine emergency.

PUR

The watermakers chosen by Steve Callahan for his ditch kit are made by PUR. The Survivor 06 costs $500 (West Marine), weighs but 2.5 pounds, and can produce a pint of water in 30 minutes. The Survivor 35 weighs 7 pounds and produces 1.4 gallons an hour. The PUR watermakers are the only hand-operated reverse osmosis watermakers in the world. Reverse osmosis consists of forcing seawater through a membrane so that pure water passes while salts do not. The recovery ratio equals roughly one part pure water for every 10 parts of seawater pumped through.

DIRECTION'S COURSE

(Rockwell Kent) The skipper headed for a small fjord that lay before us. On a faint breeze that hardly gave us headway, in silence so profound that it became the murmur of the rain, we turned the headland. There, between mountain walls, sheltered and peaceful, we anchored. Down in the cabin I took the anchor's splash as a signal to serve supper.

For an hour after the others had gone to bed I sat in the trim little fo'castle writing pages of my diary through that grateful midnight calm and stillness while rain fell on the deck. The motion woke me. We were rolling violently. I heard steps on deck, voices calling out, the sound of hawser being paid. "Oh well, we're at anchor. No one has called." Suddenly we careened so far that I was catapulted out. I dressed hastily. In the cabin the skipper was in bed.

"She's drifting to both anchors," called the mate.

"Give 'em more rope," answered the skipper.

I reached the ladder just when something rolled us over and the green sea came pouring in. "Damn . . . I'd made everything so neat!" We rummaged beneath sacks of coal for the third anchor. I had set a lighted cigarette upon the chart table. This, as I worked, was always in my mind, so from time to time I'd pause to move the cigarette so as not to burn the wood. We found the anchor, made it up, and hoisted it up the ladder.

Just then a great sea lifted us. I hung halfway out the cabin and stared at an oncoming wall of rock so near astern it seemed about to crush us. Then came another sea that hurled us and the land together. And the impact of that shock was only less than those that followed for half an hour until *Direction* sank.

That half an hour! A giant sledge hammer striking a granite mountain; a hollow hammer, and within it a man. Picture yourself the man. I stayed below, and was. See me as Adam; set full-blown into that pandemonium of force and the huge, terrifying presence of the unknown. Adam and Man and me in that compacted miniature of man's universe, the cabin of the yacht *Direction* on the rocks of Greenland.

Matches: They're in the fo'castle cupboard. I get out a lot. Next: Keep 'em dry. A big tin on the shelf. Lentils! I pour them out, pack in matches, put on the cover. Kerosene: The 5-gallon tin's too big to get ashore. The 1-gallon is buried under stores. Alcohol: I find a small bottle. I partly fill a duffle bag with blankets; put in the chronometers; add the sextant; my silver flute, my movie camera; more blankets. Over my writing table in the fo'castle was my sweetheart's picture. Tuck it for safety next my skin. Carry it ashore, last thing. Then on my return, with not so much modesty as to hide my valor, I'll tell her how in that hour of confusion and terror I had thought of her. So I took her down and—wading, climbing, dodging, holding on for dear life—made my way out and to the deck.

—*adapted from* N x E

SHEET BEND

Used most often for joining lines of approximately the same size, the sheet bend entails passing the end of one line through a bight in the other line, round both parts, and back underneath its own.

Hervey Garrett Smith (from *The Arts of the Sailor*)

BE SAFE

Safety that ignores these twin realities is no safety at all. To be safe we have to deal not only with the dangers of the deep but with "not that crap again!" and "damn the torpedoes!" We have met the danger, and it is us.

Safety is the Coast Guard's mission, its very reason for being. Out of experience, seamanship, and a grip on human nature, the Coast Guard begins with "forehandedness." In a room full of hundreds of men, Admiral Paul Welling is the sort of guy you might pick out as a square-rigger captain. You'd be right. When he was master of USCG barque *Eagle*, he explained the drill:

Overshadowing the individual safety rules is forehandedness. All hands must anticipate potential problems and take action to avoid them. Through this anticipation and preparation (plus execution and technique) we constantly teach safety. We expect that an attitude of safety-consciousness will grow in every member of the crew, imparted in some measure by the ship herself, and in some part by our shipboard evolutions. These things are not pro forma. These are real and challenging situations. We want our people to come back with all their fingers.

Before he became chief designer for Boston Whaler, Bob Daugherty was a shop teacher for nearly 20 years in the Boston high schools. Noticing a missing knuckle on Daugherty's left hand, his interviewer got up the nerve to ask him about it:

"It's tough to beat the law of averages with those saws, isn't it Mr. Daugherty?"

"Hell," Daugherty replied, "I could see those saws coming a mile away. That wasn't how I lost the finger. I was helping unload a truck and the crate slipped. Strapping caught my wedding ring and ripped the finger off before I knew it."

The stakes at sea run higher than fingers and toes.

Be safe.

You have to be a complete person— mature, sensible, and responsible.

—*John Ridgeway,*
How We Rowed the Atlantic

BE PREPARED

Between the Boy Scouts and Tom Lehrer, "Be Prepared" is very much of a cliché. It is still the beginning that works best toward a happy ending.

THE FIRST STEP   *(Cdr. Chip Barber, USN)*
Statistics show that of all accidents at sea, 85 percent stem from unsafe human action while just 15 percent are due to unsafe conditions. One of the best ways of addressing the human element is addressing attitude. During a race, crewmen work together to achieve speed. At sea, all hands should be working together in the same way to achieve safety.

LOOK AHEAD   *(Rich Wickenden)* I've been sailing most of my life. I've been in the merchant marine for over a decade. This wasn't my first transatlantic. It's embarrassing. We were in our second week out, almost to the halfway point. *Black Seal* was running nicely before quartering seas in about 20 knots of breeze. Skipper Tim Trautman and his wife Mary were off watch. Two other guys and I were on deck.

"Whoa. . . ."

Not more than a mile off our starboard bow we saw a container ship, looking as big as any I'd ever seen. Helm down, harden up, heavy trim, and we were clear of her track—but not without a few accelerated heartbeats. It was unnerving to have her come "out of nowhere" like that. She'd "snuck up" on us in the blind spot behind our liferaft. Where it says "keep a lookout at all times," I'd add a special asterisk and say "even when you're 1,000 miles from land."

WHAT'S NEXT TO GODLINESS?

(Tania Aebi) Cleanliness is next to godliness; and not only that, it's good seamanship. At least that's what I think. Not only is it a pleasure for the eyes to feast on a well-organized, dustless, greaseless environment, but the small extra effort to sustain that tidiness will always pay for itself in a pinch. You will immediately find that 6-millimeter wrench to bleed the engine before the boat makes contact with the rocks. And it's much easier to cook a meal with pots and pans that are in predictable places.

For me, much to friends' and family members' disbelief as I vacuum up *cous cous* from the carpet after a meal, maintenance is even more important at sea than it is on land. It was a lesson I learned the hard way, after many stray, yet indispensable items were washed overboard.

Ever since my enlightenment in the realms of order, I don't know how many times disaster was averted because it took me only a split second to find a manual. If you spend several minutes a day picking up, stowing, and wiping, then major clean-ups are never necessary. I am not incredibly technical and I don't have tons of earth-shattering revelations or advice. However, through plenty of trials and errors I learned that an organized boat enhanced my quality of life aboard—and it still does ashore.

SUIT YOURSELF

(John Rousmaniere) Whether skipper or crew, your enjoyment of your time on the water depends on bringing suitable clothing when you come aboard. Going barefoot seems salty, but broken toes, falls, and lack of sure-footedness are the

price. Wear deck shoes with special nonskid soles or ribbed-sole sneakers. Sea boots over warm cotton socks are the best! Be realistic about your resistance to cold; go aboard over-prepared. Carry foul-weather gear, a thick sweater, and anything else you might need.

WATCH FOR WIRES

(Tina Sherman Harnden) The incident was, sadly, typical:

> *All-American sailor John Stewart Walker was killed at age 28 when he received a shock from an overhead powerline while unrigging a Lightning at the edge of the parking lot of the Wacamaw Sailing Club in Whiteville, NC.*

Overhead powerlines are officially responsible for half a dozen deaths per year. Look out. Look up!

LIGHTNING PROTECTION

(Richard Frisbie) A sailboat on the water with its metal mast poking toward the sky like a lone tree in a pasture is a notorious lightning target. Fortunately it can be protected from lightning damage by grounding the rigging to a conductor below the waterline. The mast then acts as a lightning rod and offers a cone-shaped *zone of protection* from its tip outwards and down.

The ideal underwater ground-plate is a copper sheet about 1 foot square. Make connections with stranded copper wire (#8 or bigger).

- The path from the highest part of the system to the water should be as short and straight as possible.
- The ground wire can be bolted to the base or step of a metal mast.
- Unless the wire lead is more than 6 feet away from them, heavy metal masses (like the engine) should be connected individually to the ground wire.
- Don't let the ground system pass through turnbuckles, centerboard pivot pins, or other weak points that might be damaged by a lightning jolt.

—adapted from Basic Boatbuilding

Galley Fire

(Janet Groene) Over the years I've watched three boats burn. Two of the three were lost to fires that started in the galley. Both had stoves considered to be the "safest"—alcohol and electric.

The late Ernie Braatz, manager of technical services for Boat/U.S., said, "Most galley fires boil down to operator error. People try to hurry an alcohol flame along without waiting for the prime, or they leave a flame unattended. And, of course, a stove that's caked with grease and grime isn't safe no matter what its fuel.

"People get too complacent about propane because of all the new safety devices. Inspect those lines regularly for chafe and, for heaven's sake, turn the gas off before you leave the boat."

In short, the safety differences between the possible fuel systems are significant, but NONE come without the need for respect, understanding, care, and common sense to make them safe. Even electric cooking is subject to faulty wiring, and something as elegant and useful as the butane hot plate I use might still seep fumes into the bilge. I take it home when we're off the boat.

In the area of fire extinguishers, the more the better. Backups can be lifesavers. Stowage and positioning can be critical to having a fire extinguisher available when you need it.

The Right Stuff

(C. S. Forester) Barbara was having to hold on tightly, and now that she looked up at him, she was obviously not quite as comfortable inside as she might be. Hornblower felt both amusement and pride. He was on the point of teasing her when common sense and his own tenderness for his wife saved him and made him remember with enormous clarity how much he hated the whole world when he was being seasick.

"You're fortunate not to be sick, my dear," said Hornblower, "but then you have a good stomach. I'm afraid I'm feeling the gravest doubt about my own, as I always do at the start of a voyage. But you are your usual happy self."

—*adapted from* Commodore Hornblower

Upper and Downer

(RR) My own career in regard to seasickness has ranged from "iron man" to "basket case." I've learned not to pull my foul-weather gear over a hangover head, and that it feels good to throw up instead of fighting it. The only true wisdom I might impart on the subject comes courtesy of my wife.

Carol enjoyed waves not at all and big waves not in the slightest. She'd had her head in a bucket across most of the oceans where we'd ever sailed. For some inscrutable reason, though, she was determined to make a Bermuda Race. I'd read of the phenergin/ephedrine combination. There must be a classier one now, but in the early '80s it was cutting edge. A muscle relaxant keeps you from throwing up and an upper keeps you from nodding off. You have to start on the medication a week before heading to sea, though. It also spaces some people out.

Carol did all she was supposed to and weathered a bouncy, fetid, sweltering, and dank race. No queasiness and only an occasional endearingly goofy grin. Two years later she did the same combination and smiled through an even rougher race.

Despite its host of limitations and notwithstanding pharmacological advances of recent years (e.g., scopolamine patches), the phenergin/ephedrine combination worked wonders before my very eyes.

Stay with the Boat!

(Phil Steggall) It should be like the seat belt in your car—a conditioned reflex. Hook up! The easier you make it for yourself, the more you'll wear your harness. I hate untangling harnesses. Walter Greene made a vest for me with the harness sewn into it. That helped a lot. I also wear wet-weather gear that has a harness built in.

I run "trolley wires" the length of the boat, port and starboard—not really wires (which can roll underfoot and sometimes mask chafe) but webbing like harnesses are made from. It's flat under foot, strong, and the carabiners ride easily over it without binding. I position the trolley lines so that if I fall over and fetch up, I will be held high enough off the water to grab the gunwale (or toe-rail) at about eye level. If you're by yourself and you have to reach an arm's length or more over your head to grab the toerail, you probably won't make it back aboard.

I also give myself a second tether, fitted with a snaphook and with the length adjustable so I can tie myself off comfortably wherever I need to work.

I know I won't do it unless I make it easy for myself, so I focus hard on making it as easy as possible.

READY ANCHOR   *(RR)*

Some people carry their anchors in the bottom of lockers. If I were drifting engineless toward a bridge, I'd rather have mine where I could get at it. I like to carry an anchor "at the ready" on the bow or secured in the bow roller. At the very least, lash your anchor on deck and tie it so you can release it quickly.

SAFETY GEAR

The hardest knife ill-used doth lose his edge.

—*Shakespeare,*
Sonnet 95

Safety gear is, quite simply, any piece of kit that makes you and/or your boat safer. It extends from an EPIRB to the tape that wraps the ends of cotter pins, from a serviceable bosun's chair to a decent mask and snorkel, from a chafe-proof chain "leader" on your anchor to a swamp-proof muffler on your exhaust.

CARRY A KNIFE   *(MB)*

- When *Lazy Daisy* capsized off the northeast coast of Scotland, Lionel Miller and his crew took to their inflatable liferaft. They soon realized that although the catamaran was inverted, she was not about to sink. They decided to retrieve the dinghy from the bridge deck to take with them. Regrettably, it was impossible to untie the painter to free the dinghy, and *none of them had a knife!*
- When the Bristol Channel pilot cutter *Sea Breeze*, skippered by redoubtable yachtsman and mountaineer Bill Tilman, was lost after grounding off a Greenland fjord, he was left on board alone holding the weighted end of the leadline, with a survivor ashore holding the other end. He felt that 7 pounds of lead around his waist might be a hindrance if it came to swimming, so *he went below for a knife* to cut it off!
- Peer Tangvald, adrift in his 7-foot plywood dinghy and some 55 miles off the Grenadine Islands after *Dorothea*'s shipwreck, had to jettison much of the gear with which he had "grossly overloaded" the boat. Having lightened her, he found she was floating like a

cork, and set about constructing a jury rig. He then discovered *he'd forgotten to bring a knife.*

- George Marshall was navigator of the 44-foot ocean racer *Guia III*, eastward-bound transatlantic, when she hit and was holed by a whale. Water flooded into the forepeak through the sail bins, and Marshall went back aft to *get the knife that was always available in the galley.*

Carry a knife—on a lanyard round your waist—at all times, even when turned in!

THE INDEPENDENT BILGE ALARM

(Doug Terman) It is that ultimate, glorious night at sea, the stars smeared overhead from horizon to horizon, winds Force 4 from the southwest, the seas stretched out in long, lazy swells. The old girl's making 6 knots on a beam reach.

Odd. She feels a bit sluggish.

You decide to go below. Five steps down the companionway your right deck shoe takes on a load of salt water. The floorboards are floating, along with the soggy remains of all manner of cardboard cartons, plastic bags, and settee cushions. You yell for all hands and switch on the saloon lights. Nothing. The batteries are shorted out; the electric bilge pump must have died a long time ago from lack of juice.

The generator . . . the main engine . . . nothing!

All you've got for illumination is your Boy Scout flashlight as you grovel on hands and knees, seawater up to your armpits, trying to find where the leak is. . . .

Let's give this one a happy (but improbable) ending. You and your crew bail like hell all night, get the water down to the cabin sole, discover that the galley seawater pump's plastic filter bowl has fallen off due to faulty hasp. You'll make Antigua with all souls still alive and kicking, but the ship's batteries are shot, the main engine and generator will have to be rebuilt, both freshwater and diesel fuel tanks are contaminated, the teak veneer on your cabin woodwork is delaminating, and a good deal of your food is inedible.

To prevent the above scenario, I offer the *Entry Level Bilge Alarm System.*

Purchase:

- a float switch such as a Rule-A-Matic (which sells for $15.99 in the West Marine Products catalog, Model 214957)
- a solid-state sonic alarm (available at Radio Shack)
- a 3-foot length of ¼-inch nylon line

Run wire from the float switch in the bilge to the sonic alarm, which should be placed in an area that is high and dry and will allow the alarm to be heard both below decks and from the cockpit.

Splice electrical wires to the float switch terminal wires with a soldered *lineman's splice.* The wires to be joined must be shiny clean. Twist them together, then hold the soldering iron to the wire to heat it. Touch the wire—not the iron—with the solder; it should flow like quicksilver over the whole joint. Anywhere the solder does not adhere isn't clean enough. Use heat shrink tubing (dual wall or heavy wall—*not* thin wall) to cover the joint to fashion an immersible connection.

A short in any circuit wired directly to the battery will create a dead short across the batteries, so fuse this circuit as close to the battery as possible.

Mount the float switch so it will make contact and set off the sonic alarm when *no more than two gallons of water are in the bilge.*

Attach the ¼ inch nylon line to the float and lead it up through a hole bored in the cabin sole. Knot the line so it won't slip back into the bilge. The purpose of the line is to lift the float and sound the alarm when you give it a gentle tug.

Instruct all crewmembers as to why the bilge alarm circuit is there, how to test it, how much water in the bilge will set it off, where the manual pumps are located, and how much water each pump sucks out of the bilge per stroke. Each watch is responsible to pump the bilge to insure that no water is accumulating, and to log the number of pump strokes that were necessary to clear the bilge.

GEAR TO GO *(Cam Lewis)*

"Hey Lewie, want to sail around the planet with me?"

On the phone was Bruno Peyron, and he was asking me along on his quest to circle the globe in less than 80 days. Though I'd been sailing all my life and been in some scrapes already, my family and friends all bid me good-bye like this was going to be my last voyage. But as crewman in charge of safety and survival gear for *Commodore Explorer*, our 86-foot catamaran, I was determined to prove them wrong.

What did I know about safety gear? I'd never been to a seminar or anything, but I knew the basics. I also considered how many of my good friends are now sailing the heavens and not the seven seas.

The effort began with a list of potential problems (generated from our combined experience, reading, and consultation with offshore "masters" and competitors aboard *ENZA*). Then came the list of equipment necessary to deal with the problems (see accompanying table).

We had some advantages. We would be tracked during our sprint by Argos; if we met disaster, at least they'd know where we were.

Our first rule was "Stay aboard!" We averaged 14.39 knots for 79 days. At those speeds, man overboard was a terrifying prospect. We tried to remind each other not to get too close to the edge. This was followed by all of the other important rules:

- Wear your safety harness with lifejacket.
- Hook onto the trolley lines to move around.
- Wear your personal EPIRB and carry a whistle, strobe, and knife.
- Keep track of your shipmates, and notify your watchmate if you're crossing the boat, even just leaving the cockpit.

COMMODORE EXPLORER'S SAFETY GEAR MASTER LIST

POSSIBLE PROBLEMS

	Equipment	Man Overboard	Dismasting	Capsize	Collision	Broken Steering	Power Loss	Injury	Evacuation/Basic Survival
6	Henri Lloyd survival suits			•	•				•
1	Plastimo 6-man life raft			•	•				•
3	Argos beacons w/emergency capability			•					•
1	EPIRB/SARSAT beacon			•	•				•
2	Survival Technologies Man Overboard Modules (No. 9 series)	•							•
2	Gale Rider sea anchor/drogues (36", 18")		•	•	•	•			•
2	Steiner heaving lines	•							•
2	Steiner rescue buoys	•							•
2	Boxes assorted fishing gear								•
1	Drysuit and assorted SCUBA gear	•	•		•	•			•
6	Bilge pumps and buckets			•	•				•
1	Large PVC hull cover (for major underwater damage)				•				•
12	Watertight bulkheads (to seal off parts of hulls)			•	•				•
5	Sea Marshall personal EPIRBs with signalling alarm on board	•							•
6	Safety lines for moving across or fore and aft on board	•							•
5	Musto safety harnesses with inflatable life jackets and whistles	•							
6	Underwater flashlights with spare bulbs and batteries	•		•			•		•
8	Petzl Headlamps			•			•		
6	ACR personal strobe lights with whistles	•		•					•
24	Cyalume glow sticks	•							•
24	Plastimo handheld red flares			•	•				•
4	Plastimo white flares			•					•
2	Plastimo orange smoke flares			•					•
6	Plastimo white parachute flares			•	•				•
2	Plastimo signal mirrors			•	•				•
2	Hacksaws with spare blades		•			•			•
2	Cans orange spray paint (for writing "SOS" on bottom of hulls)			•					•
2	Complete medical kits w/manuals, 2 emergency blankets	•		•				•	•
1	Trimble handheld GPS					•			•
2	ICOM handheld VHF radios with waterproof bags			•	•				•
1	Sextant and tables			•			•		•
5	Musto offshore dry suits	•	•						•
1	Spare rudder and emergency tiller					•			
1	Extensive epoxy/carbon/glass repair kit				•	•			•
9	10-liter jerrycans for water			•					•
1	Backup Honda generator w/fuel			•			•		

With the hectic shakedown and departure, it wasn't until our fourth day into the record run that we slowed down long enough to have a safety briefing. We should have done it earlier, but we set the rules, familiarized ourselves with the gear, and sped on.

On the 52nd day we lay a-hull with bare poles 200 miles from Cape Horn. We were pounded by monstrous breaking seas. Gusts went as high as 82 knots. We lashed the sails to the tramp and boom, with crew movements on deck protected by a security rope belayed by another crewmember. Sure we were scared, but we had to fight, and we had confidence in each other, the boat, and our equipment. It was this confidence that kept our fear and fatigue from hindering our survival.

We pulled through unscathed, underway again less than 24 hours after "parking." We were shaken and a bit gun shy, but the excitement of passing the Horn and the sprint up the Atlantic soon dulled the scare from the tempest. Finishing just under the 80-day mark was nice, too.

AUTOMATIC BILGE PUMP TIMER

(*Doug Terman*) Automatic bilge pumps are dandy but have an insidious built-in flaw. Let's say you've got a seawater intake hose to the engine that has split just below the hose clamp—where you can't easily notice it. Water weeps in while you're at anchor, but the electric bilge pump easily takes care of it. So every weekend you check the bilges—nice and dry, just like always. But eventually the hose will fail completely, and most of the seawater in the anchorage will make a beeline for your bilge. You'll probably never know why the boat sank.

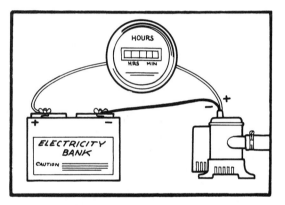

Automatic Bilge Pump Timer

The best insurance to prevent the above scenario is to insert a *Hobbs* meter in the automatic bilge pump circuit. A Hobbs meter is simply an engine-hour meter; purchase one from a marine-engine dealer for about $40 or less. It records the minutes and hours that current flows through the circuit it's inserted in. With a Hobbs meter installed between the positive terminal of your battery bank and the positive terminal of your automatic bilge pump, the meter will record how long the bilge pump has been running since last you noted it. Note the reading when you leave the boat, and compare that with what you find when you come back. At sea the off-going watch should record the Hobbs meter reading in the log. More than a minute of running time over a three hour watch should be cause for deep and protracted concern. [Readily available cycle counters are an acceptable alternative. They have a reset, like an automotive odometer, and they are available from West Marine and others for around $50.—eds.]

HANG IN

(RR) I knew Steve when he was just another sailor looking for pier-head jumps along the docks in Newport. When I saw the picture of him suspended from the Fore River Bridge by the harness he was selling, I didn't rush to support his young company; I just thought "crazy Steve." Then summer came and I needed a harness. I bought one of his. Why not? Whether or not Steve's a master marketer, he sure can sew.

Twenty years later Steve is still crazy and I still wear my Lirakis. I'm not real sure what else is out there, but for comfort, convenience, and security, I hope to be wearing my Lirakis harness for another 20 years, anyway. (Lirakis Safety Harness, Inc., 18 Sheffield Ave., Newport, RI, 02840, phone (401) 846-5356.)

THE ULTIMATE PFD

PFDs and survival suits are designed to keep crews afloat long after the mother ship has slipped below the waves. But if the boat had her own PFD, consider the advantages:

- The boat has food and water aboard, unlike the liferaft.
- Survivors are on a familiar, user-friendly platform.
- Radio contact with potential rescuers might be available.
- A floating object, however low in the water, is a better radar target than a sunken one.
- The vessel herself most likely will be saved.

US regulations require boats under 19 feet to be "unsinkable" and everything over 80 feet to have watertight doors. That leaves the bulk of recreational boats to "sink or swim."

Yachtsaver, a system of portable, deployable, self-contained flotation—a PFD for the boat—gives you an option other than jumping ship. Starting with a CO_2/nitrogen-inflated bag, Yachtsaver uses multiple floats and restraining webs to fashion systems for boats of all sizes. The fire-retardant gas provides nearly 2,500 pounds of lift per bag. Suit the flotation to your displacement, and deploy them where you can inflate them in an emergency. A single bag (including a 10 x 15 x 22-inch carryall) costs $995.00. Quad-packs (which provide 8,860 pounds of lift) come for $2,495. (Yachtsaver, Moxie Cove Rd., Round Pond, ME 04564.)

HAPPY TRAILS

(Herb McCormick) Getting a man-overboard victim back aboard presents problems. If you are alone and the swimmer is bigger than you are (your husband/significant other in the case of a cruising couple), you've got extra problems. The Lifesling, developed by the Seattle Sailing Foundation, helps to solve them.

The sling consists of a throwable flotation collar attached to a floating (yellow polypropylene) rope. In addition to the option of throwing the float, this system provides the ability to trail the collar astern at the end of its tether and circle the victim—so that he/she can grab the collar and don it. Now stop the boat and "reel" the swimmer in. During our tests (*Cruising World*, December 1992) a woman of average stature brought aboard a passive, wet, 200-pound victim in 12 minutes (see illustration, page 265).

Lifesling's collar, similar to those used to hoist downed flyers into rescue helicopters, makes an ideal "hoist" for lifting the victim aboard. Winch the swimmer aboard on a halyard, or fasten the sling to a block-and-tackle system to give you the needed mechanical advantage. Lifesling doesn't do much for an unconscious victim, and there is a danger of drowning the victim if the mother ship fails to stop when contact is made and tows the victim too fast. Still, no other system I've seen, patented or otherwise, covers so many bases—contacting the swimmer, attaching him or her to the boat, and getting him or her aboard. Many have died because those problems weren't solved. (Port Supply/Lifesling, phone (800) 621-6885.)

EXPERIENCE

The knowledge, will, and skill to prepare for what you can prepare for is not only a keystone of safety, it is also an essential in meeting that which you cannot prepare for. Buddy Melges says racers can't "get out ahead of the bow plate" unless they're happy and confident with everything aft of the bow plate. Get yourself safe for sea by wringing the most from the experience that you have.

By far the highest rate of casualties to infantrymen on the ground in Vietnam came during their first week in country. Make it through that "baptism" and you had a better-than-average chance of making it home.

The more we do, the more we know.

BAIL YOURSELF OUT   *(Tino O'Brien)*

More than hunger, thirst, enemy action, or drowning, the primary cause of death among lifeboat castaways in the North Atlantic during World War II was exposure. The trawler sailors who ferried arms from England to occupied Norway were extremely vulnerable. Faced with the daunting challenge of surviving at sea, many victims faded into inactivity and premature death. One sailor, who had survived two previous "dunkings," grabbed the drain plug from his overloaded boat and threw it overboard. Those who would live were forced to bail constantly to stay afloat. All did, and all survived!

AS YOU WERE   *(Capt. James Cook)* I was conscious latterly of an increasing sense of dis-ease. This is something that I have learned never to disregard, for it has saved us many times from danger, though not on the occasion of our grounding on the Barrier Reef when I had no such feeling but was asleep. This unease that I have sometime felt is a most strange thing, very common among masters and captains who have spent long periods at sea in the same ship. It were as though captain and ship were one, and the ship capable of communicating the awareness to the one person who can order action to avert it.

After the lamplight in the cabbin, it was a little while before I had accustomed my eyes to the darkness; I made out the unmistakable shape of Bona Vista Island. I had not forgotten the SW-going current in the neighborhood of the Cape Verde Islands; indeed I had warned

The greatest obstacle to be faced at sea is the fear of the unknown.

—*Robert J. Meura,*
Survival Guide for the Mariner

> *I used to worry all the time about what I would do if the wind went around into the northeast, things like that. Now that I know what to do, I don't worry so much.*
>
> —*Patrick Ellam*

Mr. Bligh before going below, but either our position at noon was at fault or the current was a good deal stronger than I had expected. Now it became clear that we could barely make enough speed through the water to counteract the current setting us down on the island. Our situation was very alarming, so much so that I did not dare sound the bottom for fear that the rocks would be as close to the keel as the coral had been under Endeavour Reef, and that the leadsman crying the depth should cause so new and inexperienced a crew to lose their nerve. For those few minutes I held my breath, as I imagine did the other officers, the roar of breaking waves so close in the darkness and audible over the sounds of the ship driving through the water.

Once we were clear, I noted that Mr. Bligh was shouting his orders which, though natural, was regrettable, all of us feeling that same sense of relief but not expressing it.

—*adapted from* The Last Voyage, *a fictional diary by Hammond Innes*

GONZO

(Walter Greene) We'd been running our 55-foot tri off for the whole night. I didn't have my harness clipped on. I didn't want to be tethered to the boat if she turned over. A big wave broke right over me. We capsized at the same time. I swam around the underside of the cross arm and climbed on top. Through the portholes into the cabin I could talk to my crew. They handed me a saw so I could cut a hole to get in. You'd be surprised at how fast you can cut a hole under those circumstances.

—*adapted from* The Cruising Multihull, *Chris White*

FROM THE INFERNO

September 1, 1923—*Empress of Australia*, a 615-foot luxury liner under Capt. Sam Robinson's command, was ready to cast off from her pier in Yokohama when screeching, then smoke, then tremor announced an earthquake. Robinson looked inland to see the street collapse as though furrowed by a monster plow. Fires erupted all along the waterfront. The pier rippled like a caterpillar. Crewmembers lowered rope ladders to people below, but Robinson had the gangplank run out, opening the ship to wounded and refugees. (She eventually took over 2,000 aboard.)

Still at her pier, *Empress* was threatened by burning lighters, junks, and barges, all broken loose and drifting before 70-knot winds. If the ship stayed alongside, she would be set afire. Astern, between her and open water, lay *Steel Navigator*, a freighter seemingly without crew, her two bow anchors out on cables.

Robinson called for speed astern. "We'll ram her and carry us both clear of the flames." As the big ship gathered way, hulks that had drifted down acted like a buffer between the two ships, forcing *Empress's* stern to swing clear. Almost free, the big ship's starboard prop snagged *Steel Navigator's* port cable.

Robinson then negotiated to have *Steel Navigator* manned and fired up so she might back out towing *Empress*. Before they got underway the fire resumed, licking its way across the harbor front, spouting plumes of flame. Just before it reached the two ships, the freighter sounded her whistle and the two slid weirdly away. Fanned by a freshening land breeze, the fire now began racing out into the harbor. Robinson poured power to his remaining screw and raced across the flame path to safety 10 minutes before the anchorage was engulfed.

Empress still had to clear the breakwater; she was dragging a cable, and her bow could not be brought 'round to head into the channel. Robinson tried snubbing his bow anchor, but each time he kedged up short, it would free and let her drift closer to the shoals. He saw, however, the small tanker *Iris* and convinced her to act as his towboat. On her third try she swung *Empress* enough for the liner's screw to be engaged. Though *Empress* wobbled dangerously under the pull from the cable, she answered her helm well enough to negotiate the turn and slide out into the open water of the Gulf of Tokyo, where she remained at anchor and became the relief headquarters for the ruined city.

—*adapted from* A Sailor's Tales*, Bill Robinson*

No Worries

When he first started racing, Ted Turner had green crews often and was sometimes short-handed. "That's when I worried most about safety," he says. "Later I was fortunate enough to put together full, competent, and experienced crews that didn't have to be babied. Thanks to them, even in the tough ones like the '79 Fastnet (which we won), I never felt I had to worry much about safety."

Reality Bites

(Dan Dickison) If you're young, careless, and adventuresome, there's no need to heed this counsel, but in any case I'd suggest it. I once signed on to deliver a 90-foot brigantine 400 miles across the Caribbean. Adventure had bitten me like a rabid dog. On board with me were only the crusty captain, his wife, the first mate, two extremely green but game passengers, and my very capable friend.

On the first night out—my watch—I leaned under the boom to identify some lights and WHACK! The lazy boom lift—a ¾-inch steel cable—had been left slack, and as the ship yawed, it knocked out my two front teeth. It felt like a savage hook from Mike Tyson, and I reeled accordingly. But when we mentioned it to the skipper below, he simply said, "If he's hurt, give him some rum."

Eight days later—it was a slow passage—we made landfall, and I managed to get my teeth attended to. The skipper would spend the next couple of months dodging my requests for medical reimbursements, and I'd spend the rest of my life saying: "Know your shipmates before you weigh anchor."

Experience Analyzed

(MB) The crew aboard *Westering* included Ed, a New York crane operator with no seagoing experience, along with Anabel, the children (Miranda, 6, and Bill, 4), me, and an Australian woman who happened to be my mother-in-law.

All those months ago when we'd first sailed this converted Royal National Life Boat Institute lifeboat from Dartmouth, England, on our great adventure, it had been a lovely blue and sunny day. As we slipped our lines, Rachel Lambert had called out, "Good luck Badhams. God be with you. It's always so much easier to be brave when the sun is shining, isn't it?"

That was then.

On this passage the sun seldom shone. Near dusk on the eighth day, we picked up Gibb's Head Light on Bermuda's southwest corner. By early morning, Ed coaxed the port engine back to life and we closed at last with St. George's Harbor. We covered 847 miserable and damaging miles in nine dreary days.

I learned some things—about starting a voyage on the thirteenth, about the mythical quality of midwinter "weather windows," about the incredible good nature of wives and children, even about the pluck and forbearance of mothers-in-law. I learned, too, that what you know and what you do are not always consistent.

When I was invited to initiate a course on leadership at the Royal Naval College, Dartmouth, it was a valued precept that delegation of duty in hazardous situations is good leadership—so those being led don't find themselves suddenly leaderless. Why then did I find myself "hogging" *Westering*'s wheel through most of the rough weather when I had a fit and capable young man ready to take over?

In such violent and frankly menacing conditions, I couldn't have gotten much sleep anyway. At every crunching smash into a wall of water, with every puff or change in the weather, I would have been racing up top to check that Ed—and

the boat—were still in one piece. So, in the face of theory, I did most of it myself.

THE LIMITS OF EXPERIENCE

(Webb Chiles) Just before 1030 *Chidiock* slid down a wave, hit something, and pitchpoled. I felt as though she were sinking. I had swamped her before and made preparations, but, despite my experience, I had not foreseen the situation as being as chaotic as was reality.

—*adapted from* Open Boat Across the Pacific

LEARN WELL

The sea is a great, if brutal, teacher. Learn the lessons of safety whenever and wherever you can.

MASTER TEACHER   *(Irving Johnson)*

I am sure that surviving over these many years as skipper and seaman was due to Capt. Jurs of *Peking*. There was always something of him aboard all of the *Yankee*s that we sailed. A ham-handed mountain of a man, he could do anything on the ship better than any of us. Once, when a sailor fell off a yard, he grabbed the spanker halyard tail and dove over the stern. He came up with the man like an otter comes up with fish. With him it was never a case of "good enough."

—*adapted from* The *Peking* Battles Cape Horn

CHARLIE BARR   Renowned as one of this century's best racing sailors, record-setter in *Atlantic* from Sandy Hook to the Lizard, and three-time winner of America's Cup, Charlie Barr was, says L. Francis Herreshoff, "known for his crews. He took great pleasure in sailing, and so did they. He trained his first mate to always have his eye upon him. At the slightest signal the crew would calmly execute a tack, jibe, or sail change with very little sound or fuss. He had them all executing their roles virtually without thinking, with the result the ship had but a single brain."

A GOOD TURN   *(RR)* A Fourth of July race on Buzzards Bay aboard *Fianna* marked the first time Will and I had ever raced together. Crouched by the jib winch, my son was poised for the tack.

"Watch out Will, you're standing in the bight," said skipper Brian McSweeny, as we maneuvered for the start.

Will was set up in the "slingshot" formed by the jibsheet under load as it came from the lead block, through the turning block, and forward to the winch. "It's not blowing too hard today, but it's a very bad habit to get into—standing in the bight—anytime, anywhere." Will looked a bit sheepish as he adjusted his spot, but we were both happy to be aboard.

CHILLING IMAGE

(RR) It was early in the season. We were grinders aboard *American Eagle* and we were still tickled with the power of our cross-linked coffee grinders. When it came time at the dock to send bowman Dooie Isdale aloft, we gave him a 100-foot express ride. He was shaken but smaller than any of us, so when he came down spluttering, it was just part of the game.

Next time we really cranked and had him going megaspeed by the time he reached the lower spreaders. "Whoa!" came the bellow from deck boss John Nichols. "Have you assholes figured out what would happen to him if he got his foot caught under a shroud tang on the way up going at that speed?" With that picture in mind, we put a "governor" on the elevator for the rest of the campaign.

FIRST THINGS FIRST

(Adm. Paul Welling, USCG) It was somewhere in the Pacific. We were days from making port. As we normally do, we put over the ship's boat. The boat is used to pick up a man overboard, and we practice the evolution underway daily.

The procedure is to start the boat's engine before the boat is lowered, and to make sure the engine is running well before casting off. On this occasion the boat was cast off before the engine started. The boat lay dead in the water. I chose to sail on.

The boat was almost hull down over the horizon before her crew got the engine started. They then began chasing us and came back alongside within the half hour. To all of us aboard who watched the boat disappear, and perhaps most powerfully to those in the boat watching *Eagle* disappear, I hope the correct launching sequence and the reason for following it became a bit clearer.

ORDERS

Your average afternoon daysail with friends is a long way from Gen. Jackson's battlefield, but orders and obedience to them are the lifeblood of boating, too.

Acknowledge orders. Often it's best to repeat them. "Aye-aye" works well. Yelling and screaming don't. It's a dialogue:

"Ease the jib."

"Easing."

"That's enough."

"Holding."

There's a middle ground between cat 'o nine tails

The obedience to orders, instant and unhesitating, is not only the lifeblood of armies and navies but the security of states.

—Stonewall Jackson

authoritarianism and the mushiness of command by marshmallow. Good skippers are continuously seeking it.

THE VEST IS BEST

(Bruce Kirby) I designed the Laser more than 20 years ago, but I still sail them every now and again. In the old days, before PFDs were compulsory under Laser class rules, I used to make it a point to be the first one into my lifejacket when the breeze piped up. Some people said that was the "Poppa Bear" in me. I don't mind people calling me Poppa Bear or a wimp, or whatever, but I don't want anyone saying "Kirby's not wearing his, so why should I wear mine?"

It goes beyond that, though. I had the same feeling in International 14s and Finns. In my Sonar racing today, too, even in a self-righting boat, it makes sense to me to get a PFD on. I feel more comfortable and I can concentrate on the race without having to worry overmuch about my delicate but beautiful body. A lifejacket ain't much use if it's in the boat when you're in the water.

COOKED

(MB) On the bridge on passage south from Hong Kong, the sky was overcast, the sun was invisible, and I was shirtless. After I'd gone below, I found my body scorched, with a temperature to match. At 15 knots the breeze had kept me cool. My CO admonished me that in the Royal Navy such carelessness is punishable. A "self-inflicted wound" rendering the perpetrator unfit, possibly, to carry out his duties was judged dereliction of duty and should be dealt with accordingly. The rules would be waived in my case, however, he added. I was in enough pain already.

SEAMEN FOR ALL SEASONS

(Capt. Jay Bolton) The heart of seamanship is safety consciousness. It begins by going beyond safety "information" to a due diligence in all respects, on the part of all hands, to make a vessel seaworthy before she goes to sea. It extends to all aspects of material readiness. It extends to people, too. If the operator of a vessel has a known latent defect, like a heart condition or impaired vision, and he does not provide a backup, he renders his boat unseaworthy (and he renders himself liable under Admiralty law).

I've been master of supertankers and of square-riggers. In all cases it's been my first responsibility to foster safety consciousness in all aboard. The guy that skins down the ratlines and lands like Captain Blood on the deck is putting himself at risk. That puts everyone at risk; that sets the wrong example. The great boathandler who uses the minimum of power to get the job done and keeps his options open as much as possible adds measurably to the safety of the vessel. Which one would you want aboard?

I concentrate on the little things. I find the big things take care of themselves.

—*Toby Baker, Sailing Coach, Tabor Academy*

BY THE BOOK

Arthur Knapp was famous for the glass case bolted to the bulkhead near the companionway ladder aboard *Weatherly*. Knapp was one of the original quartet of skippers to vie for the renewed America's Cup in 1958. A pipe-smoking veteran of Long Island Sound's cutthroat interclub wars, and a racing tactician known nationwide, he collected much of his wisdom into *Race Your Boat Right*, a best-seller in go-fast circles and a widely acclaimed encyclopedia of speed. On the glass case aboard *Weatherly* were bold red letters that said, "In Case of Emergency Break Glass." Inside the case was Knapp's book.

Knapp was jettisoned from *Weatherly* after her first campaign. The book followed shortly thereafter when Bus Mosbacher was installed as skipper. Then Bill Luders chopped and channeled *Weatherly* into a lighter, sprightlier racer. She won the right and defended the Cup in 1962.

> *It doesn't matter what you know if you're too lazy or insecure to put it down on paper.*
> —Bill Tierney, lacrosse coach, Princeton University

Tierney has taken his Ivy League players to three NCAA Division I Lacrosse National Championships in the past five seasons. The Tigers' disciplined play seems to emanate, at least in part, from a well-respected playbook.

Play by the book?

In the movies "the book" is stiff, inflexible, myopic. *The Rules, City Hall, the Navy way, the system*—to Hollywood they're only there for endearingly rebellious heroes to fight against. And it's true that in real life there are Blighs, Queegs, and Ahabs by the boatload, waving "the book" and making sea time sweat time. Preaching, tight-assed, hypocritical safety czars can pop up as soon as you cast off, and they use "the book" as their cat o' nine tails.

It isn't easy setting safety standards at sea. Can the book help?

- How about *COLREGS*? The International **Col**lision **Reg**ulations are the Rules of the Road. Ever read them?
- How about a "Defect Book?" Whenever anyone notices anything frayed, rusted, frozen, etc., you write it down. As the jobs are done, you cross them off.
- How about an "Emergency Book"? In it the skipper puts step-by-step, person-by-person evolutions for abandoning ship, dealing with dismasting, responding to a grounding, and handling other emer-

> *And it occurred to me. There is no manual that deals with the real business of motorcycle maintenance, the most important aspect of all. Caring about what you are doing is considered either unimportant or taken for granted.*
>
> —Robert Pirsig,
> Zen and the Art
> of Motorcycle Maintenance

gencies that might be anticipated.

- How about a tide book (like *Eldridge's Tide and Pilot Book*) or an almanac (like *Reed's*) to give the comfort of knowing how high the water is and which way it's running?

- How about *First Aid Afloat* or some equally authoritative and specific guide for keeping people healthy at sea?

- How about a crew work chart? Mark Lindsay, like many boatbuilders, races with all sorts of people. He usually gives each person in the crew a number and has them check out a simple diagram that clarifies their roles during key maneuvers. It takes two minutes.

- How about a logbook? British yachtsman Errol Bruce wrote the following standing orders in his: "In an emergency the mate of the watch should use his discretion and take any action that he deems necessary, but tell me as soon as possible. Please tell me at once if:
  (a) the weather changes
  (b) visibility falls below one mile
  (c) outside the 100 fathom line any vessel is sighted
  (d) any vessel is to pass within one mile
  (e) land, lights, or navigation marks are sighted
  (f) a sail change seems necessary
  (g) damage occurs to sails, rigging, equipment, or hull.

Never fail to call me, whatever the circumstances, if help or advice is needed."

- How about sea stories, yarns, and sailors' tales? Experience embodies lessons; yarns can be passports to safety.

DIESEL WILL BURN

(Norrie Hoyt) The book says fire danger from diesel fuel is minimal, as diesel will put out a flaming match thrown into it. Bill Buell and I learned that our *Niagara* burned up in a diesel fire anyway.

Circumstances had resulted in the boat sitting at a dock in Florida for a month, subsequently losing power on her next transit (condensation in the fuel?) and being sailed (in 30 knots of wind) to the marina in Fort Pierce. There an expert mechanic climbed over and around the engine (a Mitsubishi block marinized in England with Swedish parts). We surmise that perhaps he did no good to the heavy copper lug connecting the 150-amp alternator to the battery bank.

With power restored, Bill's brother Dexter and his parents left the marina and motorsailed against light winds—with the fully battened mainsail strapped tight and adding about 3 knots—until Dexter noticed a white fog emerging from the sail locker. We think the battery cable broke loose and tagged the pressure line to the injector, providing a "fog" of diesel. The automatic fire extinguisher may have gone off and suppressed the fire briefly.

Dexter yelled below to his parents who were, appropriately, as it turned out, listening to *Die Gotterdammerung*. They admitted a healthy gust of fresh air when they opened the engine compartment, a spark ignited the fuel, and the crew had three minutes to unlash and board the rubber dinghy.

The main went up in a 100-foot tower of flame. The boat burned to the waterline while the Coast Guard poured water and flame retardant on the flaming hull, and it sank as cooking-gas tanks exploded and blew the side out. Everything was too incinerated to offer evidence beyond our guesses when the boat was raised and barged to EPA-regulated disposal.

A FESTIVE FOURTH

(Bill Robinson) The yacht club dedication took place on the open porch of the new clubhouse on the Fourth of July. During the speeches, those of us who had come by boat began to cast an eye on

a bank of purple-black clouds building in the northwest. Soon we could see a line of foam advancing toward us ahead of dark wind streaks. The storm walloped us hard, with a wind shift to the north that screamed up to 60 knots in seconds.

I was just casting *Maiwara* off and didn't get a chance to get her motor started before I was blown up on the sedge bank below the porch. I was still trying to start the engine when two large teenagers galumphed aboard with the grace of Newfoundland puppies. In trying to help me, one crushed the engine cover while the other let all my halyards go. I persuaded them not to help me anymore and towed the boat, painter over my shoulder, chest-deep in water with waves slapping in my face, to a quieter cove as the squall subsided.

Contemplating the wreckage of my engine box and a jammed shaft, it seemed the only way I could get the boat out of there was to sail her. The halyards were flapping tantalizingly halfway up the mast. I took a good grip and eased myself up about halfway. The mast was wet, I slipped, and I slid back down like someone on a greased pole. My foot slid down onto the horn of the main halyard cleat and was impaled there, almost an inch deep. A month on a cane was time enough to reflect upon Good Samaritans and my career as an aerialist.

—*adapted from* A Sailor's Tales

THE WAVE

(Daniel Hays) Day 178. On January 6, just after I got our noon position and wrote "can't risk approaching Diego Ramirez in this visibility," a gale clomped down on us—with Force 8 winds and gusts to Force 9. In the afternoon I came on deck and besides seeing that Dad was working hard at the tiller, the seas and sky looked furious.

It's hard to see a wave (in photos, impossible). You see the mass of it—not much height—then you rise slowly as the water floods beneath you and you're on top. I was at the helm watching this really big one and suddenly I knew *Sparrow* hadn't risen and 20 feet of wave was straight up over us.

We surfed for a moment and fell off it to starboard, flat into the water. The boat didn't seem to tip over but the port rail rose up suddenly above

me as I slid down. What I'd been standing on was above my shoulder level. I was in the ocean! My tether was yanked tight as *Sparrow* came up level, surfed again, and fell over to port, the starboard deck and rail shooting up over my head. I kicked my legs and paddled for a minute in free water, then *Sparrow* righted and I was scooped on deck.

By the time all this happened, it had been 36 hours since I'd had a fix on the sun. My dead reckoning put us near Diego Ramirez (50 miles southwest of Cape Horn). But you can't steer accurately in a gale, so I was jumpy.

The gale broke at 0100 and, with the moon full, there it was: a frozen wave at the end of the continent. A featureless gray hump. The Horn.

—*adapted from* My Old Man and the Sea

STOP THE MUSIC

(Bill Black) To ingratiate ourselves with the sea gods on our passage from Kushiro, Japan, to the Aleutian chain, we made an offering of rum and lilacs. We were soon enveloped in fog, dodging drift nets which we missed by inches. Cheers for rum and lilacs.

Our Valiant 40 *Foreign Affair* was well equipped. In addition to our canopied liferaft, survival suits, and winter clothing, we carried a 406 EPIRB, a GPS, an SSB, a weatherfax, and radar. Cold and relatively uneventful, our fog-shrouded passage from Kushiro to Attu took 10 days.

Our game plan in the Aleutians was to play "musical chairs" with the fast-moving lows and fronts—move in good weather, hole up when it's nasty. Six hours after we left Massacre Bay on Attu, we were in trouble. A "developing low" had been upgraded to a storm. Fifty-knot winds were forecast to catch us well short of our landfall at Kiska. We doubled back. Retrospectively, this was a lucky break—a new chance to really explore Attu.

While we danced in rain and squalls at the end of our anchor rode, we read aloud from *The Thousand-Mile War* the detailed account of the recapture of the island from the Japanese by American forces in 1943. When the clouds lift, the scenery is awesome and you forget the days of gray skies and fog.

THE SECOND TIME AROUND

(Rich Wilson) Our first attempt to break *Northern Light*'s record for sailing from San Francisco to Boston ended in Holland. That's where we were deposited by *New Zealand Pacific* after she picked us up from our capsized and re-righted trimaran off Cape Horn. Now as we left the Horn astern and cut inside the Falklands on our way north in *Great America II*, I could not help but think of our first boat, a great boat, washed up on the coast of South Georgia. She was found by a French sailor 13 months after we abandoned her.

We were hoping for a better finish this time. We were hoping for a record passage, to be unique in that way, but whatever happened, we felt we were breaking new ground by sharing the adventure with thousands of people ashore. Via programs through Student Ocean Challenge and the American Lung Association, we were reaching 250,000 students who were, in turn, capable of interacting with us via weekly articles, *National Geographic* and NOVA specials on the voyage, a daily recording from the boat available by calling 1-900-820-BOAT, and a Monday through Friday schedule on Prodigy for computer "news conferences" involving direct questions via the Internet. Double-handing for more than two months at an average of over 9 knots was tough enough. Being "on" constantly for our followers was another full-time job.

Great American, our 53-foot Nigel Irens-designed tri, was a thoroughbred. Tough enough to take all that our course dished out, responsive enough to make our tactics look reasonable, and fast enough to match and surpass *Northern Light*'s 280-mile days, she helped us feel "we were three."

It was no surprise to those who had been sharing the voyage but still a great thrill that afternoon in March of 1993 to leave Boston Light close abeam and complete the trip—69 days, 19 hours, and 44 minutes for the 15,300-mile track. A new sail-powered record.

KEEP THE FAITH

(Robert Cox) I arose at 0530 and crept out of Manasquan Inlet in the densest fog I have ever seen. I ran straight offshore for about a mile, almost colliding with another cruiser trying to find the Inlet. Then I headed roughly north along the New Jersey coast toward Sandy Hook. For the first time ever, I was relying totally on loran. I'd determined that my compasses weren't reliable, so I put the Whaler up to just over 15 knots, turned on the automatic pilot, and concentrated on watching the latitude and longitude readout on the loran.

There is something about the loss of reference points that can induce panic. Back in my Miami/Nassau racing days, we would occasionally come across boats in the middle of the banks between Bimini and Northwest Channel. On that kind of gray, misty, overcast day, people begin mistrusting their compasses and imagining that they see islands where there are truly only pumped-up waves. Occasionally they will have a real panic attack. We would see them stop their engines and put on their lifejackets and sit there blubbering until "rescued" by someone to follow.

Running those loran lines from Manasquan to Sandy Hook in the fog, I felt something of that, even though I am supposed to be sophisticated enough to know better. What if my one engine quit? What if the headings weren't right and I was charging off to nowhere? What if? What if!

After two hours of "what-iffing," I hit the markers at Sandy Hook dead on the nose. From there I headed into Lower New York Bay, found some buoys in the fog, and then proceeded to get truly lost.

MAN OVERBOARD

Explosion, collision, capsize, trauma, fire—all happen, but 80 percent of the fatalities recorded by the Coast Guard stem from falling overboard. Of the people who drowned, says the Coast Guard, only one in six was wearing a lifejacket.

THE LONGEST HALF HOUR

(Phil Steggall) Not long ago our 27-foot trimaran was doing about 15 knots under spinnaker in a building sou'wester off Newport, RI, when a crewman fell overboard. I am embarrassed to say it, but it took us *half an hour* to get the guy back aboard.

We got the spinnaker down, but because we had no bag, we had to hold it. Finally we stuffed it down the companionway—and it popped back out. What a menace! Next we tried to start the outboard but couldn't. The owner was the only guy who knew how the kill switch worked. (He, of course, was the guy in the water.) At one point the jib sheets flogged free of their lead blocks—no stopper knots—and that complicated things further.

With no engine, under main alone, we didn't get upwind very well. Then we had the devil of a time heaving-to next to the guy. We missed him a couple of times going by so fast that he couldn't grab on. It's not a huge boat, but the two of us had our hands full handling it in this air. Our efforts weren't made any more relaxed by our fears about what was happening to our man in the water. Luckily he had on a silly, lime-green hat. We never lost sight of it. It was the best piece of safety gear on the ocean.

[Steggall, a professional sailor for decades, is unquestionably one of the most expert sailors on the planet. He won his class in the 1980 OSTAR, and as a "multihull expert," ranks with the best in the world. This "simple" retrieval, however, became a nightmare of frustration. It can happen to the best of us.—eds.]

FIRST TIME, LAST TIME

(Robin Lee Graham) I was sleeping in my harness when *Dove* was dismasted off the Cocos Islands in the Indian Ocean. I detached the harness when I came on deck because it was rigged to the boom, which was overboard. I struggled to get the mast and rigging back aboard, getting myself all cut up. Suddenly the boat lurched and, for the first time in my life, I fell overboard. If *Dove* had been underway, I would have been food for the sharks, but within seconds, long enough, I was able to grab the rail and heave myself aboard.

—adapted from Dove

ALMOST HOME

(Jack Weston) I had spent consecutive watches on deck as we battled Gulf Stream squalls aboard *Scylla* racing to Bermuda. It was sometime after midnight when I detached my lifeline, which I'd been using constantly, and started down the hatch to the cabin. When I was hip-deep in the companionway, *Scylla* lurched violently and fell away, down and sideways. I was catapulted out of the hatch, slid over the trunk, and down to the leeward rail. A rush of water along the deck washed me underneath the lifeline and overboard. Dazed by being knocked down, I had no idea what had happened and felt nothing to grab or hold onto. My first realization that I was actually overboard came when I saw the transom disappearing over a wave.

[Weston was recovered due to his own presence of mind in shedding his foul-weather clothes, and also to a new strobe water light from Guest. It pulsed brilliantly off the low clouds. Weston swam to it—mostly underwater because he could make no headway on the surface. By the time *Scylla* returned, Weston had been in the ocean for almost an hour.—eds.]

"JUST A MINUTE, DEAR"

Michael Birch, the Anglo-Canadian who has long been one of the dominant solo racers on the planet, almost missed a brilliant career. In the early '60s he and wife Jo, and three others, were delivering the 12-meter *Kurrewa* transatlantic for her new owner, Baron Bich. Michael stood watch by himself.

Jo remembers being woken by a tapping on the hull. The tap persisted and then she heard someone calling her name. Somewhat sleepily she popped up on deck. She found Michael alongside the boat clinging to the genoa sheet as the 12-meter surged along. In the process of lowering the genoa, Birch had slipped from the foredeck. On his way astern he grabbed the trailing sheet, tapped on the side and called quietly for help, and was coolly waiting for it to arrive.

BLIND SPOTS

(RR) Cruising with our children when they were young (under four years old) produced more than its share of heart-stopping moments. We were religious about harnesses when we were underway, but at quayside or at anchor we were more relaxed. Not surprisingly, of the five "dunkings" that occurred, four were when *Shere Khan* was at a dock.

SHOUT, THROW, POINT

The first three things you should do if you're left behind when some one goes over are:

- SHOUT—to alert all hands. "Man overboard" is the accepted and recognized phrase.
- THROW—a lifering, cushion, cockpit grating, or some other "flotation device" as close to the swimmer as you can.
- POINT—Don't take your eyes off the victim until someone else has assumed the "spotter" role. Keep pointing the direction even if you lose sight of the person in the water.

Doing these things smartly and confidently helps begin a successful recovery.

SEA STOP

(Rod Stephens) No two man-overboard accidents are quite alike, and difficulties can arise in a number of quarters. I was saddened by several instances where the victim was located but perished because the boat could not be maneuvered to successfully bring him aboard in time. Let me suggest a method for bringing a sailboat to a stop and virtually "heaving to" just to weather of the victim.

The main feature of this technique is a preventer run forward from the end of the main boom in such a way that when tension is taken on the preventer, the main boom is held out to leeward. Approach the victim so as to luff to a stop just to weather of him. Drop the headsail early, and close with the swimmer on a fairly free course between a close and a beam reach, trimming and easing the mainsail to control the boat's speed. Bring her into position with the swimmer abeam and just to leeward. Now tighten the preventer to hold the boom out to the shrouds, make it fast, then tie the helm down. This form of heaving to keeps the boat from surging past or falling behind the swimmer, and leaves all hands free to assist in getting him aboard.

FINDING THE VICTIM

If you lose sight of the victim, return to the position where the accident occurred ("littered," hopefully, by the sundry floating objects that you immediately tossed over the side). Start a search plan à la that outlined by Arthur Chace in *Precision Cruising* (see illustration, and paste a copy in your log). The idea is that the boat should alternate between close-reaching and broad-reaching legs, each leg taking 15 seconds longer than its predecessor. At 6 knots this will produce a spiral with 50 yards between tracks. At slower speeds the tracks will be closer together.

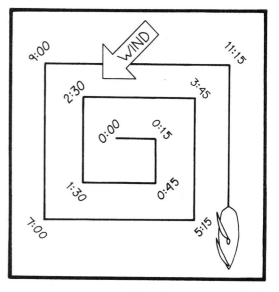

Finding the Victim

A time-tested way of fixing the spot is to note your course, steer it for a minute, turn onto the reciprocal course, and once you're squared away, sail for a minute back. Turning time and differences in speed on the two headings need to be figured precisely, however.

Most GPS and loran sets have a "Hold" button that, when punched, retains the coordinates of your position at the time. On modern sets, this button is wisely labeled "MOB" (man overboard). Punch the MOB button as soon as you can after someone goes over, and you will be able to return to the exact geographical position of the accident. Loran is reportedly more precise in terms of repeatability than GPS.

TRUE TESTIMONIAL   *(Herb McCormick)*

During our man-overboard tests, I got dunked more times than I care to count. These were serious tests, and we concluded: "Other techniques have been publicized, but our crew found none superior to the *Quick Stop*. Regardless of your sailing ability, we recommend that you practice this maneuver with every crewmember you bring aboard."

[The Offshore Racing Council's Quick-Stop Procedure is simple and lightning quick. The US Yacht Racing Union Safety at Sea Committee, the US Naval Academy Sailing Squadron, the Cruising Club of America Technical Committee, and the Sailing Foundation of Seattle, Washington, jointly conducted the sea trials that yielded Quick Stop. We feel it best addresses the critical need *to remain as close to the victim as possible throughout the retrieval.*—eds.]

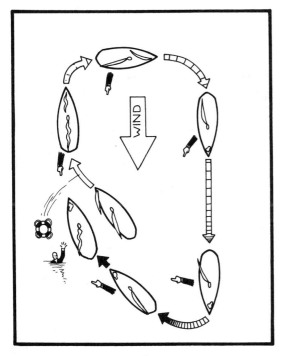

The Quick-Stop Procedure

THE QUICK-STOP PROCEDURE

1. Shout "man overboard" (port or starboard). Designate spotters to point constantly to the victim. Punching the loran's "Hold" button will retain the exact geographical position of the accident.

2. Provide immediate flotation. Deploy buoyant objects such as cockpit cushions, rolled up PFDs kept handy to the helmsman, and liferings. (The man-overboard pole rig may require too much time.)

3. Immediately tack the boat (without releasing jib sheets).

4. Allow your headsail to back and further slow and turn the boat.

5. Continue to turn until you are headed nearly dead downwind.

6. Drop the headsail(s) while keeping the mainsail centered (or nearly so). Do not slack the jib sheets while dousing so the sail will stay inside the lifelines.

7. Hold the downwind course until the victim is abaft the beam.

8. Jibe the boat.

9. Approach the victim on a course of approximately 45 to 60 degrees off the wind.

10. Establish contact with victim with heaving line or other device. [Naval Academy sailors use a "throwing sock," containing 75 feet of light floating line and a kapok bag that can be thrown into the wind.—eds.]

11. Effect recovery. [Over the leeward side is best in most cases. It will tend to be lower and more sheltered, and it will be easier to lash the boom to the lee shrouds and sling a hoisting tackle from it. In a seaway, guard against the boat slamming into the swimmer.—eds.]

You can use the Quick-Stop under spinnaker. As the boat comes head to wind, ease the pole to the headstay and lower the sail onto the foredeck during the tack. Yawls and ketches seem to fare best by dropping their mizzens as early as possible. The engine is not required, but start it in neutral in case it's needed. [Make sure nothing is in the water that can foul the prop—not the least the victim himself!—eds.]

UNDER POWER

A *destroyer turn* is simply a hard-over turn at speed. Watch out not to return too quickly and run the man down! A *Williamson turn* is more deliberate. Come to the side on which the victim fell overboard until your heading has changed 60 degrees. Steady on that course for a second, then turn hard the opposite way until you are on the reciprocal of your original heading. The Williamson turn is ideal when you have lost contact with the victim, or in low visibility or nighttime emergencies.

DANGEROUS DIP

(Garry Hoyt) After a tedious singlehanded anchor drill on top of a particularly hot afternoon sail, I was desperately anxious for the compensation of a cooling plunge in limpid Caribbean waters. Overlooked in my haste was the prosaic need to put the swim ladder in place over the side. The boat in question was a 52-foot ketch with the dinghy in davits, a high clipper bow, and a narrow bowsprit/anchor platform. It didn't take long to figure out that the anchor line was the only way back aboard, but climbing 6 feet of slick, slack nylon line proved a lot harder than it looked. Had the water been colder or I older, the outcome could have been either deadly serious or at least seriously inconvenient. (Swim ashore naked and await the next passing yacht?)

The best design solution is one of the new scoop sterns that offers a permanent platform right at water level. But if you have an older yacht, don't sneer at keeping a rope ladder where it can always be reached by arm from the water. You'll probably never need it until that moment when you really do.

SENSIBLE STEPS

("Goddard") Sometimes the man overboard can catch the painter or the tow rope of the tender. If he knows how, he can then climb into the tender over her stern even if there is some wind and sea. Should the yacht have an outboard rudder with a fancy curve to it at the waterline, then you can climb easily aboard. Most old-time sailing vessels hung two ropes from the after quarters that were called drag ropes. These were made up with Turks' heads sewed on them about 18 inches apart, so that anyone who fell over could grab these ropes.

I fell over once off a high-sided launch. It was a calm anchorage, but I couldn't find any way of getting back aboard. I had to resort to climbing aboard a nearby Friendship sloop with low freeboard. I swore to myself that I never again would have a boat or a yacht that a swimmer could not climb aboard, and so on the *Viator* there are bronze footholds or steps on either side of the rudder, one about 2 feet down and the other one a foot below the water. They are shaped like staples and cause little resistance when sailing.

—*adapted from* The Compleat Cruiser,
L. Francis Herreshoff

PRACTICE

Pointe du Hoc is a blunt, triangular cape rising sheer 117 feet from the sea. It is a salient that commands both sectors of Omaha Beach. The Germans had mounted there a six-gun 155-mm coastal battery. None of the planners believed that the American landings at Omaha could succeed unless Pointe du Hoc was neutralized.

That job was given to the 200-man 2nd Ranger Battalion of the US Army, commanded by Col. James E. Rudder. Many in the Intelligence operation believed the job could not be done—hardened positions atop a sheer cliff face with no cover, darkness, or surprise. . . .

The Ranger approach to "safety" on this, the toughest mission General Omar Bradley ever assigned, was practice. Working with 112-foot sectioned ladders, rocket-fired grappling lines, and special 100-foot aerial ladders borrowed from the London Fire Department, the soldiers scaled Swanage Cliff, near the White Cliffs at Dover, time and again.

Evidently they got it right. On D-day the landing craft with Rangers aboard hit the small shingle beach at the foot of the cliff at 0708. In just 17 minutes, 150 Rangers had command of Pointe du Hoc and the battery was silenced. Taking Omaha Beach was tough enough. Without the success of the well-oiled attack on Pointe du Hoc, it might have been impossible.

—*from* The Invasion of France and Germany,
Samuel Eliot Morison, and other sources

OVERBOARD OVER AND OVER

Someone going over the side is an emergency, but if you practice getting someone back, it need not be a fatality. Practice isn't going to make *perfect*, but give it the chance to make *possible*.

Practice a lot, and not only when the weather is warm and bright.

Use a fender tied to a bucket to simulate the man overboard—it will drift at about the same rate that a person might.

Occasionally let someone be the silent observer during a drill, then listen to their critique.

Overboard Over and Over

Brainstorm around the "what ifs."

- What if we couldn't start the engine?
- What if we lost sight of the person?
- What if the person starts to go under?

Go over the side yourself!
Whom do you call if you can't find the person?
Practice.
"Drownproofing" is achievable. Practice it.
The record of a dozen man overboard incidents shows:

- Six were successful.
- One was rescued by another boat.
- Five drowned after being brought alongside.

As part of your practice, work out a way to get the heaviest among you, possibly unconscious, back aboard. *Cruising World* had good luck with a sling fashioned from an over-size bowline. Using a tackle shackled to a halyard and fastened to the victim's harness is a good method. If you need to lead a halyard to a big primary winch in the cockpit, make your halyard tail long enough to do the job. Gang winches (lead your halyard around two winches and put a grinder on each) if you need more muscle.

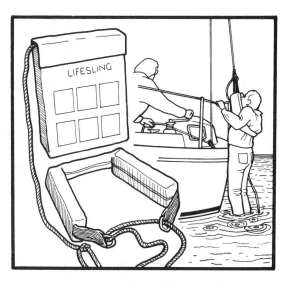

The Lifesling is designed both to "retrieve" a swimmer and to hoist him/her back aboard. For a description, see page 248.

REALLY. . .

How realistic is it to suggest practicing safety? Ask Buddy Melges or Paul Elvstrom. Titans among racing sailors, these guys are legendary for the time they spend practicing for speed.

"Mark it and set it," Melges says.

Once you're confident that you are set up right for the conditions you'll get "out front of the bow plate" and meet Mother Nature as she comes at you.

Elvstrom is a bit different: "I never marked anything. Mark it, and it's frozen. Finding what's best, what's fastest, is perpetual experimentation. The changes, refinements, and nuances deepen and develop your feel."

Mark it or not, practicing for speed is expected and accepted by sailors around the world. Practicing for safety?

- Can you see setting the hook 12 times when once will do? Teams that don't practice rarely beat teams that do. You improve your level of performance and proficiency when you practice, without question.
- Once the main's down, can you see raising it again in search of a safer way of dousing it again? Often practices are orchestrated to put more pressure on the athlete than the game. My seamanship students read and drilled and walked through demos on man-overboard

drills, but invariably the first time that they simulated the real thing on the water, "pressure" fouled them up.

- Can you see a pressure-producing practice (two men overboard, two tied together to form a 400-pound victim) perhaps rendering your crew more bullet-proof? Do you think that by surviving the drill they'd be better able to deal with the reality?

DISCOVERY

Coaches talk about building consistency. Basketball foul shooters, for instance, go through exactly the same ritual prior to every shot. Won't practice help us find and hone the routines to be the foundation for wise decisions underway? Pride comes from tradition, and pride grows out of winning, but pride comes with practice, too. Practicing safety is an investment, a commitment, and an experience that deepens your concern for safety.

Perhaps for the pleasure sailor there is no sharp dividing line between practice and "the game." Every time we cast off, every time we set sail, every time we turn on the engine or fix our position, if we're not doing it well and safely, we'll know soon enough. Maybe the distinction between "practice" and "the real thing" is a phony distinction in lots of ways. Maybe it's simply a question of putting what we know about being safe into practice.

THE BUNTLINE HITCH

(John Rousmaniere)

This is like two half-hitches except that when the first hitch is made on the outside of the standing part, the second hitch is made on the inside. This "balanced" knot grows tighter and tighter with strain. Even a bowline can flog loose, especially one with a short tail, and they are heavy knots that take up a fair amount of space. That's why I like to tie sheets into a jib with the incredible, compact *buntline hitch*. You might have to hack them off at the end of the season, but they'll do a great job all year long.

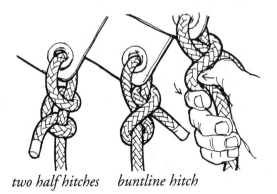

two half hitches   buntline hitch

Jim Sollers (from *Elements of Seamanship*)

In Conclusion

We bring our forum to a close, with thanks to the participants. Looking back through these pages, we find no pat conclusions, no hard-edged last words with which to summarize hard-won knowledge. Sea wisdom, it seems, is like a parable—open to interpretation.

Yet good sailors have a way of divining the correct interpretation for the situation at hand. They seem to make their own luck, while never neglecting to pay homage to Aeolus and the gods of fortune. To the schoonermen, a favorable breeze for the next port of call was "a good chance along." To you, we wish fair winds and a following sea.

ABOUT OUR CONTRIBUTORS

Adair, Mike & Anne   Freelance writer/photographers, they lived aboard their Out Island 41 *Snorkey*, in the Bahamas and the southeastern U.S. From scuba diving to security, from provisioning to fendering, their "how-to" pieces are expert and practical.

Aebi, Tania   He thought she was "going nowhere," so Tania's father dared her to sail around the world. Eighteen-year-old Tania took the challenge and aboard 26-foot *Varuna* became the youngest singlehander to complete a circumnavigation (and the first American woman, as recorded in her book *Maiden Voyage*). Today she has two children (boys 4½ and 2), and lives in Vermont. She and her husband still do boat deliveries.

Allen, Richard B.   Editor and compiler of *The Atlantic Fisherman's Handbook*, he offers financial, technical, and regulation-management guidance to commercial fishermen.

Anderson, Bob   Captain Bob, a retired U.S. Navy submariner, has done dinghy racing in England, the 1967 Fastnet, the English Channel, the Caribbean, San Francisco and Tokyo bays, and Hawaii, but loves best "gunkholing my beloved coast of Maine."

Archibald, Jim   From the Rhode Island yards of Williams & Manchester, Newport Offshore, and Merrifield Roberts, he joined Jamestown Boatyard (Jamestown, RI) in 1987. Jim set up a blister-cure facility for Nautor (Swan) in Hong Kong and now runs Jamestown's anti-blister operations, both mobile and yard-based.

Baker, Toby   Passagemaker, cruiser, and coach, Toby served Interscholastic Sailing so well they named the national championship trophy after him. He's won it, and his Tabor teams have been singled out for sportsmanship and service awards. His four transatlantics, two on his 41-foot Camper Nicholson *Torch*, he recalls as "over 10,000 miles—no snafus."

Barber, Chip   Chairman of the New York Yacht Club's Seamanship Committee, a Director of the American Sail Training Society, and member of the U.S. Sailing Association's Safety at Sea Committee, he was Director of Sailing at the U.S. Naval Academy, where he oversaw a 300-boat fleet and trained 2,000 midshipmen annually. He navigated the 1979 Fastnet Race ("in the silver") and (with 10 midshipmen and a 20-year-old Swan) won the 1992 Newport-Bermuda Race. His yacht management firm is in Charlottesville, VA.

Barnes, Howard   Howard Barnes retired after 38 years teaching high school science and wrote *Backyard Boatyard*. His five boats included a Seagull sloop, a sailing canoe, a Gar Wood ex-rum runner, and a Maine-built gaff cutter. An accomplished salt, his nickname is "Dry Rot."

Barton, Humphrey & Mary   Humphrey made his 20th Atlantic crossing at age 75. He was one of Jack Laurent-Giles's original partners and a marine surveyor from 1936 until 1959. In 1954 he founded the Ocean Cruising Club. (One need only complete a 1,000-mile passage in a boat under 70 feet overall to belong.) Mary, his widow, is currently hard-working Admiral of the OCC. He won the Cruising Club of America Blue Water Medal.

Bates, Chandler   A "yachtsman sail and power" for better than 50 years, he lives in Greenwich, CT. His trawler had starting difficulties; a 25-cent part was to blame.

Bennet, Erni   A Girl Scout troop leader, Erni took young people to sea until, in 1974, she "took over" *Adventuress*, a 101-foot schooner built in 1913. With volunteer crews and without winches, she has been getting people of all ages onto Puget Sound ever since.

Bill, David   Director of the Tabor Academy waterfront, David maintains a fleet of more than 70 small boats. Aboard his J/24 *Island Time*, he teaches sailing in the summer. A veteran one-design and offshore racer, he does deliveries, writes instructional articles (*SAIL*), teaches seamanship, and heads Tabor's Boat Donation program.

Bingham, Bruce   Illustrator, author, boatbuilder, photographer, and naval architect, he drew (for more than 10 years) the "Sailor's Sketchbook" that appeared in *SAIL* and now creates the "Workbench" column for *Cruising World*. At work now on half a dozen projects, he "gets up ridiculously early and works obscenely late."

Biwenga, Bill   After early sailing near Chicago, he was the only American aboard *Flyer* (Whitbread Round the World Race winner, 1981–82). He's done three more Whitbreads, set (with Rich Wilson) a San Francisco– Boston speed record, and become expert in applied meteorology and offshore gear. He's vanished, we hope temporarily, into the sunset in search of the perfect woman.

Black, Bill & Mary   Aboard their Valiant 40 *Foreign Affair*, they circumnavigated (Seattle, across the Pacific to the Indian Ocean, the Mediterranean, Straits of Magellan, Hawaii, Kodiak, AK) in 1975–79 and received the CCA Blue Water Medal. In 1991, they crossed the North Pacific and returned via Japan, the USSR, and the Aleutian Islands.

Bliss, Martha Robinson   RR's younger sister, she grew up sailing small boats on the Shrewsbury River (Rumson, NJ). Confined now to a Pennsylvania lake, she and husband Dan make the most of getaway charter opportunities. Her five children have, she says, helped her refine cruise organization to "a high, fine art."

Bode, Richard   His mentor was Captain Harrison Watts, a legendary racing skipper and waterman on Long Island's Great South Bay. *Blue Sloop at Dawn*, his autobiographical novel, takes its title from "a boat I saw and admired long before I knew she'd be mine." *First You Have To Row a Little Boat* contains his reflections on "life as illuminated by sailing." His *SAIL* article, "To Climb The Wind," won the Excellence in Writing Award of the American Society of Journalists and Authors.

Bolger, Philip   There's no hiding his eccentricity or his talent. Designer of *Dovekie*, the folding schooner, an "aquariark" (to take fingerlings from the Amazon and incubate them into whoppers while crossing to sell them by the pound in the Orient), plus hundreds more real and unbuilt boats, Phil asks that his biography read, "Phil has been designing boats full-time under his own name since 1952. In 1994, he and Susanne Altenburger formed PHIL BOLGER & FRIENDS, Inc., to design boats fit for the 21st century and service Phil's extant designs." His most recent book is *Boats with an Open Mind* (International Marine, 1995).

Bolton, Jay   A graduate of Tabor Academy, Jay lives in Old Lyme, CT, and has been master of ships as diverse as a 1,000-foot supertanker and the replica of HMS *Bounty* built for the MGM remake of the well-known movie and recently donated by Ted Turner to the city of Fall River.

Bombard, Dr. Alain   Shortly after World War II, he crossed the Atlantic in an inflatable dinghy *L'Heretique* with only a (sealed) box of emergency rations, "sustained only by the sea's bounty: seawater, drifting weed, fish/juice, and plankton."

A source of inspiration and a magnet for controversy, Bombard's voyage is a landmark in sea survival, but *don't drink seawater*!

Bradford, Ernle   He ran away from Norfolk, England, to the Royal Navy at 18. After destroyer service in the Mediterranean during World War II, he returned in a yacht to explore. His books about Gibraltar, the Great Siege of Malta, and the underpinnings of the Odyssey (*Ulysses Found*) resulted. He also wrote books on Nelson, Barbarossa, and Henry the Navigator, and crossed the Atlantic three times under sail.

Brantley, Duncan   A lacrosse player in college, he found work at *SAIL* before signing on with *Sports Illustrated* as yachting writer. Now freelancing and living on an estate (as caretaker) in Bridgehampton, Long Island, he has sold one screenplay to Universal Studios and is working on several sea stories he hopes will be blockbusters.

Brogdon, Bill   Retired from a 30-year career in the Coast Guard, Captain Brogdon writes regularly for major boating magazines. He's also author of the highly-acclaimed *Boat Navigation for the Rest of Us*.

Brown, Jim   Called "Trimaran Jim," he learned from multihull Godfather Arthur Piver. In the early days in San Francisco, he championed "sea-steading" and designed Searunner tris to do it in. He developed Constant Camber backyard cold-molding and helped native fishermen on Lakes Victoria (Tanganyika) and Titicaca (Peru) resurrect fleets. He and his family spent five years cruising from the West Coast to the East Coast, mostly in Central America and Mexico. He lives now in a converted chicken house in North, VA, and has recently patented the Windrider "tri-yak "that "swims" to weather. Jo Anna, Jim's wife, edited *Wind Vane*, the bulletin of sea-steading. They recently returned from cruising Cuba.

Buckley, William F., Jr.   Awards, honorary degrees, Presidential appointments, publication credits—Bill's resume is crammed with them (plus writing the play *Stained Glass*, playing solo harpsichord with the Phoenix Symphony Orchestra, and

getting 13 percent of the mayoral vote in New York City in 1965). His public knows him as editor of the *National Review* and host of *Firing Line* on TV, but he's a sailor. Five of the 36 books that he's written are based on his offshore voyages, and he's crossed the Atlantic (but his four-page *cv* doesn't say how often).

Buehler, George   Born in Oregon in 1948, he's "been messing about with boats" ever since his Sainted Mother gave him a copy of *Scuppers the Sailor Dog*. George resides with his wife and two dogs on Whidbey Island, WA, where he is known for the sterling qualities of his friends, his kindness to stray dogs and abandoned boats, and his collection of bad habits. He's a fair shot with a pistol and a Croquet Ace. (And, unlike some other naval architects, he writes good books—like *Buehler's Backyard Boatbuilding*—and readable thumbnail biographies.)

Burke, Katy   An author (*The Complete Liveaboard Book: The Handbook for Non-Macho Sailors* and *Cruising Under Power*) and practicing naval architect, she makes her home aboard the restored schooner *At Last* and has perfected the art of keeping seaborne plants green and thriving.

Burkhardt, Karl   For years a bureau chief for the *Cleveland Plain Dealer*, Karl's new job is editor of the Bentonville (AR) *Daily Record*. A regional edition of the Little Rock paper has just moved in. "A good newspaper war is like an Olympic regatta. I love it." He sailed throughout his Ohio tenure. "There are some nice lakes near here. When and if . . . . "

Calahan, H.A.   "Sage of the Sound," he wrote just before and after World War II and instructed generations of sailors and seamen in the wisdom he'd acquired by "haunting the waterfront" all his life. Dedicated often to "the boys" at his lunch table at the New York Yacht Club, his work spoke to novice and expert with equal grace. Among his best are *Back to Treasure Island*, *Learning to Cruise*, *Learning to Race*, and *Ship's Husband*.

Calder, Nigel   At 13, he got his first motorcycle, and he has been a diesel mechanic for more than 25 years. He is also a boatbuilder, cabinetmaker, and machinist. He and his wife finished their 39-foot cruising ketch *Nada* in 1984 and have spent over a dozen years exploring the Caribbean. He wrote the *Cruising Guide to the Northwestern Caribbean* but is best known for his work on boat systems. *Marine Diesel Engines, Refrigeration for Pleasureboats*, and his mega-work, *Boatowner's Mechanical and Electrical Manual*, have won a grateful following.

Callahan, Steve   After 22 years boatbuilding, designing, teaching design, writing, and doing boat deliveries, he is still best known for his 76-day ordeal alone in a liferaft. His *Adrift* (a nation-wide best seller) remains a classic. "My own telling of my story is but an imperfect rendition of what I experienced," he writes, but he presents and probes it with exceptional skill. He has since logged 60,000 nondrifting miles. Second (aboard a monohull) in the 1986 TwoStar, he won two Multihull Bermuda Races, and made one single-handed plus three double-handed transatlantic crossings. He's written over 100 magazine articles, another book—*Capsized* (about *Rose Noelle's* ordeal)—and is a *Cruising World* associate editor.

Candage, Howard E.   Chosen "Young Agent of the Year" in 1987, he was a self-employed fisherman before entering the insurance business. His back-ground in marine surveying has helped him develop clients among towing firms, marine contractors, and boatyards. His agency has recorded $2,000,000 a year in premium value.

Casey, Don   As a university student in Texas he read about Robin Lee Graham and *Dove* in *National Geographic*, "discovered" sailing, and moved to Florida to spend all his spare time on the water. First a Bristol 27, then an Alberg, then "I took a very early retirement from being a banker, bought an Allied Seawind 31 (*Richard Corey*) and began full-time sailing." He began writing, too. *Sensible Cruising: The Thoreau Approach*, a "cult-classic" and ongoing success, was followed by *This Old Boat, Sailboat Hull and Deck Repair, Canvaswork and Sail Repair*, and *Sailboat Refinishing*. Also, he's an editor who can make, as he did with this book, sprung

and perilous prose into (hopefully) sound stuff.

Chew, Clifford, Jr.   Now in his 70s, he "spent more years than I can remember in wheelhouses and engine rooms of North Atlantic draggers." After a quarter-century running his own boats out of Cape May, NJ, he "retired" to become a preacher in the Church of the Nazarene. "Moonlighting" now finds him doing engine repair, and net work "for those that still 'go down to the sea in ships, that do business in great waters.' *Psalms* 107: 23, 24."

Chiles, Webb   Born in St. Louis, MO, he wrote once that "the only important facts in my life have been my desire to sail alone around the world by way of Cape Horn, and to write." Currently he can say, "I have circumnavigated three times, twice alone, twice around Cape Horn, and twice setting world records" (fastest circumnavigation solo in a monohull—202 days, San Diego–San Diego, and longest open-boat voyage ever—in 18-foot *Chidiock Tichborne*). He has written and published *Storm Passage, The Open Boat*, and *The Ocean Waits*. He lives with his wife Carol aboard their 37-foot *Hawke*, preparing for another sail around.

Colas, Alain   A crewman with Eric Tabarly, he won the 1972 OSTAR, then took their 70-foot trimaran *Pen Duick* (which Colas rechristened *Manureva*) on a one-stop circumnavigation of the world in 1973. In *Around the World Alone*, he artic-ulated the spirit of seafaring and the power of its challenge well enough to earn him a spot with the masters. He disappeared during the 1982 Route du Rhum Race.

Coles, Adlard   Yachting publisher and author, ocean racer and long-distance cruiser, he won the 1950 Transatlantic Race, class honors in the 1957 and 1963 Fastnets, and Yachtsman of the Year recog-nition in 1957. He is best known for *Heavy Weather Sailing*, a "Bible."

Colgate, Steve   He showed talent as a teacher when he taught RR how to tie a bowline in mid-At-lantic in 1963. Teaching professionally, he started with a single boat; today his Offshore Sailing School has facilities around the world and more than 60,000 graduates. Maybe his five transatlantics, two America's Cup campaigns, 12 Bermuda Races, seven Fastnets, and the Olympics are reflected in the curriculum. His works include *Steve Colgate on Sailing*, *Colgate's Basic Sailing*, *Manual of Racing Techniques*, and *Steve Colgate on Cruising*.

Conner, Dennis   Son of a commercial fisherman, he crewed in San Diego (for Carl Eichenlaub and others) until he could afford a four-year-old Star. He was World Champion his first season. Ted Turner chose him to call tactics aboard the slow *Mariner*, and the America's Cup career of all began: starting helmsman with Ted Hood (*Courageous*); skipper of *Freedom*, *Liberty*, and the pursuant *Stars and Stripes*. First ever to lose the Cup, he was also first to get it back. Master of boat preparation, he can mount a world-class campaign in just about anything. Tight-lipped, even defensive in competition, his books, particularly *Sail Like a Champion*, are candid, far-reaching, and generous of his expertise.

Cox, Robert   Longtime manager of Lauderdale Marina in Ft. Lauderdale, his adventures on the water have appeared in *Southern Boating*, *Offshore*, and many other magazines.

Coyle, Jay   He draws upon his varied background, sail and power, north and south, as technical editor of *Yachting* magazine.

Cudmore, Harold   Visit the oldest known yacht club (the Royal Cork in Crosshaven, Ireland, 1720) and you'll see his picture. From early days, the lad has been winning dinghy and offshore races enough to become the Fin McCumhail (mythic Hibernian warrior king) of the international sailing wars. Known on the match race circuit for inventive starts and aggressive application of the rules, his St. Patrick's Day parties at the Congressional Cup are legendary.

Curry, Manfred, M.D.   Recognized as "without doubt the greatest expert on the theoretical side of sailing of his day," Curry published his *Aerodynamics of Sail* in German, French, and Turkish as well as English in 1925. He was 18 when he wrote it. *Yacht Racing* appeared in 1948, dedicated to his father "who died on his yacht during a regatta in 1935." Truly open-minded, Dr. Curry married theory and experiments (with models, wind tunnels, and full-sized boats), and was recognized as "a master of racing tactics and top-notch skipper."

Dempsey, Paul   The author of 18 books, his *Small Engines* is a mini-classic.

Dey, Richard Morris   Boyhood on Barnegat Bay, student skipper aboard *Tabor Boy*, a commercial fisherman, owner of the 50-foot schooner *Bequia World*, and teacher now aboard *Spirit of Massachusetts*, Rick has lots of sea time. Not all of his poems are "sea poems," but most of what he's written over the past 25 years deals with people, places, and themes you encounter by casting off. His books include *Bequia Poems* and "*Loss of the Schooner 'Kestrel*'" *and Other Sea Poems*. His first novel is *The Abandonment of* Rachel Delano. When he's not at sea he explores New England estuaries with his two sons in the 13-foot skiff *White Cap*.

Dickison, Dan   After "thrashing about in El Toros and Sunfish" during his California youth, Dan gravitated to island sailing ("and island time") doing deliveries, charter skippering, and hanging out. "I can remember consciously eschewing racing as overly aggressive and antagonistic." But, before long, he was bitten. One Rolex regatta and he was hooked into five years on the circuit (mostly as bowman), a berth on the USVI Olympic team, and finally an editor's slot with *Sailing World*. One year there, he competed on 26 different kinds of boats. He's retired to "the Carolina lowcountry" and a dry, shoreside seat in real estate. "It's sometimes hard to get a ride on weekends around here, though," he writes." I may just be forced to become a boatowner again."

Doyle, Robbie   He won his second Sears (Junior National Championship) Cup, then went to Harvard (where he studied applied physics and became a sailing All-American), and then off to an apprenticeship with Ted Hood. Aboard *Courageous* in

1977, he earned "we owe it all to Robbie" from Ted Turner. He founded his own loft in 1982 and has seen Doyle Sailmaking grow to embrace 26 lofts in 11 countries. He was the host for the PBS instructional series "Under Sail" and now spends time watching his kids sail Optimists.

Dove, Tom   A writer/editor, Tom once was an instructor who ran the first "learn to sail in a weekend" program and the first flotilla cruises on Chesapeake Bay at Annapolis Sailing School. He was also teaching high school science. A technical editor now for *Chesapeake Bay Magazine*, he also works with Frommer's Guidebooks and *SAIL* and has had some 900 articles published since he left the blackboard.

Duncan, Roger F.   Editor of the *Cruising Guide to the New England Coast*, he also sails (aboard his Friendship sloop *Eastward*) between Newport and Eastport. He and his wife have run cruises since 1956 "for young people—and not-so-young," involving seamanship, and coastal cruising. From 1945 until 1981, he taught English and coached rowing at Belmont Hill in Belmont, MA, and was headmaster (1978–79). The first editor of *Practical Sailor*, his anthology (under that title) includes the best from his four-year tenure. Other books include: *Eastward*; *Sailing in the Fog*; and *Coastal Maine, A Maritime History*. He led the reenactment of Benedict Arnold's invasion of Quebec in 1975.

Edles, Peter   A marine surveyor in Annapolis, his expertise extends well beyond the head.

Ellam, Patrick   One of the world's most experienced sea adventurers, and veteran of countless ocean voyages, including yacht deliveries on nearly every ocean (his Patrick Ellam Yacht Deliveries was a pioneer firm in the field), he also helped found the Midget Ocean Racing Club. His double-handed Transat (with Colin Mudie) aboard the 19-foot *Sopranino* in 1951 helped demonstrate the capabilities of modern small boats and is a landmark in offshore voyaging.

Fenger, Frederic A.   Born in Chicago in 1882, "Frits" spent his life designing, sailing, or writing about "little vessels." His first sailing was as a boy in Denmark, but when he was 19 he sailed *Yakaboo*, an ocean canoe of his own design, from Grenada to the Virgin Islands. After Cornell and MIT, he became a naval architect. His 50-foot schooner *Diablesse* had a rig acknowledged to be the forerunner of the modern wishbone. A charter member of the Cruising Club of America, his *Cruise of the Diablesse* describing adventures with "an old boat and a new wife" deserves its status as a classic.

Fletcher, Abbot   Active since the 1930s, mostly in Maine, Ab has raced 225 Gulf of Maine Circuit races and won 77 of them. He was first in class in the 1991 Marion-Bermuda Race (third overall), with 10 class wins in 28 Monhegan Island Races. For relaxation he went as watch captain aboard Newbold Smith's *Reindeer* up Greenland's west coast. He is retired from Bath Iron Works and coaches sailing at Bowdoin College.

Fontaine, Ted   Though his training was in traditional plank-on-frame building at the Washington County Vocational Technical Institute in Eastport, ME, he has been employed for the past 18 years with the Ted Hood Design Group. As chief designer he has worked on more than 200 designs; not one has been traditionally planked. He picks *American Promise* (for Dodge Morgan's record-breaking round-the-world voyage) as his best-known design and lives in (and sails out of) South Dartmouth, MA, with his wife and four children.

Fox, Uffa   Renowned for his dinghy designs (Daysailer), his winners among International 14s, his championship helmsmanship, and his prolific writing (10 books), Fox also designed lifeboats deliverable by parachute (Atlanta mini-cruisers). In *Racing, Cruising, and Design* he wrote, "Throughout my life people have been very kind to me, and I hope that these pages . . . are equally friendly, for they reflect the generosity shown me by all the people with whom I have come in contact."

Franzel, David   Founding director of the Boston Sailing Center, he built on his experience to put together a teaching/racing/social mix that has helped BSC grow year-by-year through the 1970s, 1980s, and 1990s. A crack Soling and Sonar skipper, he also does boat deliveries. His book, *Sailing: The Basics*, benefits from his ability to be at once "in-depth" and accessible.

Fraser-Harris, A.B. Fraser, DSC   Fraser wrote a number of yacht evaluations for *Nautical Quarterly*. Prior to that, Commodore Fraser-Harris, DSC, RCN, retired voluntarily and took command of the Caribbean-based 100-foot charter ketch *Ring Anderson*, bought several yachts for charter work, and finally swallowed the anchor at Annapolis, MD, where he was a marine surveyor and was a sailing coach at the U.S. Naval Academy. He's a member of the Society of Naval Architects and Marine Engineers, American Boat and Yacht Council, and Associate Member of the Royal Society of Naval Architects. His Distinguished Service Cross came from the sinking of German cruiser *Konigsberg*, Oslo Fjord, 1940.

Full, Giffy   G.W. Full & Associates, Marblehead, MA, have been in the surveying business for some 50 years. Says Ferenc Maté in *Shipshape*," In the time I spent with him surveying a wooden boat, Giffy impressed me as one of those few who really do care, who loves nothing better than going through a boat he's hired to survey and coming up with nothing wrong. What too often happens, though, is that he finds so many things wrong that he barely has the heart to tell the anxious owners, who are waiting with their champagne bottle and bright eyes full of stars."

Gabert, Barbara, M.D.   One of a pair of "floating Docs" who wrote a column in *Wind Vane*, "The Bulletin of Seasteading" (circa 1977), we never learned where she studied (or even where she got the cat that she prescribed as the best defense against fish poisoning: "Feed the cat a scrap of fish in the morning. If the cat's still alive by dinner, cook the fish and eat it").

Gast, Robert de   A writer/photographer, he has had "more boats to name than grandchildren to kiss." *Qui Vive*, then *Timesweep*, then "a wonderful couple of years on a Gemini catamaran named *Telltale*." Most recently he sailed a Dovekie (*Fiddler*) and made her the center of his book (now in its second printing), *Five Fair Rivers*. He lives in San Miguel Allende, Mexico, subject of his *The Doors of San Miguel*.

Gerr, Dave   Since 1983, Dave has been designing boats—commercial and pleasure. Based in New York, he is working on a 42-foot, tunnel-drive motor cruiser; three new patrol boats for "a Northeast-area law enforcement agency"; a 76-foot voyaging cutter; a Class-1 BOC racer; and a 72-foot charter schooner. In more than 100 articles, he has been *Offshore* magazine's eye on the technical side, and he is a contributing editor for both *Yachting* and *Professional Boatbuilder*. He wrote *The Propeller Handbook* (now in its sixth printing) and *The Nature of Boats*, and he is at work on *Boat Strength*, a handbook on structures, "the first ever of its type."

Gladstone, Bernard   Long the editor of "Boat-Keeper" in *MotorBoating & Sailing*, his rapport with his readers is remarkable, and his hardcover book *BoatKeeper* a well-thumbed reference.

Goetz, Eric   There's no sign outside, but it might say "three America's Cup–class boats built here." Eric started Goetz Custom Boats in 1975; since then, *Stars & Stripes*, *Young America*, and *America³*, plus three-time World Maxi-boat champion *Matador*, speed merchant *Route 66*, offshore powerboat champ *Popeye*, fast cruisers like *Red Herring*, and Whitbread veterans like *The Card* have come from his Bristol, RI, shop."He's the best boatbuilder in America," says Cup winner Bill Koch. Eric sailed at Brown, is an innovator with carbon fiber and composite ingredients, and is the son of a German father and Japanese mother. His shop closes on Friday at five. "I don't believe in overtime."

Gougeon, Meade   Meade is President and CEO of Gougeon Brothers, Inc. With brother Jan in a small shop on the Saginaw River, they built iceboats bonded with epoxy. Now they market their own brand, West System, of epoxy and related products worldwide, though they still build the occasional one-off sailboat. He lives in Bay City, MI, with his wife Janet and five of their 10 children, has won the world championship in DN iceboats, and races either a 35-foot tri or a 32-foot cat, "depending."

Graham, Robin Lee   Robin cast off from California at 16 to sail *Dove* around the world. He returned five years later with a pregnant wife, a new Dove, and millions of followers thanks to *National Geographic*. He, Patty, and infant Quimby went inland, built a house, and led the simple life. "Somehow along the way we acquired a construction business and all the faxes and computers to go with it. Ah, simplicity! We haven't lost our adventurous spirit, though; it's at work in Quimby, now 26."

Graul, Donald O.   Clients in Australia, England, Ireland, Italy, and the U.S. get D.O. Graul & Associates' (New York) marketing and public relations counsel. *Los Angeles Times* reporter, *One Design & Yacht Racing* and *Yachting* editor that he once was, Don has crossed to the other side of the information highway, but with 23 Mackinac Races, 17 SORCs, two Sydney-Hobarts, and the Olympic Trials behind him, his stories are salty. Then he talks about being communications director in the "Anderson for President" Campaign.

Graumann, Warren   He learned to sail "with tiller in one hand and instruction book in the other" on a 16-foot Grumman Flyer in the Thousand Islands (NY). In his O'Day 22 (*Waltz, Mathilda!*), he has cruised Lakes George and Champlain, the Hudson, and Block Island. He moved to Maine, where he sells heavy trucks and sails Casco Bay.

Gray, Ron   An editor with *MotorBoating & Sailing* with an address of "Capitain de Porto, Zihutenejo, Mexico." No wonder he doesn't answer RR's letters.

Greene, Walter   The "G" in Nathanial "G." Herreshoff is for Greene, and Walter is a builder/sailor/innovator in the family tradition. He has raced monohulls with masters like Ted Hood and mavericks like Gerry Milgram and been called "the most valuable guy aboard" virtually everywhere. Greene Marine in Falmouth, ME, built OSTAR winner *Moxie* and Mike Birch's *Olympus Photo*, which won the Route du Rhum in 1978. Walter came in fifth (of 100) in the 1980 Transat; three

boats he built were in the top five. He's been rescued after turtling in mid-Atlantic in mid-October. "I seem somewhat fixated on the Atlantic. I stopped counting after 22 crossings."

Groene, Janet   With her husband Gordon she has been part of a full-time writer/photographer duo for more than 20 years. The Groenes specialize in travel, particularly water travel. She is a nationally recognized expert on camp and galley cookery and cuisine. They have won the National Marine Manufacturers' Association Award for marine journalism and Janet received the 1995 Achievement in RV Travel Journalism Award. They have 25 books in print, including *The Galley Book* and *Experts' Guide to Hints, Tips, and Everyday Wisdom* and are working on a guide to the Caribbean. Gordon is a pilot.

Gross, Tom   A graduate of the Shrewsbury Sailing and Yacht Club Woodpussy fleet and a lacrosse player, Tom went into the Coast Guard where his way with engines helped him become a helicopter mechanic. He flew SAR missions for three years. After college and med school, he's back in the Guard as a base doctor. In addition to sailing with his family, he studies the art and application of cloaking devices.

Hammick, Anne   Longtime skipper of *Wrestler of Leigh* out of Falmouth in Cornwall, England, she is editor of the Ocean Cruising Club journal *Flying Fish*. Her *Ocean Cruising on a Budget* has been a consistent seller on both sides of the Atlantic. Her second book, *Atlantic Crossing Guide*, is a pilot of impressive authority.

Hammond, Steve   Steve is an ex-naval officer, smallboat builder, and sailor. He is presently designing light steel barges and houseboats and building a boatshop in Woolwich, ME. He is a kayaker and claims "to have mastered the first half of the Eskimo roll."

Hancock, Brian   The first stop on the Whitbread Round-the-World Race is Capetown, South Africa. In 1978, 16-year-old Brian jumped a ride and has been sailing hard ever since racing competitively in 23 countries and sailing top boats in Admiral's Cup,

Sardinia Cup, Bermuda Race (five) and Fastnet Race (four) competition plus, two transatlantics, the 13,000-mile Parmelia Cup Race, and three more 33,000-mile Whitbreads—the third with the Russians on *Fazisi*. He says bringing her to America ended the Cold War. He lectures on adventure sailing (250 appearances worldwide) and works for Doyle Sailmakers.

Hannay, Ian   Vice-chairman of the Amateur Yacht Research Society in England, and coordinator for "Design and Racing Rules" for the AYRS bulletin, he is also its editor.

Harken, Peter   He and brother Olaf rented a 60-foot garage in Pewaukee, WI, in 1967 to make parts and gear they needed to race scows and iceboats. Their landlord was a tool and die maker, and he put them in business. With "a coup d'etat the details of which are not taught in Harvard Buisiness School," they secured a contract to build International 470s. Besides dinghies and fittings, the brothers have also dabbled in Everest expeditions, Olympic luge development, the World Landsailing Champion-ship (won by Peter's *Millenium Factor*), NASA space station assembly, boat shoes, pedal boats and more. "Still," says Peter, "people in Pewaukee say my dog Mac is the smartest one in the shop."

Harnden, Tina Sherman   She came to *SAIL* from the University of New Hampshire, edited America's Cup coverage and sailing news, wrote features on cruising, boatwear, and trailer boats, and was reigning GHOST champion of the office. She, her husband, and two children now live in Maine.

Hays, Daniel   Co-author of *My Old Man and the Sea* with father David, he has published in *Northeast*, *Esquire*, *SAIL*, and *Sailing* magazines and is a teacher in a school for troubled teens in Idaho. Aboard *Regina Maris*, he studied whales and taught celestial navigation. He has a masters' degree in environmental science, and holds a 25-ton license and a second-degree black belt in Tae Kwan Do. Before their Cape Horn adventure, Dan and his father crossed the Gulf Stream in a 9-foot dinghy and sailed from Nassau to New London in a catboat.

Herreshoff, L. Francis   Graduate of the University of Rhode Island and son of "Capt. Nat," the family progression was characterized by historian Maynard Bray: "His father's designs shone with engineering perfection, his with artistic brilliance." He lived from 1890 to 1972, commanded patrol boats and developed underwater detection equipment for the Navy during World War I, and lived in "The Castle" in Marblehead, MA. The H-28, Alerion, Mobjack, and *Ticonderoga* (among many others) all came from his board. He also wrote five books including a biography of his father, the whimsical instructional book *Commonsense of Yacht Design, Sensible Cruising Designs*, and *The Compleat Cruiser*.

Heyerdahl, Thor   Famous for drifting westward from Peru across the Pacific in the balsa-log raft *Kon Tiki*, seen next crossing the Atlantic in reedboat *Ra* (as he surmised the Egyptians had done), then sailing a ship from 1,000 years before Christ east from the Tigris to "show how the seeds of civilization and culture were spread by sailors," he has sailed thousands of miles through prehistory. Underlying all of his expeditions, his work on the origins of the cultures of Oceania (*Aku-Aku, Fatu-Hiva*, and *The Art of Easter Island*), and his *Early Man and the Ocean* is his conviction that ancient sailors were more capable and far-ranging than modern historians allow. Born in Norway, he lives now in Italy.

Hill, Annie   *Badger* was Lord Nelson's first command; *Badger* is what Annie and her husband named their junk-rigged (Jay Benford–designed) 36-footer. Twelve years after casting off, Annie wrote *Voyaging on a Small Income*, distilling from the miles both practical lessons and philosophical priorities: "The Chinese rig is the handiest in the world.. We may not point as high or sail as fast as some, but that last five percent of efficiency comes very expensively. Sailing more miles for less money with fewer worries—to us it makes sense."

Hinckley, Hank, Jr.   President of Great Harbor Yachts, Hank grew up in a boatbuilding family "working around the yard" in Southwest Harbor, ME. His experience includes custom building, production management, designing, and running large service yards. He has been Service Manager, Production Manager, and President of HRH & Co., Manager of Sailboat Development for Glastron, and President of Ocean Cruising Yachts (which he co-founded). His book on fiberglass construction and repair is soon to be published.

Hiscock, Eric and Susan The 1950 edition of *Cruising Under SAIL* is dedicated to "Roger A. Pinckney, who taught me and many others how to cruise without fuss." Eric and Susan completed their three-and-a-fraction circumnavigations very much without fuss. Sailors who met on the Isle of Wight, they almost completely explored the globe and always self-sufficiently. Their writings, which also included *Voyaging*, *Under Sail*, the *Wanderer* adventures (volumes I through V) and countless magazine pieces, made them household names. MB knew them as remarkably generous with help and advice. Their most frightening moment, they wrote, was a ride through the streets of London aboard their boat cradled atop a 10-ton trailer.

Hodsdon, William Growing up in Mamaroneck, NY, Bill "had a boat in one basin—East or West—from the age of 14." A launch driver in later youth, he next acquired a Blue Jay. She is now 31. "My grandchildren are 7 and 9, and I'm shooting to get the boat in shape so they won't miss the good times I've had." He lives now in Maine and cruises Muscongus Bay while racing aboard a J/24 out of Portland Yacht Club.

Hoyt, Garry Sunfish World Champion, Olympic Finn racer, and founder of Freedom Yachts, Garry is an author and designer. His latest boat is *Escape*, for Sunfish/Laser. His latest book is the pot-stirring *Ready About*. His "The Need for Speed" column was voted "most read" by *Sailing World*'s audience. He now has a column in *SAIL* magazine. On top of everything, he devotes serious time to "removing the physical barriers that discourage people from sailing." His high-boomed, wind-instrumented, roller-furled, electric-trolling-motor-equipped trainer is one example. He is President of R & D, Inc., Newport.

Hoyt, Norris D., Ph.D. As a non-swimmer "bun-dled like a balloon" on the weather rail, Norrie began sailing in the fourth grade. "Injected" into swimming by a nervous mother, he captained Yale's swim team and set records. Married 55 years to Kitty, they've shared "five Atlantic crossings and the better part of Europe and North America" (with cruising articles in *National Geographic*, *McCall's*, *Nautical Quarterly*, and more). He's done 23 transatlantics, 16 Bermuda Races, and 12 Fastnets. He has not only written about the America's Cup (*Sports Illustrated*, *SAIL*, et al) but broadcast races on radio and TV and chaired a Cup syndicate. "I now cruise rivers, canals, and estuaries. Alongshore we rebuild the natural world as we will it to be. My biography ends with a cruise of the Tennessee-Tombigbee waterway and a little history of the freshwater mussel industry's progress from goldmine to disaster to cottage industry; as we remake the world into a human artifact, it's not too late to do it right."

Innes, Hammond Scottish author of 20 novels, the last 15 worldwide best-sellers, he was a financial journalist in London until his royalties allowed him to write fiction fulltime. He takes a break occasionally ocean racing in *Mary Deare*, the 42-foot steel sloop he launched in 1959. He and his wife, the former Dorothy Lang, actress and kinswoman to Sir Walter Scott, have explored Europe from Scandanavia to Turkey. Having read *The Wreck of the Mary Deare*, his page-turner set in *les Minquieres*, a jagged colony of surface-piercing rocks off the Brittany coast, RR did a 20-mile detour to miss "The Minkies."

Irving, John He was co-author with E.G. Martin of the encyclopedic *Cruising and Ocean Racing*, and coauthor with Douglas Service of *The Yachtsman's Week-end Book*. Sailors in the early 1900s were well-advised not to leave port without consulting Irving.

Isler, Peter An All-American and Intercollegiate Sailor of the Year, he's achieved top ranking on the international match racing circuit and coached the Olympic Sailing Team. Two-time America's Cup winner as navigator aboard *Stars & Stripes* (both 12-meter and catamaran), he also served as analyst on ESPN's Cup broadcasts (1992 and 1995). Says Dennis Conner, "The publicity surrounding the

Cup has introduced millions of Americans to sailing." Peter's *Let's Go Sailing* speaks directly and creatively to them. His wife JJ is an Olympic medalist and champion sailor. They live in La Jolla, CA, with their daughter, Marly.

Jerome, Jerome K.   Author of the oft-referenced *Three Men in a Boat*, he was better-known as a playwright ("one of the brightest lights of Victorian and Edwardian theater") with hits like *Fanny and the Servant Problem. Second Thoughts of an Idle Fellow* was one of his most popular books. Co-founder of the popular magazine *The Idler*, he died in 1927.

Jobson, Gary   After learning to sail in an Atlantic City catboat ("it had a brace on the bow to hold it together") and race on New Jersey's Barnegat Bay, Gary went to the New York Merchant Marine Academy at Ft. Schuyler. He was two-time Intercollegiate Sailor of the Year. "I could sail, but when my coach in college (Graham Hall, himself an Olympian) got me to sail for fun, I was unbeatable." Tabbed by Ted Turner as tactician aboard *Courageous*, he called the shifts and managed the skipper to victory. He survived the 1979 Fastnet storm, a 1981 drift to Bermuda with Walter Cronkite, Herbert von Karian's learning curve, and a last in the Congressional Cup to become perhaps the premier spokesperson for today's sailors. His books sell well, he is the "voice of America's Cup" on televison, and his Annapolis-based Jobson Sailing thrives. He and Janice have three children.

Johnson, Bob   A rarity among designers, he has a master's degree in naval architecture from MIT. He started Island Packet Yachts in 1979 and designed its full line, including the *Packetcat*. He also drew the Endeavour 40, the Compac 19, and the Lightfoot 21 (a cat ketch sharpie). He is a National Marine Manufacturers Association Director and serves on its international technical committee . His wife Geri is a charter broker.

Johnson, Irving and Exy   Born on the Fourth of July, 1905, Irving was the eighth generation of his family at their Hadley, MA, farm, but ached for the sea, read "all the books" and built his body by going aloft on telephone poles. Eventually, he ran away to join the monster four-master *Peking*. Captain Jurs whipped ship and men toward 50 degrees South; when Cape Horn combers broke aboard, Irving climbed the mainmast and took movies. He and his bride, Exy, began, in 1933, four decades on Yankees taking students from Mystic around the world to return on time. Eventually *National Geographic* came along, bringing generations of readers. A plus-perfect seaman, colorful leader, and powerful teacher, Irving made great copy and wrote a dozen books. In their 70s, the two "retired," built a ketch for two, visited old ports, explored canals, and even descended the Nile. Irving died in 1990.

Johnstone, Jeff   A sailor from age 5, Jeff crewed for his father (designer Rodney) in Falcons and 470s, raced for Connecticut College, then founded J-World Sailing School, which now has campuses in Key West, San Diego, Newport, and Annapolis, and has bareboat as well as racing courses. In 1988, he became President of J-Boats, Inc. He lives in Newport with his wife and two daughters and campaigns actively on the world J-24 circuit.

Kemp, Peter   Educated at the Royal Naval College, Dartmouth, he joined the *London Times* after submarine and naval intelligence service in World War II. He then became head of the Naval Historical Branch/British Ministry of Defense. Published on naval, military, and maritime subjects, he also wrote childrens' novels. He died in 1992. He was editor of the *Oxford Companion to Ships and the Sea*.

Kielhorn, William V.   Bill went to sea off Nova Scotia as cabin boy and worked aboard a square-rigger. During World War II, he was aboard the cutter *Spencer* and in the little-known Coast Guard destroyer fleet. Master of a dozen seagoing ships, he earned a master's degree in oceanography and has taught at the U.S. Coast Guard Academy, the U.S. Naval Academy, and UCLA. He pilots single and multi-engine land and sea planes and has written scientific books. His *Basic Motorboat Seamanship* teaches through simplicity and common sense. He lives now in Naples, FL.

Kiley, Deborah Scaling   Born on a ranch in West Texas, she attended Colorado Springs School, where the curriculum was built on Outward Bound principles. She dropped out of the University of Texas to go sailing. Royalties from *Albatross*, her book about the sinking of the 44-foot *Trashman*, now go to Outward Bound. She lives with her husband, John, a naval architect and circumnavigator, and two children on Cape Cod.

King, Bill, DSO, DSC, RN   His solo circumnavigation (late 1960s) and 30,000 miles of ocean racing (including winning the Fastnet) were eventful, but one wonders if they didn't seem sedate in comparison to his service during World War II, when he served continuously, through every year of the war, on patrol as a submarine commander.

Kirby, Bruce   Born in Ottawa, he sailed in three Olympics for Canada. An editor at the *Montreal Star*, he became editor of *One-Design Yachtsman* (now *Sailing World*) in 1965. A "hobbyist" in boat design, his International 14s and the acceptance of his Laser (drawn on a napkin in 1969 and now the most-popular class in the world) encouraged him to design full-time. The San Juan 24 followed, then centerboard racer/cruisers, sharpies, IOR successes, and pleasure-sailers (Ideal 18, Fox, and Sonar). In 1983, he designed *Canada I*. His second 12-meter, *Canada II*, sailed off Fremantle in 1987. He helped draft the new International America's Cup Class Rule, and is designing a boat for a new Canadian syndicate for the upcoming Cup contest. He and his wife, Margo, live in Rowayton, CT

Kirkman, Karl   A naval architect "who operates," in the words of John Rousmaniere, "at the interface between hydrodynamic theory and sailing practice," he has conducted research that led, for the first time, to the ability to rank boats in order of capsize resistance and to predict the length of time that a given boat will take to right herself after capsize at sea.

Klaus, Horst   Since 1982, Horst has been a consultant and overseer of "turnkey power projects" in Niagara Falls, NY, specializing in "uninterruptable power" from marine and portable generators. For the past 15 years, he has also been winterizing engines. He has written for *Lakeland Boating, Power Boating Canada*, and others.

Koechl, Victor   At the Tabor Academy summer program in Marion, MA, he learned to sail. Retired now from architecture, he creates maps and graphics by computer. *Oh My!*, his Pearson Ensign, is moored in Norwalk, CT. He sails the Sound, wondering if others lose their halyards.

Kyselka, Will   A geologist, he wrote *Maui, How it Came to Be* while teaching at the University of Hawaii. He accompanied the storied *Hokule'a* from Hawaii to Tahiti in 1980 and returned aboard the canoe. In addition to *An Ocean in Mind*, his books include *Stars in Mind* (with Lee Kyselka) and *North Star to Southern Cross*.

Launer, Don   His present boat is a fiberglass Ted Hermann–designed lazy-jack schooner, which he built himself and keeps at his home in Forked River, NJ. He holds a USCG Captain's license and writes for *Cruising World, Offshore, SAIL*, and the *Waterway Guide*.

Letcher, John S., Jr.   A Cal Tech graduate, John got his sea legs between California and Hawaii and Alaska —first by himself in the 20-foot *Island Girl*; later, with his wife, Patty, aboard 26-foot twin-keeler *Aleutka*; then with Patty and their three daughters aboard the Cherokee 32 *Antares*. His book on self-steering (1974) helped thousands overcome "the tyranny of the tiller." Since 1973, his company, Aero-Hydro, Inc., of Southwest Harbor, ME, has pioneered computer applications in boat design. He now serves more than 1,000 naval architects worldwide, and AeroHydro has helped design three America's Cup winners.

Lewis, Cameron C.   Cam has devoted his life to sailboat racing. At Vinalhaven, ME, he won his first race at age 6. He has won four world championships (two Finn Gold Cups and two 505 Worlds), been on the crews of the catamaran *Stars & Stripes* and *America³*, and teamed with Bruno Peyron to pilot *Commodore Explorer* around the world in less than 80 days. Rolex Yachtsman of the Year in 1993, he set a new East-West Transat record (9 days, 8 hours, and 58 minutes) aboard *Primagaz* with Laurent Borgnon. His Lewis Sailing in Lincolnville, ME, sells Dragonfly sailboats and provides professional sailing services. His first book, *Around the World in 79 Days*, has just been published.

Lewis, Dr. David   Born in New Zealand and educated in the UK, he practiced medicine in Great Britain until (in his early 40s) he began seafaring and became legend. Third in the first (1960) OSTAR, his trimaran *Rehu Moana* was the fastest multihull in 1964. He took her around the world with his wife and two small daughters and then explored the Pacific, making a 2,500-mile passage without charts or instruments to a landfall just 26 miles in error. He also voyaged solo to Antarctica (and eventually circumnavigated the continent, alone and without heat). Then he spent years ranging the atolls, learning from indiginous navigators (*We, the Navigators*). Looking back, he says, "I treasure most the dolphin tatoo on my thigh. It is a sign from the *palu* ('men of the sea'). I am one of them."

Lewis, Jonathon Samuel   A graduate of Brookline (MA) High School (where RR was his English teacher), Jonathon has led a varied life. Underwater photography, teaching, and thoroughbred racetrack management number among his careers, and Massachussetts, California, Florida, Costa Rica, Italy, and the Virgin Islands his homes. He and his wife, Betsy, headed down-island from Boston in their lightweight *Tranquility Base* and returned after four years—to Brookline—where he wrote *Claire & Friends*, a self-illustrated story for children, and started Creative License Press.

Lie, Arne Brun   Imprisoned in six Nazi concentration camps before he was 20, Arne was one of the few to survive. He and RR collaborated on *Night and Fog*, a book of his wartime (and maritime) experiences, published in 1989. He helped design *Tresbelle*, his 39-foot cutter, and sailed her twice transatlantic. A member of the Royal Norwegian Cruising Club, he sails out of Ipswich with his wife, Ellen, and two children.

Linden, Louis F.   As executive director of the *Constellation* Foundation, Louis oversaw restoration of that 1,400-ton Civil War warship. He has been a lawyer, financial consultant, charter/delivery captain, and worker on the restored barque *Elissa* and has "sailed aboard most historically significant tall ships." A contributor to *Proceedings* of the Smithsonian Institution, *SAIL*, and *USA Today*, he also edited *The Champion* for criminal defense lawyers.

Lindsay, Mark   A sailor from Gloucester, he is one of America's premier sailboat builders. His dinghy experience includes years in Interclubs (National Champion) and 505s (former National Champion). After MIT, he apprenticed with Joe Duplin (Stars) and Dick Carter (yacht design). His 20-something business has world and Olympic champions in the Flying Dutchman, Fireball, and 505s to its credit. He is known for his work with underwater foils and builds carbon fiber rudders for America's Cup contenders. Working now on a series of 39-foot, high-tech epoxy Bruce Farr designs (IMS racers), he says,"I think I've brought a one-design focus to offshore boats." He sails a winged, carbon 30-footer he designed and built for a client "who just likes to go fast."

Linskey, Thomas   Olympic medalist (in 470s with Dave Ullman) and circumnavigator (aboard boats, self-built and otherwise, named *Freelance*), he has consistently chronicled the realities of both "lives" in the pages of *SAIL*, where he is an associate editor.

Lord, Walter   One of the world's best-read authors of popular history, he was born in Baltimore in 1916. His interest in the *Titanic* (which led to *A Night to Remember*, 1955) began when he crossed the Atlantic aboard SS *Olympic* at 10. A graduate of Princeton, he was a financial journalist and copywriter before his *Titanic* success led him into histories. *Day of Infamy* (Pearl Harbor), *A Time to Stand* (the Alamo), and *The Dawn's Early Light*, (the Battle of Baltimore in 1812) were among his biggest. He averages two years of research for every year of writing and works nine to five in coat and tie "to discipline myself."

Loutrel, Liz   She and husband Steve have been cruising Newfoundland and Labrador "time out of mind." "We've gone in kayaks, a traditional 40-

foot yawl, and an experimental [Steve's design] motorsailer." The latter, veteran of a decade's expeditions, has plug-in wheels that let the Loutrels run her ashore to take multiday hikes to the interior. She is also self-righting, self-bailing, and has positive flotation.

Loya, Art   A live-aboard for three years, he cruised the Gulf of Mexico, the Florida Keys, and the Bahamas aboard his Morgan 38 *Rumgod*. He is a computer consultant and amateur astronomer.

Luray, Martin   Mentor, inspiration, and friend, we dedicate this book to him.

McCallum, Frank   Deputy Editor of the British *Sailing Life*, Frank lives now in Glasgow, Scotland.

McConnell, Malcolm & Carol   They met (he in the Foreign Service, she with the Voice of America) in North Africa, ran a charter boat together out of Rhodes, and recorded their transatlantic baptism aboard the 30-foot *Matata* in *First Crossing*. He has written three novels, she has contributed to *Vogue*, *SAIL*, and *Yachting*. They live and write now in Queenstown, MD, and sail *Matata* each summer on the Turkish Coast.

McCormick, Herb   Executive Editor of *Cruising World*, he chose a career in journalism when he discovered he was too short to be a tight end in the pros. Co-author (with George Day) of *Out There*, still one of the premier books on the BOC, he was media manager for the 1994–95 BOC Challenge. He's sailed transatlantic (aboard the catamaran *British Airways*) and Australia to Antartica and return (aboard *Spirit of Sydney*). He lives aboard (six months a year) his C&C 33 named *Marra* (the Aboriginal word for "wind") by his Aussie fiancée.

McCullough, Virginia   Living aboard *Sojourner*, their 40-foot wooden ketch, with her husband and two children through an Annapolis winter, she has come ashore to write (more than 250 magazine articles plus two co-authored books) and focus on health care and interpersonal issues.

McCurdy, Sheila   Daughter of Faith and Jim McCurdy, she cannot remember a time when there wasn't sailing. She has amassed 60,000 offshore miles, has a 50-Ton USCG license, and was watch captain aboard the family boat (*Selkie*—second overall in the 1994 Newport–Bermuda Race). She serves on the U.S. Sailing Association Fales Committee on Seamanship, wrote a sailing manual for the Association, has authored numerous boat reviews, and is married to Dave Brown, President of SUNY at Ft. Schuyler.

MacGregor, Brodie   Owner/manager of the Concordia Yacht Yard in South Dartmouth, MA, this energetic Scotsman uses savvy and skill to keep the gates of "Heaven" open.

McHutchison, Jim   He once, albeit briefly, owned three 40-footers—at once. He has cruised to Labrador, raced to Bermuda (first in class in the 1981 Marion Race), explored the Caribbean, and left few East Coast anchorages unvisited. He lives now near St. Michael's, MD.

McHutchison, Suzanne   She split time between Marshfield and Wellfleet (MA) growing up. With husband Jim, she cruised and raced "between St. Pierre and Bermuda," raised two daughters, and helped run a small advertising agency. She is now a yacht broker.

MacLean, David   An author with 3 million books in print, David was a chief in the Navy from World War II to Vietnam. Now a training specialist for a defense firm, he also writes instructional material (*Everything You Always Wanted to Know About Boating*) for the Coast Guard. His *Small Craft Electronic Equipment Care & Repair* is remarkably clear and expert.

McSweeney, Brian   An orthodontist in Marion, MA, he has one of the most enviable racing records on Buzzards Bay (in Shields, a Baltic 55, and the Baltic 38 *Fianna*. The secret? "It's a bitch getting a crew together, so I try my best to make it fun so they'll come back."

Maggio, Joe   He holds a Class A Masters' license, but Joe didn't go to sea until he returned from Vietnam. A war correspondent and author of the war novel *Company Man*, he was taken "not so much by the romance but by the reality" of tall ships. He became master of the schooner *William H. Albury* in 1974 and has been operating her on sail training, adventure, and film-making cruises since. In 1988, he had the 85-foot topsail schooner *Heritage of Miami* built. She is Miami's official tall ship. In 1993, he co-wrote *Randolph Wardell Johnston*, a biographical tribute to the Bahamian artist.

Manry, Robert   Known best for his Atlantic crossing to England in 13-foot *Tinkerbelle*, he was raised in India and took his first sail on the Juma River at Allahmabad. He went with his minister/father to Canton, escaping the day before the Japanese invasion of China. An infantryman in World War II, he became a court reporter and then a copy editor. Married with two children, he toured the eastern U.S. in a 26-footer before he died in 1972.

Marchaj, C.A.   His *Sailing Theory and Practice* appeared in 1962 and became one of the most influential books in sailboat racing. A Polish small-boat skipper and research assistant in aeronautics at Southampton University in England, Tony applied theorems from "pure science" to the racecourse through experiments and informed analysis. Though abstruse and formula-laden in parts, his book produced insights, perceptions, and techniques that brought new levels of performance. His *Aerodynamics of Sailing*, published 20 years later, uncovered both new certainties and time-honored mysteries. In the 1980s, *Seaworthiness: The Forgotten Factor* led a reexamination of the International Offshore Rule in the wake of the 1979 Fastnet disaster. *Sail Performance: Theory and Practice*, a massive revision of the 1962 book, was published in 1996.

Marples, John   A mechanical engineer and design partner with Jim Brown, he built his own airplane and flew it coast-to-coast. He also built a Searunner 37 trimaran and won the 1972 multihull Transpac. He manufactures and sells marine hardware in St. Augustine, FL.

Marshall, Roger   Born in England and trained at Southampton University, Roger has been practicing naval architecture in the U.S. since joining Sparkman & Stephens in 1973. He has worked on America's Cup design, most notably on modifications to

Courageous. He has written *Designed to Win*, *Race to Win*, *Designed to Cruise*, and *Sail Better*, and publishes *Marshall's Marine Review*, a monthly digest of technical, consumer, and design information. He also teaches naval architecture at Roger Williams College (Bristol, RI) and lives in Jamestown with his wife, Mary.

Martin, Gretchen   Her extensive cruising has been primarily in Chesapeake Bay.

Martin, Tink   Her "Adventures in Boating Mishaps" is *Offshore* magazine's most-read column. She has been on the water most of her life, sailing and canoeing as a child, rowing on the Wellesley College crew, and data-gathering for *Boating Almanac* ("I visited every marine facility from Calais, Maine, to Rye, New York") and *A Cruising Guide to Narragansett Bay and the South Coast of Massachusetts* (with Patrick and Lynda Morris Childress). A consultant in leadership development and adult learning systems, offshore cruising and driving a ski boat are her passions. She lives in Winthrop, MA.

Maté, Ferenc   Author of six books on boats, among them *Shipshape* and *The Finely Fitted Yacht* (which contains over 200 projects for upgrading and fitting out), he has also written two novels (*Finisterre* and *Behind the Waterfall*). Born in 1945 and educated at the University of British Columbia, he has designed and built floating houses, written for television, and completed a Westsail 32 from a bare hull (hence *From a Bare Hull*). With his wife, Candace, he directs the Vancouver-based Albatross Press. His boat's name is *Warm Rain*.

Melges, Buddy (Harry, Jr.)   Zenda, on Delavan Lake in Wisconsin, was once famed as "winter home of the Ringling Brothers Circus." Buddy was born there and has made the locals forget clowns and elephants. Too poor to buy a bicycle, the story goes, he traveled by dinghy, took passengers for 10 cents a ride, and bought a sailboat. Olympic medalist (bronze in FDs in 1964, gold in Solings in 1972), three-time Mallory Cup (Men's National) Champion, three-time 5.5 world champ, two-time Star world champ, and helmsman aboard *America³*, the "Wizard of Zenda" is on everyone's short list of the world's best racers. Sailing iceboats helped, especially with jibing angles. He calls tacking and jibing "the blocking and tackling" of sailing, and has always built on the basics of boathandling and practice as ways to "get ahead of your boat. You have to be out there ahead of the bowplate if you're going to be successful meeting Mother Nature." He has received the Herreshoff Trophy as "the person who has done the most for yachting in North America."

Mellor, John   His 40 years under sail include racing dinghies and sailing Thames barges. A Royal Naval Seaman officer for five years, he spent the next 30 as professional delivery skipper, trawler master, sailing school manager, and navigation instructor. Of his 12 books, most recent are *Young Crew, Smallcraft Emergency Procedures*, and *Handling Troubles Afloat*. He lives on the Isle of Skye and sails a Cornish fishing lugger.

Merriam, Robert W.   Founder of Merriam Instruments, Inc., in East Greenwich, RI, Bob has long monitored marine electronics and writes "Sea Circuits" in *Fishing Gazette*. "Don't wire a boat like a car," is one of his repeated cautions. A practical seaman, he sings the virtues of simplicity, "but you don't have to give up sophisticated solutions to problems provided that those solutions have been reduced to simple terms."

Minnoch, James   A U.S. Coast Guard–licensed captain and seaplane pilot, he works in municipal planning for the state of New Hampshire. He keeps his Bristol 33 *Springtide* at Petit Manan Point in Maine, where the tidal range is considerable, but goes beyond personal experience in *Aground*, to draw lessons, advice, and techniques from 42 USCG-recorded groundings.

Mino, Eric   One of the ablest student executive officers ever aboard *Tabor Boy*, he strengthened ties between the ship and student body and instilled superior crew morale. A stellar naval architecture student, he is a graduate of the Massachussets Maritime Academy.

Miranda, Rosalind   Navigatrix on scores of European ocean races and veteran of a four-year Pacific cruise "where we had no electricity, never mind electronics," she invented her own brand of celestial navigation. *Miranav* (the title of both her system and the book outlining it) requires no theory, just addition, subtraction, and the capacity to follow clear, concise instructions. "My method is not for the dry, stable classroom; it's for the realities of motion, cold, hunger, and wet. The plastic edition is waterproof— excellent in a lifeboat." Rosalind, recently married, is a member of the Royal Institute of Navigation and a frequent contributor to *Multihulls* magazine. She offers reasonably priced one-week navigation courses on a bed-and-breakfast basis from her 400-year-old home in sunny Spain.

Moeller, Jan and Bill   They had never sailed before they came from the Midwest to New York to make their fortunes writing and doing photography. Eventually, they owned four boats, the last a 32-foot Dutch cutter. More than 10 years of living aboard culminated in a seminal 1977 book, *Living Aboard: The Cruising Sailboat as a Home*. The Moellers ranged the East Coast, following the seasons into the 1980s and compiling *The Intracoastal Waterway, Norfolk to Miami: A Cockpit Cruising Handbook*, now in its fourth authoritative edition. In recent years, Jan and Bill have ranged the continent in a liveaboard RV, writing and photographing books of the American West. They have also written several RVing guides, including *RVing Basics* and *RV Electrical Systems*.

Moitessier, Bernard   Few moments in ocean sailing are more famous or instructive. Bernard Moitessier rounded Cape Horn in 1969, abandoned the Golden Globe (solo, nonstop, around-the-world) Race, which he was leading, and bore away on a second circumnavigation. "His kinship with the sea was as nearly complete as is possible for a land mammal," some said. Born in Saigon in 1925, he set off alone in 1953. Eighty-five days out of Singapore, he wrecked his Siamese junk *Marie Therese* on Diego Garcia. He was prospering as a fisherman until a shark tore off half his foot, but eventually he earned enough to build *Marie Therese II*. She was wrecked in the Caribbean, but his best-seller *Vagabond of the South Seas* made him a folk hero in France. A naval architect built his experience into a new design, a steel fabricator begged to build it, and *Joshua* was launched in 1963. Married now, he and Francoise sailed the 39-foot ketch to Tahiti and back, before he was "shamed" by his celebrity into entering the long race. After withdrawing, he radioed a passing freighter, "I am going away to save my soul." He finally lit in Tahiti after 37,455 uninterrupted miles. He eventually returned to France and finished *Tamata*, his autobiography, before he died in 1994.

Moore, Jim *By Way of the Wind*, Jim's book on building a 36-footer and taking her, and his wife, Molly, around the world, is witty and wise. For their second voyage (1990–91), from Hawaii east via the Panama Canal, see *Swan: The Second Voyage*. They live in Wilmington, NC.

Morawa, Phillip Information and imaging manager (Joseph Meritt & Co., Hartford, CT), he readies documents for the courtroom on CD-ROM and "litigation imaging" software. He has lived aboard his Aquarius 23, studied at Westlawn School of Yacht Design, built boats "professionally and for fun," and moors in Greenport, NY.

Morgan, Dodge A record-setting solo sailor, you'd expect him to be "one of a kind," and you'd be right. His first boat was a tarred-over shipping box for a Johnson outboard in which he failed (at age 12) to cross Harwichport Harbor. He taught himself to sail in a 110 while learning to fly jets in the Air Force, then took a 35-year-old Murray Peterson schooner from Maine to Alaska ("mostly alone after my first wife left early"). He founded an electronics company in a garage while living aboard a "gorgeous 31-foot Peterson schooner with absolutely no electronics." He grew the company to $40 million a year, sold it, and traded the schooner for *American Promise*," which had much electrical gear, not much of which worked when I was finished." He is building a 52-foot Hood-designed cutter now for polar explorations; "I'll try electrical gear again." In the late 1980s, he bought the *Maine Times*, a weekly newspaper.

Murphy, Tim A *Cruising World* associate editor, Tim grew up—from age 13—aboard a 41-foot

Garden-designed ketch based in Lake Ponchartrain, and exploring the Gulf and Bahamas. He completed one high school year via correspondence courses, but he's studied in Paris and Berlin (where he taught sailing under the eye of East German gunboats) and sailed in New Zealand, Greece, and transatlantic from the Canaries to the Caribbean.

Mustin, Henry Henry, from Marblehead, MA, is a surveyor recognized internationally and the only American member of the Yacht Designers and Surveyors Assn., Ltd., in England. He is also certified by the National Association of Marine Surveyors in the U.S. He specializes in fiberglass, composite, steel, and alloy construction and wrote *Surveying Fiberglass Sailboats* (1992). His next book will be about powerboat survey and construction methods.

Naranjo, Ralph With Lenore and their children he did a five-year circumnavigation aboard 41-foot *Wind Shadow*. Now Technical Editor of *Cruising World*, he has written for magazines, published books (like *Wind Shadow West*), occupied the Van-derStar Chair at the U.S. Naval Academy, and managed the waterfront at Seawanhaka Corinthian Yacht Club and Boatyard in Oyster Bay, NY.

Newby, Eric Of his fifteen books on travel and adventure, *The Last Grain Race* stands apart. He shipped as an apprentice aboard the 320-foot barque *Moshulu* in Australia and worked his way through her 91-day race to be first home to Queenstown, Ireland.

Newick, Dick Designing and building boats from age 12, Dick first used multihulls in his day charter business in the Virgin Islands in 1956. Within four decades, he'd reached such preeminence that from 1968 to 1996, his trimarans had finished 1-2-3-4-5-10 in the 100-boat OSTAR. *Moxie* (Phil Weld), the first American OSTAR winner, *Third Turtle* (Mike Birch), the 36-foot *Val* that finished third in 1976, and *Cheers* (Tom Follett), a proa now in a French museum, are his best-known, but bird-like grace and ruthless simplicity distinguish them all. He also used adaptations of his easily driven hulls as workboats in the underfunded fisheries of Latin America and India. When asked, "Why trimarans?" he replies, "Because I like to *sail*."

Newman, Jarvis He went to high school in Southwest Harbor, ME, before getting an associate's degree in aircraft maintenance in 1956. He wrote technical manuals, developed helicopter engines, and installed hydraulic elevators before going to the H.R. Hinckley Co. (of Southwest Harbor) as construction manager. In 1967, he started his own shop. Surfhunter (C. Raymond Hunt), Newman PowerBoats (Lowell & Spalding and Ralph Stanley), and 800 Newman tenders plus the Dictator and Pemaquid Friendship sloops followed before he sold the business and opened Newman Marine Brokerage.

O'Cain, Jimmy Owner of the Cape Dory 30 *Annabell Lee*, he keeps her in Charleston, SC. "She is a fine sailing cutter and is for sale."

Pardey, Lin and Larry Three weeks after they met in 1965, they became a cruising couple. Married three years later, they've voyaged 92,000 miles in their own boats plus 60,000 miles in races and deliveries. Their first boat, *Seraffyn*, a 24-foot Lyle Hess–designed wooden cutter they built themselves, had her European, Mediterranean, and Oriental adventures recorded in popular books before she gave way to *Taleisin* (a 29-foot Hess cutter they built for $38,000). They've visited 66 countries, become citizens of three, and seen most of the world's exotic islands; they've won readership, navigation, and seamanship awards; and they've done it together and paid for it as they went along. Their *Self-Sufficient Sailor, The Capable Cruiser, The Care and Feeding of the Sailing Crew,* and *Storm Tactics Handbook* show a determination to "pay back the debt we owe cruising" with lessons they've learned. Having refit *Taleisin* in England, they are "primed for new adventures."

Paris, Jay E., Jr. He began studying yacht design at 12, was published in *Rudder* at 17, and studied at Webb Institute and MIT. Stints working at Sparkman & Stephens put him in touch with talented coworkers and challenging projects. He has been an oceanographer (at Woods Hole Oceanographic In-

stitute), and designed state-of-the-art winches, and designed boats like the 61-foot teak ketch *Lone Star*, the Freedom 33 cat ketch, and his new 32-foot oceanworthy trailerable. Longtime technical editor of *SAIL* magazine's Buyer's Guide, he lives with his wife, Phyllis, dog Puka, and yardful of antique cars near Brunswick, ME.

Payne, Robert "Bob" of "Bob's Broadsides" in *SAIL*, cook on an all-woman-crew, "the other hand" on a double-handed transatlantic catamaran crossing with Chay Blyth, an intrepid cruiser exploring Europe, Asia, Australia, and the Pacific, and a tenderfooted walker from Boston to New York, Bob has amused and delighted readers for three decades. His first novel is unfinished, but his *International Marine Boat Manager* sold out its first printing. He has three children and lives with his wife, Diane, in Milton, MA.

Payson, H.H. "Dynamite" A Maine craftsman "with common sense and uncommon humor" he has been building boats (mainly a flotilla of varied Phil Bolger creations from plywood), writing books, and selling plans by mail since the mid-1960s. *Instant Boats* is a mini-classic and *Build the New Instant Boats* is in its ninth printing. He can be reached at Pleasant Beach Road, South Thomaston, ME 04858.

Payson, Herb He grew up sailing on Casco Bay, ME. In the early 1970s, he gave up playing the piano in clubs and went cruising. He and his wife, Nancy, spent almost a decade island-hopping the Pacific in *Sea Foam*, their 36-foot gaff-rigged ketch. Then came trailer-sailing from coast to coast and across much of the heartland. A longtime contributor to *SAIL* whose self-deprecating and perceptive stories won him thousands of fans, he wrote *Blown Away* and *You Can't Blow Home Again*.

Peale, Barry As vice-president of Milford Boat Works (Milford, CT) he sailed, sold, built, and serviced sailboats for years. Recently retired and living in Steamboat Springs, CO—Stonington, CT, in the summer for a saltwater fix—he's now building them for fun as Mudlark Marine. His first project is the Little America 23, a trailerable sharpie schooner. Long a writer for *SAIL* and other marine magazines, he is a master of sailors' secrets from maintenance to protocol, from sailing fast to seakindliness.

Perry, Robert H.   The biography on the back of his *Sailing Designs* states, "Unlike familiar 'boy-designer-makes-good' stories, Bob was not designing dinghies when he was in high school." In the Introduction, though, Bob says he started collecting designs from magazines when he was 14. Whatever he did as a kid, Bob Perry has blossomed into one of the giants of sailboat design. His Valiant 40 made "performance cruising" a reality, and he's worked with over a dozen builders refining that ideal and staying a step ahead of the crowd. He's also developed a following for his *Sailing* design reviews unequalled today. Boat names? The only thing that makes *Eye of Newt* sound noble might just be *Ricky Nelson*.

Phillips, Chuck   A Green Beret and then a "counter-intelligence operative" in Asia, the fact that he's still alive proves that he knows a little bit about firearms.

Piailug (Mau)   Born on Satawal, in the Carolines, he is a rare navigator of Oceania. Noticed first when he guided double-canoe *Hokule'a* from Maui to Tahiti (using the traditional star paths and wayfinding techniqes that enabled his ancestors to criss-cross the Pacific long before sextant and compass), he taught Stephen Thomas, the American apprentice who wrote *The Last Navigator*, much of what he knows so it might be passed to modern sailors.

Pickering, Charlie   Retired now, he and Gail live in Marblehead "close enough to the Eastern YC to spit on it," (not that a flag officer would comport himself thus). His tales include being rescued from pursuing gendarmes off the beach in Haiti by a heaven-sent schooner from Boston and "playing some small part" in teaching Ted Hood to sail. *Warlock*, his Nonesuch 30, prowls the New England coast. If he ever gets to Bermuda again, he promises not to do any

more back flips off the stern rail.

Poulnot, Carlton   A licensed master and yacht broker in Charleston, SC, he's sailed for over 50 years.

Reid, Capt. George H.   A Merchant Marine officer since 1944 with experience as mate and master of seagoing and harbor tugs, tankers, freighters, and passenger vessels, George is also a licensed U.S. Master (oceans unlimited) and 1st Class Pilot (unlimited tonnage), St. Thomas, VI. *Primer of Towing* (1975) was his first of eight books on shiphandling , salvage, and beach discharges. *Marine Salvage for Boaters and Divers* is the most recent. He is President of Harrison Reid & Associates, marine surveyors and engineers, of Cape Canaveral, FL.

Rice, Bob   He got his meteorological training in the Air Force. Since 1960, he has been getting ever deeper into "special project" weather (most often weather-routing). The track record that he's established began with balloonists (in 1976, Maxie Anderson's *Double Eagle II* was the first hot-air balloon to complete a transatlantic), extended to yachtsmen (Phil Weld's first-ever American victory in the OSTAR in 1980), and now has encompassed round-the world routing such as Dodge Morgan's *American Promise* (1984). One of his recent achievements was to help *Kiwi Magic* win America's Cup with near-flawless short-term forecasts. A legend among ocean racers and voyagers, Rice is currently at work on a book on marine weather to be published by International Marine.

Richard, Ron   Founder/teacher of the Marshfield High School boatbuilding program, his 31 students built 10 wooden boats (three Shellback dinghies, two Nutshell prams, and five six-hour canoes) and sold them all last year. A teacher in building trades, he says, "There's something about building a boat that brings the best out in kids." He sails his O'Day Daysailer *Harumbee* from his home on Bartlett's Island and has lent RR an estimated 357 tools during their 25-year friendship.

Robinson, Alice   RR's youngest sister, she astounded the family with full-power Whaler landings at age 11 and Blue Jay prowess later in *Ace of Spades*. Having cruised Europe, the Med, and much of the Caribbean, she was a charter broker at John G. Alden in Boston before getting into real estate "at the bottom of the market." She lives in a 150-year-old house in Scituate, MA, watches birds at both ends of the flyway, and has left very little of the Caribbean unexplored. She sails her Marshall 18 catboat *Buelah* on Duxbury Bay.

Robinson, Bill RR's father, his career at *Yachting* (correspondent 1947–57, associate/executive editor 1957–67, editor 1967–79, and editor-at-large 1979–87) and 30 books make him almost as well-known as his son. He learned to sail in a "Baby Rainbow" on Nantucket and, mostly with his wife, Jane, has raced, cruised, and explored over much of the planet. A Princeton graduate (class of '39), he has been attending (as sports writer, cheering parent, and fan) home football games since 1933. RR's favorites of his works include *A Sailor's Tales, Legendary Yachts, Great Yacht Designers, Over the Horizon, Where the Trade Winds Blow, The Science of Sailing,* and *Best Cruising Spots Worldwide*. No one ever called his boats beautiful, but *Mar Claro, Tanagra,* and *Brunelle* are remembered with affection.

Robinson, Carol A Sunfish sailor on Lake Wallenpaupack, she married RR in 1968, enjoyed a one-day honeymoon on Nantucket, and started work teaching summer school the next day. RR has been trying to set things right ever since: the Greek Islands, Dalmatian Coast, Tahiti, Virgins, Bahamas, Finnish islands, Irish coast...he's still trying. She (quite literally) nursed her family through five summers in the Med on the 25-foot *Shere Khan*. "Once the two kids got so big that we had to buy an airline ticket for each of them; we quit and shipped the boat home." Her nautical ambitions are modest. "Let me sail my Sunfish and paddle my kayak around the creeks in Marshfield or jet me back to Tahiti."

Robinson, Sam RR's great-uncle, he was master of steamships beginning with British troopships in World War I and extending to the flagship of the Canadian Pacific Line, *Empress of Japan,* in the early 1930s. As captain of *Empress of Australia,* he was decorated by half-a-dozen countries for saving and evacuating people from the nightmarish Yokohama earthquake of 1923, events that inspired Bill Robinson's novel, *Destruction at Noonday*.

Robinson, Will RR's son, an engineering student at University of Rhode Island, he hit the North River in his Whaler at 12 and learned enough to qualify (some years later) as assistant harbormaster in Marshfield. Architect/builder of the family's 120-foot dock, he keeps house, cars, fleet, and father running. Having raced to Bermuda, cruised *Shere Khan* on his own, and bought a Laser, he is that rare sailor who can replace a head gasket, apply the Rules of the Road, jibe a spinnaker in 30 knots, reattach a headboard in the Gulf Stream, and cook pasta to perfection.

Roth, Hal An expert mountaineer and member of the Explorer's Club, he took Margaret to sea aboard their 35-foot sloop *Whisper,* and their circumnavigation yielded the CCA Blue Water Medal and produced the enduring *After 50,000 Miles* (1972). *Always a Distant Anchorage* marks the next stage—still cruising after all these years. Quite late in life, Hal accepted even greater challenges and made the 1986–87 BOC Race (*Chasing the Long Rainbow*); he came back in 1990–91 (*Chasing the Wind*) to make yet another rounding and author yet another (his eighth) book.

Rousmaniere, John Once an associate editor at *Yachting,* he's gone on to write a dozen books on sailing and log 30,000 miles. Lean prose, relentless research, and the authority of having been there distinguish his work. *Fastnet, Force 10,* and *The Golden Pastime* are among his best. His *The Annapolis Book of Seamanship* has taken a place of preeminence among with the most-valued reference/teaching texts; his fixation with potatoes, however, remains an enigma.

Rubin, Steve Retired from teaching at SUNY Oneonta, he and his wife Gail lived aboard *Jenny's Run* for most of a decade in the Bahamas. He writes on a variety of marine topics for popular magazines and completed a transatlantic "mostly navigating below." The couple live now in Charlottesville, VA.

Saunders, Mike   His *The Walkabouts* (1975) is a family adventure story whose title (a reference to the aboriginal rite of passage by ordeal in the desert) fits perfectly. Born in Johannesburg and living in Rhodesia, Mike, his wife Liz, and their four children took to the sea to escape the politics at home. Their 18-month odyssey took them to Brazil, the Eastern Caribbean, the Azores, and on to England. Mike's seamanship articles appeared in *SAIL*, "among others."

Schumacher, Carl   His 20-year tenure, international clientele, and 30 or so completed designs support both the "light is right" philosophy and the sound, open-minded, meticulous way he's implemented it. He apprenticed with Bill Lapworth, worked under Gary Mull, and has designed custom performers like *Heart of Gold* (second in class in the 1991 Transpac) and *Cepheus* (the 40-foot racer-cruiser that won her class in the 1992 Newport-Bermuda Race). His production boats (Express 27, 34, and 37; Olson 911S; Alerion Express 20 and 28) have also done him proud. The Express 34 was *Sailing World's* Boat of the Year in 1994. A graduate of Cal State Polytechnic Institute, he lives with his wife and children in Alameda, CA.

Seidman, David.   An editor of *Boating* magazine, David is a longtime marine writer, author, and columnist who specializes in simplifying the complicated. He's the author of *The Complete Sailor* and *The Essential Sea Kayaker*.

Sentsey, Paul   Owner of a construction company in upstate New York, he enjoys finding materials and techniques from his work that help him maintain his boat.

Service, Thomas B.   Captain Service is a deep ocean search and recovery salvage master for the U.S. Navy Supervisor of Salvage; he owns and runs White Star Marine; and he and his family made a four-year circumnavigation aboard their 44-foot cutter *Jean Marie* (while raising and educating two daughters). Using side-scan sonar and remote-op-erated vehicles he has recovered wreckage from high-performance airplanes, and he designed, rigged, and operated the system for removing (lowering more than 150 feet) the center span (360 tons, 620 feet) of the Sunshine Skyway Bridge. White Star Marine is in St. Petersburg, FL.

Sharp, Don   Mechanic of the first palm, authority on maritime history, and one-time associate editor at the one-time *MotorBoat* magazine, he rebuilt RR's diesel inboard for two cases of beer. Eloquent and elegant in print, iconoclastic and colorful in person, he has been with *Sea* and *Boating* and other periodicals, but none of his old friends knows where he's gone. Few, if any, are wiser concerning the internals of infernal combustion engines.

Shaw, Tom   A member of the U.S. Coast Guard Auxiliary, he is also a regular contributor to the popular newsletter *Messing About in Boats*.

Siemens, David F.   Captain Dave holds a USCG 100-ton Master's license with endorsements and has delivered more than 200 boats to destinations as diverse as Chile, Alaska, and the Dominican Republic. He taught basic powerboat handling, advanced power cruising, and offshore sailing in Florida and has captained a number of charter boats. He has recently completed, with his wife Lesley and "Cruisin' Cat," a 12-month cruise of the Western Caribbean aboard *Zindagi*, their 37-foot sloop whose name means "life" in Urdu/Hindi. He writes frequently for consumer and trade publications and lives now in San Francisco.

Slocum, Joshua   Famous for his solo circumnavigation, the first on record, he had an up-and-down career as a ship's master before, and a frustrating, demeaning grind after, his celebrated sail. Once he was master of the American flagship *Northern Light*; his crew mutinied, and he killed a man. He once owned and sailed "a little bark which, of all man's handiwork, seemed nearest to perfection," but "quit her deck on the coast of Brazil, where she was wrecked. My home voyage was made in the canoe *Liberdade* without accident." His book *Sailing Alone Around the World*, about the voyage aboard

Spray, reveals a hero-sailor but does little to clarify the questions that surround his life and death. He disappeared at sea in November of 1909.

Smeeton, Miles and Beryl Brigadier General Miles took the surrender of the Japanese Imperial Army in Burma. After World War II, he and Beryl, neither of whom had ever sailed, bought *Tzu Hang*, a 45-foot ketch, taught themselves to sail by going transatlantic, then set sail for Cape Horn. They were pitchpoled during a survival storm in the Southern Ocean. Beryl was thrown overside, and the housetop ripped away. With crewman John Guzzwell they made temporary repairs and limped into Chile. On Boxing Day 1957, within miles of where they'd been rolled before, *Tzu Hang* heeled hard over and turned turtle. Masts broken, hatch gone, they made Valparaiso. Then they refit and made an east-about (seven-year) circumnavigation. In their 60s, the Smeetons still felt the call of Cape Horn. They rounded successfully at last on December 18, 1968.

Smith, F. Newbold A football tackle and championship wrestler, Newbold didn't let partial paralysis from a riding accident snuff his venturesomeness. He took his Swan 43 *Reindeer* to Spitsbergen (82 North) and back—three and a half months, 10,500 miles, and the right to say he'd sailed closer to the North Pole than any pleasure yacht had ever been. He won the CCA Blue Water Medal in 1976 and, in his Farr-designed *Reindeer*, has been cruising and racing north and south with similar success ever since. *Down Denmark Strait* is his book about the sail to Spitsbergen.

Speiss, Gerry A schoolteacher from Minnesota, he learned to sail in Acapulco on his honeymoon, built 10½-foot *Yankee Girl* in his garage, tested her for two years on the lakes, and sailed her successfully (54 days, from Virginia Beach, VA, to Falmouth, England) transatlantic. In surviving years, he designed and built more boats.

Sprague, Phineas, Jr. President of Portland Yacht Services, which specializes in wooden boat restoration, he made a circumnavigation (1972–77) in the 1931 72-foot Alden schooner *Mariah* and holds

the speed record (12 hours, 20 minutes) between Portland and Yarmouth, Nova Scotia. He has been relief captain on *Nantucket* lightship, is past president of the schooner Bowdoin Association, and rowed an eight-oared shell in the Head of the Charles Regatta. He graduated from Harvard in 1972.

Spurr, Dan The editor of *Practical Sailor*, he began sailing in Michigan at 15 on a Rhodes Bantam. His first boat was a Snipe, which he transformed into a day cruiser. He has since owned and upgraded a twin-keeled Alacrity, a Silhouette, Mk. II, a Pearson Triton, and a Pearson Vanguard. In 1981, he left hospital administration and went to *Cruising World*, where he became senior editor before joining *Practical Sailor*. He has written fiction (his short story "Wreck of the Juniper" has been anthologized), personal narrative (*Steered by the Falling Stars: A Father's Journey*), and history (tentatively titled *Looking for LaSalle* plus a soon-to-be-published history of fiberglass boatbuilding) as well as *Spurr's Boat Book: Upgrading the Cruising Sailboat* and *Yacht Style*. He currently owns a 1975 Tartan 44 and a yard full of dinghies.

Steggall, Phillip A transplanted Kiwi, his 30-year sailing career has been a love affair with wings. *Gipsy Moth* class winner in the 1980 OSTAR (aboard the nobly named *Jeans Foster*), he has gone on to consult on a number of soaring edge projects including his swept-back ground effect tri that lacked only the sponsorship to get off the water. Wherever you have flown, Mr. Steggall, and Beth and the kids, thanks for staying aboard.

Stephens, Olin J., II Master of America's Cup competition and designer of six Cup winners (*Ranger*, *Columbia*, *Constellation*, *Intrepid*, *Courageous*, and *Freedom*) his long (he founded Sparkman & Stephens in 1929) and varied career has additional high points. *Dorade*'s 1931 transatlantic win led to a Wall Street tickertape parade; S & S boats won three Fastnets in succession (1931, 1933, and 1935). He designed the Lightning, the Blue Jay, and Bolero, plus two

Whitbread winners. The CCA, IOR, and IMS rules all benefited from his involvement, as did the new International America's Cup Class formula. His views on: aesthetics ("something that's too pretty can easily become ugly"); stability ("the range of positive stability is much more important than its limits"); tank testing ("the tank won't design a boat. It will only answer a question"); and dream boats ("if I ever own a boat again, I'll want it to be very small and very simple") are always worth hearing.

Stephens, Roderick, Jr.   As accomplished a sailor/engineer as his brother Olin was designer, he rigged and sailed S & S creations through seven decades. Renowned as a milk drinker, often seen taking five flights of stairs double-time, the captain of the Scarsdale High football team, a man who went aloft often in his 70s, his "perfect lunch" at sea was an apple: "You can throw it away if something goes wrong. It's not that simple with a sandwich." He once showed Capt. Nat Herreshoff movies of superboat *Ranger*, only to realize his audience "was two or three steps ahead of me explaining aspects of our deck layout we hadn't figured out yet." An expert, teacher, and champion, he was a lifelong learner and died in 1995.

Stokes, Francis   He first sailed "duck boats" and "sneakboxes" at the Jersey shore and became an early singlehander in his Comet on Barnegat Bay. World War II, college, life, and family pushed sailing aside until 1968, when family-style racing and cruising his Cal 25 "led to a solo voyage to England in 1970 and the OSTAR races of 1976 and 1980." He has made nine transatlantics (five solo), many Bermuda Races, and the BOC Solo Challenge (during which he rescued fellow-competitor Tony Lush in mid-leg). A yachtbroker, he sold *Mooneshine*, his Garden-designed 39-footer, after that race. He lives in Kittery Point, ME

Storm, Eliot   An orthodontist from White Plains, NY, he wired up a solid fix when his Universal diesel's heat exchanger had some cavities.

Stout, Gordon   "You cannot hear the waves if you have Madonna coming over your Walkman,"

he says. A 30-year cruiser, he's crossed the Atlantic over half-a-dozen times—each way—cruised Alaska and South America, the Suez and Panama Canals, and the inland lakes of Ireland. "The real disasters as cruising boats are the ones between 55 and 85 feet—too big to handle yourself, too small to let you get away from your crew."

Street, Donald   A lifelong sailor who cut his teeth in Long Island Sound, he wrote the popular *Cruising Guide to the Eastern Caribbean*. His "other" book, *The Ocean Sailing Yacht*, has been identified by its publisher, W.W. Norton, as by far the best-selling of their nautical offerings, ever. Rakish, red, and (it's tempting to say) rust-streaked, his *Iolaire* is perhaps "Squeaky's" *piece de resistance*. He has sailed his engineless 44-foot yawl, born before he was, just about everywhere he's wanted to go including more than 10 transatlantics and over 35 years of sailing around home-base in Grenada. He splits time between the islands and the south coast of Ireland, where he lives with his wife Trich and represents Lloyd's of London.

Tabarly, Eric   Who else has won the Fastnet, two OSTARs, broken the *Atlantic*'s transatlantic record, and honed the edge of offshore speed for four decades? A "pen duick" is a black Brittany waterbird, but you can't hear the name without thinking of him. Apostle of light displacement (*Pen Duick III*, a lightweight schooner, won the Fastnet, Sydney-Hobart, and TransPac Races all in the same year); unrivalled solo racer; pioneer with hydrofoils, spent uranium, and mega-spinnakers; a career naval officer and Legion d'Honneur recipient, Eric is a household celebrity in France and a model for sailors everywhere.

Taft, Dr. David, DDS   A dentist in Harpswell, ME, he learned to sail in Megansett, MA, where he raced Cape Cod Knockabouts. He eventually became club champion and finished second in the Knockabout Junior Nationals. From 1966–70, he sailed at Tufts, where he captained the freshman sailing team and was on the victorious MacMillan Cup (big-boat collegiate championship) crew. He's raced Jollyboats, Finns, Tempests, and more; navigated many Gulf of Maine Ocean Races; owns a Laser; keeps a Sabre 28; and charters often.

Taylor, Diane   Mate on the multihull *Isla*, she found it too far for Domino's to deliver when she and her crew were wrecked and stranded for nearly a week in the Bahamas.

Taylor, Jim   Preeminence didn't come overnight for this Marblehead, MA, designer. Five years' apprenticeship with Ted Hood (including overseeing modifications to *Courageous* for the 1977 America's Cup), work in Mini-Ton/MORC racers, evolution of a "maxi-trailerable," and establishment of his name (Taylor 38) all came first. His focus on IMS (the Taylor 40 was the first grand prix IMS boat) and his work on the *America³* design team pushed him toward the top, and since the launching of the Taylor 41 (1-1-1-1-1 in her first regatta) and the market success of his Sabre 362 (*Sailing World*'s Boat of the Year) he's been busy. His most recent projects include the Resolute rowing shell (built of carbon fiber by Eric Goetz), a new trainer for Offshore Sailing School, and several new Admiral's Cup boats. He lives with his wife, Ann, and pre-teen naval architect Nat.

Taylor, Keith   Born in New Zealand, he was a Sydney newspaperman until he traveled to the States to cover the America's Cup. One of the founding miscreants of the Society of International Nautical Scribes (SINS), he was also RR's editor at *SAIL*. He works now with professional sailing and maritime iterations on the Internet and lives in Marshfield, MA, with his wife Karen and two post-college children.

Templin, Doug   He built his first boat in eighth-grade shop and now owns Detco Marine, manufacturing varnish and caulking and distributing Sterling polyurethane coatings. He has maintained his bluewater wooden boats for 35 years and consults in the marine coating field.

Terman, Doug   The sailor with the bright idea for this book, Doug gets to write his own biography: "Doug Terman is a sailor with 160,000 miles

under his wobbly keel and leaking garboards. He now resides safely on dry land in the mountains of Vermont, where he tells lies to landlubbers—normally in the form of sailing novels. He is still waiting for the call from Hollywood." His friend MB would add: "A Mr. Fix-it without peer and a damn fine novelist, his ideas are dangerous."

Textor, Ken   A USCG-licensed captain, Ken has been sailing and writing about boats for 20 years. His yarns have appeared in two books, including *Innocents Afloat*, and articles for magazines including *SAIL*, *Cruising World*, *Offshore*, *Down East*, and *Northeast Sailing Life*, sharing his local knowledge of Maine and the waters beyond. He is also the editor of *The New Book of SAIL Trim*.

Thomas, Stephen   A navigator and delivery skipper before he was 25, Steve sought "something more" by apprenticing to traditional navigator Mau Piailug on Satawal. For nearly two years, he lived, sailed, ate, and drank with the master on his atoll. *The Last Navigator* records not only that rich, quirky, and involving adventure, but the heretofore secret principles and lore of navigators like Piailug. Steve appears now on the Public Broadcasting System television show *This Old House*, where he succeeded Bob Vila as host, and recently won the Shields Class nationals.

Thompson, Jeremy   A recent graduate of Tabor Academy and prime scoring weapon on RR's lacrosse team, he has caught "tuna enough to feed a small army" fishing with his brother and father out of their home in Ft. Lauderdale, FL

Tierney, Bill   A graduate of SUNY Cortland and one-time assistant coach at Johns Hopkins, he has created a remarkable winning tradition as head lacrosse coach at Princeton. His Tigers have won three of a possible five national championships in recent seasons. Among the keys to that success is a well-thumbed playbook. "We take 'being on the same page' very literally."

Toppa, Mike   A sailmaker for North Sails for 17 years, he was raised in Newport, RI. Currently active in the Snipe and Melges 24 classes, he co-authored, with Gary Jobson, *Speed Sailing*. A veteran of four America's Cup regattas, he has won twice (with *Freedom*, 1980, and *America³*, 1993). He's also won the Swan, 12-Meter, and maxi-boat world championships.

Trautman, George   Practice partner of football ironman Chuck Bednarik at Penn, he earned the nickname "Nails." In the Marines, teaching and coaching, and on the squash court, it stuck. Now he's headmaster of Avon Old Farms School in Avon, CT, and everyone calls him "Sir." He's even taken up the effete pastime of sailing (but attacked it with characteristic passion). From virtual scratch, he rehabilitated a 50-year-old Rhodes 27. Now, he ranges the East Coast in his 45-foot Kiwi-built Herreshoff Mobjack ketch (named *Epimandanos* after the Theban general whose victories saved the city-state from Spartan conquest.).

Vanadia, Peter   When he learned his cancer was incurable, Peter set out to complete a long-dreamed-of expedition to the Arctic to find and recover the ships of British explorer John Franklin, lost in his 1840 search for the Northwest Passage. A boat, sponsor, and film crew were organized, but he ran out of time. His death in August 1995 punctuated, nonetheless, a very full life. Master of *Young America* and *Northern Light*, and navigator aboard SEA's *Westward*, he was a superlative teacher. Through Safety at Sea Seminars and articles in *Sea History* and *Cruising World*, he informed sailors; as president of Philadelphia Marine Services, he met their needs. Cameraman, director, race car driver, stuntman, and husband, he set an inspiring standard.

Van Voorhis, Richard   The stage and the sea are passions he shares unstintingly with the students at Tabor. His resurrected Rhodes 18 *Pyg* (for Pygmalion) is testament to the shipwright skills he helps them develop in his boat/set design shop.

Vigor, John   Former managing editor of *Sea* magazine, he was a dinghy champion and newspaperman in South Africa before voyaging to Ft. Lauderdale in his 31-foot boat in 1987 with his family. His children's novel *Danger, Dolphins, and Ginger Beer* was followed by two future standards for sailors: *The Practical Mariner's Book of Knowledge* and *The Sailor's Assistant*.

Vigor, June   Creative cruiser and authoress (*SAIL*) in her own right, she has, like her husband, sailed well over 10,000 miles offshore. John and June live in Oak Harbor, WA.

Villiers, Alan   A larger-than-life Australian seaman, he shipped out at 15, sailed numerous windjammers, then, in the mid-1930s, skippered full-rigged *Joseph Conrad* around the world with cadets. He brings the authority of his time under sail to maritime history. The growth of sea exploration and waterborne trade, he maintains, was due not so much to improved ships and instruments as to perfection in the seamanly art of how to handle them. "To multiply ships and lack mariners is to set armor upon the coast and provide no one to wear it," said Queen Elizabeth in 1597. Chosen as master of the *Mayflower* he re-enacted her crossing and has kept a vision of working sail alive. In his foreword to *Men, Ships & The Sea*, Melville Grosvenor (National Geographic Society) says, "This book could only be written by one who knows ships intimately, has lived the sea and writes it with all of the might and flavor of the sea itself. Such a man is Alan Villiers, the greatest sea writer of our time."

von Rieschoten, Cornelis   Descended from ship captains and ship fitters in Rotterdam, Conny sailed and organized two boats named *Flyer* to two consecutive Whitbread Round-the-World Race wins (1977–78 and 1981–82), recruiting and motivating his crew; selecting, equipping, maintaining, and driving his boats; and learning weather and seamanship enough to girdle the planet. Then he took *Flyer* around again, "just cruising."

Warren, Nigel   His work for Vospers, Ltd., in ship design led to *Metal Corrosion in Boats*. "While metal corrosion is not exactly a 'black art,' it is nonetheless an area where the presence of so many variables dictates the absence of any hard and fast rules." A keen sailor, he lives with his wife on the Isle of Wight.

Watson, James R. There must be a million and one uses for epoxy; chances are J.R. knows most of them. He has worked for Gougeon Brothers for 20 years. He began as a boatbuilder, but he has been technical advisor for the past 16 years. If anything beats his expertise getting the most from epoxy, it's his knack for spelling out complicated procedures in simple terms. He has written more than 50 articles.

Way-Nee, Chris His Vancouver 27 took a seven-month cruise and now is enjoying a two-year refit. Marine technologist Chris works for a marine repair company in Vancouver, BC.

Welch, Dr. Ethan L., M.D. A vascular surgeon who practices in Rochester, NY, he has sailed "everything from frostbite dinghies to ocean-going catamarans." For years, he has chartered, with friends, from bases around the world. "Several incidents caught me unprepared, despite my medical training, because the first aid kits provided by charter companies proved inadequate." His Sea Pak is an answer, and one geared "to prepare the first-aid giver, as much as possible, to handle the stress of emergency situations."

West, Gordon He grew up aboard a 72-foot powerboat and runs a radio school in Costa Mesa, CA. He is an Extra-class amateur radio operator (WN6NOA) and a participant in the Radio Technical Commission for Marine Services. He consults with companies, advises consumers, and writes books (like *Boat Owners' Guide to Marine Electronics* —co-authored with Freeman Pittman) and articles (like those in *SAIL, Boating Industry, Worldradio News*, and *Radio!*).

West, Jack Jack is the author of *Modern Powerboats* and *Boat-owner's Guide to Radar*, among other books, and father of Gordon.

White, Chris Author of *The Cruising Multihull*, he designed *Juniper*, his exquisite cruising tri and a fleet of trend-setting cats including the Atlantic 42 and Jim Hunt's 44-footer hailed as "the cruiser for the next millenium." He lives in South Dartmouth, MA.

White, Joel Interested in boats since childhood, Joel ran Brooklin Boat Yard in Brooklin, ME from 1960 to 1990. His son Steve now runs the yard. Joel "a builder first" has designed dinghies (like Shellback), daysailers (like *LaLa* and the Haven 12½), and full-blown cruiser/racers up to 73 feet. His opponents call him a "light air wizard" no matter the boat. He is the son of the late essayist E.B. White.

White, Ridge Now in charge of Robert E. White Instruments, Inc., he is a champion dinghy sailor, confirmed cruiser, and has coached interscholastic sailing.

Wickenden, Rick A merchant officer, he grew up at Tabor Academy in Marion, MA, where his father taught history. He has cruised and raced from a very early age, and during shore time between offshore assignments he makes valued guest appearances in the Naval Science Department at Tabor.

Willoughby, Capt. R.M., MRIN, FNI "Mike" went to sea in 1927 as third mate of a coasting schooner. He served in the merchant navy and then as a Royal Naval Reserve submarine captain during World War II, commanded the schooner *Te Vega*, was chairman of the Shipbuilders' Association, skippered *Sir Winston Churchill* and *Regina Maris*, and designed the *Captain Scott*, the brig *Astrid*, and half a dozen tall ships including the 2,500-ton *Sailiner*, a power-assisted windship for commercial service. He is also a prolific and talented marine painter.

Wilson, Rich An MIT graduate, he was a member of Wind Ship, a private firm dedicated to fostering the use of sail power in commercial shipping. He skippered his family's *Hoger Danske* to overall victory in the 1980 Bermuda Race and broke (aboard *Great American* with Bill Biwenga) the clipper ship passage record between San Fransisco and Boston. President now of Classroom Afloat, he brings nautical adventure, through correspondence, video, and real-time computer interaction, to schools across America.

Worth, Dr. Claud   One of the most expert and experienced British yachtsmen at the turn of the century, he wrote *Yacht Cruising* and *Yacht Navigation and Voyaging*. A keen observer of hull shape, rigging, and construction, he named his boats *Tern* (I, II, III, and IV) operating, of course, on the premise that one good tern deserves . . . .

Wright, Dermot   An English author, he says *Marine Engines and Boating Mechanics* was meant "to bring maritime mechanics up to automotive standards of care-free reliability."

Wunderlich, Dr. Bebe, M.D.   A longtime cruiser and one-fourth owner of the world-girdling *Boston Light*, she is medical consultant to *SAIL* magazine, lectures and writes on medical safety at sea, and practices "what I preach . . . most of the time."

Zarella, John   With his wife, Donna, he owns and operates North River Marine in Scituate, MA. He pretends little interest in sailboats but was known to buy a resurrected Manchester 17 because "she looked sweet" and is learning to handle his 13-foot sprit-rigged Melonseed from his daughters. He has put up with RR's nickle-diming for 20 years and learned, over time, to drive three out of every four pilings passably straight.

BIBLIOGRAPHY

Many of the books in this list are out of print, but still available in libraries and second-hand bookstores. Of the latter, two of the best are Columbia Trading Company, (508) 778-2929, and Armchair Sailor, (401) 847-4252. Both offer mail-order fulfillment.

Aebi, Tania, and Bernadette Brennan. *Maiden Voyage: The First American Woman & Youngest Person Ever to Circumnavigate the Globe.* New York: Simon & Schuster. 1989.

Allen, Richard B (editor). *The Atlantic Fisherman's Handbook.* Fisheries Communications, Inc. 1982.

Bailey, Maurice, and Maralyn Bailey. *One Hundred Seventeen Days Adrift.* Dobbs Ferry, NY: Sheridan House. 1992.

_____. *Staying Alive.* New York: David McKay.

Barnes, Howard. *The Backyard Boatyard.* Camden, ME: International Marine. 1982.

Beiser, Arthur. *The Proper Yacht.* Second Edition. Camden, ME: International Marine. 1978.

_____. *The Sailor's World.*

Bingham, Bruce. *Sailor's Sketchbook.* Camden, ME: International Marine. 1983.

Bode, Richard. *Blue Sloop at Dawn.*

_____. *First You Have to Row a Little Boat: Reflections on Life & Living.* New York: Warner Books. 1996.

Bolger, Philip C. *Boats with an Open Mind: Seventy-Five Uninhibited Designs & Concepts.* Camden, ME: International Marine. 1994.

Bowditch, Nathaniel. *The American Practical Navigator: Being an Epitome of Navigation.* Scholarly. 1977.

Bradford, Ernle. *Ulysses Found.* London: Hodder & Stoughton.

Briggs, Vernon. *Around Cape Horn to Honolulu on the Bark Amy Turner.* Library Editions, Ltd. 1970.

Brogdon, Bill. *Navigation for the Rest of Us.* Camden, ME: International Marine. 1995.

Brown, Jim. *The Case for the Cruising Trimaran.* Camden, ME: International Marine. 1979.

Buckley, William F., Jr. *Atlantic High.* Boston: Little, Brown & Co. 1982.

Buehler, George. *Buehler's Backyard Boatbuilding.* Camden, ME: International Marine. 1990.

Burke, Katy. *The Complete Liveaboard Book.* Camden, ME: International Marine. 1982.

_____. *Cruising Under Power: An Insider's Guide to the Pleasures of Powerboat Cruising.* New York: G.P. Putnam's Sons. 1991.

_____. *The Handbook for Non-Macho Sailors.* Camden, ME: International Marine. 1985.

Calahan, H.A. *Back to Treasure Island.*

_____. *Gadgets and Wrinkles.* Macmillan. 1938.

_____. *Learning to Cruise.*

_____. *Learning to Race.*

_____. *The Ship's Husband.* Macmillan. 1946.

_____. *The Yachtsman's Omnibus.* MacMillan.

Calder, Nigel. *Boatowner's Mechanical and Electrical Manual: How to Maintain, Repair & Improve Your Boat's Essential Systems.* Camden, ME: International Marine. 1989.

_____. *The Cruising Guide to the Northwest Caribbean: The Yucatan Coast of Mexico, Belize, Guatemala, Honduras & the Bay Islands.* Camden, ME: International Marine/McGraw Hill. 1991.

_____. *Marine Diesel Engines: Maintenance, Troubleshooting, & Repair.* Camden, ME: International Marine. 1987.

_____. *Refrigeration for Pleasureboats: Installation, Maintenance & Repair.* Camden, ME: International Marine/McGraw Hill. 1990.

_____. *Repairs at Sea.* Camden, ME: International Marine. 1988.

Calder, Nigel. *The Weather Machine.* Viking Press, 1974.

Callahan, Steve. *Adrift: Seventy-Six Days Lost at Sea.* New York: Houghton Mifflin Co. 1996.

Casey, Don. *Canvaswork and Sail Repair.* Camden, ME: International Marine. 1996.

_____. *Sailboat Hull and Deck Repair.* Camden, ME: International Marine. 1996.

_____. *Sailboat Refinishing: Painting, Varnishing, and Cosmetics.* Camden, ME: International Marine. 1995.

_____. *This Old Boat*. Camden, ME: International Marine/McGraw Hill. 1991.

Casey, Don, and **Lew Hackler.** *Sensible Cruising: The Thoreau Approach.* Camden, ME: International Marine. 1990.

Chichester, Sir Francis. *Gipsy Moth Circles the World.* Coward-McCann. 1967.

_____. *The Lonely Sea and the Sky.* New York: Paragon House. 1964.

Chiles, Webb. *The Ocean Waits.*

_____. *Open Boat Across the Atlantic.*

_____. *Open Boat Across the Pacific.* New York: W.W. Norton. 1982.

_____. *Storm Passage: Alone Around Cape Horn.* Random House. 1977.

Colas, Alain. *Around the World Alone.* Hauppauge, NY: Barron's. 1978.

Coles, Adlard, and **Peter Bruce.** *Heavy Weather Sailing.* Camden, ME: International Marine. 1992.

Colgate, Steve. *Colgate's Basic Sailing.* Offshore Sailing School, Ltd. 1991.

_____. *Fundamentals of Sailing, Cruising, & Racing.* New York: W.W. Norton. 1978.

_____. *Manual of Racing Techniques.*

_____. *Steve Colgate on Cruising.* Offshore Sailing School, 1990.

_____. *Steve Colgate on Sailing.* New York: W.W. Norton. 1991.

Conner, Dennis, and **Michael Levitt.** *Sail Like a Champion.* New York: St. Martin's Press. 1992.

Conrad, Joseph. *Typhoon & Other Stories.* Alfred A. Knopf, Inc.. 1991.

Cooper, Bill, and **Laurel Cooper.** *Sail Into the Sunset.* Dobbs Ferry, NY: Sheridan House.

_____. *Sell Up and Sail: Taking the Ulysses Option.* Dobbs Ferry, NY: Sheridan House. 1990.

Cornell, F.M., and **A.C. Hoffman.** Edited by William B. Hayler. *American Merchant Seaman's Manual.* Centreville, MD: Cornell Maritime Press. 1981.

Corry, Will. *Sea Lion.*

Curry, Manfred. *The Aerodynamics of Sails.* 1925.

_____. *Yacht Racing.* 1935.

Dana, Richard Henry. *Two Years Before the Mast.* Viking Penguin. 1981.

De Gast, Robert. *The Doors of San Miguel de Allende.* Pomegranate. 1994.

_____. *Five Fair Rivers.* Johns Hopkins University Press.

Dempsey, Paul. *Small Marine Engines.*

Dey, Richard Morris. *The Abandonment of* Rachel Delano.

_____. *The Bequia Poems.*

_____. *The Loss of the Schooner* Kestrel *and Other Sea Poems.*

Donaldson, Sven. *A Sailor's Guide to Sails.* New York: Dodd Mead & Co. 1984.

Duncan, Roger F. *Coastal Maine, A Maritime History.* New York: W.W. Norton. 1992.

_____. *Eastward.* Camden, ME: International Marine. 1976.

_____. *Sailing in the Fog.* Camden, ME: International Marine. 1986.

Duncan, Roger F., et al. *The Cruising Guide to the New England Coast.* New York: W.W. Norton. 1995.

Eldridge Tide & Pilot Book. Boston: Robert Eldridge White.

Ellam, Patrick. *Yacht Cruising.* New York: W.W. Norton. 1983.

Elsevier's Nautical Dictionary. Compiled by J.P. Vandenberghe and L.Y. Chaballe. Elsevier. 1978.

Fenger, Frederic A. *The Cruise of the Diablesse.* Belmont, MA: Wellington Books. 1958.

Forester, C.S. *Admiral Hornblower in the West Indies.* Little Brown & Co. 1989.

_____. *Commodore Hornblower.* Little Brown & Co. 1945.

Fox, Uffa. *Racing, Cruising, and Design.* Camden, ME: International Marine. 1985.

Franzel, Dave. *Sailing: The Basics.* Camden, ME: International Marine. 1985.

Frisbie, Richard. *Basic Boatbuilding.* Henry Regnery Co. 1975.

Gerr, Dave. *The Nature of Boats.* Camden, ME: International Marine. 1992.

_____. *The Propeller Handbook.* Camden, ME: International Marine. 1989.

Gladstone, Bernard, and **Tom Bottomley** (editors). *Boatkeeper: The Boatowner's Manual to Maintenance, Repair, & Construction.* New York: William Morrow & Co. 1984.

Glennie, John, and **Jane Phare.** *The Spirit of* Rose Noelle. New York: Fawcett/Random House. Robert Hale & Co.

Global Weather Experiment. 1978. From the Global Atmospheric Research Programme, administered through the United Nations' World Meteorological Organization.

Graham, Robin Lee. *Dove.* New York: Bantam, William Morrow & Co. 1972.

Griffith, Bob, with **Nancy Griffith.** *Blue Water: A Guide to Self-Reliant Sailboat Cruising.* Boston: Sail Books, Inc. 1979.

Groene, Gordon, and **Janet Groene.** *The Right-Seat Handbook: A Cockpit Passenger's Companion.* TAB Books. 1992.

Groene, Janet. *Cooking Aboard Your RV.* Camden, ME: International Marine. 1993.

_____. *Cooking on the Go.* Revised edition. Hearst Marine (William Morrow & Co.). 1987.

_____. *Dressing Ship.* Hearst Marine (William Morrow & Co.).

_____. *The Galley Book.*

_____. *How to Live Aboard a Boat.* Hearst Marine (William Morrow & Co.).

_____. *Living Aboard Your RV.* Camden, ME: International Marine. 1993.

Hammick, Anne. *Ocean Cruising on a Budget.* Camden, ME: International Marine. 1991.

_____. *Atlantic Crossing Guide.* Camden, ME: International Marine. 1993.

Hauser, Heinrich. *Fair Winds and Foul: A Narrative of Daily Life Aboard an American Clipper Ship*, by Frederick Perry. Cruger, NY: E.M. Coleman Enterprises. 1980.

Hayler, William B., John M. Keever, and Paul M. Seiler. *American Merchant Seaman's Manual*. Centreville, MD: Cornell Maritime Press, Inc. 1981.

Hays, Dave, and Daniel Hays. *My Old Man and the Sea: A Father and Son Sail Around Cape Horn*. Algonquin Books of Chapel Hill. 1995.

Herreshoff, L. Francis. *Commensense of Yacht Design*.

_____. *The Compleat Cruiser: The Art, Practice and Enjoyment of Boating*. Dobbs Ferry, NY: Sheridan House, Inc. 1956.

_____. *Sensible Cruising Designs*. Camden, ME: International Marine. 1991.

Herron, Jeannine. *The Voyage of Aquarius*. New York: Dutton/Penguin.

Heyerdahl, Thor. *Aku-Aku*.

_____. *Easter Island*. New York: Random House. 1989.

_____. *Early Man and the Ocean*. New York: Doubleday. 1979.

_____. *Fatu-Hiva: Back to Nature*. Buccaneer Books. 1992.

_____. *Kon-Tiki*. Amereon. 1976.

_____. *Ra*.

Hill, Annie. *Voyaging on a Small Income*. St. Michaels, MD: Tiller Publishing. 1993.

Hiscock, Eric, and Susan Hiscock. *Cruising Under Sail*. London: Oxford University Press. 1950.

_____. *Voyaging Under Sail*. London: Oxford University Press. 1959.

Homer, *The Odyssey*. Translated by Robert Fitzgerald. New York: Random House. 1990.

Hoyt, Garry. *Ready About!* Camden, ME: International Marine. 1987.

Innes, Hammond. *The Last Voyage: Captain Cook's Lost Diary*. Alfred A. Knopf, Inc. 1978.

_____. *Sea and Islands*.

Innes, Hammond. *The Wreck of the Mary Deare*. Carroll & Graf. 1985.

Irving, John, and Douglas Service. *The Yachtsman's Weekend Book*. New York: Dutton/Penguin.

Isler, Peter. The American Sailing Association's *Let's Go Sailing*. Hearst Books. 1993.

Jerome, Jerome K. *Second Thoughts of an Idle Fellow*.

_____. *Three Men in a Boat*. Viking Penguin. 1978.

Jobson, Gary. *Storm Sailing*. Hearst Marine (William Morrow & Co.). 1983.

Johnson, Irving. *The Peking Battles Cape Horn*. Sea History Press. 1995.

Kemp, Peter K. (editor). *The Oxford Companion to Ships & the Sea*. Oxford University Press. 1994.

Kent, Rockwell. *N x E*. Hanover, NH: University Press of New England. 1996.

Kielhorn, William V. *Basic Motorboat Seamanship*.

Kiley, Deborah Scaling, and Meg Noonan. *Albatross*. Boston: Houghton Mifflin Co. 1994.

Knapp, Arthur. *Race Your Boat Right*. Princeton, NJ: Van Nostrand. 1952, 1960.

Knight, Kathryn Lasky. *Atlantic Circle*. W.W. Norton.

Kyselka, Will. *An Ocean In Mind*. Honolulu, HI: University of Hawaii Press. 1987.

_____. *Stars in Mind*.

Kyselka, Will, and Ray Lanterman. *North Star to Southern Cross*. Honolulu, HI: University of Hawaii Press. 1976.

Lathem, Edward Connery. *The Poetry of Robert Frost*, edited by Edward Connery Lathem. New York: Henry Holt & Co., Inc. 1969.

Lawrence, T.E. *Seven Pillars of Wisdom*. New York: Doubleday. 1935.

Letcher, John S., Jr. *Self-Steering for Sailing Craft*. Camden, ME: International Marine. 1974.

Lewis, Cam, and Michael Levitt *Around the World in Seventy-Nine Days*. Bantam Doubleday Dell. 1996.

Lewis, David. *The Voyaging Stars*. Curtis Brown (Aust) Pty Ltd.

_____. *We, the Navigators: The Ancient Art of Landfinding in the Pacific*. Honolulu, HI: University of Hawaii Press. 1975.

Lie, Arne Brun, and Robby Robinson. *Night and Fog*. New York: W.W. Norton. 1990.

Linden, Louis F. *The Champion*.

Lord, Walter. *A Night to Remember*. New York: Holt Rinehart & Winston. 1955.

McConnell, Malcolm, and Carol McConnell. *First Crossing: The Personal Log of a Transatlantic Adventure*. New York: W.W. Norton. 1983.

McCormick, Herb. *Out There*. Hearst.

McKibben, Bill. *The End of Nature*. New York: Random House. 1989.

McKinney, Sam. *Bligh*. Camden, ME: International Marine. 1989.

MacLean, Dave. *Everything You Always Wanted to Know About Boating*.

_____. *Small Craft Electronic Equipment Care & Repair*.

McPhee, John. *Looking for a Ship*. New York: Farrar Straus Giroux. 1990.

Marchaj, C.A. *Aero-Hydrodynamics of Sailing*. Camden, ME: International Marine. 1989.

_____. *Sail Performance: Theory and Practice*. Camden, ME: International Marine. 1996.

_____. *Sailing Theory and Practice*. New York: Dodd, Mead. 1982.

_____. *Seaworthiness: The Forgotten Factor*. Camden, ME: International Marine. 1987.

Marsden, Peter. *The Wreck of the Amsterdam*. Stein & Day. 1974.

Marshall, Roger. *Designed to Cruise*. New York: W.W. Norton. 1990.

_____. *Designed to Win*.

_____. *Marshall's Marine Sourcebook: Where to Find Absolutely Everything Nautical*. St. Martin. 1993.

_____. *Race to Win*. New York: W.W. Norton. 1980.

_____. *Sail Better: 101 Tips and Techniques*. St. Martin's Griffin. 1996.

Martin, E.G., and John Irving. *Cruising and Ocean Racing: A Complete Manual on Yachting*. Gordon Press. 1977.

Maté, Ferenc. *The Finely Fitted Yacht*. New York: W.W. Norton. 1979.

_____. *Finisterre*.

_____. *From a Bare Hull: How to Build a Sailboat*. Albatross/W.W. Norton 1983.

_____. *Shipshape: The Art of Sailboat Maintenance*. New York: Albatross/W.W. Norton. 1986.

Matthiessen, Peter. *Killing Mr. Watson*. New York: Random House, Inc. 1990.

Meisel, Tony. *Under Sail*. New York: Macmillan. 1982.

Mellor, John. *The Art of Pilotage*. Dobbs Ferry, NY: Sheridan House. 1990.

_____. *Handling Troubles Afloat*. Dobbs Ferry, NY: Sheridan House. 1996.

_____. *Smallcraft Emergency Procedures*.

_____. *Young Crew*. Voyageur Press. 1994.

Melville, Herman. *Moby Dick*. Holt Rinehart & Winston. 1966.

Meurn, Robert J. *Survival Guide for the Mariner*. Centreville, MD: Cornell Maritime Press. 1993.

Miller, Conrad. *Small Boat Engines, Inboard and Outboard*. Dobbs Ferry, NY: Sheridan House. 1970.

Miller, Conrad, and E.S. Maloney. *Your Boat's Electrical System*. New York: Hearst Marine (William Morrow & Co.). 1988.

Milton. *Paradise Lost*. Buccaneer Books. 1983.

Minnoch, James E. *Aground*. John deGraff, Inc. 1985.

Miranda, Rosalind. *Miranav*.

Mitchell, Carleton. *The Wind's Call*.

Moeller, Jan, and Bill Moeller. *The Intracoastal Waterway, Norfolk to Miami: A Cockpit Cruising Handbook*. Camden, ME: International Marine. 1991, 1996.

_____. *Living Aboard: The Cruising Sailboat as a Home*. Camden, ME: International Marine. 1977.

Moitissier, Bernard. *The Long Way*. Dobbs Ferry, NY: Sheridan House. 1995.

Moore, Jim. *By Way of the Wind*. Dobbs Ferry, NY: Sheridan House. 1991.

_____. *Swan: The Second Voyage*. Dobbs Ferry, NY: Sheridan House. 1994.

Morgan, Dodge. *American Promise*. Boston: Houghton Mifflin. 1989.

Morison, Samuel Eliot. *The History of United States Naval Operations in World War II*. Boston: Little, Brown and Company. 1947.

Mostert, Noel. *Supership*. Random House.

Mowat, Farley. *The Serpent's Coil*. Boston: Little Brown & Co. 1961.

Moxon, Lloyd M. *Lay Her Before the Wind*. New York: Doubleday. 1978.

Mustin, Henry. *Surveying Fiberglass Sailboats*. Camden, ME: International Marine. 1994.

Nalepka, James, and Steven Callahan. *Capsized*. Harper Collins. 1992.

Naranjo, Ralph. *Wind Shadow West*.

Newby, Eric. *The Last Grain Race*. Viking Penguin. 1986.

Nicolson, Ian. *Customize Your Boat*. W.W. Norton. 1990.

O'Brian, Patrick. *Post Captain*. William Collins Sons & Co. (W.W. Norton). 1972.

Pardey, Lin, and Larry Pardey. *The Capable Cruiser*. New York: W.W. Norton. 1987.

_____. *The Care and Feeding of the Offshore Crew*. New York: W.W. Norton. 1980.

_____. *The Self-Sufficient Sailor*. New York: W.W. Norton. 1982.

_____. *Storm Tactics Handbook*. Paradise Cay Publications. 1995.

Payne, Bob, and Nick Ellison. *The International Marine Boat Manager: Your Vessel's Custom Handbook of Operating and Service Procedures*. Camden, ME: International Marine. 1992.

Payson, H.H. "Dynamite." *Build the New Instant Boats*. Camden, ME: International Marine. 1984.

_____. *Instant Boats*. Camden, ME: International Marine. 1979.

Payson, Herb. *Blown Away*. Dobbs Ferry, NY: Sheridan House 1995.

_____. *You Can Never Blow Home Again*. Hearst Marine (William Morrow & Co.). 1984.

Perry, Robert H. *Sailing Designs*, Volumes 1, et al. Port Publications. 1994.

Pirsig, Robert. *Zen and the Art of Motorcycle Maintenance*. New York: Bantam Books/William Morrow & Co. 1974.

Reid, George H. *Marine Salvage: A Guide for Boaters and Divers*. 1996

_____. *Primer of Towing*. Centreville, MD: Cornell Maritime Press. 1975.

Rietschoten, Cornelis van, and Barry Pickthall. *Flyer: The Quest to Win the Round the World Race*. New York: W.W. Norton and Cambs, United Kingdom: A&C Black (Publishers) Limited. 1979.

Robertson, Dougal. *Survive the Savage Sea*. Harper Collins. 1973.

Robin, Bernard. *Survival at Sea*. Random House UK Limited.

Robinson, Bill. *Best Sailing Spots Worldwide*. Hearst Marine (William Morrow & Co.). 1991.

Robinson, Bill. *Destruction at Noonday*. Dobbs Ferry, NY: Sheridan House. 1992.

_____. *Great Yacht Designers*.

_____. *Legendary Yachts*. Eaton Press. 1971.

_____. "Man Overboard." *The Best From Yachting*. Charles Scribners. 1967.

_____. *Over the Horizon.*

_____. *A Sailor's Tales.* New York: W.W. Norton. 1978.

_____. *The Science of Sailing.*

_____. *South to the Caribbean.*

_____. *Where the Trade Winds Blow.*

Roth, Hal. *After Fifty Thousand Miles.* New York: W.W. Norton. 1972.

_____. *Always a Distant Anchorage.* New York: W.W. Norton. 1988.

_____. *Chasing the Long Rainbow.* New York: W.W. Norton. 1990

_____. *Chasing the Wind: A Book of High Adventure.* Dobbs Ferry, NY: Sheridan House. 1993.

_____. Recipe for *Jolie Brise* onion soup, in *Yachting* magazine.

Rousmaniere, John. *The Annapolis Book of Seamanship.* New York: Simon & Schuster. 1983.

_____. *Fastnet, Force 10.* New York: W.W. Norton. 1980.

_____. *The Golden Pastime: A New History of Yachting.* New York: W.W. Norton.

_____. *The Sailing Lifestyle: A Guide to Sailing and Cruising for Pleasure.* New York: Simon & Schuster. 1985.

Saunders, Mike. *The Walkabouts.* 1975.

Seidman, David. *The Complete Sailor.* Camden, ME: International Marine. 1995.

Sheldon, Paul. *First Aid Afloat.* Cornell Maritime Press.

Slocum, Joshua. *Sailing Alone Around the World.* Dobbs Ferry, N.Y.: Sheridan House, Inc. 1954.

Smith, Newbold. *Down Denmark Strait.*

Spurr, Dan. *Spurr's Boat Book: Upgrading the Cruising Sailboat.* Camden, ME: International Marine. 1983.

_____. *Steered by the Falling Stars: A Father's Journey.* Camden, ME: International Marine. 1992.

_____. *Yacht Style.* Camden, ME: International Marine. 1990.

Street, Donald M., Jr. *Street's Cruising Guide to the Eastern Caribbean.* Volumes 1, et al. New York: W.W. Norton. 1985.

_____. *The Ocean Sailing Yacht.* New York: W.W. Norton. 1973.

Tabarly, Eric. *Pen Duick.* London: Adlard Coles, Ltd.

Tazelaar, James, and **Jean Brussiere.** *To Challenge a Distant Sea.*

Textor, Ken. *Innocents Afloat.* Dobbs Ferry, NY: Sheridan House. 1993.

Thomas, Stephen D. *The Last Navigator.* New York: Henry Holt & Co. Ballantine. 1988.

Toppa, Mike, and **Gary Jobson.** *Speed Sailing.*

Vigor, John. *Danger, Dolphins, and Ginger Beer.* New York: Athenium. 1994.

_____. *The Practical Mariner's Book of Knowledge.* Camden, ME: International Marine, 1994.

_____. *The Sailor's Assistant.* Camden, ME: International Marine, 1995.

Villiers, Alan J. *Cruise of the Conrad.*

_____. *Men, Ships & The Sea.*

_____. *The Way of a Ship.* Scribner's. 1953.

Warren, Nigel. *Metal Corrosion in Boats.* Camden, ME: International Marine. 1990.

Watson, Lyall. *Heaven's Breath.*

Watts, Alan. *Instant Wind Forecasting.* Dobbs Ferry, NY: Sheridan House. 1988.

_____. *The Weather Handbook.* Dobbs Ferry, NY: Sheridan House. 1994.

Webb, Barbara. *Yachtsman's Eight Language Dictionary.* Clinton Corners, NY: John de Graff, Inc. 1977.

_____. *Yachtsman's Ten Language Dictionary.* Revised by Michael Manton. Dobbs Ferry, NY: Sheridan House. 1995.

West, Gordon. *Boatowner's Guide to Marine Electronics.* Camden, ME: International Marine. 1993.

West, Jack. *Boatowner's Guide to Radar.* Camden, ME: International Marine, 1988.

_____. *Modern Powerboats.* Camden, ME: International Marine, 1975.

White, Chris. *The Cruising Multihull.* Camden, ME: International Marine, 1996.

Whiting, John. *On Deck.*

Worth, Claud. *Yacht Cruising.*

_____. *Yacht Navigation and Voyaging.*

Wright, Dermot. *Marine Engines and Boating Mechanics.* David & Charles Publishers. 1973.

INDEX

The following publishers have generously given permission to use extended quotations from copyrighted works: